FELICIA HEMANS

FELICIA HEMANS

SELECTED POEMS, PROSE, AND LETTERS

edited by

Gary Kelly

broadview literary texts

National Library of Canada Cataloguing in Publication Data

Hemans, Felicia Dorothea, 1793-1835
    Felicia Hemans : selected poems, prose, and letters

(Broadview Literary Texts)
ISBN 1-55111-137-3

I. Kelly, Gary   II. Title.   III. Series
PR4780.A4 2001   821'.7   C2001-903144-0

Broadview Press Ltd. is an independent, international publishing house, incorporated in 1985.

North America:
P.O. Box 1243, Peterborough, Ontario, Canada K9J 7H5
3576 California Road, Orchard Park, NY 14127
TEL: (705) 743-8990; FAX: (705) 743-8353;
E-MAIL: customerservice@broadviewpress.com

United Kingdom:
Thomas Lyster Ltd.
Unit 9, Ormskirk Industrial Park
Old Boundary Way, Burscough Road
Ormskirk, Lancashire L39 2YW
TEL: (01695) 575112; FAX: (01695) 570120; E-mail: books@tlyster.co.uk

Australia:
St. Clair Press, P.O. Box 287, Rozelle, NSW 2039
TEL: (02) 818-1942; FAX: (02) 418-1923

www.broadviewpress.com

Broadview Press gratefully acknowledges the financial support of the Book Publishing Industry Development Program, Ministry of Canadian Heritage, Government of Canada.

Broadview Press is grateful to Professor Eugene Benson and Professor L. W. Conolly for advice on editorial matters for the Broadview Literary Texts series.

Text design and composition by George Kirkpatrick and Kelly Liberty

PRINTED IN CANADA

FOR ISOBEL AND LEN FINDLAY

FELICIA HEMANS

Contents

Acknowledgements • 11
About this Edition • 12
   Abbreviations and Website • 14
Introduction • 15
Felicia Hemans: A Brief Chronology • 86

Selected Poems, Prose, and Letters • 91

From *Poems* (1808) • 93
   "To the Muse" • 93
   "A Tribute to the Genius of Robert Burns" • 93
   "The Farewell" • 95
From *England and Spain; or, Valour and Patriotism* (1808) • 96
From *The Domestic Affections, and Other Poems* (1812) • 103
   "Sonnet to Italy" • 103
   "War-Song of the Spanish Patriots" • 103
   "The Domestic Affections" • 106
From *The Restoration of the Works of Art to Italy* (1816) • 112
From *Modern Greece* (1817) • 124
From *Translations from Camoens, and other Poets* (1818) • 142
   from Camoens:
      Sonnet 282: "Wrapt in sad musings" • 142
   from other poets
      da Filicaja: "Italia, Italia! O tu cui diè la sorte" • 143
   from Original Poetry
      "Guerilla Song" • 144
From *Tales, and Historic Scenes* (1819) • 145
   "The Widow of Crescentius" • 145
   "The Wife of Asdrubal" • 173
From *A Selection of Welsh Airs* (1822) • 177
   "The Rock of Cader-Idris" • 177
From *The Siege of Valencia ... with Other Poems* (1823) • 179
   from "The Siege of Valencia" • 179
   from "Other Poems" • 196
   "Songs of the Cid" • 196
      "The Cid's Departure into Exile" • 197

"The Cid's Death-bed" • 198
"The Cid's Funeral Procession" • 201
"The Cid's Rising" • 205
from "Other Poems" • 207
from "Greek Songs" • 207
"The Voice of Scio" • 207
"The Spartan's March" • 209
"The Tombs of Platæa" • 211
"England's Dead" • 213
"The Voice of Spring" • 215
From *The Vespers of Palermo* (1823) • 219
From *The Forest Sanctuary; with Other Poems* • 227
from the first edition (1825) • 227
"The Forest Sanctuary" • 227
from "Miscellaneous Pieces" • 299
"The Treasures of the Deep" • 299
from the second edition (1829)
"Casabianca" • 300
"Evening Prayer at a Girls' School" • 302
"The Lost Pleiad" • 304
"The Breeze from Shore" • 305
From *Records of Woman: with Other Poems* (1828) • 307
from "Records of Woman" • 307
"Arabella Stuart" • 307
"The Switzer's Wife" • 318
"Properzia Rossi" • 323
"Pauline" • 328
"The Grave of a Poetess" • 332
from "Miscellaneous Pieces" • 334
"The Homes of England" • 334
"To Wordsworth" • 336
"Körner and His Sister" • 337
"The Landing of the Pilgrim Fathers in New
England" • 340
"The Palm-tree" • 342
"The Child's Last Sleep" • 344
"The Illuminated City" • 345
"The Graves of a Household" • 347
"The Image in Lava" • 348

From *The Amulet* (1829) • 351
   "Woman and Fame" • 351
From *Songs of the Affections, with Other Poems* (1830) • 353
   from "Songs of the Affections" • 353
      "Woman on the Field of Battle" • 353
   from "Miscellaneous Poems" • 355
      "Corinne at the Capitol" • 355
      "The Ruin" • 357
      "The Song of Night" • 360
      "The Diver" • 362
      "The Requiem of Genius" • 364
      "Second Sight" • 366
From *Hymns on Nature, for the Use of Children* (1833) • 369
   "To a Younger Child" • 369
From the *New Monthly Magazine* (1834) • 370
   from "Scenes and Passages from the 'Tasso' of Goethe" • 370
From *Scenes and Hymns of Life, with Other Religious
   Poems* (1834) • 374
   Preface • 374
   from "Scenes and Hymns of Life" • 375
      "Prisoners' Evening Service" • 375
   from "Miscellaneous Poems" • 381
   from "Female Characters of Scripture" • 381
      "I. Invocation" • 381
      "II. Invocation Continued" • 382
      "IV. Ruth" • 382
      "VII. The Annunciation" • 383
      "IX. The Penitent Anointing Christ's Feet" • 384
      "XV. Mary Magdalene bearing Tidings of the
      Resurrection" • 384
      "Communings with Thought" • 385
   from "Sonnets, Devotional and Memorial" • 387
      "I. The Sacred Harp" • 387
   from "Miscellaneous Poems" • 388
      "Elysium" • 388
From *National Lyrics, and Songs for Music* (1834) • 392
   from "National Lyrics" • 392
      "Introductory Stanzas: The Themes of Song" • 392

"Rhine Song of the German Soldiers after
Victory" • 394
from "Miscellaneous Poems" • 396
"Books and Flowers" • 396
"Scene in a Dalecarlian Mine" • 398
From the *New Monthly Magazine* (1835) • 400
from "Thoughts During Sickness" • 400
"Intellectual Powers" • 400
"Sickness like Night" • 400
"The Recovery" • 401
From *Poetical Remains* (1836) • 402
from "Records of the Spring of 1834" • 402
"V. A Thought of the Sea" • 402
"XII. A Remembrance of Grasmere" • 403
"XIII. On Reading Paul and Virginia in
Childhood" • 404
from "Records of the Autumn of 1834" • 405
"I. The Return to Poetry" • 405
"II. On Reading Coleridge's Epitaph Written by
Himself" • 405
"VII. Design and Performance" • 406
"IX. To Silvio Pellico, on Reading his
'Prigione'" • 407
"X. To the Same, Released" • 408
"To the Mountain Winds" • 408
"Sabbath Sonnet" • 410

Appendix A: Selected Letters • 411

Appendix B: Views and Reviews • 446

Select Bibliography • 489

Acknowledgements

I am grateful to students in classes and seminars at the University of Keele, the University of Alberta, and the University of Bologna for helping me to a better understanding of Felicia Hemans's poetry. My great debt to colleagues and fellow critics and literary historians is partly recorded in the notes to my Introduction. The dedication is a small indication of my gratitude for 33 years of personal, political, and professional friendship, without which I would not be able to do the work that I do here, such as it is. I could not have carried out the work for this edition without the funding provided by the Social Sciences and Humanities Research Council of Canada and the University of Alberta. In preparing the edition I have been helped by Kim Feyen, Kirsten MacLeod, Theresa Daniels, Jennifer Kelly, Evelyn Erizpe, Nigel Leask, Diana Holmes, Paula Feldman, and the staffs of the University of Alberta Library and especially Bruce Peel Special Collections, the Huntington Library, McGill University Library, the British Library, the Bodleian Library, and the Liverpool Public Records Library. Susan Wolfson offered helpful suggestions and valuable information. Don LePan and Broadview Press have been loyal and patient beyond the call of duty or publisher's interest. For references to Hemans in nineteenth-century literature, thanks to David Amigoni, Janice Schroeder, Tia Berger, Doris Meriwether, Austin Meredith, and Elizabeth Miller. Thanks to the Huntington Library, British Library, Liverpool Public Library, McGill University Library for permission to quote manuscript materials.

Edmonton
May 2000

About this edition

Range of texts: The material conditions of production and sale of editions such as this necessarily enforce selection from Hemans's work. I argue that Hemans consciously constructed a public poetic career, in a continuing dialectical relationship with the literary, cultural, social, political, and publishing conditions of her time, and that as she became established as a national poetic voice her career and public standing became part of those conditions. Accordingly, I have tried to give a selection of work, over the span of her career, that represents the range of her interests and of the forms she used, as I see them in relation to the likely interests of readers and students today.

Texts used: Hemans first published many or most of her poems in magazines and literary annuals, and then collected these poems, with hitherto unpublished poems, in volume form. This was a way of maximizing earnings from her writing. I believe that Hemans and her readers and critics would have regarded magazine and annual publication as tending toward the ephemeral, and publication in book form as the texts' claim to greater permanence and cultural authority. Republication in second and third editions would have been regarded as mainly though not entirely a commercial matter. I argue that Hemans's literary production was a constant and continuing response to the conditions around her, as she understood them and intended to shape them. Accordingly, in most cases I have chosen to use first publication in book form as base text, giving substantive variants from earlier publication in magazines or annuals. In fact, Hemans made relatively few major alterations to her texts after first publication, except in *The Restoration of the Works of Art to Italy*, and a few shorter poems. Insertion or deletion of exclamation marks is not usually considered a substantive change, but such marks may be associated with "sentimental" and expressive poetry, especially of the Romantic period, and these traits have been matters of controversy in Hemans criticism. Accordingly, I have recorded change from statement to exclamation (in Hemans's work, less frequently from exclamation to statement), as well as changes of emphasis (from italic to roman, or vice versa), since these were conventional markers of expressivity in Hemans's day. Hemans also published none of her work that was humorous, parodic, or satirical; accordingly, I include some of this work on my Hemans website (see below).

Introduction, annotation, commentary, supporting documents, and website: Knowledge about Hemans, her work, and the conditions of its literary production is not yet as highly developed or as widely circulated culturally as knowledge about some of her contemporaries. To enable users of this book to get as much out of reading Hemans as possible, I have aimed to identify significant textual changes, to identify quotations and allusions, to explain references that may now be obscure, and to define words and phrases that have changed their primary meaning since Hemans's day or that were used mainly in literature at that time. I have not assumed that all readers in a multi-cultural society such as Canada, or other places where Broadview texts are available, will have substantial knowledge of texts that are supposed to have circulated formerly more widely, such as the Bible and certain once familiar literary texts in English, and European literature as known in her time. Accordingly, I have been more particular in explaining such references and terms than some readers perhaps would like. In order to provide a context for reading Hemans now, I provide an Introduction and Chronology that attempt to outline her career and her major works in what I see as their literary, cultural, social, political, and publishing context. For Hemans, those contexts were European (indeed, global) as well as British, and the Introduction and Chronology are framed accordingly. The supporting documents are also designed for this purpose, and I have included a section of "Letters To, From, and About Hemans" and a section of "Views and Reviews" of her and her work from the 1810s to the 1873. Hemans purposely constructed herself as a specifically "feminine" poet, or poet of the personal, domestic, local, and quotidian. She also constructed herself as a "feminine" poet of a certain social class – the gentrified upper middle class – that is, as a "lady." She succeeded in being taken as such, though her motive in doing so was to address and to alter the public, political sphere of her time, and beyond. Accordingly, I have tried to construct and annotate the sections of Letters and Views and Reviews so that they can be read as continuous narratives of the processes of construction of Hemans as a figure in and for the inescapably politicized public culture of the nineteenth century and now, again, in the twenty-first. This book is designed, then, to be a self-contained resource for reading and study of Hemans, but not to contain, in the sense of limit, such reading and study. Accordingly, I provide a website with additional materials (including unpublished poems) by, about, and relating to Hemans and what she represented and may represent now.

Abbreviations

Chorley   Henry F. Chorley, *Memorials of Mrs. Hemans with Illustrations of Her Literary Character from Her Private Correspondence*, second edition, 2 vols (London: Saunders and Otley, 1837).

Hughes   [Harriet Mary Browne Hughes, later Owen,] "Memoir of the Life and Writings of Mrs Hemans. By Her Sister." In *The Works of Mrs Hemans*, 7 vols (Edinburgh and London: William Blackwood and Sons, 1841), vol. 1.

Lawrence   *The Last Autumn at a Favourite Residence, with Other Poems; and Recollections of Mrs. Hemans* (Liverpool: G. and J. Robinson, and Evans, Chegwin, and Hall; London: John Murray, 1836).

Liverpool   Liverpool Public Library, Public Records Library.

FH   Felicia Hemans.

Website

http://www.arts.ualberta.ca/hemans. This includes additional texts, letters, reviews, etc.

Introduction

Felicia Hemans, the Reading Public, and the Political Nation

Felicia Hemans was the most widely read woman poet in the nineteenth-century English-speaking world.[1] Furthermore, nineteenth-century reprint editions of her poetry appeared in series with the half-dozen most widely read men poets from the Romantic period.[2] Such popularity indicates that she successfully addressed the interests and values of a large part of the reading public in her time and through the nineteenth century. Hemans built this success from three main elements. First there were the values, knowledge, and outlook she acquired in her family and native city, region, and country. These were the values, knowledge, and outlook of what was at that time the revolutionary class. Then there was her energetic adaptation of new developments in both British and European Romantic literature—developments that were designed to further the interests of the revolutionary class throughout Europe and in its colonies and former colonies. Finally, Hemans responded passionately to the unfolding national and international politics of her day—the revolution in which she and her reading public were implicated.[3] For throughout Britain, Europe, and indeed the New World, people with backgrounds and values similar to hers were attempting to found modern states in the aftermath of Revolutionary and Napoleonic cataclysm, against the restoration of reactionary and repressive monarchic regimes, and in face of emergent working-class political movements. Hemans and those like her formed the majority of the reading public at that time; these predominant-

---

1   Donald H. Reiman, introduction, *Felicia Dorothea Hemans, Tales and Historic Scenes*, etc. (New York and London: Garland Publishing, 1978) v.

2   Advertisements for "Standard Editions of Poetry" published by Frederick Warne and Co., London and New York, in the 1880s and '90s.

3   For a detailed account of one aspect of Hemans's poetic response to current events, see Nanora Sweet, "The Bowl of Liberty: Felicia Hemans and the Romantic Mediterranean," unpub. PhD. diss, University of Michigan, 1993.

ly middle-class reading publics were also those who had just become or were demanding to become the political nation—people with direct interest in state affairs, who were founding modern liberal states much as we still have them. These reading publics and political nations, in the English-speaking world, made Hemans the popular poet she was and remained until the early twentieth century.

Family, Region, and Nation: Enlightenment Legacy and Liberal Politics

Hemans's social, intellectual, and cultural formation prepared her well for this public literary role. She was born in 1793, at one of the most violent moments in Revolutionary Europe, into the merchant class in Liverpool. At that time Liverpool was a major world port with international business that included the slave trade and that was highly sensitive to the unfolding international crisis. Felicia Browne's family was well placed to bring her benefits from such a situation. Her father, George Browne, was a wine merchant of Irish background; her mother, Felicity Wagner Browne, was the daughter of the Liverpool consul for Austrian-ruled Tuscany, and she claimed German-Italian extraction and culture. These international and cosmopolitan connections would have a continuing influence for Felicia Hemans the poet, and would have been reinforced by developments in Liverpool itself. Like many provincial towns in late eighteenth-century Britain, and indeed throughout Europe and beyond, Liverpool was increasingly dominated by the "town gentry," or coalition of professional and commercial middle-class people, often including religious Dissenters. This social coalition were forming their own culture, distinct from and at times opposed to the social and cultural hegemony of the regional county gentry, to the political and economic dominance of London and the home counties of southern England, and to the political and ecclesiastical establishment of the state. In Liverpool, as in Norwich, Birmingham, Bristol, and similar places in Britain, Continental Europe, and beyond, the "town gentry" were leaders in provincial or regional Enlightenments set up to counter the historic dominance of metropolitan establishments of church and state, and historic privileged interests of court monarchy, aristocracy, and landed gentry. The "town gentry" developed local cultural resources and identities, advanced economic and social modernization, and pressed for those political and other reforms that they considered necessary to continue this work and thereby promote their own interests. As Nanora Sweet puts it, this culture of "disestablishment" of the Old Order aimed to transfer history "from an aristocratic to a bourgeois basis."[1] Yet these cultures were not merely provincial, or narrowly parochial. Resistant as they were to the hegemony of a metropolitan, centralist establishment, they frequently looked beyond national boundaries to claim authority and validation from a wider, cosmopolitan, European culture. Hemans's family background and education gave her access to that wider culture, inherited from the European Enlightenments and building a cosmopolitan liberalism.

Hemans's family was directly connected to the cosmopolitan yet provincial Enlightenment in Liverpool, for its leader was the lawyer, banker, and reform campaigner William Roscoe (1753-1831), whom Hemans knew and whose son helped arrange publication of her early poems. William Roscoe the elder supported reform causes of many kinds, was a close friend of Joseph Johnson, the main London publisher of the English provincial and other Enlightenments, and, through Johnson, Roscoe also befriended the Revolutionary feminist Mary Wollstonecraft. Among his many activities Roscoe wrote two cultural histories celebrating earlier urban renaissances in Italy,[2] thereby validating that of his own day in Liverpool. The social, cultural, and political re-formation of towns such as Liverpool was recontextualized and catalyzed, however, by the national and international crises that ensued from the outbreak of the French Revolution in 1789 and that flared on through

---

1   See Nanora Sweet, "'Lorenzo's' Liverpool and 'Corinne's' Coppet: The Italianate Salon and Romantic Education," in *Lessons of Romanticism: A Critical Companion*, ed. Thomas Pfau and Robert F. Gleckner (Durham and London: Duke University Press, 1998) 244-60.
2   *Life of Lorenzo de' Medici* (1796); *Life of Leo X* (1805).

Hemans's childhood, youth, and early adulthood. In places such as Liverpool, two major effects of the Revolution debate were the emergence of politicized working-class movements and division among the "town gentry" over whether or not to forge a reform coalition with such movements. The outbreak of war between Britain and Revolutionary France in 1793, with the two decades of global military and economic conflict that followed, exacerbated these divisions and forced a reconsideration of the relation between reform and patriotism. Despite her youth, Felicia Browne the poet would address this crisis and propose a distinctly feminist negotiation of the tension between reform and patriotism.

The wars also damaged Britain's economic stability and international trade, and George Browne's business was one of many affected. Some investments failed, he wound up his business, and retired with his family to north Wales. Later he would re-engage in business and go to Canada, where he died, probably in 1812. In north Wales Felicia Browne was educated at home, under the supervision of her mother and apparently in a permissive and undisciplined way. She had a tenacious memory and quick apprehension and seems to have read widely in English and continental European literature, travels, and history, and she had opportunity to learn modern languages. This reading gave her a cosmopolitan, internationalist outlook, encouraged by her mother, which prepared her for a lifelong engagement with European liberalism and Romanticism. Though she was still young when removed from Liverpool and its provincial Enlightenment, nonetheless she remained close to it in ideology, culture, and values.

Home Front and Global War: Building a Poetic Career

Felicia Browne's first volume, *Poems* (1808), was published at Liverpool while she lived in North Wales with her mother and sister and was characteristic of such a work by a young female poet at that time. It was published by subscription, with a predominantly regional clientele, though headed by the Prince of Wales (at that time still associated with Whig, reform-oriented politicians) and including many members of the aristocracy and gentry, as well as clergymen, professional and military men, and their wives and daughters. Most of the poems deal with subjects commonly found in late eighteenth-century women's verse, including occasional poems about events in family life, loco-descriptive pieces, apostrophes to such abstractions as genius, hope, and mirth, and some religious poems. The poems use conventional and familiar verse forms after respected eighteenth-century Augustan and Sentimental poets, from Alexander Pope to William Cowper, and include sonnets of the kind made fashionable by Charlotte Smith and others. Publication of the book was managed by William Roscoe the younger and was probably designed to show the Liverpool provincial Enlightenment's readiness, in the cause of social and cultural progress, to nurture youthful, and perhaps especially female, artistic endeavour. Significantly, however, the book also includes a number of patriotic and political poems. According to social and cultural conventions of the time, such topics would usually be considered unfeminine, but here they were given justification by the author's having two brothers, George and Henry, in the army. Thus the conventional "To Patriotism" is followed by "To My Younger Brother, on His Entering the Army." The collection also includes a few poems reflecting on the poetic vocation itself, such as "To the Muse"; such poems would form a continuing thread in Hemans's work, merging in a major theme of her last years—the contradictions of female literary fame. Broadly, the poems comprise an anthology of themes from reform-oriented Sentimental culture, couched in forms familiar from approved eighteenth-century authors.

Meanwhile, the great patriotic struggle against Napoleonic France was absorbing the British public's attention, centred especially on the Peninsular War in Spain, where Felicia Browne's two brothers were serving in the British army. Early British military intervention went badly, however, and many at home blamed the corruption and inefficiency of a government dominated by the royal court and aristocratic interests and patronage. Felicia Browne's *England and Spain; or, Valour and Patriotism* (1808), appropriately in heroic couplets, represents

Britain's engagement as a renewal of the nation's libertarian traditions, derived from classical republicanism, and linked to the kind of independent civic culture celebrated by William Roscoe the elder. The political theme in *England and Spain* may have been one reason why the republican and pacifist Percy Shelley, who did not know the Brownes, wrote to Felicia Browne with the pretext of dissuading her from support for war and belief in a god.[1] This criticism, and the dangerous attentions of a young man of such obviously radical political and religious views, may have influenced "The Domestic Affections" (1812), the major poem in her collection with that title. The poem, which is again in the heroic couplets conventionally prescribed for elevated public themes, links patriotism to a renewed middle-class domestic ideology designed to oppose upper-class decadence, and it re-emphasizes the wish for peace expressed in *England and Spain*. Thus *The Domestic Affections and Other Poems* continues a line of late eighteenth- and early nineteenth-century irenic poems by women that deplore the domestic cost of war and especially its cost to women, conventionally the custodians and nurturers of the domestic sphere.

Seeking further acceptably feminine ways of consolidating her career and assuming the role of public poet, Felicia Browne turned to translating poetry from the modern languages. This was considered appropriately feminine literary work because it did not transgress on learned studies and discourses that had historically been the preserves of men, and because it could be seen as modest service to the supposedly original genius of male authors. Nevertheless, Felicia Browne pursued this work with the public and political sphere in view. Her mother inquired about the possibility of her daughter acquiring a commission to translate an anti-Napoleonic poem by Napoleon's brother.[2] Felicia Browne may have done more: Ugo Foscolo was one of many Italians who had welcomed Napoleon's inter-

---

1   Percy B. Shelley to Miss FD Browne, Bronwhilfa, St Asaph, FlintS[hire]; 49 Lincolns Inn Fields, [London,] 13 (?) March 1811, Bodleian Library MS Don. *c.* 180, fols. 13-16.
2   See letter 4 here.

vention in their country in the late 1790s as a step to reform of the Old Order and the establishment of an independent and unified country, but who turned against Napoleon when they realized that he intended to control Italy himself. Foscolo expressed his disillusionment and his liberal patriotic politics in an autobiographical novel, *Ultime lettere di Jacopo Ortis* (1802), about double disappointment—in Napoleon as betrayer of liberal patriotism, and in love. The novel links political and subjective alienation and exile in a way that became common in liberal Romantic literature. Foscolo became a political exile in London and Felicia Browne was already involved in translating poetry with a liberal patriotic cast and with linked themes of disappointed love and political exile; an English translation of Foscolo's novel, by "F.B.," was published in 1812 at London, where many readers would welcome such an anti-Napoleonic yet liberal patriotic work, and one with a Romantic personal element.[1]

Soon the poet could claim new authority for her patriotic yet acceptably feminine work, as "Mrs Hemans," the title by which she would be known to literature thereafter. In July 1812 she married Capt. Alfred Hemans, who was considerably older and a veteran of the Peninsular War and by whom she had five sons in six years. The couple had been in love for some time but marriage was delayed by her parents because of her youth. The couple went to live with the Brownes in north Wales, and for a time in Northamptonshire (where Capt. Hemans had a command). During this time, her poetry turned increasingly to leading issues in the public political sphere. In Britain, the transition from wartime to peacetime economy produced economic distress and social conflict, pressures to reduce government expenditure and especially the armed forces, and demands for what was called "radical reform" in order to achieve these aims more expeditiously and thoroughly. Hemans responded to these issues as the wife and sister of army veterans, but risking transgression of gendered boundaries of discourse of that time. Two apparently unpublished verse

---

1 Douglas Radcliff-Umstead, introduction, *Ugo Foscolo's Ultime lettere di Jacopo Ortis: A Translation* (Chapel Hill: University of North Carolina Press, 1970).

satires, "The Army" and "Reform—a Poem" (see the present editor's Hemans website), address linked public issues of the immediate post-war years in Britain.

Both poems are in heroic couplets, the long-established form for such public and satirical discourse. "Reform" attacks "radical reformers" in general and one reform orator in particular—Charles Phillips. For a central issue in the poem is the politics of discourse, or oratory as the art of persuasion in a broad sense. The poem associates the stylistic excess of radical reform oratory with that of the so-called Della Cruscan poets of the late 1780s, who had by this time become infamous for uniting literary, political, moral, and even linguistic subversiveness. "Reform" ridicules phrases from Phillips's speeches as excessive and illiterate, thereby associating reform discourse with the undisciplined, ill-educated, and plebeian. "Reform" aims to contain this transgressive language in its own chaster diction, regular verse form, and literary and learned allusions (substantiated by footnotes). Hemans apparently decided against publishing "The Army" and "Reform," however, probably because such overtly satirico-political verse would have been considered by many to be unfeminine. Nevertheless, manifest formal and stylistic discipline would be a distinctive characteristic of her poetry throughout her career, implicitly opposed to what many considered the excesses of more politically radical Romantic poets. This characteristic would also enable Hemans to become a widely respected and widely read poet, though at the cost of being relegated by critics to a lesser rank than her more overtly experimental and transgressive male contemporaries.

Hemans did not relinquish ambitious and potentially "unfeminine" subjects, but rather framed them in ways that would seem acceptably feminine. This strategy is seen in the two ambitious poems she published next, both addressing the post-Napoleonic condition of Britain and Europe. *The Restoration of the Works of Art to Italy* (1816) and *Modern Greece* (1817) ostensibly deal with the arts, which were conventionally accepted as a legitimate interest of cultivated women, or "ladies." At the same time, these poems are written from a broad historical and cultural perspective and comment on large national and international political issues. After the final defeat of Napoleon, Britain found itself the unrivalled European superpower, expected by many at home and abroad to exercise global leadership for reform, liberalization, and modernization. Britain, with a constitutional monarchy supposedly balancing interests of the historic landed class and "the people" (i.e., the emergent middle classes), was also the model for reformists and liberals throughout Europe and the New World. Yet the British government found itself acting, though often unwillingly and against public opinion, in concert with reactionary Continental European powers, while facing strong demands for reform at home. Hemans's ability to comment on this situation through literature had been bolstered by the work of Germaine de Staël, at that time the most widely known and influential woman writer in Europe, and especially her widely read novel *Corinne, ou l'Italie* (1807), which was powerfully enabling for Hemans and many other women writers.

Both the classical republicanism of Hemans's Liverpool background and the liberal nationalism of Staël and her circle inform *The Restoration of the Works of Art to Italy*.[1] It celebrates the return of sculptures and paintings taken by the French during their occupation of Italy (selections from the poem are included in this edition). This poem, too, uses heroic couplets as the conventionally appropriate form for serious public themes, especially when couched in neoclassical terms. For the poem draws on a major theme in the critical historiography of Enlightenment and eighteenth-century classical republicanism. This was the contrast between peoples with a glorious independent ancient civilization and their degenerate and subjugated modern descendants; here the arts are seen as symptomatic of the condition of the entire civilization. Like the heroine of Staël's *Corinne*, the narrator of Hemans's poem presents Italy's major artworks as embodiments of a once independent nation-

---

1 See Nanora Sweet, "History, Imperialism, and the Aesthetics of the Beautiful," in *At the Limits of Romanticism: Essays in Cultural, Feminist, and Materialist Criticism*, ed. Mary A. Favret and Nicola J. Watson (Bloomington and Indianapolis: Indiana University Press, 1994) 170-84.

al identity and culture that endure despite centuries of foreign
and despotic rule. Hemans chooses cities (Venice, Florence, and
Rome as second Athens) and artworks celebrated by historians
in a tradition from classical republicanism to Revolutionary
sympathy to Romantic liberalism, from J.J. Winckelmann to
William Roscoe to J.C. Sismondi. The poem implies that
return of and to classical artworks and to the political culture
that created them can inspire Italy's return to freedom and
independence—and also ensure the independence, freedom,
and resulting cultural creativity of ancient Rome's modern
heir—Britain. The poem was well received, especially among
liberals (Byron, for example), but Hemans made major changes
in the second edition to appeal to a broader range of the
reading public. She added explicitly patriotic passages praising
the British armies that had defeated Napoleon and thus
ensured the restoration of the works of art to Italy. She added
learned endnotes identifying sources and allusions, thereby
claiming more cultural authority for herself. More important,
she added description of and praise for christian art (specifi-
cally Raphael's "Transfiguration of Christ"), declaring that the
religion informing such art is inherently superior to classical
pagan culture. The last change may have been motivated by
caution or criticism. Religious piety was considered admirably
feminine at the time, while unqualified veneration for a pagan
classical antiquity could seem unfeminine.

Modern Greece similarly addresses the condition of Britain
and Europe in the Napoleonic aftermath, but is even more
ambitious in theme, form, and scope. Accordingly, Hemans was
careful to keep her name off the title page. The poem also takes
several new directions. It turns from a recent event in the arts
on the Continent—the return of artworks from France to
Italy—to a recent artistic controversy in Britain—the pro-
posed government purchase of Lord Elgin's "marbles," or frag-
ments of ancient Greek sculpture. Hemans again links a partic-
ular issue to a vast historical and cultural survey, but now con-
trasts ancient with modern Greece. In the eighteenth century,
western European writers represented the modern Greeks, like
the modern Italians, as degenerate versions of their glorious

ancient forebears, who were accordingly subjugated by later and more vigorous foreign civilizations. These writers often suggested similar degeneration was at work in modern states and would have similar results unless there was liberalization, reform, and modernization. One way recommended to avoid national decline and fall was through regeneration by the arts, reviving classical republican models. In *Modern Greece*, Hemans implies that state acquisition and public exhibition of the Elgin marbles would place the artistic expression of Athenian republican greatness at the centre of modern British culture, thereby enabling the reconstruction of Britain as a modern Athens. This liberal reformist programme is reinforced by Hemans's turn, paradoxically, from a neo-classical verse form to a renaissance one, from heroic couplets to a version of the stanza used by Edmund Spenser in his patriotic christian romance, *The Faerie Queen* (1590-96). This verse form had recently been revived by British liberal Romantic poets such as Thomas Campbell (in *Gertrude of Wyoming*, 1809), and Byron (in *Childe Harold's Pilgrimage*). Like Campbell, Byron, and others, Hemans also expands the argument of her poetic text through certain devices. She includes numerous prose endnotes that explain allusions to a wide range of literary texts, historic events and sites, and artworks. She also cites sources and parallels from a wide range of writers, including Enlightenment historians, antiquarians, and travellers; Romantic writers such as Chateaubriand; and liberal reform-oriented writers such as Henry Holland and C. Pouqueville, Napoleon's former consul in Albania.

After these two ambitious and well received poems, Hemans published *Translations from Camoens, and Other Poets, with Original Poetry* (1818), collecting work from the 1810s that presents personal and public themes, implying a connection between them. The personal theme is absent or lost love; the public theme is loss of national independence. As in Foscolo and numerous other liberal Romantic writers, these themes are linked: the unreformed social and political world is hostile to autonomous, sovereign (or self-governing) subjectivity, which is manifested in the capacity for romantic love, among other things, and thwarted love is implicitly an effect of that hostility, in turn producing alienation and exile. Like other Romantic writers, Hemans appropriates earlier literature to this liberal Romantic theme. Luis de Camoens, or Camões (1524-80), wrote *Os Lusiades*, a renaissance epic celebrating Portugal's golden age of exploration and empire, and during the Peninsular War the British reading public was interested in all aspects of Spanish and Portuguese history and culture. Hemans translated his lesser known love complaints, however, with translations on similar themes from other European poets. These poems express obliquely Felicia Browne's separation from Capt. Hemans before they were married, though a few months after the book was published Capt. Hemans left his then pregnant wife for Italy, and did not return. Separation and loss would be a recurring theme in Hemans's poetry for the rest of her life. She would merge it, however, with a leading theme of liberal Romanticism—exile—and she begins that work here, using a favourite device of Romantic poets—the unstated intertextual connections between poems in a collection or set. For example, Hemans includes translations of such poems as Vincenzo Filicaja's seventeenth-century sonnet deploring the subject condition of his native Italy, and personal loss is implicitly linked to loss of national independence, as expressed in the original poem, "Guerilla Song" (both poems are included in this edition).

The Feminization of History

This connection is made explicit in Hemans's next volume, *Tales, and Historic Scenes* (two of the volume's nine poems are included in this edition; others are posted on the editor's Hemans website). It was published in 1819 when post-war economic, social, and political conflicts were reaching a crisis that would last for several years and, in the opinion of many, pushed Britain to the brink of revolution. Similar crises seemed imminent all across Europe. Hemans places this national and international scene of struggle within a correspondingly broad historical and geographical context. She gives poetic and fictionalized treatment to a number of turning points in history that could be seen as analogous to her own times, and presents these moments as experienced by individuals, often women, and always victims, through exacting vengeance in death. The poems' settings range through Europe and especially the Mediterranean world, from the second century BC to the fifteenth century AD. This range implies that recurring themes have general historical validity and significance for Europe and its empires — past, present, and future. Each poem is set in a conflict between great historic national and imperial rivals or between internal factions in a single state, and often the two levels of conflict are related. No temporal setting comes closer than three centuries to Hemans's day. Yet the poems clearly reflect on the conflicts of the Revolutionary and Napoleonic wars, and the poems are set in various places that figured in those struggles, and where despotic, reactionary regimes were restored after the final defeat of Napoleon in 1815. *Tales, and Historic Scenes* reflects on the social and political conflicts caused by these restorations, and anticipates the confrontations and revolts that would occur in these places from the early 1820s on.

The book presents these conflicts from a Romantic feminist viewpoint, showing the deaths of individuals, communities, nations, and empires in the cycles of "masculine" history. Death is a major theme in Hemans's work, and more prominent there than in the work of any other poet of her time — perhaps of any time. Some critics in her own time, and many critics and readers through the nineteenth century, saw her interest in and treatment of death as sentimental, for better or worse. Death is often seen as a transhistorical fact of human existence, defying culture and discourse; but death is a cultural as well as a biological fact, and cultures of death are socially and historically particular. Hemans was the major poet of what might be termed Romantic death. This culture of death was a response to what many saw as the meaningless mass death of the Revolutionary and Napoleonic cataclysm, and indeed of most of human history. Mass death and widespread and historic human misery were preoccupations of Enlightenment philosophers and theologians. Whether caused by natural or human agency, these evils challenged both Enlightenment belief in humanity's power to improve its condition and the religious doctrine of theodicy, or the ultimate benevolence of the divine plan for humanity.

Many Enlightenment philosophers rejected religious consolations for these evils. They advocated, on the one hand, a classical republican stoicism in the face of unavoidable human misery, and on the other hand a revolution in the social and political order that was blamed for much of the misery and mass death, past and present. The French Revolutionaries and their sympathizers in other countries aimed to end such evils, and some with extreme views even believed that human progress would eliminate sickness and death. But the Revolution and its Napoleonic sequel used mass death as an instrument of policies and programs that, in the eyes of many, eventually came to seem futile and even counter-productive. Accordingly, post-Revolutionary and Romantic culture assigned meaning to death by individualizing it, locating it in the individual subject, in contrast to Revolutionary death which was seen to annihilate the individual in an abyss of mass death and oblivion. Revolutionary and Napoleonic death were seen to have sacrificed the individual in the name of generalizations or abstractions such as the "rights of man" or "the people," without achieving revolutionary change. Romantic culture proposed to achieve such change another way, making death meaningful by focusing on the individual, who is immortalized in the memory of other individuals, memorialized in art (one of Hemans's favourite subjects was funerary art[1]), and thereby made exemplary in public and political culture. In this way, Romantic death served the liberal ideology of the autonomous sovereign subject.

Hemans gives a Romantic feminist turn to Romantic death in the context of human history, past and present. She does so in order to bring about a future liberal state that will supposedly alter the nature of that history and, in effect, end it. Hemans constructs her Romantic feminist representation of death in several ways. She emphasizes the importance of memory as "record," one of her favourite words, which comes from the

---

1   See, for example, "The Child's Last Sleep" in this edition.

Latin *cor/cordis*, for heart, as conventional symbol of the humane and social feelings. Not only does Hemans represent "records" as the transcendence of death and mortality in individual feeling, but she also uses poetry to create a literature of such "records," against the merely documentary records which provide the materials both for the institutions of state power and for historiography as the narrative of that power. Hemans's strategy is to write the heart, in several ways. She represents central human relationships as those of the feelings, particularly those then called the "domestic affections," which included friendship based on mutuality of feelings and interests. Especially in her narrative poems, she creates an authorial persona that clearly sympathizes with the poems' subjects. Throughout her career, but increasingly so, however, she writes personal expressive lyrics in authorial voice. Most prominently at this stage of her career, she reconstructs history, particularly in her narrative poems, but also in her dramas and many of her shorter poems.

Since the seventeenth century, at least, critics had pointed out that historiography dealt mainly with the public and political sphere, because this sphere produced and preserved the majority of documents on which historians depended. Consequently historiography was supposed to be unable to depict the private feelings and private lives of even famous persons, let alone obscure individuals; subjective and private experience, it was argued, were better represented by romance, or fiction of various kinds. Hemans and other liberal Romantic writers took these views farther. They saw historiography, written almost exclusively by men, as a record of conflict, war, and destruction caused by and for men. Such history may elicit from women a specifically feminine kind of heroism, but it also victimizes women and what they represent—especially the autonomous subject, the "domestic affections," and the local as a site of particular human and social meanings that make authentic community possible. Hemans, like other women writers of her time, suggests that the way to break the cycle of masculine history is to refeminize history for the future. She does so by feminizing the "masculine" discourse of historiography with what many at that time considered to be the "feminine" discourse of "romance," or fiction.

In *Tales, and Historic Scenes* and Hemans's other historical narrative poems, history and romance are not merged but placed in tension. Each poem centres on a particular historical moment of crisis, with prefaces and notes indicating facts and sources, but this moment is fictionalized and feminized by being represented from the viewpoint of a female or feminized male protagonist and in terms of individual subjective and emotional experience and the "domestic affections." A similar method was used by women writers of Sensibility and the Revolution debate, from Clara Reeve to Charlotte Smith. This method privileges the subjective and domestic over the public and political, implying that the latter should be based on the nature and needs of the former. In *Tales, and Historic Scenes*, this implication is supported by formal devices of textual structure, narration, and description. Each poem in the set has a prose preface drawn from some historical work, followed by an often lyrical poetic version of the event referred to or described in the prose. Most of the poems also have author's prose endnotes, often lengthy, apparently validating the poetic treatment of the subject by the "facts" of historiography and other learned discourses. Many of these factual and learned sources promote social, economic, and political modernization; they range from travel books, through literature in several languages (often associated with a cosmopolitan European culture of broadly liberal character), to liberal historiography by such writers as Sismondi, a member of Staël's circle.

The effect of this textual structure is complex, however. The verse romance is framed by prose fact and literary parallels or sources. The verse narrative and the feminized experience it represents and valorizes are at the centre; the supposedly authoritative and authorizing discourses of fact and literature (here, mostly by male writers) are marginalized. Prose and verse discourses are placed in contrast, tension, and even conflict. The centrality of the feminine is reinforced by handling of narration and description. All the poems are in third-person omniscient narration, with the narrator clearly sympathetic to the poems' protagonists. Lyrical description is used to empha-size this narratorial sympathy and author's imaginative respon-siveness, and expressive language and exclamations are used by the narrator, though relatively sparingly. Hemans constructs the poem's narrator as an implied model consciousness similar in values and sympathies to the authors she cites, who range from Milton to Staël, and many of whom readers could consider more or less "liberal" in politics and sympathies. The narrator is the central character in the poetic part of each text, implicitly joining the company of these authors.

By now this implied claim of Hemans's was being validated by literary critics, publishers, and public literary institutions. One early reviewer found her "possessed of a powerful imagi-nation and of a commanding mind," with a praiseworthy "strain of piety" in her work.[1] Another reviewer was "aston-ished by her powers," thought her only rival among women poets was Joanna Baillie, and declared that "even compared with the living *masters* [i.e., men] of song ... she is entitled to a place of very high distinction."[2] The political dimension of her work was noted by a reviewer who declared, "When Liberty strings her lyre, she frequently rises into a more elevated and impressive strain of poetry ...."[3] One reviewer had thought *Modern Greece*, which was published anonymously, "to be the work of an academical" writer, that is, a classically educated man, probably at a university, "and certainly not a female" writer. Responding perhaps to Hemans's easy command of the heroic couplet form, the reviewer thought her poetry resem-bled that of Alexander Pope and, more recently, Reginald Heber.[4] These comments imply that, for some critics, at least, Hemans transcended the supposedly "naturally" limited powers of women and the socially limited education and public expe-rience available to them. Another reviewer, however, found her poetry better than that of any female contemporary but still limited in a supposedly characteristic feminine way, lacking

---

1   See item 1 in Views and Reviews here.
2   Item 2 in Views and Reviews.
3   Item 3 in Views and Reviews.
4   Item 5 in Views and Reviews.

"that uniform deep colour of poetic feeling, by which the touch of a master-poet is so easily distinguished."[1] A reviewer of *Tales, and Historic Scenes* noted that Hemans's style of narrative poetry differed from that of her male contemporaries in focusing on (and evoking) feeling rather than action and adventure.[2] Reviewers agreed that Hemans's style, while it had faults, was chaste, pure, elegant, and classical, avoiding the "excesses" of much contemporary poetry, and that her narrative poems were highly descriptive.

Responding to such reception, Hemans published a series of reflective poems connected to public issues, including *The Sceptic: A Poem, Stanzas to the Memory of the Late King, Wallace's Invocation to Bruce* (all 1820), and *Dartmoor: A Poem* (1822); the last two won poetry competitions with cash prizes. Such competitions were established ways of attracting public attention for young men seeking professional appointment, like her friend Reginald Heber and his poem *Palestine*, which Hemans admired. Almost all professions were closed to women, but Hemans may have felt that winning a poetry competition would help her career-building in one of the few professions that were open to women, and which she had taken up — writing. Urged on by Heber, she also began work on a major religious poem, "Religion and Superstition," which, however, was not completed.

Hemans's response to her growing recognition as a public voice is indicated in "The Rock of Cader-Idris" (included in this edition), from *A Selection of Welsh Melodies* (1822). The book contains folksong imitations of a kind much practised by Romantic liberal nationalist writers, and Hemans herself would produce a large amount of such material, including "Songs of the Cid" (1823), "Greek Songs" (1823), and "Lays of Many Lands" (1825). Hemans also acquired an extensive library of similar material from Continental European languages. In Britain, middle-class professionals and intellectuals collected, imitated, "edited," and forged folksongs, from Thomas Percy's *Reliques of Ancient English Poetry* (1765) through Walter Scott's

---

1   Item 3 in Views and Reviews.
2   Item 2 in Views and Reviews.

Minstrelsy of the Scottish Border (1802-03)—both of which Hemans knew. The early folklorists saw folksongs and popular ballads, with folk culture in general, as fragments of a once universal national culture. Folksong collection and imitation appropriated a centuries-old plebeian oral and print culture for the emergent professional middle-class institution of "national" literature, inscribing that culture in an invented "national" tradition, history, identity, and destiny. Romantic liberal nationalism gave a particular turn to this discourse in Britain. Wales and other remote and supposedly uncorrupted regions, such as western Ireland and the Scottish Highlands, were used as figures for the essential or "true" Britain, marginalized by the unreformed hegemonic order but a potential source of national, social, political, and cultural renewal, regeneration, reform, and reconciliation. Hemans's songs in *Welsh Melodies* are built around a recurring trope in this kind of literature: the mountain land as home (or refuge) of a free people who, because they are free, are also rich in patriotic song. This people may be invaded, oppressed, and even occupied by an (implicitly corrupt and rapacious) alien power, but they are inspired by their tradition of patriotic song to continued or renewed resistance, led by their national bards. In "The Rock of Cader-Idris," Hemans places herself in the line of these bards. At the same time, however, the poem suggests that to become a national poetic voice risks madness or death—in other words, loss of the very selfhood that distinguishes the sovereign subject of liberal ideology. In *Welsh Melodies*, Hemans appropriates the liberal Romantic and nationalist discourse of folksong while constructing herself as a Welsh Corinne.[1] This figure anticipates her later self-construction in her poems as conflicted public voice and therefore exemplary liberal subject.

Hemans gave complex dramatic representation to the figure of the (female) national and patriotic voice in her next two major works, dramas published in 1823. "The Siege of Valencia: A Dramatic Poem" and many of the shorter poems pub-

---

1   In fact she has been included in the modern monograph series Writers of Wales, published by the Welsh Arts Council: Peter Trinder, *Mrs. Hemans* (Cardiff: University of Wales Press, 1984).

lished with it address national and international crises of the early 1820s by alluding to several layers of Spanish history, from ancient times to the present, and by drawing elements from several literary works with resonance for European liberalism. Hemans states that the action of "The Siege of Valencia" is set in the time of El Cid, a mostly legendary eleventh-century Spanish military leader who had seized Valencia just before his death. He then came to be celebrated in popular ballads as a figure for Christian resistance to the Moors. This literature was later revived and imitated when El Cid was made a figure for patriotic Spanish resistance to Napoleon, and then as a symbol of the patriot in other European liberal nationalist movements. Hemans's "dramatic poem" is written as a "closet" drama (i.e., meant to be read privately rather than performed in the theatre) modelled on those of Hemans's friend Joanna Baillie. Baillie's dramas, beginning with *A Series of Plays on the Passions* (1798), were designed to urge social reconciliation in the Revolutionary aftermath, largely through a feminization of social relations and culture, and Hemans's poem "The Last Constantine," published with "The Siege of Valencia," was based on Baillie's play *Constantine Paleologus*. Structurally, however, Hemans's play is modelled on the later historical dramas of Friedrich Schiller, which became favourites with European liberals and which were also based on legendary historical figures, such as Wilhelm Tell and Jeanne d'Arc. Hemans dramatizes a fictitious but historically-based event—the siege of Valencia, then ruled by El Cid, undertaken by a new wave of muslim Moors invading Spain from North Africa. In Hemans's play the Moors, led by the cruel Abdullah, besiege Valencia, governed by the christian Alvar Gonzalez. Gonzalez's sons have been captured by Abdullah, who offers to spare them in exchange for surrender of the city; Gonzalez's wife Elmina pleads the superior claim of the domestic affections over the public interest, but he maintains his public duty and family honour. Elmina visits the Moorish camp to plead a mother's right, but fails to persuade Abdullah. The citizens of Valencia, beset from without by the Moors and from within by plague, consider surrender, but their will to resist is reinforced by Hernandez, a priest and former warrior of unyieldingly masculine patriotism and fanatically religious motivation, and by Ximena, Gonzalez's daughter. She has abandoned her femininity to lead the patriotic cause, but dies from the strain of assuming this "unnatural" public role. The siege is raised by arrival of the christian king and his army, though Gonzalez dies, heroic victim of the conflict within his family and his own heart more than victim of the Moors.

Hemans's second play of 1823, *The Vespers of Palermo*, fictionalizes a popular Sicilian uprising in AD 1282 against the foreign rule of Charles of Anjou. The episode was known as the "Sicilian Vespers" because it broke out in a church at vespers, or evening service. The revolt was followed by a massacre of the French. The island became a republic comprised of free communes, but had to submit to a monarchic regime in exchange for the support of Pedro III of Aragon against Charles's attempt to retake the island. Once again Hemans fictionalizes history to represent the conflict of private and public spheres in an unmodernized, illiberal state. In her dramatization, the count di Procida, loyal follower of the former ruler, Conradin, and motivated as much by revenge as patriotism, returns from exile to lead a revolt of discontented Sicilian nobility against the French viceroy, Eribert. The plot is supported by Vittoria, the betrothed of the murdered Conradin. She is courted by Eribert, and agrees to lure Eribert and his French entourage to their deaths during a banquet—one of Hemans's favourite tropes was representing death in the midst of festivity. The rebels seize Palermo, but Procida finds vengeance unsatisfying, and the conspirators grimly await a French counter-attack. Procida's son Raimond loves Eribert's sister, Constance, however, and is suspected of betraying the conspiracy; Procida places country above family and condemns his son to die. When the French do counter-attack, the remorseful Vittoria releases Raimond to lead further resistance, but she dies from the effort of supra-feminine patriotic heroism. Raimond is mortally wounded and dies before his repentant father and Constance, who rebukes Procida; the play closes with Procida calling in vain for his son's word of forgiveness.

For Hemans's readers, the themes and allusions in these plays would have highly topical reference to recent or continuing liberal nationalist revolts in Spain, Portugal, Italy (including Palermo), Greece, Russia, Poland, Mexico, and elsewhere.[1] To the dismay of many, Britain stood by while these revolts, claiming to seek British-style constitutional monarchy, were suppressed by a league of reactionary continental monarchic powers, including France and Austria. The plays' themes were also relevant to the recent divisive national debate in Britain over the "trial" of queen Caroline, which precipitated a near-revolutionary crisis. The crisis revived a long-standing and politically destabilizing conflict within the royal family, which Hemans had already alluded to in *Stanzas* on the death of George III (1820). The "queen Caroline affair" also revived Enlightenment critique of women's role in affairs of state under monarchic court governments, whether as royal mistresses or as rulers. In the 1820s there were powerful women ruling directly or indirectly in several European dominions, including Spain and certain Italian states, sometimes favouring liberal reform but more usually obstructing it. In her two plays, Hemans addresses these European and British issues from a Romantic feminist standpoint. She does so partly by adapting the structure and character relations of Friedrich Schiller's later historical dramas, which had become favourite texts with European liberals. Hemans sharpens Schiller's contrast between weakly feminine and fatally masculinized women, brutally masculine and nobly feminized men. More important, these plays show the cost of armed struggle led by men, however patriotically motivated, to women, to the social values and practices they represent, and to their potential for feminizing history and thereby enabling the formation of modern liberal states.

Hemans's Romantic feminist critique of masculine history seems even stronger in her "Songs of the Cid," originally published in the liberal *New Monthly Magazine*, where similar poems by other authors were appearing in the early 1820s in sympathy with the liberal revolt in Spain. "Songs of the Cid" were republished with "The Siege of Valencia" and linked to it

---

1   For the British reading public's linked cultural and commercial interest in Spain and its former empire, see Nanora Sweet, "'Hitherto closed to British enterprise': Trading and Writing the Hispanic World circa 1815," *European Romantic Review* 8 (Spring 1997): 139-47.

by the ballads sung by Ximena in the play. Hemans was and is seen as participating in the Romantic revival of medieval chivalry, but chivalry had already been revised and imbued with middle-class values in eighteenth-century literature and cultural historiography. Romantic culture carried this revision further, associating chivalry with liberal patriotism and national revival, for which El Cid was made a symbol in several European literatures. Hemans's refiguring of El Cid and chivalry is more elegiac than celebratory, however, centring on her recurring themes of exile and death. "Songs of the Cid" ignores the hero's triumphs, or his positive presence in history and legend, to give him a bizarrely negative presence, or presence by absence—another of Hemans's favourite tropes. The instances chosen by Hemans from the Cid stories are his exile from family lands and home; his deathbed, when he instructed that after death his body be dressed for battle, put on horseback, and sent against the Moors besieging Valencia; the resulting victory over the Moors; and his ghost's heroic role in defeating the Moors at the battle of Las Navas de Tolosa in AD 1212, blocking further Moorish expansion. Paradoxically, Hemans's Cid achieves his historic patriotic role in absence and death; an otherwise supermasculine hero is strangely demasculinized but apparently is no less effective in the national cause, because he remains a figure of legend, or ideology.

By now Hemans herself was becoming recognized as an important public voice, largely by avoiding sacrifice of her feminine identity. One reviewer claimed, "She is especially excellent in painting the strength, and the weaknesses of her own lovely sex, and there is a womanly nature throughout all her thoughts and her aspirations, which is new and inexpressibly touching." This ability gives Hemans her public authority: the reviewer quotes lines from "The Siege of Valencia" that "only" a mother could have written (scene 1, ll. 424-62, included in this edition) and declares, "When a woman can write like this, she *ought* to write. Her mind is national property."[1] Another reviewer praised "Songs of the Cid" and the ballads in "The Siege of Valencia": "A chivalrous and even a mar-

---

1   See *British Critic and Quarterly Theological Review*, 20 (July 1823) 50-61.

tial strain flows freely from her lyre, which never sends forth nobler sounds than when it celebrates the battles of freedom or the achievements of romance." The reviewer links this strain directly to the current situation in Spain, calling for a modern-day Cid to rescue his country from internal and external oppression.[1] Hemans's next major work, *The Forest Sanctuary* (1825), responds in terms of Romantic feminism. If "Songs of the Cid" represents a chivalric hero who is strangely demasculinized yet still an effective national leader, *The Forest Sanctuary* goes farther and represents a feminized warrior as model liberal subject for the future.

In November 1824 Hemans told a friend that the poem's subject "relates to the sufferings of a Spanish Protestant in the time of Philip the Second; and is supposed to be narrated by the sufferer himself, who escapes to America."[2] The poem, which Hemans would consider her best work, is set in the mid-sixteenth century and the protagonist-narrator is a former Spanish conquistador. As the poem opens, he is living in exile in a remote forest somewhere in eastern North America. He longingly recalls his home in Spain, and then recounts why and how he fled his native country. He relates that, on returning to Spain from fighting in Peru, he had come upon a procession of those about to be burned alive after having been condemned for heresy by the Inquisition. He was shocked to see in this procession his comrade-in-arms, Alvar, who had saved his life in a battle against the native people in South America. Also in the procession were Alvar's two sisters, who had adopted their brother's unorthodox religious views and thus had to share his fate. The narrator's faith in church and state was radically shaken by this instance of institutionalized oppression, and he sought solace in a cathedral, where a picture of Christ walking on the waters moved him to adopt a form of Protestantism. Being a soldier, he was accustomed to comradely frankness and unaccustomed to hide his beliefs, and so became imprisoned for heresy. Eventually he escaped from prison and fled to the New World with his wife, Leonor, and their son. Leonor did

---

1   Item 6 in Views and Reviews.
2   See letter 12 here.

not share her husband's new beliefs, however, and accordingly believed he was doomed to hell after death. Her grief wore her down and she died on the voyage and was buried at sea. In South America, the narrator found that the conflicts and oppressions of the Old World had been transported to the New, and he took his son to a "forest sanctuary" beyond the limits of European settlement, in North America. He closes his narrative contemplating his sleeping son, the American wilderness, his continued longing for Spain, however irredeemably conflicted, his doubtful religious faith, and an uncertain future for himself and child. In the manuscript version of the poem, the ending is significantly different, and Leonor is also characterized as much more the victim of religious superstition, or false ideology.

This narrative is less about the story than about the narrator, however, for the poem is designed to represent, as a figure from the past, the modern liberal subject who is alienated and exiled by a repressive ideology (here, Catholicism) that is in turn sustained by an unmodernized society and enforced by a despotic state. Accordingly, Hemans casts her narrative as a dramatic monologue—a form in which a historical or fictitious character describes his or her situation or feelings, usually addressing a person other than the reader. The form developed partly from the long tradition of verse complaint in letter form, going back to classical antiquity, and partly from the monodrama, a brief play for one character, sometimes with chorus and often with musical accompaniment, designed to exhibit the subjective experience of a particular historical or fictitious person, in many cases a victim of social injustice or human limitations. Significantly, most verse complaints and monodramas have an afflicted female protagonist. By the early nineteenth century, these forms were being used to address the interests of a largely middle-class reading public in individual subjectivity as the basis of personal identity and political rights. During the 1820s Letitia Landon used the dramatic monologue to advance her version of Romantic feminism, notably in *The Improvisatrice* (1824). In developing this form, both Landon and Hemans anticipated the next generation of male poets, including Alfred

Tennyson and Robert Browning, who took up the dramatic monologue in the 1830s and in the following decades developed it into a major Victorian poetic form. In doing so they became major public voices, while the contribution of Hemans and Landon was forgotten.[1]

The Forest Sanctuary also participates in Romantic literary appropriation of Renaissance romance and the Spenserian stanza (see discussion of Modern Greece, above). For male poets such as Campbell, Byron, Percy Shelley in The Revolt of Islam (1818), and Keats in "The Eve of St Agnes" (1819), using the Spenserian stanza advertised participation in a line of heroic "patriotic" poetry adapted to new and even revolutionary themes and subjects of national and imperial importance. Because of the form's association with these male writers, and because it was considered technically challenging, some saw it as inherently "masculine." Wordsworth, for example, advised a woman poet against attempting it, declaring it to be "a fine structure of verse, but also almost insurmountably difficult."[2] Hemans uses this stanza form to make the same claims that her male contemporaries did and, like them, she exploits its combination of flexibility and strong closure. With its two linked but distinct iambic pentameter quatrains (ababbcbc) and final rhyming couplet of an iambic pentameter with an iambic hexameter line, the form enables the poet to sustain narrative impetus and variation along with poetic formality, proceeding by verse units that are similar in structure but that may be diverse in subject, pace, and tone.

During the Romantic period (as the term suggests), the romance, which had earlier served an aristocratic feudal culture of chivalry, was remade to serve the interests of the middle-class reading public. Earlier romance was constructed around a plot of moral and ethical testing and education of the individual in a world that seemed mysterious and menacing. Eighteenth-century critics and writers initiated a comprehensive embour-

---

1 Neither Landon nor Hemans is mentioned in books on the dramatic monologue by Alan Sinfield (1977) and Elisabeth A. Howe (1996).

2 The Letters of William and Dorothy Wordsworth: The Later Years, ed. E. de Selincourt, 3 vols (Oxford: Clarendon Press, 1939) 2.58, pointed out to me by Susan Wolfson.

geoisement of romance and chivalry, remaking them in the image and interests of a gentrified middle-class culture and civil society. Romantic romances from Jane Porter's novel *The Scottish Chiefs* to the poems and novels of Walter Scott extended and developed this process by representing the formation of a liberal sovereign subject in an inhospitable or even hostile social and political world. As Marlon Ross points out, Hemans uses Romantic romance to foreground subjectivity rather than masculine action.[1] *The Forest Sanctuary* uses romance to represent the reformation of the sovereign subject, as a process of feminization in response to masculine history. Like Renaissance romance, Hemans's poem recounts an adventure on a journey from home, to a scene of trial and battle, and back home again; but for Hemans's knight errant the real romance journey is not external but inward, not martial and imperial but subjective and spiritual. It begins when he returns from his military expedition to learn that home, whether national or domestic, is for him irredeemably divided and conflicted. His encounter with the Inquisition—the execution of his friends and his own subsequent imprisonment as a heretic—reveals that the unmodernized, illiberal state depends on institutionalized violence. His wife's fatal religious difference from him reveals how such a state is internalized in subjectivity and the domestic sphere. These revelations prepare for the protagonist's conversion from the state's masculinist ideology to a feminized one, through an image of the central feminized figure in European culture and history—Christ—a direct contrast to the masculine martial hero of medieval romance and imperialist history.

The feminized ideology is represented in this poem as a Protestant form of christianity, for many Romantic liberals considered the Catholic Church, past and present, to be complicit in what Hemans would see as masculine history, and thus an obstacle to formation of the liberal state. This issue was highly topical, for the major political controversy in Britain during the mid and late 1820s was over Catholic emancipation,

---

1 Marlon Ross, *The Contours of Masculine Desire: Romanticism and the Rise of Women's Poetry* (New York and Oxford: Oxford University Press, 1989) 271-72.

or repeal of laws that withheld certain civil liberties from Roman Catholics in Britain and Ireland. In a letter to a friend written some months after the publication of *The Forest Sanctuary*, Hemans worried that the poem had appeared at a moment that "gives it some apparent coincidence with the great subject of national debate—the Catholic question." She declared that her poem "was however written without the slightest view to such coincidence, (which in my opinion Poetry should always avoid,) a considerable period having elapsed between its composition and appearance before the Public."[1] Nevertheless, the "Catholic question" was involved in the struggle to found a liberal state, in Britain and throughout Europe. Hemans was dubious about Catholic emancipation, and this attitude seems illiberal now. Like many who sympathized with reform, however, Hemans associated the ideology of the sovereign subject with middle-class Protestantism. She associated Catholicism with a pre-modern or unmodernized social structure, customary culture, and collective consciousness; these were widely seen at that time as obstacles to achieving a modern liberal state, as alien and "not British." When living in Ireland in her last years, for example, Hemans found a mass political demonstration by Catholics to be sublimely incomprehensible, and the domestic religious piety of her Catholic neighbours seemed a vestige of the customary folk culture represented by Gothic novelists such as Ann Radcliffe.[2] As Linda Colley has argued, this suspicion of Catholicism was deeply rooted in English and British culture and was a powerful force in shaping Romantic nationalism in Britain.[3]

In *The Forest Sanctuary* Hemans represents the Catholic Church as an arm of a despotic monarchic and imperialist state, centred in the ideological and political institution of the Inquisition. The long history of this institution had just come to an end when Hemans's poem was published. The Inquisition was established by Ferdinand and Isabella after their conquest of Granada, the last Moorish kingdom in Spain, in 1492, and was

---

1   Letter to the Rev. S. Butler, 5 May 1826, British Library Add. MS 34586 g. 192.
2   FH to ?; 20 Dawson Street, Dublin, 29 Jan. 1833; in Chorley 2.263-4.
3   *Britons: Forging the Nation, 1707-1837* (London: Pimlico, 1992).

designed less to police converts and heretics than to consolidate the centralized monarchic state. In following centuries, down to Hemans's day, the Inquisition was used by established interests to resist modernization of Spain and its empire. Writers such as Hemans's friend Joseph Blanco White treated the Inquisition as both symptom and cause of Spain's decline and inability to modernize as a progressive civil society. The Inquisition was abolished by Napoleon, to the approval of Spanish reformers, but restored in 1814 with the Spanish monarchy, to be abolished again for good during the revolution of the early 1820s, to the applause of liberals everywhere.

Hemans goes further, however, and treats the Inquisition as another instance of the problem of evil—the long-standing topic of theological and philosophical debate that was given new relevance in Hemans's lifetime by a seemingly unending series of wars, revolution, suffering, and mass death. As in *Tales, and Historic Scenes*, Hemans gives a specifically Romantic feminist turn to the issue, showing that the problem of evil, of which the Inquisition and Spanish history are instances, is characteristic of masculine history down to the present. *The Forest Sanctuary* also shows, however, that history of this kind can precipitate a transformation in individual subjects, feminizing them according to the divinely provided pattern of Christ's sacrifice—a sacrifice that is supposedly transhistorical and that enables the individual, through redemption and salvation, to escape from history as evil into eternity. Thus, according to long-established Christian doctrine, evil produces good in the divine plan. In Hemans's Romantic feminist version of this argument, historic absolutist regimes paradoxically bring about the formation of liberal subjects, who in turn anticipate the advent of the modern liberal state. Such an argument of historical and transhistorical consolation would be just what religiously committed liberals would want to read in the aftermath of suppression of liberal revolts all over Europe in the early 1820s. This argument of the poem's story and plot is reinforced by the devices of dramatic monologue and romance form, which foreground the sovereign subjectivity of the narrator-protagonist. In Hemans's poem this liberal subject is projected into the past, thereby anticipating and validating the liberal subjects of the present (Hemans's readers), and implicitly preserving such a subject for the liberal state of the future. The religious dimension of the poem gives that historic subject divine validation, making it transhistorical.

Hemans was by now an established poet and public figure on both sides of the Atlantic, as shown by reviews of her work, by the high fees paid her by editors and publishers, by remarks of those who knew her, and strikingly by published poetic tributes to her.[1] In 1826 the *Literary Magnet*, a magazine of general literature, devoted an article to her as the first woman and the second subject in the series "The Living Poets of England" (the first poet considered was Wordsworth).[2] The article begins, "Mrs. Hemans is unquestionably the first *female* poet—the mistress-mind of the day." There were also personal tributes; the writer Anne Grant told her some time in the mid or late 1820s that she was "Praised by all that read you,—loved by all that praise you,—and known, in some degree, wherever our language is spoken."[3] Across the Atlantic, Hemans was seen as a poet who particularly addressed the self-consciously liberal, Christian, civil society of the new United States of America. The *North American Review* boasted in 1827, "There has been no age, ... there has been no people, where the efforts of mind, directly connected with the preservation of elevated feeling and religious earnestness, are more valued than they are by the better part of our own community."[4] The article goes on, "Where the public mind had been thus formed, the poetry of Mrs Hemans was sure to find admirers." Hemans was seen as contributing to the development of this modern liberal state: passages of *The Vespers of Palermo* "have already found their way into an excellent selection of pieces for schools, and thus contribute to give lessons of morality" to children, while her shorter poems have circulated so widely in newspapers "that

---

1   See reviews included in this edition, and Paula R. Feldman, "The Poet and the Profits: Felicia Hemans and the Literary Marketplace," *Keats-Shelley Journal* 46 (1997): 148-76.

2   *The Literary Magnet*, new series, 1 (March 1826): 113-21.

3   Quoted in Hughes (see Abbreviations), 1.120.

4   *North American Review* 24 (April 1827): 443-63, p. 444.

throughout a great part of this country there is not a family of the middling class, in which some of them have not been read." Two years later, the American *Christian Examiner* saw Hemans as part of a revolution in poetry that expressed and promoted a liberal revolution in society and state.[1] Tricia Lootens argues that Hemans's works "helped to inspire and authorize an explicitly, even vehemently public and political strain of nineteenth-century American women's poetry," as seen in the early work, at least, of Lydia Sigourney, who became known as "the American Hemans."[2]

"Mrs Hemans," Woman, and the Modern Liberal State

Hemans's next major work, "Records of Woman" (1828),[3] capitalizes on that fame in particular ways. Even before the work was published it received a poetic tribute from "Genevra" in *Blackwood's Magazine*.[4] "Records of Woman" develops the form and themes of Hemans's earlier *Tales, and Historic Scenes*, and takes them in new directions, informed by Hemans's Romantic feminism. Like the earlier work, "Records of Woman" is a set of poems on related subjects and shows the cost of "masculine" history, as conflict, war, and destruction, to individuals — especially wives and mothers — and to families, nations, empires, and entire peoples. But "Records of Woman" gives greater prominence to women, seems less optimistic about their potential for feminizing history, and emphasizes the heroism and sacrifice of women in the face of history as meaningless death. As Paula Feldman puts it, "Placed in intensely trying situations, [Hemans's] heroines evince uncommon

---

1 *Christian Examiner* 6 (March 1829): 35-52.

2 Tricia Lootens, "Hemans and her American Heirs: Nineteenth-Century Women's Poetry and National Identity," in *Women's Poetry, Late Romantic to Late Victorian: Gender and Genre, 1830-1900*, ed. Isobel Armstrong and Virginia Blain (Basingstoke: Macmillan Press, 1999) 243-60.

3 Here I use *Records of Woman* as the short title for *Records of Woman: with Other Poems*, the book published in 1828, and "Records of Woman" for the set of poems so titled, forming part of the book.

4 "To Mrs Hemans, On her intended Publication, entitled, 'Records of Woman,'" *Blackwood's Magazine* 23 (May 1828): 642.

strength of character, courage, and nobility of spirit."[1] Such uncommonness, however, is shown to have a cost, like female fame—a major theme of Hemans's later work.

This darker view of the condition of women and the woman artist may have reflected on Hemans's own situation after the death of her mother in 1827, the marriage and removal of her sister soon after, and her husband's rejection of her proposal for reconciliation. These events left her feeling abandoned and isolated, even as her literary fame was established. Recent criticism of Hemans has emphasized this personal theme of loss in Hemans's later work. But published poems are not private documents, or cease to be only such documents once they are published; they are then public and rhetorical statements, with meanings created by their circulation in public fields of discourse. Like other contemporary women writers such as Mary Shelley and Letitia Landon, Hemans generalizes her personal situation and experience in her work in order to do what she had always done—address effectively the major and pressing issues of the public and political sphere. Paradoxically, doing so now required Hemans to assert a specifically feminine poetic authority, and in ways that would be apparent to her readers. For critics and readers increasingly saw her work's excellence as essentially "feminine"; if she were not to become limited by that view she had to find ways of using it to maintain her standing with the reading public, thereby both developing the career on which she and her sons depended and continuing to intervene in history as a Romantic feminist.

Accordingly, in "Records of Woman" Hemans concentrates on women, and particular women in history, thereby claiming an authority peculiar to the woman writer, as a woman. Furthermore, Hemans takes care to demonstrate her cultural knowledge and literary skill, thereby claiming authority as a poet—a particular kind of master of literary discourse. Finally, she merges the theme of women in history with the issue of

---

1   Paula R. Feldman, Introduction, Felicia Hemans, *Records of Woman with Other Poems*, ed. Paula R. Feldman (Lexington: University Press of Kentucky, 1999).

female fame, or woman in the public sphere, claiming authority through her established public identity—a woman who has emerged from private and domestic life into history. In doing so, Hemans moves beyond *The Forest Sanctuary* to suggest that she herself, or rather she as "Mrs Hemans" the female author, as well as (or more than) the assumed historical or fictitious characters in her poems, is the model liberal subject waiting in exile for the advent of the modern state. Through this identity Hemans asserts the ability and right to speak for and to all those like herself—an implied liberal reading public waiting to become the political nation. Through the particular themes and forms of "Records of Woman," the established public figure "Mrs Hemans" calls upon this reading public to assume the particular feminized liberal subjectivity she represents through her female characters, historical and fictitious, but also through the character "Mrs Hemans" constructed in her many poems in author's voice.

"Records of Woman" is designed to convey broad cultural knowledge and poetic mastery and thus ideological authority. It is manifestly ambitious in both form and subject matter. The nineteen poems are diverse in subject, genre, and stanza form, yet the set has a coherence, complexity, and resonance between and across individual poems.[1] This demonstration of authorial mastery is reinforced by the figure of the implied author in the poems. Some of these poems use the technique of third-person sympathetic narration that Hemans had developed from Byron and others, in which the story is filtered through a manifestly sympathizing and even autobiographizing narrator. These poems include "The Switzer's Wife," "Joan of Arc, in Rheims," "Pauline," and "The Queen of Prussia's Tomb," as well as most of the other poems.[2] The set of poems is concluded by one of the collection's three personal lyrics, "The Grave of a Poetess," suggesting as closure an identification of author with subjects

---

1 See the full text, scrupulously edited and fully annotated by Paula R. Feldman.
2 These include "Gertrude, or Fidelity till Death," "Imelda," "Edith, a Tale of the Woods," "The Indian City," "The Peasant Girl of the Rhone," "Indian Woman's Death-Song," "Juana," "The American Forest-Girl," "Costanza," and "Madeline, a Domestic Tale."

for the set as a whole.[1] This suggestion is reinforced by two features: some third-person narrative poems include lyrics in the protagonist's voice, and the set includes two dramatic monologues — "Arabella Stuart" and "Properzia Rossi" (both included in this edition).

The poems in "Records of Woman" adapt a number of literary forms and traditions and draw on a range of literary and historical sources, reworking them to serve Hemans's liberal Romantic feminism, with particular contemporary relevance. For example, in "Arabella Stuart," the opening poem in the set, Hemans turns to the dramatic monologue form much practised by her widely read contemporary, Letitia Landon, known from her published signature as "L.E.L." Hemans emphasizes that her protagonist is a historical personage, and cites as her source an essay by the well known antiquarian and scholar Isaac D'Israeli, which contains extracts from Stuart's letters. Hemans purports to give poetic form to these historical documents. According to the discursive and generic conventions of Hemans's day, such poetic formulation would be taken as inherently more immediate, more intensely personal than prose. Hemans gives greater force to this effect of immediacy in the construction of her poem, as successive sections express the fluctuating emotions of the heroine from desire for imminent reunion with her lover-husband, through expectation, disappointment, fear, disillusionment, sense of betrayal, to a final blessing of her husband as she realizes that the emotional torment of disappointed desire is leading to her death. Hemans's use of the dramatic monologue form here, in one of her best poems, is close to that of the form's major source—monodrama—in which a female protagonist enacts a succession of intense emotional states.

The poem is more than an intensely expressive statement of female desire, however. Certainly the poem is built around the narrator's longing for her absent lover-husband. This version of one of Hemans's favourite themes — the intense subjective and emotional experience of absence—is an unusual venture by

---

1   The other two personal lyrics are "The Memorial Pillar" and "The Queen of Prussia's Tomb."

her into the poetics of erotic desire that "L.E.L." made her specialty. In a way, "Arabella Stuart" is Hemans's response to Landon's work, or it comes as close to Landon's style and subject matter as Hemans was willing to go, or perhaps willing to risk; but there are important differences between "Arabella Stuart" and Landon's work. Thwarted female desire has a politics as well as a poetics in Landon's work, which addresses the reading public's anxiety about their social and political aspirations in relation to contemporary forms of aggressive mercantile and industrial capitalism. Such forces of economic transformation could be felt—if not intellectually understood—to commodify individual identity and social relationships, making them into objects of circulation and exchange in which desire for them had to remain ever about to be achieved, but not actually achievable, or possible.

Hemans's "Arabella Stuart" also gives literary expression to these anxieties, but the poem's politics are more overtly related to the liberal ideology shared by much of the reading public, and to familiar themes of middle-class literature that criticized the ideology of court monarchy and the courtly culture of the Old Order. For "Arabella Stuart" fictionalizes a kind of historical figure then receiving renewed attention in liberal Romantic historiography and literature. By Hemans's day, Arabella—properly Arbella—Stuart (1575-1615) was well established as one of a number of historical female figures, including most famously her aunt Mary Queen of Scots, who were portrayed as victims of the conflict between their own femininity, and especially erotic love, and the institutions of state and political intrigue under court monarchy. Stuart was of royal lineage and her children would have a claim to the throne, so she could not marry without permission of the reigning monarch. When she did so, she was imprisoned and died. Hemans had already represented such figures in her earlier poems and plays. As Isaac D'Israeli puts it in Hemans's acknowledged source, "A writer of romance might render her [Stuart] one of those interesting personages whose griefs have been deepened by their royalty, and whose adventures, touched with the warm hues of love and distraction, closed at the bars of her prison gate: a sad example of a female victim to the state!"[1]

In "The Switzer's Wife" Hemans gives a Romantic feminist turn to a well known historical moment, often celebrated in European liberal literature, and to its most influential literary representation, in Friedrich Schiller's play *Wilhelm Tell* (1804), which is still performed annually in Switzerland as the great national patriotic drama. In the late eighteenth and early nineteenth century, reformers throughout Europe portrayed Switzerland as an idyllic, simple, and pure mountain pastoral democracy free from the "corruption" and "vices" of societies and countries ruled by court monarchy. Consequently, European liberals were shocked when Napoleon invaded Switzerland in the late 1790s and set up a puppet Helvetic Republic. Switzerland was soon represented as a symbol of anti-Napoleonic liberal nationalism in Schiller's play, which advocates reconciliation of different classes and regions in the national cause, promotes a form of democratic rule by middle-class men, condones violence only in a "just" and historic cause, and rejects violence for selfish or personal ends, such as revenge. Hemans's poem is based on an episode in the play, as its epigraph indicates, but Hemans again recasts her source to emphasize the specific role of women and the feminine in liberal nationalism. Schiller presents three principal female characters. There is Tell's wife Hedwig, who is critical of the men's resistance to the foreign oppressor, seeing it as contrary to the interests of property, home, and family. In contrast, the aristocrat Berta draws her suitor Ulrich into the patriotic cause and resigns her class status at the end. Finally, placed between these two is Gertrud Stauffacher, who is the domestic yet inspiringly patriotic "Switzer's Wife" of Hemans's poem. These characters represent alternative female roles in liberal nationalism, but Hemans presents only Gertrud Stauffacher, the bourgeois domestic inspiration of national resistance. Furthermore, "The Switzer's Wife" generally follows the exchange between her

---

1   Isaac D'Israeli, *A Second Series of Curiosities of Literature: Consisting of Researches in Literary, Biographical, and Political History; of Critical and Philosophical Inquiries; and of Secret History*, 3 vols (London: John Murray, 1823) 1.264.

and her husband in act 1, scene 2, of *Wilhelm Tell*, but Hemans increases Schiller's emphasis on the domestic basis—and cost—of patriotism by introducing the figure of the boy, concern for whose fate almost disables the Switzer from his patriotic duty, until his wife's intervention.

In "Properzia Rossi" Hemans turns from public woman as divinely inspired domestic patriot to public woman as imaginatively inspired artist. The poem deals directly with the insufficiencies of fame for the female artist and engages critically with a long tradition of representing women, especially women artists and intellectuals, as victims of and limited by their passions. Properzia de'Rossi (*c.* 1490-1530), from Bologna, was known in cultural history as the only woman among the 142 subjects in the first edition of Giorgio Vasari's influential biographical work, known in English as *The Lives of the Artists* (1550). Vasari represents Rossi as an autobiographical artist whose major work expressively depicts a transgressive erotic passion—that of Potiphar's wife for her servant Joseph in the Bible—parallel to Rossi's own for a young man not her husband. According to Vasari, both the strength and weakness of Rossi's work and career came from the personal womanly failing of her (thwarted) erotic desire. Later, Rossi was compared to other mythic female victims of erotic passion, such as Sappho and Medea.[1] This explanation of the relation between Rossi's art and her (feminine) character was the dominant one down to Hemans's day, but by then attitudes were changing.

Hemans's acknowledged source is a painting by Jean-Louis Ducis, one of four entitled *Arts under the Empire of Love*, exhibited at the Paris Salon of 1822. It shows Rossi with supposedly her last sculpture, a bas-relief of Ariadne, another victim of transgressive love. In classical myth, Ariadne helps Theseus escape from death and they elope, but she is later abandoned by him. Her story was represented numerous times in drama from the sixteenth century on, and in Romantic literature Ariadne became a figure for self-sacrifice leading to exile. Ducis represents Rossi depicting the abandoned Ariadne. He thereby

---

1   Fredrika H. Jacobs, "The Construction of a Life: Madonna Properzia De'Rossi '*Schultrice*' Bolognese," *Word and Image,* 9:2 (April-June 1993): 122-32, p. 123.

turns Rossi into a feminist artist, one whose work portrays both the historic wrongs of woman, including her own, and the force in the arts of a self-transcending subjective absolute—love, whether transgressive or not. Implicitly, the arts here are themselves a powerful force in the historic civilizing process that liberals claimed to lead. Ducis makes Rossi a transhistorical subject who represents the beneficial feminization of the arts in the public interest and thus he radically alters Vasari's Rossi. Ducis's work also expresses the liberal and feminist view that the unfortunate fates of such women were due to systemic gender bias in society, culture, and politics rather than to an essential deficiency in female "nature." Accordingly, such women can represent the emergent model of the liberal sovereign subject, man or woman, whose needs and rights were not yet realized in the existing social, cultural, and political order.

Hemans gives a specifically Romantic feminist turn to this figure by diminishing the importance of feminine erotic desire in Rossi's situation, as compared to Vasari's and even Ducis's representation, and by presenting Rossi as victim of the contradiction for a woman between the "affections" (or feelings) and fame, between on the one hand sovereign subjectivity and its imperatives, which inspire art and earn fame, and on the other hand fame when unaccompanied by affections, or perhaps implicitly when the cost of fame is loss of the affections. As in "Arabella Stuart," Hemans also gives greater rhetorical immediacy and directness to this conflicted figure by representing Rossi through dramatic monologue. Hemans's handling of the form, without the distancing dramatic irony more characteristic of Victorian dramatic monologues, facilitates readers' tendency to identify the poem's author with its protagonist. This tendency is encouraged by the closing poem in "Records of Woman," an elegy in author's voice entitled "The Grave of a Poetess." The poem refers to Mary Tighe and has an epigraph taken from Staël's *Corinne*, where a tombstone bears a motto which may be translated, "Don't feel sorry for me—if only you knew how much sorrow this tomb has saved me!"[1]

---

1 Germaine de Staël, *Corinne; ou, l'Italie* (3 vols, 1807) 3.283 (book 18, ch. 3), where the phrase is on an epitaph in a church in Florence.

Thus "Records of Woman" opens and closes with poems about the conflict between subjective and public identity. There is a significant and complex movement, however, across "Records of Woman" from "Arabella Stuart" to "The Grave of a Poetess." This movement is from past to present, from assumed persona to direct authorial voice, from woman entangled in the political sphere to woman poet engaging with the public sphere. This movement marks Hemans's openly assuming for herself the role of model liberal subject in her texts. She is able to do so precisely because she is a public woman but also a domestic woman — the "Mrs Hemans" on certain of her title pages, in reviews of her work, and generally as her known public title. Knowledge of her situation as abandoned wife and mother also seems to have been widely circulated. Paradoxically, it is because she is a famous woman — and even subject of gossip — that she can discourse publicly and with authority on the insufficiency of fame to the private and domestic self, and, by implication or parallel, on the insufficiency of the present state of society and politics, where fame circulates, to the authentic, liberal subject.[1]

Woman and Fame: The Poetess as Exemplary Liberal Subject

A year after the appearance of *Records of Woman; with Other Poems*, Hemans published a poem entitled "Woman and Fame" (included in this edition) in *The Amulet*, an annual giftbook containing fashionable *belles-lettres* and engravings, of a highly feminized character, and relying for sales largely on public recognition of its contributors' names.[2] The poem moves

---

1 Kevin Eubanks gives a different motivation for Hemans's assumption in her later work of a specifically feminine public poetic identity; see "Minerva's Veil: Hemans, Critics, and the Construction of Gender," *European Romantic Review* 8 (Fall 1997): 341-59. See also Glennis Stephenson, who argues that Hemans accepts a male-prescribed femininity whereas her contemporary Letitia Landon resists it: "Poet Construction: Mrs Hemans, L.E.L., and the Image of the Nineteenth-Century Woman Poet," in *ReImagining Women: Representations of Women in Culture*, ed. Shirley Neuman and Glennis Stephenson (Toronto: University of Toronto Press, 1993) 61-73.

2 On the feminized and feminine character of the giftbook annuals, see Sonia Hofkosh, *Sexual Politics and the Romantic Author* (Cambridge: Cambridge University Press, 1998) 86-87.

beyond even the direct authorial voice of "The Grave of a Poetess." "Woman and Fame" declares the superiority of "affection" and "words of home-born love" to fame, especially fame of masculine, martial kinds, and especially for "the sick heart" and "the drooping reed." As Susan Wolfson observes, the very existence of the poem as a public document and artefact, with all of those by Hemans that had gone before and would follow, resists understanding the text as promoting a submissive feminine domesticity.[1] The very context of publication—an annual that used authors of established fame, and paid accordingly—complicates and perhaps ironizes the poem's implications. Moreover, the figure of the author in the poem is a construction, and one designed to represent not only the feminine against the masculine but the public against the private and domestic; the poem may also imply that the feminine and private are oppressed by the masculine and public. When "Woman and Fame" was republished by Hemans's family in her collected *Poems*, they added an epigraph from her own poem "Corinne at the Capitol" (included in this edition), underlining her self-identification with Staël's heroine, a poetess and national voice, who is killed by the conflict of her public and private identities. Hemans's family were only collaborating in her textual self-construction as afflicted and conflicted woman of fame, and thereby both exemplary liberal subject and authoritative national voice in an as yet illiberal state.

This self-figuration was appearing increasingly in her published work, in the work of others, and in socially circulated views of her. Bernard Barton, the Quaker bank clerk and poet, whose work Hemans admired, first represented Hemans in one of his own poems, published in 1824, as a religious poet and therefore unlike her famous Romantic contemporaries (such as Shelley and Byron). In 1827 he represented her in verse again, but now as the woman whose literary success could not compensate for her private loss and subjective afflictions, but who

---

1 Susan J. Wolfson, "'Domestic Affections' and 'the spear of Minerva': Felicia Hemans and the Dilemma of Gender," in *Re-Visioning Romanticism: British Women Writers, 1776-1837*, ed. Carol Shiner Wilson and Joel Hafner (Philadelphia: University of Pennsylvania Press, 1994) 128-66, p. 160.

must turn away from this world to god for consolation.[1] Anne Grant met Hemans in fashionable society in the late 1820s and wrote to a friend, "She is feminine & natural, & very pretty. But she sings like a nightingale with a thorn at her breast"[2]—a reference, probably picked up from Byron, to the Philomel of classical legend and literature, who was transformed into a nightingale and who pressed her breast against a thorn to keep herself awake through the night singing her plaintive song of betrayal, rape, and mutilation.

In the same year that Hemans published "Woman and Fame," her public standing as the poet of the feminine was authorized by the leading critic Francis Jeffrey, in one of the leading literary periodicals of the day (passages of the review are included in this edition).[3] Jeffrey was a Scottish judge, man of letters, and a founder and editor of the Whig-leaning *Edinburgh Review*. This was one of the first of a new generation of professionalized critical magazines that, in the early decades of the nineteenth century, addressed and helped to form the reading public as political nation in waiting.[4] As a Whig, Jeffrey had reformist and liberal political and literary sympathies; he was highly critical of Wordsworth and the "Lake school" of poets, but appreciated elements in the poetry of Byron, Keats, and Shelley. Reviewing the second editions of *The Forest Sanctuary* and *Records of Woman* in 1829, Jeffrey follows a common view of the time in arguing that women's poetry was inevitably different from and more limited than men's because of differences between the sexes that were partly natural, but mainly imposed by social, educational, and cultural practices. Jeffrey elaborates the common doctrine of separate spheres, claiming that, while women may be excluded by convention from the public sphere and thus from the grander passions and intellectual accomplishments, they are specialists in the feelings, the domestic affec-

1   "To Mrs. Hemans," from *Minor Poems, including Napoleon* (1824) and "To Felicia Hemans, on the Death of a Friend," from *A Widow's Tale, and Other Poems* (1827).
2   See item 7 b in Views and Reviews.
3   See item 8 in Views and Reviews.
4   See Jon P. Klancher, *The Making of English Reading Audiences, 1790-1832* (Madison: University of Wisconsin Press, 1987).

tions, and the aesthetics of everyday life. Although Jeffrey suggests in some places that gender difference is non-hierarchical, in other places it seems that the masculine is inherently superior to the feminine.

This ambiguity or contradiction was common in liberal ideology and, paradoxically, seems to have been central to progressive middle-class reform movements of the time, and for long after, partly accounting for the continued exclusion of women from the electorate and from much of the public political sphere. On the one hand, liberal ideology hypostatized subjectivity, domesticity, and quotidian and local life as the prospective basis for the new political nation and liberal national state. On the other hand, women were excluded from direct participation in both political nation and state until the twentieth century—long after the founding of modern liberal states. For much of the century, at least, liberal political discourse characterized that sphere as unreformed, unjust, and unequal—a scene of conflict and struggle dominated by a decadent social order, often morally degrading and ideologically contaminating to the middle-class men who engaged in it, and even more dangerous for middle-class women. Such women, as the supposed embodiments of an idealized version of middle-class values and practices, were to be kept from that sphere to preside over the domestic and local spheres, which were represented as the nurse, school, and refuge of liberal sovereign subjectivity. In gendering middle-class identity and assigning the sexes separate spheres, liberal political discourse was developing a long-standing theme in reformist middle-class critique of the public sphere as dominated by upper-class decadence on the one hand and working-class indiscipline on the other, with both obstructing modernization.

Accordingly, the private sphere was constructed as an idealized and necessary domain of feminized nurture for middle-class men and their refuge from the conflicted and unreformed public sphere. This gendering of public and private spheres informs Jeffrey's gendering of poetic discourse in his review of Hemans. The review's opening paragraphs claim that women poets, though few, exemplify the natural, social, and cultural differences between the sexes. Jeffrey goes on to treat Hemans's work as "a fine exemplification of Female Poetry": "It is infinitely sweet, elegant, and tender—touching, perhaps, and contemplative, rather than vehement and overpowering." Jeffrey insists, however, that Hemans's achievement accords with "the very essence of poetry"—"the fine perception and vivid expression of that subtle and mysterious analogy which exists between the physical and the moral world," or, as he puts it later, "that fine accord she has established between the world of sense and of soul—that delicate blending of our deep inward emotions with their splendid symbols and emblems without." For Jeffrey, the public role of the poet is to enable the reading public to perceive or understand the world in this way—as an extension, analogy, or creation of its sovereign subjective self. Since liberal ideology made this self the basis of the modern state, poetry and literature as Jeffrey defines them would be instrumental in founding and maintaining such a state. Accordingly, Jeffrey anticipates "enduring fame" for Hemans, though he urges her to keep to "short poems," or "occasional verses," by which he means brief expressive lyrics predominantly in author's voice. In fact, Hemans did just that.

The Literary Magnet had offered the same advice in 1826, declaring:

> It is a high, but it is also a deserved compliment, that we mean to pay Mrs. Hemans, when we express a wish that she would oftener be to us an unveiled prophetess; and without the intervention of history, ancient or modern— classical or romantic—impart to us her own impressions on subjects that come more immediately home to the human heart, and are more intimately connected with the course of human life.[1]

This advice was linked to her established identity as not only the leading woman poet of the day, but also an essentially "feminine" poet. In this, the last phase of her career, Hemans capi-

1 *The Literary Magnet*, new series, 1 (March 1826): 119.

talizes on her now established reputation and public standing as a poet, particularly a woman poet, and particlularly an afflicted woman. Paradoxically, she claims to be a national voice by foregrounding her (afflicted) private self in her texts, by emphasizing her feminine identity, by suggesting that her femininity is afflicted despite or because of her fame. Recent criticism of Hemans tends to see her accepting and even advocating a limited feminine and domestic ideology.[1] This pose was, however, a rhetorical strategy. By seeming to accept, and in fact emphasizing that she is a woman and a woman poet, Hemans claims in her poetry to represent liberal subjects in general, who, like her, like her female and male protagonists, like Staël and her Corinne and many similar authors and their protagonists in her time, and throughout Europe and beyond, are afflicted by an unreformed, illiberal social and political order. As Angela Leighton points out, this self-construction by Hemans clearly has a feminist purpose: "the evidence of a great deal of Hemans' poetry is that the estranged heart belongs as much to women as to men." Leighton also draws the connection, however, between this sense of estrangement and the wider liberal Romantic culture of Hemans's day.[2] It is because she is a woman and a prominent poet that Hemans can renew her public political authority.

Throughout her career Hemans had practised acceptably and conventionally "feminine" forms and subjects, avoiding overt transgression of gendered canons of discourse and knowledge. She had also, however, pursued increasingly ambitious forms and material. That care in building her career obtained her an established reputation as the first woman poet of her day, and one of the leading poets regardless of sex. Viewed in one way, she seems to accept a gendered literary identity, as "poetess." In fact, she did so in order to exploit further her established public identity and to expand her authority as a public

---

1 For example, Anthony John Harding, "Felicia Hemans and the Effacement of Woman," in *Romantic Women Writers: Voices and Countervoices*, ed. Paula R. Feldman and Theresa M. Kelley (Hanover, NH, and London: University Press of New England, 1995) 138-49.

2 Angela Leighton, *Victorian Women Poets: Writing Against the Heart* (Charlottesville and London: University Press of Virginia, 1992) ch. 1, p. 26.

voice. For now her public standing enabled her to represent herself as victim of the contradictions of woman and fame, private and public identity, and thereby to represent herself as exemplary liberal subject in an as yet illiberal state. By appearing to accept the identity of "poetess" she is not submitting to a limiting identity imposed by a male-dominated literary establishment but using the gendered character of the literary discursive order to promote herself, her career, and her gradualist liberalism.[1] Appropriately enough, she takes this turn in her public self-construction at the same time that Britain and several other countries in Europe and its former colonies were being transformed, though more or less violently, into modern liberal states.

She does so in several ways. First, she henceforth gives the appearance of turning from a certain kind of poetic ambition to another, from large and historical subjects to the "affections" and religion in everyday life, from large forms to small ones. Here she was again following the advice offered in 1826 by the *Literary Magnet*, which declared her shorter poems, like those of other leading poets of the day, to be her "undying lays."[2] This turn to the personal lyric is indicated by the titles of her remaining books—*Songs of the Affections, with Other Poems* (1830), *Hymns on the Works of Nature, for the Use of Children* (1833), *National Lyrics, and Songs for Music* (1834), and *Scenes and Hymns of Life, with Other Religious Poems* (1834). The titles indicate that these volumes are made up of shorter poems, dealing with conventionally "feminine" topics, including the domestic affections, childhood, everyday life, and devotional religion. Even the "national lyrics" represent domesticity, quotidian life, and localism as the basis of national identity and patriotism.

Secondly, Hemans changes her public self-representation in relation to leading men and women poets and writers of her day as well as the past. Since her earliest work she had used a

1 Cf. Donna Gaye Berliner, "The Female Romantic Imagination" (unpub. Ph.D. diss., University of Texas, 1994); Margaret H. Linley, "'Truly a Poetess, and a Good One': Christina Rosetti and the Cultural Category of the Poetess" (unpub. Ph.D. diss., Queen's University at Kingston, 1996).

2 *The Literary Magnet*, new series, 1 (March 1826): 114.

number of devices to associate herself with certain literary groups and traditions, from established English and Continental European classics such as Shakespeare and Camoens to leading contemporary European and American Romantic liberals. These devices include direct reference in prefaces, dedications, notes, and poems addressed to other writers; quotations and epigraphs from other writers; and similarities in themes and forms between her work and others'. Hemans constructs herself not as follower of these writers, but associate, sympathizer, and—with men poets—feminine re-interpreter, thereby implying her membership in certain poetic traditions and certain contemporary literary movements. These are generally liberal in character. In her early and middle career Hemans associated herself with respected English women writers such as Joanna Baillie and with respectable liberal, patriotic, and religious men poets, from Thomas Campbell through Reginald Heber and the American William Cullen Bryant to Bernard Barton.

Hemans had also associated herself, however, with the two most famous writers in Europe at that time—Staël and Byron—both of whom were prominent liberals and both of whom were also controversial, partly through their merging of authorial persona with transgressive characters in their works. Hemans had also maintained an interest in Shelley, who was by the mid-1820s an even more controversial figure. Hemans now distanced herself from Shelley (she had his name removed from the epigraph to one of her poems, though she retained the epigraph itself).[1] Now Hemans also implicates Staël and Byron in her self-representation as victim of the contradictions of private and public identity, subjectivity and fame, and therefore representative liberal subject. In "The Fountain of Oblivion," for example, published in *Songs of the Affections* (1830), she takes her epigraph—"*Implora pace!*" (Pray, peace!)—from Byron, in a footnote citing his wish to have the phrase placed above his grave. Death, as in most of Hemans's poems, is here the repose from the conflicts, both external and internalized, of

---

1 FH to William Blackwood; Rhyllon 14 Feb. [1828?]; National Library of Scotland MS 4719 fol. 89.

a masculinist, unreformed, illiberal world. In "Corinne at the Capitol" (included in this edition), also from *Songs of the Affections*, Hemans brings Staël and Byron together, with an epigraph from the former and a quotation from the latter, in a poem declaring the insignificance of Corinne's public recognition as national voice compared to the satisfaction of the woman who "makes the humblest hearth / Lovely but to one on earth!"

In Hemans's later work this self-construction through association with a certain version of Staël and Byron is reinforced by her public adoption—and adaptation—of Wordsworth as moral and literary inspiration.[1] She had long admired certain of Wordsworth's works, and in 1826 published a poem, "To the Author of the Excursion and the Lyrical Ballads," in the *Literary Magnet*, republished as "To Wordsworth" among the miscellaneous poems with "Records of Woman." Hemans's friendship and correspondence with Maria Jane Jewsbury, an open disciple of Wordsworth, together with scandalous revelations about Shelley's and Byron's private lives, suggested to Hemans the advantage of shifting her predominant literary association from writers such as Staël, Byron, and Shelley to Wordsworth. After her death, Hemans's biographers and critics represented her admiration for Wordsworth as a salutary, transformative influence. For example, David Moir wrote in *Blackwood's Magazine* two months after her death:

> In her earlier works [to *The Forest Sanctuary*] she follows the classic model as contradistinguished from the romantic, and they are inferior in that polish of style and almost gorgeous richness of language, in which her maturer compositions are set. It is evident that new stores of thought were latterly opened up to her, in a more extended acquaintance with the literature of Spain and Germany, as well as by a profounder study of the writings of our great poetical regenerator—Wordsworth.[2]

---

1 For another reading of the relationship of Hemans and Wordsworth, public and private, see Deborah Kennedy, "Hemans, Wordsworth, and the 'Literary Lady'," *Victorian Poetry* 33 (Fall 1997): 267-86.

2 *Blackwood's Magazine* 38 (July 1835): 99.

Nineteenth-century critics followed this line, but she continued to cite Byron and other liberal Romantic writers, and her self-association with Wordsworth served her own interests. Anne Mellor points out that "Hemans enrolled the leading male poets of her time within" her construction of feminine Romanticism.[1] Marlon Ross argues that "Her change from Byron to Wordsworth is ... not a true alteration because she simply comes to believe that Wordsworth represents more closely than Byron what she desires a male poet to be."[2] Hemans's private view of Wordsworth and her motives for adopting him publicly as a mentor were complex, however (see extracts from letters included in this edition).[3]

For Hemans, public association with Wordsworth was a timely response to the reading public's interests. In the year of Hemans's death, the critic Thomas De Quincey claimed that "Up to 1820 the name of Wordsworth was trampled underfoot; from 1820 to 1830 it was militant; from 1830 to 1835 it has been triumphant."[4] More important, in her work Hemans reconstructs Wordsworth in her own interests,[5] and she did so fully only in *Scenes and Hymns of Life, with other Religious Poems* (1834), published a year before her death. She sent Wordsworth the dedication she wished to insert, in which she suggests that his poetry had the same power for her that he claimed memory and nature had for him, healing the damage caused to mind and spirit by an unaccommodating social and political world, thereby enabling him to assume his public poetic vocation. Marlon Ross argues that "What Wordsworth does is to restore [Hemans's] faith in the compatibility between the domestic affections and poetic genius, not so much by what he writes as by how he presents himself in his home environment."[6] Cer-

---

1 Anne K. Mellor, *Romanticism and Gender* (New York and London: Routledge, 1993) 126.

2 Ross, *The Contours of Masculine Desire*, 305.

3 See Wolfson, "'Domestic Affections' and 'the spear of Minerva,'" in *Re-Visioning Romanticism*, ed. Wilson and Hafner, 137-39.

4 Quoted in *The Oxford Companion to English Literature*, 5th edn, ed. Margaret Drabble (Oxford: Oxford University Press, 1985) art. "Wordsworth."

5 See letters 24 and 25 here.

6 Ross, *The Contours of Masculine Desire*, 306.

tainly in her proposed dedication Hemans portrays Wordsworth as a national voice because he is the poet of nature, domesticity, and Christianity—presumably the Protestantism of the state church.

Wordsworth rejected this dedication and its definition of him and his work, however. Aware of the precariousness of his reconstruction of masculine poetic identity in his work and career and of his growing public stature, he may have felt reluctant to be claimed and defined in this way, especially by a woman poet and one who had constructed herself as poet— the poet—of the feminine.[1] The Wordsworth household practised what Kurt Heinzelman calls a "cult of domesticity,"[2] which seems to have been derived from an anti-aristocratic tradition of classical republicanism. Wordsworth liked Hemans, but he was leery of "bluestockings" and "literary ladies," associating them (as many at the time did) with a decadent upper-class culture. The women of his household respected Hemans but found her to be a "bluestocking." With their own politicized gendering of private and public spheres, they were unable to appreciate Hemans's self-conscious and necessary distancing of herself from domesticity of a certain kind, perhaps derived from the Revolutionary feminist Mary Wollstonecraft. Wollstonecraft had attacked the figure of the domestic female as merely "notable woman," that is, ignorant housekeeper whose subjectivity was absorbed in and enslaved by daily domestic toil and concerns.[3] In the end, Hemans published a one-sentence dedication to Wordsworth in *Scenes and Hymns of Life*. She went on in her Preface to echo Wordsworth's self-characterization in the preface to *The Excursion* (1814) and identify herself as a religious poet with a large but as yet incomplete poetic

---

1   See Susan J. Wolfson, "Gendering the Soul," in *Romantic Women Writers: Voices and Countervoices*, ed. Feldman and Kelley (1995) 33-68.

2   See Kurt Heinzelman, "The Cult of Domesticity: Dorothy and William Wordsworth at Grasmere," in *Romanticism and Feminism*, ed. Anne K. Mellor (Bloomington and Indianapolis: Indiana University Press, 1988) 52-78; Norma Clarke, *Ambitious Heights: Writing, Friendship, Love—The Jewsbury Sisters, Felicia Hemans, and Jane Welsh Carlyle* (London and New York: Routledge, 1990) 63-65.

3   See Gary Kelly, *Revolutionary Feminism: The Mind and Career of Mary Wollstonecraft* (London: Macmillan, 1992) ch. 5.

project that aimed to bring religion more into quotidian life and relations. Hemans could do so because religion in everyday life was at that time a conventionally accepted domain of feminine knowledge and practice.

Wordsworth and Hemans may have constructed their respective poetic identities as distinctly masculine and feminine. Both did so, however, in relation to the struggle within the middle classes for ideological leadership of the reading public as the political nation, and against kinds of masculinity and femininity associated with decadent and despotic court monarchy and aristocratic hegemony, past and present. In that respect poet and poetess occupied common ground, as Hemans seems to have realized more fully than did Wordsworth or most male Romantic poets, who were defensive about their masculinity. Wordsworth and Hemans remained leading poets of a reading public that had a large ideological, cultural, and political investment in these distinctly masculine and feminine, yet similarly liberal and middle-class, identities. This fact was asserted publicly by Hemans's friend Maria Jane Jewsbury at the beginning of the reform decade of the 1830s. Jewsbury portrays Hemans as the character "Egeria" in her story "The Nonchalant" (1830), where the narrator declares, "Other women might be more commanding, more versatile, more acute; but I never saw one so exquisitely feminine."[1] A year later Jewsbury made an explicit connection between Hemans's femininity and class-based ideology, in her (anonymous) article entitled "Literary Sketches No. 1: Felicia Hemans" (extracts are included in this edition), in the recently founded liberal intellectual magazine, the *Athenaeum*.[2] Jewsbury opens the article by declaring, "Were there to be a feminine literary house of commons, Felicia Hemans might very worthily be called to fill the chair as the speaker—a representative of the whole body, as distinguished from the other estates of the intellectual realm." The parliamentary model Jewsbury adduces is the liberal one of representative democracy, in which sovereign subjects choose

---

1   Maria Jane Jewsbury, *The Three Histories: The History of an Enthusiast; The History of a Nonchalant; The History of a Realist* (London, 1830), pp. 231-32.

2   See item 9 in Views and Reviews.

an eminently sovereign subject to represent them in government and the state, and where the speaker of the assembly mediates between all representatives.

Hemans has this representative authority, according to Jewsbury, because "She writes from and to the heart." This is the effect that Isobel Armstrong calls "the gush of the feminine," which may be understood as a discourse of self-expressiveness, recognized as such in Hemans's day, and usually associated with women writers—indeed, with women generally.[1] It is revealing, for example, that Hemans uses "gush" and its variants 85 times in her poetry, more than twice as often as the nearest poet of the Romantic period—Byron. In Hemans's day "the gush of the feminine" would have been associated particularly with the reformist and oppositional culture of Sensibility, which promoted personal and expressive literary forms above all others as vehicles for representing—or inventing—autonomous subjectivity. As Angela Leighton again astutely observes, Hemans rehabilitates that culture, hitherto discredited by association with the prolonged gush of blood caused by the Revolutionary and Napoleonic cataclysm.[2] For as Jewsbury already recognized in 1830, and as critics had recognized even earlier when they praised the "classical" correctness of her style, Hemans practises the discourse of gushing in a particular, disciplined way, one that locates itself within a specific class culture. Hemans, writes Jewsbury,

> always writes like one who feels that the heart is a sacred thing, not rashly to be wounded, whilst she scorns to lower her own intellectual dignity by an ambitious straining after effect. Her matronly delicacy of thought, her chastened style of expression, her hallowed ideas of happiness as connected with home, and home-enjoyments;— to condense all in one emphatic word, her *womanliness* is to her intellectual qualities as the morning mist

---

1 Isobel Armstrong, "The Gush of the Feminine: How Can We Read Women's Poetry of the Romantic Period?", in *Romantic Women Writers: Voices and Countervoices*, ed. Feldman and Kelley (1995) 13-32.

2 Leighton, *Victorian Women Poets*, 26.

to the landscape, or the evening dew to the flower — that which enhances loveliness without diminishing lustre. To speak confidentially to our trusted friend the public, Mrs. Hemans throws herself into her poetry, and the said self is an English gentlewoman.[1]

For this reason, Jewsbury can accept the kind of gender distinction advanced by Jeffrey, while denying that this distinction is hierarchical, and arguing that the difference can be dialectical:

> There will always be a difference between the poetry of men and women — so let it be; we have two kinds of excellence instead of one; we have also the pleasure of contrast: we discover that power is the element of man's genius — beauty that of woman's: — and occasionally we reciprocate their respective influence, by discerning the beauty of power, and feeling the power of beauty.

For Jewsbury, Hemans is a leading poet and the leading woman poet for two reasons. Her work participates in a single poetics of power and beauty, and it speaks directly from one subjectivity to another, from author to reader, within a class-specific ideology and culture.

This is why Hemans is required to be "feminine" in life as in work, according to Jewsbury: "a poetess ought to be feminine. All that we know are so; and Mrs. Hemans especially." Jeffrey had made clear why this was so. The poetics and politics of Romanticism were still sustained by the rhetorical doctrine of ethos, or validation of discourse by the known character of the writer. It is this validation that gave rhetorical persuasiveness to much discourse during the late eighteenth and early nineteenth century, and indeed, beyond. Certainly many of Hemans's letters can be quoted to show that she had a personal stake in maintaining a certain character of femininity; those letters, too, of course were rhetorical performances, maintaining a particular character (or characters) with friends and acquaintances of

---

1 Item 9 in Views and Reviews.

many degrees of proximity. Private life, too, is a domain of the performative, and the Hemans of her letters (especially the letters selected by biographers determined to sustain her self-representation) is no more the "real" Hemans than is the Hemans of the poems, and especially the Hemans of the personal expressive lyrics. Hemans knew how to manage the resources of poetry, as a gendered discourse in and of her time, in order to achieve her rhetorical purpose. Paradoxically, it was by skilfully constructing herself in her work as essentially feminine that she was able to acquire her peculiar power with the reading public as the political nation.

Verse tributes from other cultivated middle-class poets, many of them women, were already bearing public witness to this power. In 1829 Amelia Gillespie Smyth, author of prose tales and of poems in the literary annuals, published a poem "On Reading 'The Records of Woman'" in *The Winter's Wreath*, an annual to which Hemans also contributed. A year later Catherine G. Godwin, author of "Sappho: A Dramatic Sketch" and other poems, published a poem "To Felicia Hemans" in another annual in which Hemans published, *Friendship's Offering*. In 1831 "E.P." sent from Leeds a poetic tribute "To Mrs Hemans" for *Blackwood's Magazine*, which published many of Hemans's later short poems.[1] "E.P." celebrates Hemans's power to express her own subjective self in verse and thereby to rouse her reader's "heart," even resulting, in this instance, in a corresponding poeticizing. In 1833 a testimony to the power of Hemans's address from subject to subject was received from distant South America by the *New Monthly Magazine*, where Hemans also published. The poem, "To Mrs. Hemans," was by the Hon. Mrs Eliza Erskine Norton, herself a published poet and political journalist; it sees Hemans as an expressive poet of overflowing subjectivity, inspired by the spirit of ancient republican Greece, dwelling with Beauty, speaking for nature as the divine spirit, engaging her readers directly and immediately, subject to subject, in a transcendent community.

Implicitly, this is a community of liberal sovereign subjects.

---

1   *Blackwood's Magazine*, 29 (April 1831): 667.

Accordingly, Hemans's poetics, as defined by Jewsbury, Norton, and other commentators, is also a politics. The connection is suggested by Marlon Ross, in a fine summary of Hemans's intended effect:

> Upon finishing one of Hemans's romances — or lyrics, for that matter — the reader discovers the deepness and broadness of her own heart in the guise of another's suffering or joy (though usually it is suffering). In this way, Hemans teaches the power of beauty, to women as well as to men. But the difference between knowing powers and limits is so subtle that we could almost say that it is basically the same lesson, a lesson that tends to dissolve the rationale for gender difference as it demonstrates the similar effect of heart-knowledge on men and women. What women must learn is that heart-knowledge cannot protect them from the demands of public life, from the political strife of the state. What men must learn is that heart-knowledge is the basis for all their public actions, for all the motivations and aims that make them the more visible agents of state guardianship.[1]

In assigning human and social value to Hemans's poetry, Ross here seems to place himself in the position of Hemans's contemporaries such as Jewsbury and Norton.

What must be added is that Hemans's design gives a Romantic feminist turn to a class-based ideology because it merges a conventionally accepted domain of feminine knowledge and authority — the private feelings and domestic affections[2] — with a particular social and cultural education and practice of the aesthetic — "beauty" — that was at that time, in effect, available only to the middle and upper classes, and in practice mainly pursued by the professional middle class. As Jewsbury makes clear in her essay on Hemans, beauty here

---

1 Ross, *The Contours of Masculine Desire*, 275.
2 See Stuart Curran's groundbreaking essay on late eighteenth- and early nineteenth-century women poets, "The I Altered," in *Romanticism and Feminism*, ed. Anne K. Mellor (Bloomington and Indianapolis: Indiana University Press, 1988) 185-207.

means the power to rouse feeling—the root sense of "aesthetic." Put another way, this is the power to rouse or bring into being and self-consciousness the sovereign subjectivity that was (and is) also available only to people with certain education and cultural opportunities. What Jewsbury terms the power of beauty is designed to call into being the liberal political nation of sovereign subjects. As Marlon Ross puts it, again, speaking of what would later become notorious as Hemans's "sentimentality":

> There is no doubt that Hemans sees her goal as the feminization of culture at large. Bringing her readers to tears is not simply a way of sensitizing them individually; it is more importantly a way of transforming them collectively into a community of shared desire.[1]

The fact that she succeeded is indicated by the response of two leading architects of the liberal state in nineteenth-century Britain. In 1824 the teenaged son of a Liverpool merchant gave his favourite sister, whom he later credited with his moral and religious education, a specially bound volume containing three of Hemans's poems—*The Sceptic, The Restoration of the Works of Art to Italy*, and *Modern Greece*.[2] After university, William Ewart Gladstone (1809-98) went into politics, joined Robert Peel's government in the 1830s and again in the 1840s, and went on to be the great advocate of reform and leader of the Liberal party in the second half of the nineteenth century. While Gladstone was in Peel's short-lived government of 1834-35, Peel, who also had a Lancashire commercial background and who would later go on to modernize the Tory party and promote liberal reform, was told that Felicia Hemans was ill and in straitened circumstances. While desperately trying to prop up his minority government, he took time to have a letter written to her, offering £100 and a government job for her son. In the letter, Peel declared that this was "only the fulfilment of a public duty, which I feel incumbent on me as the King's Minister,

---

1   Ross, *The Contours of masculine Desire*, 292.
2   The volume is in the Huntington Library, San Marino, California.

to prevent the reproach which would justly attach to me, if I could permit a Lady so distinguished for literary exertions, which have aided the cause of virtue, and have conferred honour on her Country and her sex, to suffer from privations, which official station gives me the opportunity of relieving."[1] Peel was the re-inventor of the Tory party as a major force in remaking Britain as a liberal state; Gladstone was the popular voice of liberalism through a great part of the later nineteenth century. Like Hemans, they advocated a gradualist reform and liberalization in order to achieve the modern state, based on the ideology of the sovereign subject (however trammelled by assumptions of race, ethnicity, class, and gender) that Hemans prominently, but among many others, had helped to circulate by means of the commercial and public cultural institution of literature.

Hemans spent her last years in Ireland, where her brother was chief of the Dublin police. She spent time with his family, often in the country, with members of the Graves family, and with the circle of William Rowan Hamilton, professor of astronomy at Trinity College, Dublin, whom she had met while visiting the Wordsworths in 1830. In Dublin Hamilton had a friend who was "dying" to meet her and who said he "could be content to marry [her] blindfold for the sake of her poetry alone."[2] Hemans felt ambivalent about Ireland, however. She herself seems to have socialized only with the protestant Anglo-Irish. Like many English people of her time, she regarded the majority of the Irish as an alien people who seemed to be still enmeshed in a pre-modern customary and collective culture, indicated by their devotion to Catholicism, and made more menacing by mass political organization. Her brother's policing responsibilities would have reinforced her sense of this collective otherness, against which Hemans now manifested her sovereign subjectivity even more insistently in her published work. As she told her friend, the scientist William Rowan Hamilton, in 1832, "I am going soon to employ myself upon a

---

1   See Letter 33 here.
2   Hamilton to Aubrey de Vere, 7 Nov. 1832, in Robert Perceval Graves, *Life of Sir William Rowan Hamilton*, 3 vols (Dublin and London, 1882) 1.622.

volume of sacred poetry, upon which I shall earnestly desire to pour out my whole heart and mind."[1] She continued to publish a stream of personal lyrics, most now of an explicitly religious character conformable to the established state religion of anglican Protestantism. Many of these poems also refer to her personal, domestic, and physical afflictions, with religion as a specific consolation. In this way, her poet's soul is aligned with the divine being against a persistently hostile social world and intimations of mortality, where her afflicted physical body is associated with a conflicted material and social reality. She does continue to use forms other than the personal lyric, such as the dramatic scene, translation, and the poem based on a historical figure, which were major elements in her earlier work. Now these forms, too, are made explicitly religious, however, as Hemans continues to revise and reinterpret her own earlier work, sources, influences, and practices, and to reconstruct her authorial persona as exemplary sovereign subject.

For example, "Prisoners' Evening Service" (included in this edition), from a set of dramatized dialogues in *Scenes and Hymns of Life, with Other Religious Poems* (1834), is based on an incident in Helen Maria Williams's series of *Letters* from France during the 1790s. Williams was the principal British eyewitness observer of the French Revolution and a leading writer of the culture of Sensibility, and her *Letters* from France gendered the Revolution as a struggle between malevolent and beneficial, destructive and constructive, masculinized and feminized forces.[2] This representation was highly influential and Hemans adapts it again here, in the aftermath of the Great Reform Bill of 1832, dramatizing an act of defiant domestic piety in a prison setting during what Williams had portrayed as the destructively masculinist, Revolutionary Jacobin Terror. The sonnets entitled "Female Characters of Scripture," also from *Scenes and Hymns of Life*, resemble "Records of Woman" and many of the poems from *Tales, and Historic Scenes*, representing sympathetically women in various situations of conflict and suffering

1 Graves, *Life of Hamilton*, 1.603.
2 See Gary Kelly, *Women, Writing, and Revolution 1790-1827* (Oxford: Clarendon Press, 1993), ch. 2.

(selections are included in this edition). The sources for "Female Characters" are Biblical and sacred rather than secular, however, ranging from Ruth, the best known exile of scripture, to Mary Magdalene, the best known fallen woman, and the poems are lyric rather than narrative. These features indicate obliquely the shift of the well known "Mrs Hemans" to a poetics and politics now centred on a religiously grounded authorial subject. In the personal lyric "Communings with Thought" (also from *Scenes and Hymns of Life*, and included in this edition), Hemans transcendentalizes herself, as she reviews the topics of her earlier work, from ancient Greece to chivalric romance, and exhorts her thoughts to soar higher, to the martyr's grave and the scenes of woman's suffering, and higher still, to "shoot the gulf of death" and beyond, to eternity.

The movement to religion as the basis of a sovereign subjectivity is made clear in Hemans's two sonnets to Silvio Pellico (included in this edition), published in *Blackwood's Magazine* at the end of 1834. Pellico was a liberal dramatist and patriot imprisoned by the Austrian rulers of northern Italy; while imprisoned he underwent a religious experience and when released he published his account of this as *Le mie prigioni* (*My Prisons*, 1832). Many liberals maintained the Enlightenment tradition of religious scepticism and anticlericalism, but many also wanted a dialogue with established religion and the state church. Pellico's book became a classic for European moderate liberals, presenting personal religious experience both as a divine validation of the sovereign subject central to liberal ideology and as a consolation where the liberal state was yet to be achieved. By aligning herself with Pellico, Hemans indicates her move to this form of liberalism.

As "Communings with Thought" indicates, Hemans also links the religious and transcendental validation of her standing as exemplary sovereign subject to the immediately preceding validation in her career—her standing as "poetess," or (afflicted) woman of poetic fame. She does so in a number of poems that join a long series dealing with the poetic vocation, going back to "The Minstrel to His Harp" in *Poems* (1808). In "The Sacred Harp" from "Sonnets, Devotional and Memorial" in *Scenes and Hymns of Life*, Hemans exhorts sacred "poesy" to fulfil again, as in Biblical times, its role in defeating worldly evil. In "Introductory Stanzas: The Themes of Song" from *National Lyrics, and Songs for Music*, which is not an overtly religious volume, Hemans declares that the "themes of song" should be those places where blood has been shed for freedom. This is a common trope in liberal verse, but the poem goes on to suggest that higher, eternal themes are human social and religious feelings — "faith, love, pity." In the sonnet "Intellectual Powers," from the series "Thoughts during Sickness" published in the *New Monthly Magazine* two months before her death, Hemans describes how physical illness breaks up the linked powers of memory, thought, and imagination that create poetry and that can only be permanently united in the life hereafter. In the sonnet "The Return to Poetry," from "Records of the Autumn of 1834" published in *Blackwood's Magazine* in 1834, she prays that heaven may henceforth guide her poetry so that it not be distracted by and diverted to worldly beauty. In the sonnet "Design and Performance" from the same series, Hemans expresses fear of being unable to achieve her remaining (and highest?) ambition, announced in the Preface to *Scenes and Hymns of Life*, "to build, / For lowly hearts devout, but *one* enduring fane" of religious poetry.

Such a turn to an expressly religious poetic calling is not a turn from politics, however. In the aftermath of the Great Reform Bill of 1832 many in Britain remained excluded from the political nation and disaffected from the new liberal state then under construction. These groups included particularly the educated and politicized working classes and many of the lower middle classes. These groups were also mainstays of Protestant religious Dissent, or those Protestants self-excluded from the state church. Hemans's design of using poetry to build "but one" church ("fane") aims to use the emergent national institution of literature to call a single devout reading public into being, transcending sectarian divisions. Her design to build this church for "lowly hearts" elides social differences of "high" and "low" in a lowness, or religiously enjoined humility, of the inward subjective self, supposedly evading hierarchical divisions of social class.

Hemans also reflects on the public vocation of poet in a rare prose essay, with translations, published in the *New Monthly Magazine* for January 1834.[1] The first (and only) in an intended series of "German Studies, By Mrs. Hemans" examines Goethe's drama "Tasso" and translates some passages from it. In the opening paragraphs (included in this edition) Hemans defines the character and role of the poet, from her position as "Mrs. Hemans," in terms of her Romantic feminism. In doing so she quotes Wordsworth and Coleridge, the leading English theorists of the (masculine) poetic identity as transcendent subject creating the world in the act of perceiving it, and representing that vision and that subjectivity for readers through poetry. Hemans insists, however, on the primacy of the human and social to this necessarily afflicted transcendent subjectivity. As she had written to a friend in 1828 or 1829, "... I fear that a woman's mind never can be able, and never was formed to attain that power of sufficiency to itself, which seems to lie somewhere or other amongst the *rocks* of a man's."[2] In the essay on Goethe's "Tasso" she writes:

> Let the poet bear into the recesses of woods and shadowy hills a heart full-fraught with the sympathies which will have been fostered by intercourse with his kind, a memory covered with the secret inscriptions which joy and sorrow fail not indelibly to write .... We thus admit it essential to his high office, that the chambers of imagery in the heart of the poet must be filled with materials moulded from the sorrows, the affections, the fiery trials, and immortal longings of the human soul.

These materials are not to be found in "the gaudy and hurrying masque of life" and the haunts of "the sons and daughters of fashion" — common phrases at that time for fashionable and courtly upper-class society.

---

1 She may have contributed an essay on and translations of Spanish ballads in *Blackwood's Magazine* 6 (Feb. 1820): 481-91, and perhaps others in the series "Horæ Hispanicæ" and the other "Horæ" series.

2 FH to members of the Chorley family? [Wavertree, late 1828 or early 1829], in Hughes, pp. 159-63.

Hemans then places this feminized poet figure in relation to forebears made familiar by Romantic literature, in particular earlier Italian poets such as Dante and Tasso who were exiled and supposedly broken by the necessity of subservience to courtly culture and by the subject condition of their native land. Significantly, Hemans criticizes Goethe for failing to show Tasso resisting these forces with more dignity; in her translations she emphasizes the feminine sympathy for Tasso by the princess Leonora d'Este of Ferrara, and she closes her essay with a quotation from Byron's "The Lament of Tasso," which portrays the Italian poet more heroically. Significantly, too, in the passage that Hemans chooses, Byron himself seems to be a religious poet, since he assigns divine validation to the identity and role of Tasso and implicitly of any poet with integrity, that is to say, with sovereign subjectivity. Implicitly, the author of this essay, whom the reading public (and certainly the readership of the liberal *New Monthly Magazine*) already knew as the afflicted poetess "Mrs Hemans," joins the line of feminized and religiously motivated poet-heroes from Tasso to Byron that the essay identifies.

Hemans, the Modern Liberal State, and the Institution of Literature: The Contradictions of Female Fame, 1835 to the Present

Hemans died on 16 May 1835, and a few months later "Delta" (David Moir) declared in *Blackwood's Magazine* that "as a female writer, influencing the female mind, she has undoubtedly stood, for some by-past years, the very first in the first rank; and this pre-eminence has been acknowledged, not only in her own land, but wherever the English tongue is spoken, whether on the banks of the eastern Ganges, or the western Mississippi."[1] Her family, friends, many admirers, and successive generations of critics quickly consolidated her self-representation as the afflicted feminine poet in her writing. The memorial tablet erected in St Asaph cathedral by her family was inscribed, "in

---

1 *Blackwood's Magazine* 38 (July 1835): 96.

memory of Felicia Hemans, whose character is best portrayed in her writings."[1] The family reinforced this figure by publishing *Poetical Remains* (1836), with poems that add the dimension of physical to Hemans's spiritual suffering. Within months of Hemans's death, her contemporary Letitia Landon published an essay and an elegy on Hemans in the *New Monthly Magazine*.[2] Both pieces represent Hemans as an autobiographical poet whose personal affliction speaks to similar afflictions in her readers. Landon identifies this affliction as unfulfilled desire, the same affliction represented in Staël's Corinne and in Landon's own poems and self-construction there. Landon thus reasserts the poetics and politics implicit in the theme of woman and fame as formulated in Hemans's later poetry. Henry Chorley, Hemans's close friend, was given access to her private papers and published a biography of her in 1836. Chorley, too, perpetuates Hemans's self-representation as a Corinne figure, but he tries to complicate this self-representation, using letters and documents that show Hemans's sense of humour, personal idiosyncrasies, political interests, and ironic references to her own literary fame. As a result, the biography was controversial, and some found in it suggestions that, rather than being afflicted by fame, Hemans enjoyed being a literary lion.[3] In the late 1830s, Hemans's family sought to monumentalize her further with a seven-volume collected edition of her poems, with some that were hitherto unpublished. This edition opens with a sentimentalizing biography by Hemans's sister, Harriet Hughes, which aims to counter the impression given by Chorley, but which also includes extracts from Hemans's numerous unpublished burlesques, parodies, and satires, presumably designed to show that Hemans was not always, as some critics complained, a morbid poet. As late as 1854, Hemans's brother Lt Col. George Browne gave a recently published complete edition of her

---

1   Paula R. Feldman, Introduction, Felicia Hemans, *Records of Woman with Other Poems*, xx.

2   See items 11 and 12 in Views and Reviews.

3   *Dublin Magazine*, 2 (Dec. 1836): 245-75, pp. 272-73; the writer even chose to deny the widely asserted view that Hemans was physically beautiful (252).

poems to Sarah B. Dalyell as one "who so fully appreciates the Virtues and Talents of The Authoress."[1]

Contradictory and usually simplistic figures of "Mrs Hemans" continued to circulate in literary and popular culture for another century at least. The predominant figure was the poet of femininity, domesticity, and patriotism, for better or worse.[2] By 1840, the mass-market publisher George Virtue could appropriate "Mrs Hemans" as presiding genius for a female conduct book and guide to domestic economy.[3] Editions of Hemans's works in various formats and at various prices were reissued frequently and included in series of "classic" or "standard" British poets.[4] These publications culminated in an early twentieth-century edition from Oxford University Press, the established provider of standard editions of "classic" English poets for the nation and empire. Hemans's shorter poems frequently appeared in "reciters"—books used for home and school performances, usually by children—through the nineteenth century and even as late as 1978.[5] At least one anthology of her shorter poems was prepared for use in schools by a mass-market publisher.[6] In 1879, The Argosy, a monthly magazine owned by the popular novelist Mrs Henry Wood and aimed at a wide readership, asserted that Hemans's "works are

1 Copy owned by the present editor.

2 See Margaret M. Morlier, "Elizabeth Barrett Browning and Felicia Hemans: The 'Poetess' Problem," *Studies in Browning and His Circle*, 20 (1993): 70-79; Virginia Blain, "'Thou with Earth's Music Answerest to the Sky': Felicia Hemans, Mary Ann Browne, and the Myth of Poetic Sisterhood," *Women's Writing* 2:3 (1995): 251-69; Tricia Lootens, "Hemans and Home: Victorianism, Feminine 'Internal Enemies,' and the Domestication of National Identity," *PMLA* 109 (March 1994): 238-53.

3 *Mrs. Hemans's Young Woman's Companion, or Female Instructor; Being a Summary of Useful Knowledge; Calculated to Form the Intellectual, the Moral, and the Domestic Character; Interspersed with Interesting Tales, Biographical Sketches of Illustrious Women &c. To Which Are Subjoined Medicinal Receipts, and Other Useful Directions Requisite for Every Female to Whom Domestic Economy is a Desirable Object.* A New Edition, Embellished with Appropriate Engravings (London: George Virtue, 1840).

4 E.g., the editions published by F. Warne and Co. in the 1880s.

5 *The Faber Popular Reciter*, ed. Kingsley Amis (London: Faber and Faber, 1978), discussed in Jerome McGann, *The Poetics of Sensibility: A Revolution in Literary Style* (Oxford: Clarendon Press, 1996) 183-84, 189-90.

6 See note 2 above.

familiar in most English households."[1] The last two decades of the century saw Hemans included in several popular volumes of biographies of domestically exemplary women writers and intellectuals.[2] These books were probably designed to give the reading public counter-examples to the popular and often controversial women writers of the day and to engage obliquely in the "new woman" debate. At the end of the century, selections from Hemans were included in a 45-volume *Library of the World's Best Literature, Ancient and Modern*, aimed at the mass market of state-educated citizenry in the United States, supposedly desirous to have in their own homes a set of approved literature.[3]

Perhaps responding to these continuingly popular figures of Hemans, male literary critics and editors such as George Gilfillan and William Michael Rossetti simplified the figure constructed by Jeffrey, Jewsbury, and Landon, in an increasingly condescending attitude to Hemans.[4] At the beginning of the twentieth century, the *Academy*, the leading literary-intellectual weekly of the time, compared Hemans to the popular poet of empire, Rudyard Kipling.[5] Serious writers, British and American, men and women, and including W.M. Thackeray, Elizabeth Gaskell, Henry David Thoreau, and Bram Stoker, could

---

1   H. Barton Baker, "Mrs. Hemans," *The Argosy* 28 (1879): 189-95, p. 189.

2   [Eva Hope,] *Queens of Literature of the Victorian Era* (London: W. Scott, 1886), including Hemans, Mary Somerville, Harriet Martineau, Elizabeth Barrett Browning, and George Eliot; Daniel Wise, *Some Remarkable Women: A Book for Young Women* (Cincinnati: Jennings and Pye; New York: Eaton and Mains, 1887), including the Brontë sisters, Hannah Adams, Elizabeth Prentiss, Sister Dora, Mary Lamb, Frances Ridley Havergal, Hemans, the Grimke sisters, and Caroline Herschel; Lucy Walford, *Twelve English Authoresses* (London and New York: Longmans, Green, and Co., 1892), including Hannah More, Maria Edgeworth, Frances Burney, Harriet Martineau, Jane Austen, Hemans, Mary Somerville, Jane Taylor, Charlotte Brontë, Elizabeth Barrett Browning, George Eliot; and George Barnett Smith, *Noble Womanhood: A Series of Biographical Sketches* (London and New York: Society for Promoting Christian Knowledge, 1912), including Princess Alice of Hesse, Florence Nightingale, Frances Ridley Havergal, Harriet Beecher Stowe, Sister Dora, Louisa May Alcott, Elizabeth Fry, and Hemans.

3   New York, several imprints from 1896 to 1902, edited by Charles Dudley Warner, George H. Warner, Hamilton Wright Mabie, and Lucia Gilbert Runkle.

4   See items 14 and 16 in Views and Reviews.

5   "Ardo": "A Literary Progenitress of Rudyard Kipling, *The Academy and Literature*, 24 (Oct. 1903): 444-45.

use "Mrs Hemans" as a familiar figure for a certain kind of too easy and too popular sentimental verse.[1] Certain of Hemans's poems were so familiar they could be used by literary satirists to burlesque various kinds of popular literature, from Edgar Allan Poe's 1845 Gothic poem "The Raven" to crime and romance novels of the 1930s.[2] A volume of parodies of Hemans's "Casabianca" was published in Boston in 1911, and a volume of humorous imitations of Hemans was published in Australia in 1944.[3] In 1972 the famous first line of "Casabianca" appeared in the song "Big 6," the first hit of the risqué reggae and ska artist Judge Dread. Even today schoolchildren continue to circulate burlesques of "Casabianca," though few know the poem's title or its author's name.[4]

Some writers and social critics, however, continued to see "Mrs Hemans" as an exemplary figure for a liberal ideology, culture, and state, though again in contradictory ways. In the United States this figure of Hemans had a very large influence in the emergent national culture, from the public to the private sphere. Hemans's "The Landing of the Pilgrim Fathers in New England" was widely circulated and set to music, becoming virtually a national anthem. For example, it was one of three poems read aloud in the "Order of Exercises, for Celebrating the Semi-century Anniversary of the Adoption, by the State, of the Constitution of the United States: at Trinity Church, R[hode] I[sland], June 25th, 1840" (the other poems were William Cullen Bryant's "Ode on the Constitution" and James Atkinson's "The breaking waves dashed high ..."). In broad social culture and ideology, Hemans was already contributing to what has been called "the feminization of American cul-

---

1   See William Makepeace Thackeray, *The History of Pendennis* (Oxford: Oxford University Press, 1994), ch. 3, pp. 30-31; Henry David Thoreau, *Walden and Other Writings* (New York: Modern Library, 1937), p. 145; Elizabeth Gaskell, *Wives and Daughters*, (Harmondsworth: Penguin, 1969), pp. 96-97; Bram Stoker, *The Annotated Dracula*, ed. Leonard Wolf (New York: Ballantine Books, 1975), ch. 5, pp. 82-83.

2   William James Linton, "Raving," from *Pot-Pourri* (London, 1875), and "Strange News for Mrs Hemans," *Punch*, 25 Nov. 1931, p. 574.

3   *Mocking Rimes: Some Parodies on "The Boy Stood on the Burning Deck"* (Boston: Carol Press, 1911); Tom Ugly, *Going Jeep, and Other Imitations of Felicia Hemans* (Sydney: Pinnacle Press, 1944).

4   Samples are in Clarke, *Ambitious Heights*, 44.

ture,"[1] through editions of her own work, that of followers such as Lydia Sigourney, and promotion of her by morally earnest male critics. So ethereally feminine did Hemans seem, that at least one man claimed that the late poet had sent him a poem through a female spiritualist medium.[2]

In Britain, a positive view of Hemans was maintained by critics and writers who were in many cases associated with reform and philanthropic movements. In September 1835, the Unitarian social reformer Mary Carpenter, in a poem "On the Death of Mrs. Hemans," envisaged Hemans continuing to instruct readers in the common bonds of humanity:

> ... Still shalt thou tell
> E'en from the tomb, how warm affections swell
> In fairest hearts;—how each to each is bound
> In joy or woe, to live, to toil, to die. —[3]

In 1845, Thomas Cooper, the working-class poet and advocate of radical reform, represented Hemans as an early feminist heralding the emancipation of women some time in the future.[4] In 1861 Jane Williams opposed the tendency of critics such as Gilfillan to trivialize Hemans and insisted that her poetry was valuable for its representation of the sovereign subject making the world in its own image (see passages in this edition).[5] Hemans retained a certain place in high literary culture; as Tricia Lootens states, Hemans "was surely the first woman poet to become a Victorian literary monument."[6] Elizabeth Barrett Browning had an intense if ambivalent interest in Hemans as woman artist, and wrote a poem entitled "Felicia Hemans." Alfred Tennyson's early poems often bear a striking

---

1 Ann Douglas, *The Feminization of American Culture* (1977; New York: Doubleday, 1988) 113.

2 Letter of Daniel Norton to Henry Hudson (1821-1901), editor of the *New England Spiritualist* (Henry Hudson Mss., Connecticut Historical Society).

3 *Voices of the Spirit and Spirit Pictures*, published posthumously for private circulation, 1877.

4 See item 13 in Views and Reviews.

5 See item 15 in Views and Reviews.

6 *Lost Saints: Silence, Gender, and Victorian Literary Canonization* (Charlottesville and London: University Press of Virginia, 1996) 67.

resemblance to Hemans's, even as he gives her themes and forms new direction.[1] Other Victorian poets quoted or referred to Hemans, including Alaric Watts, E.H. Bickersteth, William Allingham, Janet Hamilton, J.J. Murphy, J.C. Prince, Charles Swain, and H.D. Rawnsley. At the end of the century Hemans could still be eulogized by another poet, Cecil Frances Humphreys, for her power to express and to address afflicted common humanity precisely through what others dismissed as her sentimentalism. By that point, the standing and circulation of Hemans's work in literary culture became implicated, as it still is, in further broad social and cultural transformations.

In the early twentieth century, the modernist movement, which was oppositional by being both elitist and masculinist in central respects, accelerated the nineteenth-century disparagement of much Sentimental and Romantic literature. Though Hemans and other widely read Romantic writers such as Walter Scott continued to appear in schoolbooks and circulated in popular reading culture, they were ignored by high literary culture and the new institution of male-dominated university-based academic criticism and scholarship. This process refashioned the masculinization of literature and culture already inherent in Romanticism and institutionalized in the modern liberal state. The marginalization of women in the liberal state's public institution of literature corresponded to the exclusion of women from the liberal state's electorate until well into the twentieth century, and occurred despite—or because of—the instrumental role of Romantic feminism and Romantic women writers such as Hemans in constructing liberal ideology and transforming the reading public into the political nation. The gendering of literature and the electorate paralleled the marginalization of plebeian culture and the exclusion from electoral franchise of most of the working classes until late in the nineteenth century.

These processes participated in a broader hierarchization of culture and politics that privileged the interests of the middle classes and especially professional men in the modern state. In

---

1 Herbert F. Tucker, "House Arrest: The Domestication of English Poetry in the 1820s," *New Literary History* 25 (Summer 1994): 521-48, pp. 542-43.

this hierarchy, the popular was associated with the plebeian, the feminine and feminized, the sentimental, and the "merely" commercial; the popular was disparaged accordingly, and excluded from high culture, from official culture, and, to a large extent, from state and especially higher education.[1] As Marlon Ross has argued, the denigrating and forgetting of Hemans and other women poets of the period have formed part of the re-instituting of masculinist Romantic literature as definitive of literature in general.[2] Hemans and other "sentimental" writers did continue to circulate in popular literary culture, however. In 1947 Decca Records included Hemans's "The Landing of the Pilgrim Fathers" in an eight-record set entitled "Our Common Heritage: Great Poems Celebrating Milestones in the History of America" (reissued in 1960 as an LP). In 1963 the popular actor Vincent Price included the same poem in a two-day program of public readings entitled "America the Beautiful." In the same year the same poem was included in a four-record set of readings for schools, entitled "Prose and Poetry Adventures." In 1973 a recording of popular poems set to music, entitled "Songs of Love and Death," included one by Hemans. Meanwhile, popular literary culture was and continues to be dominated by epigones of poets like Hemans, from "Patience Strong" to Rod McKuen and Jewel, including the lyrics in much popular music, and the vast, almost entirely unknown writing public who produce what is called folk poetry and who publish, when they do publish, in church magazines, local newspapers, community and organization newsletters, and now the internet.[3] The occasional, superficial similarities between the themes and verse forms used by popular "sentimental" poets like Strong and McKuen and those used by Hemans make it difficult for many academically trained readers nowadays to distinguish much of her work from theirs. At the same time, the presence of poets like Hemans as an influence and

---

1 See "Popular" in Raymond Williams, *Keywords: A Vocabulary of Culture and Society* ([Glasgow:] Fontana, 1976).

2 Ross, *The Contours of Masculine Desire*, 233-59.

3 See Roger deV. Renwick, *English Folk Poetry: Structure and Meaning* (London: Batsford, 1980), and Pauline Greenhill, *True Poetry: Traditional and Popular Verse in Ontario* (Montreal: McGill-Queen's University Press, 1989).

echo in modern folk poetry attests to their continuing power to address concerns of ordinary people who want to articulate their situation and responses to both everyday life and the larger world beyond their control.

Paradoxically, the late twentieth-century revival of interest in Hemans, though still academic and university-based, owes much to recent changes in culture, society, and politics in that larger world. These changes have, according to one argument, produced the universal triumph of the modern liberal state that Hemans, with many other Romantic writers, heralded and helped achieve. From the 1960s, at least, there have been increasing demands for full participation in the public sphere, civil society, and the liberal state from groups who still had not received the franchise and civil rights, or if they had received them, were nevertheless marginalized, oppressed, or excluded. Among the foremost of such groups were women. In liberal states, many of these demands have been at least partly realized, resulting in an apparent broadening of the political nation in those states. In 1989, the fall of the Berlin wall and collapse of the soviet system and Eastern bloc accompanied so-called liberalization in Western economies and globalization of trade, culture, and politics. These events have led some commentators to announce the triumph of the liberal state as the end of history—end as goal, and end as termination, in the sense that revolutionary transformation, hitherto the characteristic of history, has been made unnecessary by the universality, or imminent universality of the liberal state.[1] Since the late 1960s there has been a rapidly increasing interest in women writers and women's literature. This interest was and is largely moved by university-based feminism, and it supports women's claims to be sovereign subjects entitled thereby to fuller participation in the public sphere and the modern state. During the 1990s, the decade that celebrated the "triumph" of the liberal state, academic scholarship and criticism became more interested in Hemans as part of this movement.

Nevertheless, this interest was slow to develop precisely

---

1 See Francis Fukuyama, *The End of History and the Last Man* (New York: The Free Press, 1992).

because of the continuing prevalence of a certain image of Hemans—an image that she used to advance her career and her political values, that helped make and keep her popular, but that was turned against her by masculinist and elitist criticism in the nineteenth century and after. The ground-breaking feminist literary history, *The Madwoman in the Attic: The Woman Writer and the Nineteenth-Century Literary Imagination* (1979), by Sandra M. Gilbert and Susan Gubar, deals almost entirely with fiction and finds no occasion to mention the most widely read woman poet of that century. The most recent edition of a standard reference work, the *Oxford Companion to English Literature* (1985), dismisses Hemans's "fluent and innocuous volumes."[1] A history of English Romantic poetry published in 1985 and aimed at students and teachers does not mention Hemans.[2] Specifically feminist criticism, too, has often been resistant to Hemans's work. As Norma Clarke points out in a pioneering feminist study of Hemans and her friends, "so absolutely has she been identified with pre-Victorian and Victorian ideal womanhood, with all its renunciation, suffering, and 'self-devoting affection,' that even feminist scholars have shown little interest in recouping her for the revised tradition" of women's writing.[3] Criticism that is sympathetic to Hemans seems often to re-present the feminine figure and ideology constructed by Hemans herself, in collusion with her contemporary critics, though for her own purposes. As Diego Saglia writes, "even criticism of a more recent period still seems caught up in methods of reading which award precedence to the text of femaleness, woman as the ultimate explanation of poetry by women, rather than to the literary artefact itself in its complex and unstable negotiations of a gendered position."[4]

For it is also paradoxical that modern feminisms and other progressive movements developed substantial critiques of the

---

1 Fifth edition, ed. Margaret Drabble, art. "Hemans."
2 J.R. Watson, *English Poetry of the Romantic Period 1789-1830* (London and New York: Longman, 1985).
3 Clarke, *Ambitious Heights*, 35.
4 Diego Saglia, "Epic or Domestic?: Felicia Hemans's Heroic Poetry and the Myth of the Victorian Poetess," *Rivista di Studi Vittoriani* 2 (July 1997): 125-47, p. 147.

sentimentalism, domestic ideology, and Romantic nationalism that Hemans and her contemporaries, both men and women, used for revolutionary transformation of the Old Order and achievement of the modern liberal state. The domestic ideology is now seen to limit or inhibit women from full participation in the modern liberal state and economy. Feminism remained leery of the "sentimentalism" used by Hemans and her contemporaries to invent and propagate the sovereign subjectivity on which the liberal state was to be based. For during the nineteenth century, "sentimentality" became associated with feminization, or rather effeminization, and with the popular, and those associations persist today.[1] Hemans's later, religious poetry is especially resistant to the highly secularized and socially insulated progressivism of much academic discourse. In recent decades a variety of often contradictory movements, including regionalism, globalization, pacifism, and the promotion of civil society, has contributed to critiques of the Romantic model of the nation state. Hemans and Romantic feminism, with Romantic literature and culture in general, now seem ambiguous cultural forces, to be re-examined in a broad critique of the modern liberal state. Both the institutional culture of the modern liberal state and its critics now have little or no place, apparently, for one of that state's founders. Reconsideration of Hemans and her work may at least, however, have a place in a new literary history that, as one aspect of Jerome McGann puts it, "assumes the past has not yet happened, that it remains to be seen.[2] It may even be that reconsideration of Hemans and her work, which this edition aims to enable but cannot determine, can help to recover something of the revolutionary potential they once had, and take that potential in new directions.

1   Ross, *The Contours of Masculine Desire*, 291-92
2   McGann, *The Poetics of Sensibility*, 180.

Felicia Hemans: A Brief Chronology

1793 Felicia Dorothea Browne born Liverpool, 25 September, one of six children, fourth child and second daughter; other children: Thomas, later Sir (1784-1855); George, later Colonel, Chief Commissioner of Police, Ireland; Elizabeth (1789-1807); Claude (1795-1821); Harriet (1798-1835); father George a Liverpool wine merchant, originally from Ireland; mother Felicity (Wagner, 1766-1827) of Italian-German parentage, daughter of Austrian consul for Tuscany at Liverpool.

1799 father winds up business because of commercial blockade of the Continent; moves family to comfortable retired home at Gwrych, near Abergele, Wales.

1804 winter with family in London.

1805 winter with family in London.

1808 *Poems*, "By Felicia Dorothea Browne," published by subscription (Liverpool, for T. Cadell and W. Davies, London), dedicated to the Prince of Wales by permission; intense interest in Peninsular War; publishes *England and Spain; or, Valour and Patriotism* (Liverpool and London: T. Cadell and W. Davies).

1809 family moves to Bronwylfa, near St Asaph, Wales; meets Capt. Alfred Hemans (1781-1827, died at Rome), their desire to marry is discouraged by her family.

1812 *The Domestic Affections and Other Poems*, "By Felicia Dorothea Browne" (London: T. Cadell and W. Davies); 28 July marries Capt. Hemans; moves to Daventry, where he is adjutant to Northamptonshire militia; Arthur born (died 1837, Rome), first of 5 children, all boys.

1813 Hemans family move to Bronwylfa, Wales, living with her mother; three more sons born: George Willoughby (1814-85; water and sewage engineer; Chief Engineer, Irish Railway); Claude Lewis (1815-93, died in USA); Henry William (baptised 1817-71, died Brazil).

1816 *The Restoration of the Works of Art to Italy: A Poem*, "By a Lady" (Oxford: R. Pearson; J. Ebers, London); second edition of *The Restoration of the Works of Art to Italy*, considerably revised, published by John Murray (London).

1817   (June) *Modern Greece: A Poem* (London: John Murray).

1818   (May) *Translations from Camoens, and Other Poets, with Original Poetry*, "By the Author of 'Modern Greece,' and the 'Restoration of the Works of Art to Italy'" (Oxford: J. Parker; John Murray, London); Capt. Hemans leaves for Italy, ostensibly for his health, but does not return; (Sept.) birth of last son, Charles Lloyd, later Isidore (1818-76, journalist and art historian, died at Lucca Italy).

1819   (May) *Tales, and Historic Scenes, in Verse*, "By Felicia Hemans" (London: John Murray); "The Meeting of Wallace and Bruce on the Banks of the Carron" awarded £50 prize and published in *Blackwood's Edinburgh Magazine* (Sept.).

1820   *The Sceptic: A Poem*, "By Mrs. Hemans" (London: John Murray); *Stanzas to the Memory of the Late King*, "By Mrs. Hemans" (London: John Murray); (April) *Wallace's Invocation to Bruce* (Edinburgh: Blackwood; T. Cadell and W. Davies, London; dated 1819); favourable review of Hemans's poems in conservative *Quarterly Review*; meets Reginald Heber; working on major religious poem, "Superstition and Revelation."

1821   *Dartmoor: A Poem*, "By Felicia D. Hemans" (London: The Royal Society of Literature); second edition of *Wallace's Invocation to Bruce*; (Sept.) second editions of *The Sceptic* and *Modern Greece*; death of brother, Claude Scott Browne, at Kingston, Upper Canada; becomes deeply interested in German literature.

1822   *A Selection of Welsh Melodies, with Symphonies and Accompaniments By John Parry, and Characteristic Words By Mrs. Hemans* (London: J. Power).

1823   (June) *The Siege of Valencia: A Dramatic Poem*; *The Last Constantine: with Other Poems*, "By Mrs. Hemans" (London: John Murray); (Nov.) second edition of *Tales, and*

Historic Scenes; (Nov.) *The Vespers of Palermo: A Tragedy, in Five Acts* (London: John Murray); (Dec.) failure of *Vespers of Palermo* at Covent Garden theatre, London; begins contributing to liberal periodical, *New Monthly Magazine*, edited by Thomas Campbell; follows progress of revolutions in Mexico and South America.

1824 becoming popular in the USA; successful production of *Vespers of Palermo* in Edinburgh.

1825 (May) *The Forest Sanctuary; and Other Poems*, "By Mrs. Hemans" (London: John Murray); interested in Polish aspirations for independence; moves family from Bron-wylfa to nearby Rhyllon; begins publishing in literary annuals.

1827 publishes *Hymns for Childhood* in USA (Boston: Hilliard, Gray, Little, and Wilkins); begins publishing regularly in *Blackwood's Edinburgh Magazine*; death of mother.

1828 *Records of Woman; with Other Poems*, "By Felicia Hemans" (Edinburgh: William Blackwood; and T. Cadell, London), dedicated to Joanna Baillie; M.J. Jewsbury summers in Wales to be near Hemans; marriage of sister; moves to Wavertree, near Liverpool; planning volume of prose sketches, "Recollections of a Poet's Childhood"; (Oct.) second edition of *Records of Woman*; (Dec.) second edition, "With Additions," of *The Forest Sanctuary*.

1829 major review of Hemans's poetry by Francis Jeffrey in liberal *Edinburgh Review*; visits Scotland; acquaintance with Walter Scott and others.

1830 *Songs of the Affections, with Other Poems*, "By Felicia Hemans" (Edinburgh: William Blackwood; and T. Cadell, London), dedicated to Sir Robert Liston; (June) third edition of *Records of Woman*; visits Wordsworth in Lake district; rents villa, Dove Nest, nearby; visits Scotland again; visits Dublin.

1831 moves to Dublin.

1832 by now virtually an invalid.

1833 *Hymns on the Works of Nature, for the Use of Children*, "By Mrs. Felicia Hemans" (London: John Mardon, "Reprinted from the American Edition" of *Hymns for Childhood*).

1834 *Scenes and Hymns of Life, with Other Religious Poems*, "By Felicia Hemans" (Edinburgh: William Blackwood; and T. Cadell, London), dedicated to Wordsworth; *National Lyrics, and Songs for Music*, "By Felicia Hemans" (Dublin: William Curry Jr. and Co.; London: Simpkin and Marshall), dedicated to Rose Lawrence; fourth edition of *Records of Woman*.

1835 second edition of *Songs of the Affections*; Prime Minister Robert Peel awards her a cash donation and a government job for her son Henry; dies Dublin, 16 May; third edition of *The Forest Sanctuary*.

1836 *Poetical Remains of the Late Mrs Hemans* (Edinburgh: William Blackwood and Sons; and T. Cadell, London).

Chronology based on Paula R. Feldman, "The Poet and the Profits: Felicia Hemans and the Literary Marketplace," *Keats-Shelley Journal* 46 (1997): 148-76, and on information generously supplied by Hemans's descendant, Margaret Nott.

SELECTED POEMS, PROSE,

AND LETTERS

FROM *POEMS* (1808)[1]

TO THE MUSE.

GODDESS of the magic lay,
Ever let me own thy sway;
Thine the sweet enchanting art,
To charm and to correct the heart;
To bid the tear of pity flow,   5
Sacred to thy tale of woe;
Or raise the lovely smile of pleasure,
With sportive animated measure.

"Oh! Goddes of the magic lay,"
To thee my early vows I pay;   10
Still let me wander in thy train,
And pour the wild romantic strain.
Be mine to rove by thee inspir'd,
In peaceful vales and scenes retir'd;
For in thy path, oh! heavenly maid,   15
The roses smile that never fade.

A TRIBUTE TO THE GENIUS OF
ROBERT BURNS.[2]

As in the lone sequester'd grove,
  The woodlark on the bending spray,
Attunes to liberty and love
      The sportive lay:

---

1 for context and commentary, see Introduction, pp. 18-19.
2 Burns (1759-96) was raised in poverty as a farm labourer; he adapted popular Scot-
   tish ballad forms and songs and the success of his *Poems, Chiefly in the Scottish Dialect*
   (1786) brought accclaim and patronage from middle-class intellectuals and profes-
   sionals; he associated Scottish patriotism with the cause of reform and sympathised
   with the early phase of the French Revolution; after his death he was sentimental-
   ized as a poet of rustic simplicity and independence, a voice of "the people"
   estranged from and not fully appreciated by the supposedly decadent culture and
   society of his time.

'Twas thus in mountain scenes retir'd,
    That Scotia's minstrel, nature's child,
Would sing, by ardent genius fir'd,
            His carol wild.

In poverty his generous heart,
With freedom and with fancy glow'd;
And native strains untaught by art,
            Spontaneous flow'd.

Oh! Burns, to every feeling breast,
    To every gentle mind sincere,
By love and tender pity blest,
            Thy song is dear.

Sweet bard! 'twas thine to soar on high,
    With inspiration and the muse;
To claim from beauty's radiant eye
            Compassion's dews;

To raise the smile of social glee,
    The patriot's manly heart to fire;
Or wake the tear of sympathy,
            With plaintive lyre.

Sweet bard! for thee the muses mourn,
    In melting lays they sing thy name;
And twine, to deck thy sacred urn,
            The wreath of fame.

THE FAREWELL.

WHEN sad the parting word we hear,
 That seems of past delights to tell;
Who then, without a sacred tear,
    Can say farewell?

And are we ever doom'd to mourn,   5
 That e'en our joys may lead to pain?
Alas! the rose without a thorn
    We seek in vain.

When friends endear'd by absence meet,
 Their hours are crown'd with every treasure; 10
Too soon the happy moments fleet
    On wings of pleasure.

But when the parting hour is nigh,
 What feeling breast their woes can tell?
With many a prayer and tender sigh   15
    They bid farewell.

Yet Hope may charm their grief away,
 And pour her sweet enchanting strain,
That friends belov'd—some future day,
    Shall meet agrain.   20

Her aid the fair deceiver lends,
 To dry the tears which sadly fell;
And calm the sorrow which attends
    The last farewell.

FROM *ENGLAND AND SPAIN; OR, VALOUR AND PATRIOTISM* (1808)[1]

Too long have Tyranny and Power combin'd,
To sway, with iron sceptre, o'er mankind;[2]
Long has Oppression worn th' imperial robe,
And rapine's sword has wasted half the globe!
5 O'er Europe's cultur'd realms, and climes afar,
Triumphant Gaul has pour'd the tide of war;
To her fair Austria vail'd the standard bright;
Ausonia's[3] lovely plains have own'd her might;
While Prussia's eagle, never taught to yield,
10 Forsook her tow'ring height on Jena's field![4]
[…]
 O'er peaceful realms, that smil'd with plenty gay,
Has desolation spread her ample sway;
Thy blast, oh Ruin! on tremendous wings,
Has proudly swept o'er empires, nations, kings!
25 Thus the wild hurricane's impetuous force,
With dark destruction marks its whelming course;
Despoils the woodland's pomp, the blooming plain,
Death on its pinion, vengeance in its train!

 Rise, Freedom, rise! and breaking from thy trance,
30 Wave the dread banner, seize the glitt'ring lance!
With arm of might assert thy sacred cause,
And call thy champions to defend thy laws!
How long shall tyrant power her throne maintain?
How long shall despots and usurpers reign?
35 Is honour's lofty soul for ever fled?
Is virtue lost? is martial ardour dead?
Is there no heart where worth and valour dwell,
No patriot WALLACE, no undaunted TELL?[5]

---

1 for context and commentary, see Introduction, pp. 19-20.
2 reference to Napoleon.
3 Ausonia] ancient name for Italy.
4 Napoleon defeated the Prussian army at Jena in Germany, Oct. 1806.
5 William Wallace, 13th-century Scottish warrior who led resistance to English occupation of his native country, but was betrayed and executed; he became a legendary

Yes, Freedom, yes! thy sons, a noble band,
Around thy banner, firm, exulting stand;   40
Once more 'tis thine, invincible, to wield
The beamy spear, and adamantine shield!
Again thy cheek with proud resentment glows,
Again thy lion-glance appals thy foes;
Thy kindling eye-beam darts unconquer'd fires,   45
Thy look sublime the warrior's heart inspires:
And while, to guard thy standard and thy right,
CASTILIANS[1] rush, intrepid to the fight;
Lo! BRITAIN's gen'rous host their aid supply,
Resolv'd for thee to triumph or to die!   50
And glory smiles to see IBERIA's name,
Enroll'd with ALBION's[2] in the book of fame!
[…]
     Hail, ALBION! hail, thou land of freedom's birth!
Pride of the main, and Phœnix[3] of the earth!   70
Thou second Rome,[4] where mercy, justice, dwell,
Whose sons in wisdom as in arms excel!
Thine are the dauntless bands, like Spartans brave,[5]
Bold in the field, triumphant on the wave;
In classic elegance, and arts divine,   75
To rival Athens'[6] fairest palm is thine;

---

figure through popular chapbooks, and in the Romantic period became a symbol of the patriot; Hemans later wrote a poem celebrating him, "Wallace's Invocation to Bruce" (1819); Wilhelm Tell was a mostly legendary 14th-century leader of Swiss resistance to foreign rule, also celebrated in the Romantic period as a patriot, in such influential texts as Friedrich Schiller's play of 1804.

1   Castilians] from Castille, region in central north-west Spain, and medieval kingdom that led the military expulsion of the Moors from Spain, and Spanish conquest of Mexico, in the late 15th and early 16th century; also scene of conflict between French and allied (British and Spanish) armies, and of effective Spanish guerilla action, at the time the poem was published.

2   Albion] ancient and poetic name for England.

3   Phœnix] in myth and literature, bird reborn from its own ashes.

4   ancient Rome was supposed to have brought peace and prosperity to its empire.

5   Sparta, a famously martial, disciplined, and puritanical city-state, led resistance in ancient Greece against foreign invaders.

6   Athens was the most powerful, rich, and cultivated of the ancient Greek city-states, and celebrated for its democratic government, though in fact it was based on a slave economy, excluded most women from public life, and ruled its dependent states with rigour.

For taste and fancy from Hymettus[1] fly,
And richer bloom beneath thy varying sky,
Where Science mounts, in radiant car sublime,
80 To other worlds beyond the sphere of time!
Hail, ALBION, hail! to thee has fate denied
Peruvian mines and rich Hindostan's pride;[2]
The gems that Ormuz and Golconda[3] boast,
And all the wealth of Montezuma's coast:[4]
85 For thee no Parian marbles[5] brightly shine;
No glowing suns mature the blushing vine;
No light Arabian gales their wings expand,
To waft Sabæan incense o'er the land;[6]
No graceful cedars crown thy lofty hills,
90 No trickling myrrh for thee its balm distils;
Not from thy trees the lucid amber flows,
And far from thee the scented cassia blows!
Yet fearless Commerce, pillar of thy throne,
Makes all the wealth of foreign climes thy own;
95 From Lapland's shore to Afric's fervid reign,
She bids thy ensigns float above the main;
Unfurls her streamers to the fav'ring gale,
And shows to other worlds her daring sail;
Then wafts their gold, their varied stores to thee,
100 Queen of the trident! empress of the sea!
[…]

235   Oh! thou, the sovereign of the noble soul!
Thou source of energies beyond controul!
Queen of the lofty thought, the gen'rous deed,

---

1 Hymettus] mountain in Attica, Greece, in ancient times source of renowned honey
   and supposed to be the site of a spring whose waters could inspire poets.
2 Britons liked to believe that Spanish imperial rule in Peru and Muslim rule in India
   (Hindostan) were excessively harsh, unlike British rule of its colonies.
3 Ormuz and Golconda] places in India.
4 Montezuma was ruler of the Aztec empire in Mexico, overthrown by the Spaniards
   in the 16th century.
5 marble from the island of Paros in the Aegean was famed for its whiteness and used
   for sculpture and architectural ornament in ancient Athens.
6 in earlier times, southwest Arabia was the source of spices and perfumes much
   prized in Europe.

Whose sons unconquer'd fight, undaunted bleed,
Inspiring Liberty! thy worshipp'd name
The warm enthusiast kindles to a flame;   240
Thy look of heaven, thy voice of harmony,
Thy charms inspire him to achievements high;
More blest, with thee to tread perennial snows,
Where ne'er a flow'r expands, a zephyr blows;
Where Winter, binding nature in his chain,   245
In frost-work palace holds perpetual reign;
Than, far from thee, with frolic step to rove,
The green savannas, and the spicy grove;
Scent the rich balm of India's perfum'd gales,
In citron-woods, and aromatic vales;   250
For oh! fair Liberty, when thou art near,
Elysium[1] blossoms in the desart drear!

      Where'er thy smile its magic pow'r bestows,
There arts and taste expand, there fancy glows;
Thy sacred lyre its wild enchantment gives,   255
And ev'ry chord to swelling transport lives;
There ardent Genius bids the pencil trace
The soul of beauty, and the lines of grace;
With bold, Promethean[2] hand, the canvas warms,
And calls from stone expression's breathing forms.   260
Thus, where the fruitful Nile o'erflows its bound,
Its genial waves diffuse abundance round,
Bid Ceres[3] laugh o'er waste and sterile sands,
And rich profusion clothe deserted lands!

      Immortal FREEDOM! daughter of the skies!   265
To thee shall BRITAIN's grateful incense rise!
Ne'er, goddess! ne'er forsake thy fav'rite isle,
Still be thy ALBION brighten'd with thy smile!
[…]

---

1   Elysium] in ancient myth, the abode of the blessed after death; and thence any land
    of ideal happiness.
2   in myth, the god Prometheus shaped man from clay.
3   Ceres] ancient goddess of harvest.

Genius of chivalry![1] whose early days,
300   Tradition still recounts in artless lays;[2]
Whose faded splendors fancy oft recalls,
The floating banners, and the lofty halls;
The gallant feats thy festivals display'd,
The tilt, the tournament, the long crusade;
305   Whose ancient pride Romance delights to hail,
In fabling numbers, or heroic tale:
Those times are fled, when stern thy castles frown'd,
Their stately tow'rs with feudal grandeur crown'd;
Those times are fled, when fair IBERIA's[3] clime,
310   Beheld thy Gothic[4] reign, thy pomp sublime;
And all thy glories, all thy deeds of yore,
Live but in legends wild, and poet's lore!
Lo! where thy silent harp neglected lies,
Light o'er its chords the murm'ring zephyr sighs;
315   Thy solemn courts, where once the minstrel sung,
The choral voice of mirth and music rung;
Now, with the ivy clad, forsaken, lone,
Hear but the breeze and echo to its moan:
Thy lonely tow'rs deserted fall away,
320   Thy broken shield is mould'ring in decay.
Yet tho' thy transient pageantries are gone,
Like fairy visions, bright, yet swiftly flown;
Genius of chivalry! thy noble train,
Thy firm, exalted virtues yet remain!
325   Fair truth, array'd in robes of spotless white,
Her eye a sunbeam, and her zone[5] of light;
Warm emulation, with aspiring aim,
Still darting forward to the wreath of fame;

---

1   chivalry] here, an idealized form of the actual medieval upper-class code and cul-
   ture of feudal chivalry, adapted in the late 18th and early 19th century to middle-
   class values.
2   lays] popular ballads, supposedly relics of medieval culture, and much collected and
   imitated in the Romantic period.
3   Iberia] ancient name for the region of Spain and Portugal.
4   Gothic] Visigoths seized the Iberian peninsula from the crumbling Roman empire
   and were in turn almost driven out by invading Moors from north Africa.
5   zone] an ornamental belt.

And purest love, that waves his torch divine,
At awful honour's consecrated shrine;   330
Ardour with eagle-wing, and fiery glance;
And gen'rous courage, resting on his lance;
And loyalty, by perils unsubdued;
Untainted faith, unshaken fortitude;
And patriot energy, with heart of flame;   335
These, in IBERIA's sons are yet the same!
[…]

   Ah! when shall mad ambition cease to rage?
Ah! when shall war his demon-wrath assuage?
When, when, supplanting discord's iron reign,
Shall mercy wave her olive-wand again?
Not till the despot's dread career is clos'd,   565
And might restrain'd, and tyranny depos'd!

   Return, sweet Peace, ethereal form benign!
Fair blue-ey'd seraph! balmy power divine!
Descend once more! thy hallow'd blessings bring,
Wave thy bright locks, and spread thy downy wing!   570
Luxuriant plenty laughing in thy train,
Shall crown with glowing stores the desart-plain;
Young smiling hope, attendant on thy way,
Shall gild thy path with mild celestial ray.
Descend once more! thou daughter of the sky!   575
Cheer ev'ry heart, and brighten ev'ry eye!
Justice, thy harbinger, before thee send,
Thy myrtle-sceptre[1] o'er the globe extend:
Thy cherub-look again shall soothe mankind;
Thy cherub-hand the wounds of discord bind;   580
Thy smile of heav'n shall ev'ry muse inspire,
To thee the bard shall strike the silver lyre.
Descend once more! to bid the world rejoice,
Let nations hail thee with exulting voice;
Around thy shrine with purest incense throng,   585

---

1 myrtle] in myth a shrub associated with Venus and thus with love and peace.

Weave the fresh palm,[1] and swell the choral song!
Then shall the shepherd's flute, the woodland reed,
The martial clarion, and the drum succeed,
Again shall bloom Arcadia's[2] fairest flowers,
590 And music warble in Idalian[3] bowers;
Where war and carnage blew the blast of death,
The gale shall whisper with Favonian[4] breath!
And golden Ceres bless the festive swain,
Where the wild combat redden'd o'er the plain!
[...]

Oh! thou! whose fiat lulls the storm asleep!
Thou! at whose nod subsides the rolling deep!
605 Whose awful word restrains the whirlwind's force,
And stays the thunder in its vengeful course;
Fountain of life! Omnipotent Supreme!
Robed in perfection! crown'd with glory's beam!
Oh! send on earth thy consecrated dove,
610 To bear the sacred olive from above;
Restore again the blest, the halcyon time,[5]
The festal harmony of nature's prime!
Bid truth and justice once again appear,
And spread their sunshine o'er this mundane sphere;
615 Bright in their path, let wreaths unfading bloom,
Transcendent light their hallow'd fane illume;
Bid war and anarchy for ever cease,
And kindred seraphs rear the shrine of peace;
Brothers once more, let men her empire own,
620 And realms and monarchs bend before the throne;
While circling rays of angel-mercy shed
Eternal halos round her sainted head!

---

1 palm] branches of this tree were associated with victory or supremacy.
2 Arcadia was a mythic land of idyllic rustic simplicity.
3 Idalia was one of the names of Venus.
4 Favonian] in ancient lore, western, hence gentle, propitious.
5 the halcyon is a bird supposedly empowered to calm rough seas; in Greek myth, Ceyx was drowned and in pity for his wife Alcyone's grief the gods transformed both into sea-birds, forbidding winds to blow during their breeding season.

FROM *THE DOMESTIC AFFECTIONS, AND OTHER POEMS* (1812)[1]

SONNET TO ITALY.

FOR thee, Ausonia![2] Nature's bounteous hand,
  Luxuriant spreads around her blooming stores;
Profusion laughs o'er all the glowing land,
  And softest breezes from thy myrtle-shores.[3]

Yet though for thee, unclouded suns diffuse
  Their genial radiance o'er thy blushing plains;
Though in thy fragrant groves the sportive muse
  Delights to pour her wild, enchanted strains;

Though airs that breathe of paradise are thine,
  Sweet as the Indian, or Arabian gales;[4]
Though fruitful olive and empurpling vine,
  Enrich, fair Italy! thy Alpine vales;
Yet far from thee inspiring freedom flies,
To Albion's[5] coast and ever-varying skies!

WAR-SONG
OF THE SPANISH PATRIOTS.[6]

YE who burn with glory's flame!
Ye who love the Patriot's fame;

---

1   for context and commentary, see Introduction, p. 20.
2   Ausonia] ancient poetic name for Italy.
3   myrtle is an aromatic evergreen shrub with white flowers, in classical myth associated with Venus and thus with love.
4   gales] poeticism for mild winds.
5   Albion] poetic name for England.
6   Patriots] name given to those Spaniards who opposed Napoleon's occupation of Spain and imposition of his brother Joseph on the Spanish throne, precipitating the Peninsular War; the Spanish patriots adopted a British-style constitutional monarchy at Cadiz in 1812; in Britain, "patriot" was a name adopted by late 18th-

Ye who scorn oppressive might,
Rise! in freedom's cause unite!
      Castilians[1] rise!
Hark! Iberia[2] calls, ye brave!
Haste! your bleeding country save:
Be the palm of bright renown,
Be th' unfading laurel-crown,
      The hero's prize!

High the crimson banner wave!
Ours be the conquest or the grave!
Spirits of our noble sires,
Lo! your sons, with kindred fires,
      Unconquer'd glow!
See them once again advance,
Crush the pride of hostile France;
See their hearts, with ardour warm,
See them, with triumphant arm,
      Repel the foe!

By the Cid's[3] immortal name,
By Gonsalvo's[4] deathless fame;
By the chiefs of former time,
By the valiant deeds sublime,
      Of ancient days;
Brave Castilians! grasp the spear!

---

century reformists; during Italian, Spanish, and German resistance to Napoleon it came to mean "nationalist" in the modern sense; FH's usage embodies older and newer sense, adopted by liberals throughout Europe.

1 Castilians] see *England and Spain*, l. 48.

2 Iberia] ancient Roman and common poetic name for Hispanic peninsula.

3 Cid] Rodrigo Diaz of Bivar, 11th-century Spanish knight who served both Muslim and Christian rulers and whose deeds were glamourized after his death in popular ballads, longer romances, and pseudo-histories; during the Peninsular War he was made a figure for Spanish patriotic resistance to outside invaders.

4 Gonsalvo] Gonzalo Fernández de Córdoba (1453-1515), known as the Great Captain, Spanish general in the service of queen Isabella of Castille; he led several successful campaigns against the Moors in Spain and the French in Italy; his military tactics were compared to those of Wellington in the Peninsular War.

Gallant Andalusians,[1] hear!
Glory calls you to the plain,
Future bards, in lofty strain,
　　Shall sing your praise!　　　　　　　30

Shades of mighty warriors dead,
Ye who nobly fought and bled;
Ye whose valour could withstand,
The savage Moor's invading band
　　Untaught to yield;　　　　　　　　35
Bade victorious Charlemagne,[2]
Own the patriot arms of Spain;
Ye, in later times renown'd,
Ye who fell with laurels crown'd,
　　On Pavia's field![3]　　　　　　　40

Teach our hearts like yours to burn;
Lawless pow'r like you to spurn;
Teach us but like you to wield,
Freedom's lance and Freedom's shield;
　　With daring might:　　　　　　　45
Tyrant![4] soon thy reign is o'er,
Thou shalt waste mankind no more;
Boast no more thy thousands slain,
Jena's, or Marengo's[5] plain;
Lo! the sun that gilds thy day,　　　50
Soon will veil its parting ray,
　　In endless night!

1　Andalusians] of Andalusia, region in southern Spain, last medieval Moorish king-
　　dom, and scene of stubborn Spanish resistance to the French during the Peninsular
　　War.
2　Charlemagne] king of the Franks who led an expedition against the Moorish rulers
　　of northern Spain in 778 but was forced to withdraw; he escaped with his army
　　thanks to a heroic and fatal rearguard action led by Roland against an army of
　　Christian Spaniards at Roncesvalles; the episode became the subject of numerous
　　romances.
3　Pavia] city in Italy where in 1525 the army of the Spanish-German emperor
　　Charles v defeated that of the French king Francis I.
4　Tyrant] Napoleon.
5　Jena in Germany and Marengo in Italy were major military victories by Napoleon,
　　in 1806 and 1800 respectively.

FROM "THE DOMESTIC AFFECTIONS":[1]

WHENCE are those tranquil joys, in mercy giv'n,
To light the wilderness with beams of Heav'n?
To sooth our cares, and thro' the cloud diffuse,
Their temper'd sun-shine, and celestial hues?
5 Those pure delights, ordain'd on life to throw
Gleams of the bliss ethereal natures know?
Say, do they grace Ambition's regal throne,
When kneeling myriads call the world his own?
Or dwell with luxury, in th' enchanted bow'rs,
10 Where taste and wealth exert *creative* pow'rs?

Favor'd of Heav'n! O Genius! are they thine,
When round thy brow the wreaths of glory shine;
While rapture gazes on thy radiant way,
'Midst the bright realms of clear and mental day?
15 No! sacred joys! 'tis yours to dwell enshrin'd,
Most fondly cherish'd, in the purest mind;
To twine with flowers, those lov'd, endearing ties,
On earth so sweet,—so perfect in the skies!

Nurs'd on the lap of solitude and shade,
20 The violet smiles, embosom'd in the glade;
There sheds her spirit on the lonely gale,
Gem of seclusion! treasure of the vale!
Thus, far retir'd from life's tumultuous road,
Domestic bliss has fix'd her calm abode,
25 Where hallow'd innocence and sweet repose
May strew her shadowy path with many a rose;
As, when dread thunder shakes the troubled sky,
The cherub, infancy, can close its eye,

---

1 the title is a common phrase used at that time for egalitarian social sympathy based
in the home and including members of the same family as well as personal (rather
than, say, business or political) friends; in the aftermath of the French Revolution
and Napoleonic Wars this idea of community was often contrasted with what was
seen as an irredeemably conflicted public and political sphere, and as the foundation
for new ideas of nation different from both monarchic models and revolutionary
republican ones.

And sweetly smile, unconscious of a tear,
While viewless angels wave their pinions near;   30
Thus, while around the storms of discord roll,
Borne on resistless wing, from pole to pole;
While war's red lightnings desolate the ball,[1]
And thrones and empires in destruction fall;
Then, calm as evening on the silvery wave,   35
When the wind slumbers in the ocean-cave,
She dwells, unruffled, in her bow'r of rest,
Her empire, home!—her throne, affection's breast! [...]

Can war's dread scenes the hallow'd ties efface,
Each tender thought, each fond remembrance chase?
Can fields of carnage, days of toil, destroy
The lov'd impressions of domestic joy?

Ye day-light dreams! that cheer the soldier's breast,   115
In hostile climes, with spells benign and blest;
Sooth his brave heart, and shed your glowing ray,
O'er the long march, thro' desolation's way;
Oh! still ye bear him from th' ensanguin'd plain,
Armour's bright flash, and victory's choral strain;   120
To that lov'd home, where pure affection glows,
That shrine of bliss! asylum of repose! [...]

Hail! sweet endearments of domestic ties,
Charms of existence! angel-sympathies!
Tho' pleasure smile, a soft, Circassian[2] queen!   155
And guide her votaries thro' a fairy scene;
Where sylphid forms beguile their vernal hours,
With mirth and music, in Arcadian[3] bow'rs;

---

1 ball] here, globe.   160
2 Circassian queen] woman from a region in the Caucasus, then controlled by
   Turkey; famed for their fair complexion and beauty, such women were prized as
   concubines in the Turkish empire, and in the sultan's harem supposedly used their
   amorous skills to gain power, or even become queen, like women in the court cul-
   ture of western Europe.
3 Arcadia is a mythic land of pastoral simplicity and love; notoriously, monarchs and
   their courtiers would play at pastoral life for amusement.

Tho' gazing nations hail the fiery car,
160   That bears the son of conquest from afar;
While Fame's loud Paean bids his heart rejoice,
And ev'ry life-pulse vibrates to her voice;
Yet from your source *alone*, in mazes bright,
Flows the full current of serene delight!

165   On Freedom's wing, that ev'ry wild explores,
Thro' realms of space, th' aspiring eagle soars!
Darts o'er the clouds, exulting to admire,
Meridian glory — on her throne of fire!
Bird of the sun![1] his keen, unwearied gaze,
170   Hails the full noon, and triumphs in the blaze!
But soon, descending from his height sublime,
Day's burning fount, and light's empyreal clime;
Once more he speeds to joys more calmly blest,
'Midst the dear inmates of his lonely nest!

175   Thus Genius, mounting on his bright career,
Thro' the wide regions of the mental sphere;
And proudly waving, in his gifted hand,
O'er Fancy's worlds, Invention's plastic[2] wand;
Fearless and firm, with lightning-eye surveys
180   The clearest heav'n of intellectual rays!
Yet, on his course tho' loftiest hopes attend,
And kindling raptures aid him to ascend;
(While in his mind, with high-born grandeur fraught,
Dilate the noblest energies of thought;)
185   Still, from the bliss, ethereal and refin'd,
Which crowns the soarings of triumphant mind,
At length he flies, to that serene retreat,
Where calm and pure, the mild affections meet;
Embosom'd there, to feel and to impart,
190   The softer pleasures of the social heart!

---

1   the eagle, whose high flight supposedly approaches the sun.
2   plastic] able to shape, a common sense at that time.

Ah! weep for those, deserted and forlorn,
From ev'ry tie, by fate relentless torn! […]

Lo! thro' the waste, the wilderness of snows,
With fainting step, Siberia's exile[1] goes!
Homeless and sad, o'er many a polar wild,
Where beam, or flower, or verdure, never smil'd;   220
Where frost and silence hold their despot-reign,
And bind existence in eternal chain!
Child of the desert! pilgrim of the gloom!
Dark is the path which leads thee to the tomb!
While on thy faded cheek, the arctic air   225
Congeals the bitter tear-drop of despair!
Yet not, that fate condemns thy closing day,
In that stern clime, to shed its parting ray;
Not that fair Nature's loveliness and light,
No more shall beam enchantment on thy sight;   230
Ah! not for *this*, far, far beyond relief,
Deep in thy bosom dwells the hopeless grief;
But that no friend of kindred heart is there,
Thy woes to meliorate, thy toils to share;
That no mild soother fondly shall assuage   235
The stormy trials of thy lingering age;
No smile of tenderness, with angel-power,
Lull the dread pangs of dissolution's hour;
For this alone, despair, a withering guest,
Sits on thy brow, and cankers in thy breast! […]   240

And thus, Affection, can *thy* voice compose   255
The stormy tide of passions and of woes;
Bid every throb of wild emotion cease,
And lull misfortune in the arms of peace!

---

1 Siberia's exile] those who offended the Russian government would be exiled to
   Siberia; the situation was fictionalized in Sophie Cottin's highly popular Sentimen-
   tal novel, *Élisabeth, ou les exilés de Sibérie* (1806), translated and frequently reprinted
   in English; it recounts the perilous journey of a young woman from Siberia to St
   Petersburg to seek a pardon for her father from the Czar.

Oh! mark yon drooping form, of aged mien,
260 Wan, yet resign'd, and hopeless, yet serene!
Long ere victorious time had sought to chase
The bloom, the smile, that once illum'd his face;
That faded eye was dimm'd with many a care,
Those waving locks were silver'd by despair!
265 Yet filial love can pour the sovereign balm,
Assuage his pangs, his wounded spirit calm!
He, a sad emigrant![1] condemn'd to roam
In life's pale autumn from his ruin'd home;
Has borne the shock of peril's darkest wave,
270 Where joy — and hope — and fortune — found a grave!
'Twas his, to see destruction's fiercest band,
Rush, like a TYPHON,[2] on his native land,
And roll, triumphant, on their blasted way,
In fire and blood — the deluge of dismay!
275 Unequal combat rag'd on many a plain,
And patriot-valour wav'd the sword — in vain!

Ah! gallant exile! nobly, long, he bled,
Long brav'd the tempest gath'ring o'er his head!
Till all was lost! and horror's darkening eye,
280 Rous'd the stern spirit of despair — to die!
Ah! gallant exile! in the storm that roll'd
Far o'er his country, rushing uncontroll'd;
The flowers that grac'd his path with loveliest bloom,
Torn by the blast — were scatter'd on the tomb! [...]

Yes! we may hope, that Nature's deathless ties,
Renew'd, refin'd — shall triumph in the skies!

---

1 emigrant] many people were displaced by the French Revolutionary and
Napoleonic wars; in particular, the French *émigrés*, many of whom were nobles
whose property was expropriated by the Revolution and who were forced to flee,
were often made figures for critical sympathy, as in Charlotte Smith's poem *The
Emigrants* (1793); political exiles were also favourite subjects of liberal writers, many
of whom were themselves exiles at this time.
2 in Greek myth, Typhon was a monster believed responsible for volcanic eruptions
and storm winds — both common figures for Revolutionary violence in Hemans's
day.

Heart-soothing thought! whose lov'd, consoling pow'r,
With seraph-dreams can gild reflection's hour;   310
Oh! still be near! and bright'ning thro' the gloom,
Beam and ascend! the day-star of the tomb!
And smile for those, in sternest ordeals prov'd,
Those lonely hearts, bereft of all they lov'd! […]

Yes! in the noon of that Elysian clime,[1]
Beyond the sphere of anguish, death, or time;
Where mind's bright eye, with renovated fire,   425
Shall beam on glories—never to expire;
Oh! there, th' illumin'd soul may fondly trust,
More pure, more perfect, rising from the dust;[2]
Those mild affections, whose consoling light
Sheds the soft moon-beam on terrestrial night;   430
Sublim'd, ennobled, shall for ever glow,
Exalting rapture—not assuaging woe!

---

1 Elysian clime] in classical myth and literature Elysium is the paradise of perfect hap-
   piness for the virtuous made immortal after death.
2 dust] common biblical and poetic term for the body, representing human mortality.

FROM *THE RESTORATION OF THE WORKS OF ART TO ITALY: A POEM* (1816)[1]

Italia, Italia! O tu cui die la sorte
Dono infelice di bellezza, ond'hai
Funesta dote d'infiniti guai,
Che'n fronte scritte per gran doglia porte;
Deh, fossi tu men bella, o almen piu forte.

FILICAJA.[2]

"The French, who in every invasion have been the scourge of Italy, and have rivalled or rather surpassed the rapacity of the Goths and Vandals,[3] laid their sacrilegious hands on the unparalleled collection of the Vatican,[4] tore its Masterpieces from their pedestals, and dragging them from their temples of marble, transported them to Paris, and consigned them to the dull sullen halls, or rather stables, of the *Louvre*.[5]

* *

---

1 Napoleon's empire brought modernization and reform to its subject peoples, but also exploited them and plundered their art treasures, as in Italy; after Napoleon's fall in 1815, many of these works were returned, but reactionary monarchic regimes were also "restored"; text from 2nd edn, 1816, much revised from the 1st, also 1816; title page of 1st edn reads "By A LADY," of the 2nd edn, "By FELICIA HEMANS"; passages added in the 2nd edn are here enclosed in square brackets; other changes were mostly minor (punctuation and fewer personifying capitalizations); substantive changes are noted; Hemans added endnotes to the 2nd edn, here placed as footnotes and indicated as hers; editor's cuts indicated by ellipses enclosed in square brackets; for context and commentary, see Introduction, pp. 22-24.

2 opening lines of sonnet by Vincenzo da Filicaja (1642-1707), probably written in 1690 in response to a French invasion of Italy; during the Romantic period it was adapted by various writers, such as Byron (see *Childe Harold's Pilgrimage*, canto 4, 1818, stanzas 42-43) in support of a liberal nationalism; see Hemans's version of the sonnet from her *Translations from Camoens and Other Poems* (1818); in the 1st edn the epigraph is from Byron's *The Giaour* (1813): "As if for gods a dwelling place" (l. 47), describing the Greek isles.

3 Vandals] Germanic tribe who, with the Goths, pillaged the western Roman empire in the 5th century AD; later the terms "Goth" and "Vandal" were applied to anyone "uncivilized" or "barbaric."

4 Vatican] the palace of the Popes, containing vast art collections.

5 *Louvre*] palace of the French kings at Paris, turned into public galleries after the Revolution; its art collections were augmented by works looted from Italy by the Revolutionary and Napoleonic armies.

But the joy of discovery was short, and the triumph of taste transitory!"[1]

Eustace's Classical Tour through Italy, vol. ii. p. 60.

Land of departed fame! whose classic plains,
Have proudly echoed to immortal strains;
Whose hallow'd soil hath given the great and brave,
Day-stars of life, a birth-place and a grave;
Home of the Arts! where glory's faded smile,   5
Sheds ling'ring light o'er many a mould'ring pile;
Proud wreck of vanish'd power, of splendor fled,
Majestic temple of the mighty dead!
Whose grandeur, yet contending with decay,
Gleams thro' the twilight of thy glorious day;   10
Tho' dimm'd thy brightness, rivetted thy chain,
Yet, fallen Italy! rejoice again!
Lost, lovely Realm! once more 'tis thine to gaze
On the rich relics of sublimer days.

Awake, ye Muses of Etrurian[2] shades,   15
Or sacred Tivoli's[3] romantic glades;
Wake, ye that slumber in the bowery gloom,
Where the wild ivy shadows Virgil's tomb;[4]
Or ye, whose voice, by Sorga's lonely wave,
Swell'd the deep echoes of the fountain's cave,   20

---

1 from the Rev. John Chetwode Eustace (?1762-1815), *A Classical Tour through Italy An. MDCCCII* (1815; 4th edition, 4 vols, London, 1817), where the passage after the asterisks precedes the first part; Chetwode was a Roman Catholic, classical republican, anti-Revolutionary, anti-Bonapartist supporter of a British constitution free from encroachments of both monarch and common people; he also advocated peace and reconciliation for the Napoleonic aftermath.

2 Etruria] ancient name for Tuscany, whose capital, Florence, was later home to Dante (1265-1321) and Petrarch (1304-74), poets who established a standard Italian literary language.

3 Tivoli] town east of Rome, famous for its renaissance palace, the Villa d'Este, and for the ruins of the emperor Hadrian's summer palace, from which many artworks were recovered over the centuries.

4 the tomb of Virgil (70-19 BC), Roman epic poet and author of the *Aeneid*, was long thought to be at Posillipo near Naples; Sorga (next line) is near Mantua, where Virgil was believed to have been born.

[Or thrill'd the soul in Tasso's[1] numbers high,
Those magic strains of love and chivalry;
If yet by classic streams ye fondly rove,
Haunting the myrtle-vale, the laurel-grove;[2]]
25 Oh! rouse once more the daring soul of song,
Seize with bold hands the harp,[3] forgot so long,
And hail, with wonted pride, those works rever'd,
Hallow'd by time, by absence more endear'd.

[And breathe to Those the strain, whose warrior-might[4]
30 Each danger stemm'd, prevail'd in every fight;
Souls of unyielding power, to storms inured,
Sublim'd by peril, and by toil matured.
Sing of that Leader, whose ascendant mind,
Could rouse the slumb'ring spirit of mankind;
35 Whose banners track'd the vanquish'd Eagle's[5] flight
O'er many a plain, and dark Sierra's[6] height;
Who bade once more the wild, heroic lay,
Record the deeds of Roncesvalles'[7] day […].

45 Yet, when the storm seem'd hushed, the conflict past,
One strife remained—the mightiest and the last![8]

---

1 Torquato Tasso (1544-95), writer of verse romances, was raised at Naples, but joined his father, also a poet, in exile.
2 in myth and literature, laurel and myrtle symbolize victory and erotic love, the main themes of Tasso's romances.
3 here, instrument with which poets of earlier times were supposed to accompany their recitations or improvisations.
4 reference to British armies led by Wellington, who had fought Napoleon in Spain and defeated him at Waterloo.
5 Napoleon adopted the eagle as his military standard, in imitation of the ancient Roman emperors.
6 Sierras are mountain ranges of Spain, scene of bitter guerila warfare and campaigns of the Peninsular War.
7 Roncesvalles] valley in northern Spain, in AD 778 site of last stand by knights of Roland (or Orlando) covering the withdrawal of emperor Charlemagne's army, a feat celebrated in chivalric romance ("heroic lay"); Roncesvalles was also the site of conflict late in the Peninsular War when Wellington's armies advanced from Spain into southern France.
8 the final defeat of Napoleon at Waterloo, Belgium, June 1815.

Nerved for the struggle, in that fateful hour,
Untamed Ambition summon'd all his power;
Vengeance and Pride, to frenzy rous'd, were there,
And the stern might of resolute Despair. 50
　　Isle of the free! 'twas then thy champions[1] stood,
Breasting unmov'd the combat's wildest flood,
Sunbeam of Battle, then thy spirit shone,
Glow'd in each breast, and sunk with life alone.

　　Oh hearts devoted![2] whose illustrious doom, 55
Gave there at once your triumph and your tomb,
Ye, firm and faithful, in th' ordeal tried
Of that dread strife, by Freedom sanctified;
Shrin'd, not entomb'd, ye rest in sacred earth,
Hallow'd by deeds of more than mortal worth. 60
What tho' to mark where sleeps heroic dust,
No sculptur'd trophy rise, or breathing bust,
Yours, on the scene where valour's race was run,
A prouder sepulchre—the field ye won!
There every mead, each cabin's lowly name,[3] 65
Shall live a watch-word blended with your fame;
And well may flowers suffice those graves to crown,
That ask no urn to blazen their renown.
There shall the Bard in future ages tread,
And bless each wreath that blossoms o'er the dead; 70
Revere each tree, whose sheltering branches wave
O'er the low mounds, the altars of the brave;
Pause o'er each Warrior's grass-grown bed, and hear
In every breeze, some name to glory dear,
And as the shades of twilight close around, 75
With martial pageants people all the ground.
Thither unborn descendants of the slain,

1　champions] a term from medieval chivalry and romance, referring to those who
fight on behalf of another.
2　devoted] here, doomed rather than (or perhaps as well as) consecrated to a particu-
lar purpose.
3　name] various fields ("meads," or meadows) and small farmhouses ("cabin") at
Waterloo were celebrated for the particular military actions that took place there.

Shall throng, as pilgrim's to some holy fane,[1]
While, as they trace each spot, whose records tell,
80 Where fought their fathers, and prevail'd, and fell,
Warm in their souls shall loftiest feelings glow,
Claiming proud kindred with the dust below!
And many an age shall see the brave repair,
To learn the Hero's bright devotion there.

85   And well, Ausonia![2] may that field of fame,
From thee one song of echoing triumph claim.
Land of the lyre![3] 'twas there th' avenging sword,
Won the bright treasures to thy fanes restored;
Those precious trophies o'er thy realms that throw
90 A veil of radiance, hiding half thy woe,
And bid the stranger for awhile forget
How deep thy fall, and deem thee glorious yet.]

Yes! fair creations, to perfection wrought,
Embodied visions of ascending thought!
95 Forms of sublimity! by Genius traced,
In tints that vindicate adoring taste;
Whose bright originals, to earth unknown,[4]
Live in the spheres encircling glory's throne;
Models of art, to deathless fame consign'd,
100 Stamp'd with the high-born majesty of mind;
Yes, matchless works! your presence shall restore
One beam of splendor to your native shore,
And her sad scenes of lost renown illume,[5]
As the bright Sunset gilds some Hero's tomb. [...]
131   Fair Florence![6] Queen of Arno's lovely vale!

---

1   Waterloo became a popular tourist site immediately after the battle, visited by many writers, whose descriptions became a popular genre.
2   Ausonia] poetic name for Italy.
3   lyre] symbol of elevated poetry, as sung by bards.
4   unknown] reference to neoplatonic notion of artistic work as inevitably flawed approximation of an ideal form or "original."
5   illume] illuminate, with a suggestion of cultural enlightenment.
6   Florence] principal city of Tuscany, on the banks of the Arno; renowned during the Renaissance for its culture, prosperity, and political power, as celebrated in *The Life*

Justice and Truth indignant heard thy tale,
And sternly smil'd, in retribution's hour,
To wrest thy treasures from the Spoiler's power. [...]
Cosmo, Lorenzo![1] view your reign once more,   175
The shrine where nations mingle to adore!
Again th' Enthusiast there, with ardent gaze,
Shall hail the mighty of departed days:
Those sovereign spirits, whose commanding mind,
Seems in the marble's breathing mould[2] enshrined;   180
Still, with ascendant power, the world to awe,
Still the deep homage of the heart to draw;
To breathe some spell of holiness around,
Bid all the scene be consecrated ground,
And from the stone, by Inspiration wrought,   185
Dart the pure lightnings of exalted thought.

There thou, fair offspring of immortal Mind!
Love's radiant Goddess,[3] Idol of mankind!
Once the bright object of Devotion's vow,
Shalt claim from taste a kindred worship now.   190
Oh! who can tell what beams of heavenly light,
Flash'd o'er the sculptor's intellectual sight,
How many a glimpse, reveal'd to him alone,
Made brighter beings, nobler worlds his own;
Ere, like some vision sent the earth to bless,   195
Burst into life thy pomp of loveliness!

---

of *Lorenzo de' Medici* (1796) by Hemans's friend William Roscoe; Florence later
became an arena for the continuing struggle between the papacy and the Holy
Roman Emperor to dominate the Italian states; it then became part of the Grand
Duchy of Tuscany, fell into decline, and was ruled or dominated by foreign powers,
including France during the Napoleonic wars.

1   Lorenzo] (*c.*1449-92) and Cosmo, or Cosimo, de' Medici (1389-1464), rulers of Flo-
    rence and great patrons of the arts.

2   mould] shape, with secondary sense of earth, or physical matter.

3   the Venus de' Medici, a statue of the ancient Roman goddess of erotic love, in a
    pose of modesty, perhaps by an Athenian follower of Praxiteles in the 1st century
    BC; in the early 17th century it was sent to Florence and displayed in the Uffizi
    gallery; the French took it to Paris in 1803.

Young Genius there, while dwells his kindling eye
On forms, instinct with bright divinity,
While new-born powers, dilating in his heart,
200 Embrace the full magnificence of Art;[1]
From scenes, by Raphael's[2] gifted hand arrayed,
From dreams of heaven, by Angelo[3] pourtrayed;
From each fair work of Grecian skill sublime,
Seal'd with perfection, "sanctified by time;"[4]
205 Shall catch a kindred glow, and proudly feel
His spirit burn with emulative zeal,
Buoyant with loftier hopes, his soul shall rise,
Imbued at once with nobler energies;
O'er life's dim scenes on rapid pinion soar,[5]
210 And worlds of visionary grace explore,
Till his bold hand give glory's day-dreams birth,
And with new wonders charm admiring earth.

Venice[6] exult! and o'er thy moonlight seas,
Swell with gay strains each Adriatic breeze!
215 What tho' long fled those years of martial fame,
That shed romantic lustre o'er thy name;
Tho' to the winds thy streamers idly play,
And the wild waves another Queen obey;
Tho' quench'd the spirit of thine ancient race,
220 And power and freedom scarce have left a trace;

---

1 for several centuries Italy had been the resort of art students from elsewhere in Europe.
2 Raphael] common appellation in English for Raffaello Sanzio (1483-1520), influential Italian painter especially revered in the 18th century as the leading exponent of the artistic ideals of classical antiquity.
3 Angelo] Michelangelo Buonarotti (?1475-1564), considered the leading exponent of the Florentine school in art, with its emphasis on *disegno*, or design.
4 phrase possibly from Hugh Downman (1740-1809), *Poems to Thespia* (1781; 1791), XII. 3: "Where custom rules, long-sanctified by time ...", but the phrase was almost proverbial.
5 O'er ... soar] 1st edn: O'er the dim scenes of life undaunted soar,
6 Venice] republican city-state on the Adriatic sea; a major commercial and naval power and centre of the arts during the renaissance; it then declined in power but remained independent until Napoleon conquered it in 1797 and passed it and its territories to Austria, under whose control it was left by the allied powers after the final defeat of Napoleon.

Yet still shall Art her splendors round thee cast,
And gild the wreck of years for ever past.
Again thy fanes may boast a Titian's[1] dyes,
Whose clear soft brilliance emulates thy skies,
And scenes that glow in colouring's richest bloom,   225
With life's warm flush Palladian[2] halls illume.[3]
From thy rich[4] dome again th' unrivalled steed[5]
Starts to existence, rushes into speed,
Still for Lysippus claims that wreath of fame,
Panting with ardour, vivified with flame. [...]   230
   Lo! where thy sons, oh Rome! a godlike train,   285
In imaged majesty return again![6]
Bards, chieftains, monarchs, tower with mien august,
O'er scenes that shrine their venerable dust.
Those forms, those features, luminous with soul,
Still o'er thy children seem to claim control;   290
With awful grace arrest the pilgrim's glance,
Bind his rapt soul in elevating trance,
And bid the past, to fancy's ardent eyes,
From time's dim sepulchre in glory rise.[7] [...]
[[...] Consummate work![8] the noblest and the last,

---

1 Titian] common English name for Tiziano Vecellio (*c.*? 1485-90–1576), the greatest
   painter of the school of Venice, famous for his advocacy of *colore* ("colour") in rival-
   ry with Raphael and followers of the classical ideal.
2 Palladian] Andrea Palladio (1508-80) championed classical antiquity in his architec-
   tural designs and theoretical writings, influencing design of buildings and towns
   throughout Europe in the 18th century.
3 1st edn: lines 223-26 placed after 230.
4 rich] 1st edn: proud; reference to the gilded mosaic decoration of the dome of the
   church of San Marco in Venice.
5 one of four bronze horses, from perhaps the 2nd century AD, wrongly attributed to
   the Greek sculptor Lysippus (flourished *c.* 370-300 BC), looted by the Venetians in
   the sack of Constantinople by Crusaders in 1204, placed on San Marco in 1265, and
   removed by the French in the late 1790s.
6 reference to collections of portrait busts and statues representing figures of ancient
   Roman history.
7 Hemans goes on to describe some of the famous art works removed from Rome by
   the French.
8 work] part of a Roman copy (about 1st century BC) of a Greek statue, by Apollo-
   nius, possibly of Hercules; it was displayed in the Belvedere Papal palace from the
   15th century until removed to Paris in the late 1790s.

380 Of Grecian Freedom, ere her reign was past.[1]
Nurse of the mighty, she, while lingering still,
Her mantle flowed o'er many a classic hill,
Ere yet her voice its parting accents breathed,
A Hero's image to the world bequeathed;
385 Enshrined in thee th' imperishable ray,
Of high-souled Genius, fostered by her sway,
And bade thee teach, to ages yet unborn,
What lofty dreams were hers — who never shall return!]

And mark yon group,[2] transfixed with many a throe,
390 Sealed with the image of eternal woe:
With fearful truth, terrific power, exprest,
Thy pangs, Laocoon, agonize the breast,
And the stern combat picture to mankind,
Of suffering nature, and enduring mind.
395 Oh, mighty conflict! tho' his pains intense,
Distend each nerve,[3] and dart thro' every sense;
Tho' fixed on him, his children's suppliant eyes,
Implore the aid avenging fate denies;
Tho' with the giant-snake in fruitless strife,
400 Heaves every muscle with convulsive life,
And in each limb Existence writhes, enrolled
'Midst the dread circles of the venomed fold;
Yet the strong spirit lives — and not a cry,

---

1 Le Torso d'Hercule paroît un des derniers ouvrages parfaits que l'art ait produit en Grece, avant la perte de sa liberté. Car après que la Grece fut réduite en province Romaine, l'histoire ne fait mention d'aucun Artiste célebre de cette nation, jusqu'aux temps du Triumvirat Romain. WINCKELMANN, *ibid.* tom. ii. p. 250. [Hemans's endnote; passage from translation of Winckelmann's *Geschichte der Kunst des Altertums* (1764, book 10, ch. 3, section 20); translated: "The torso of Hercules appears to be one of the last perfect works which art produced in Greece, before the loss of its freedom. For after Greece was reduced to a Roman province, we find no mention of any celebrated Greek artist until the time of the Roman triumvirate" — i.e., Caesar, Pompey, and Crassus, in the 1st century BC.

2 marble sculpture of an episode in Virgil's *Aeneid* (2.199-231), where the Trojan priest Laokoon and two of his sons are attacked by a sea monster; the work is a 1st-century AD imitation of a Hellenistic sculpture at Pergamon, and received considerable attention from late 18th- and early 19th-century writers and philosophers; it was taken to Paris by the French in 1797 and returned to Rome in 1816.

3 nerve] 1st edn: vein

Shall own the might of Nature's agony!
That furrowed brow unconquered soul reveals,   405
That patient eye to angry Heaven appeals,
That struggling bosom concentrates its breath,
Nor yields one moan to torture or to death![1]
Sublimest triumph of intrepid Art!
With speechless horror to congeal the heart,   410
To freeze each pulse, and dart thro' every vein,
Cold thrills of fear, keen sympathies of pain;
Yet teach the spirit how its lofty power,
May brave the pangs of fate's severest hour.

Turn from such conflicts, and enraptured gaze,   415
On scenes where Painting all her skill displays:
Landscapes, by colouring drest in richer dyes,
More mellowed sunshine, more unclouded skies;

---

1   "It is not, in the same manner, in the agonized limbs, or in the convulsed muscles of
    the Laocoon, that the secret grace of its composition resides; it is in the majestic air
    of the head, which has not *yielded* to *suffering*, and in the deep serenity of the fore-
    head, which seems to be still *superior* to all its *afflictions*, and significant of a mind
    that cannot be subdued.["] *Allison's Essays*, vol. ii. p. 400.
       Laocoon nous offre le spectacle de la nature humaine dans la plus grande douleur
    dont elle soit susceptible, sous l'image d'un homme qui tâche de rassembler contre
    elle toute la force de l'esprit. Tandis que l'excès de la souffrance enfle les muscles, et
    tire violemment les nerfs, le courage se montre sur le front gonflé: la poitrine s'élève
    avec peine par la nécessité de la respiration, qui est également contrainte par le
    silence que la force de l'ame impose à la douleur qu'elle voudrait étouffer ★ ★ ★ ★
    Son air est plaintif, et non criard ★ ★ ★ WINCKELMANN, *ibid*. tom. ii. 214.

    [Hemans's endnote; first passage from Archibald Alison (1757-1839), *Essays on the
    Nature and Principles of Taste* (1790; 4th edn, 2 vols, 1815, pp. 400-401), Hemans's
    emphases; "agonized" is "agonizing" in Alison's text; second passage from translation
    of *Geschichte der Kunst des Altertums* (book 10, ch. 3, section 16) by Johann Joachim
    Winckelmann (1717-68), German art historian and critic, whose influential work
    links great artistic achievement to political liberty; translated: "Laocoon offers us the
    spectacle of human nature in the greatest suffering of which it is susceptible, in the
    figure of a man who tries to gather against it all the strength of his soul. While the
    extremity of suffering expands his muscles, and violently strains his nerves, courage
    is displayed on his swelling brow; his breast heaves with difficulty by the need to
    breathe, which is equally constrained by the silence which the strength of his soul
    imposes on the suffering that it would suppress.... His expression is plaintive and
    not complaining."]

Or dreams of bliss, to dying Martyrs given,
420   Descending Seraphs, robed in beams of heaven.

Oh! sovereign Masters of the Pencil's[1] might,
Its depth of shadow, and its blaze of light,[2]
Ye, whose bold thought disdaining every bound,
Explored the worlds above, below, around,
425   Children of Italy! who stand alone,
And unapproached, 'midst regions all your own;
What scenes, what beings blest your favoured[3] sight,
Severely[4] grand, unutterably bright!
Triumphant spirits! your exulting eye,
430   Could meet the noontide of eternity,
And gaze untired, undaunted, uncontrolled,
On all that Fancy trembles to behold.[5] [...]
[Hence, ye vain fictions, fancy's erring theme,[6]
Gods of illusion! phantoms of a dream!
Frail, powerless idols of departed time,
Fables of song, delusive, tho' sublime!
465   To loftier tasks has Roman Art assigned,
Her matchless pencil, and her mighty mind! [...]
Oh! mark, where Raphael's pure and perfect line
Pourtrays that form ineffably divine![7]
Where with transcendent skill his hand has shed
Diffusive sunbeams round the Saviour's head;
505   Each heaven-illumined lineament imbued

---

1   the pencil symbolizes drawing and painting.
2   effective contrast of light and shade, or "chiaroscuro," was considered a central prin-
    ciple of pictorial representation.
3   favoured] 1st edn: gifted
4   Severely] 1st edn: Profoundly; Hemans is evoking the aesthetics of "the sublime,"
    characterized by grandeur beyond the power of language to represent.
5   Hemans goes on to describe the wall paintings and pictorial sculptures of ancient
    Roman art based on pagan mythology and religion.
6   in early 19th-century poetics, "fancy" was often described as a more playful power
    than "imagination," which was associated with divine inspiration.
7   The Transfiguration, thought to be so perfect a specimen of art, that, in honour of
    Raphael, it was carried before his body to the grave. [Hemans's endnote, referring
    to a major painting by Raphael, almost completed just before his death in 1520,
    depicting Christ's transformation into a spirit ascending to heaven; it was removed
    from the Vatican to Paris by the French in 1797.]

With all the fulness of beatitude,
And traced the sainted group, whose mortal sight,
Sinks overpowered by that excess of light!

Gaze on that scene, and own the might of Art,
By truth inspired, to elevate the heart!   510
To bid the soul exultingly possess,
Of all her powers, a heightened consciousness,
And strong in hope, anticipate the day,
The last of life, the first of freedom's ray;
To realize, in some unclouded sphere,   515
Those pictured glories feebly imaged here!
Dim, cold reflections from her native sky,
Faint effluence of "the Day-spring from on high!"[1]]

---

[1]   the quotation is a description of Christ by John the Baptist's father in the Bible
(Luke 1.78).

FROM *MODERN GREECE: A POEM*
(1817)[1]

MODERN GREECE.
A POEM.[2]

O Greece! thou sapient nurse of finer arts,
Which to bright Science blooming Fancy bore,
Be this thy praise, that thou, and thou alone,
In these hast led the way, in these excelled,
Crowned with the laurel of assenting Time.
THOMSON'S LIBERTY.[3]

I.

OH! who hath trod thy consecrated clime,[4]
Fair land of Phidias![5] theme of lofty strains!

---

1 text: from the 1st edition of 1817; alterations to the 2nd edition of 1821 are mostly in punctuation and spelling; Hemans's endnotes have been placed here as footnotes and indicated as hers; neither 1st (1817) nor 2nd edn (1821) has Hemans's name on title page; editor's excisions are indicated by ellipses in square brackets; for context and commentary, see Introduction, pp. 24-5.

2 the poem addresses the controversy over state acquisition of the ancient Greek sculptures known as the "Elgin marbles" after Thomas Bruce, seventh Earl of Elgin (1766-1841); Elgin's removal of sculptures from the Parthenon, or ancient religious centre of Athens, was condemned by some as vandalism and praised by others as the rescue of great art from Turkish abuse and neglect; some also felt that Elgin had prevented the French from getting the sculptures and using them to proclaim themselves as the modern successors to the glories of ancient Greece; other Romantic writers touched on the controversy, including Byron and Keats; after a parliamentary enquiry, the government bought the sculptures for the British Museum in London, where they remain, though successive Greek governments have demanded their return.

3 Liberty] from James Thomson (1700-48), *Liberty: A Poem* (1735-36), part 11, "Greece" (ll. 252-56), presenting the history of liberty from mythic pastoral times to Thomson's day; Greece is the first high point, then republican Rome; suppressed by social corruption and political despotism, liberty is revived in modern Britain, associated with achievement in the arts as sign of a country's pre-eminence among nations.

4 clime] region, with its distinctive culture, civilization, and history.

5 Phidias] sculptor (5th century BC) and supervisor of the decoration of the Acropolis at Athens, from which the "Elgin marbles" were later taken; the statesman and

And traced each scene, that, midst the wrecks of time,[1]
The print of Glory's parting step retains;
Nor for awhile, in high-wrought dreams, forgot,   5
Musing on years gone by in brightness there,
The hopes, the fears, the sorrows of his lot,
The hues his fate hath worn, or yet may wear;
As when from mountain-heights, his ardent eye
Of sea and heaven hath track'd the blue infinity?   10

II.

Is there who views with cold unaltered mien,
His frozen heart with proud indifference fraught,
Each sacred haunt, each unforgotten scene,
Where Freedom triumph'd, or where Wisdom taught?
Souls that too deeply feel, oh, envy not   15
The sullen calm your fate hath never known:
Through the dull twilight of that wint'ry lot
Genius ne'er pierced, nor Fancy's sunbeam shone,
Nor those high thoughts, that, hailing Glory's trace,
Glow with the generous flames of every age and race.   20

III.

But blest the wanderer, whose enthusiast mind
Each muse of ancient days hath deep imbued
With lofty lore; and all his thoughts refined
In the calm school of silent solitude;
Pour'd on his ear, midst groves and glens retired,   25
The mighty strains of each illustrious clime,
All that hath lived, while empires have expired,
To float for ever on the winds of Time;
And on his soul indelibly pourtray'd
Fair visionary forms, to fill each classic shade.   30

---

military leader Pericles (c. 490-429 BC) planned the Acropolis as symbol of Athens's
pre-eminence in the Greek world, though Hemans makes Phidias rather than Peri-
cles the presiding spirit of Athens and Greece.

1 wrecks of time] echoes Byron's description of ruins "Swept into wrecks anon by
Time's ungentle tide!" (*Childe Harold's Pilgrimage*, canto 1, 1812, l. 287).

IV.

Is not his mind, to meaner[1] thoughts unknown,
A sanctuary of beauty and of light?
There he may dwell, in regions all his own,
A world of dreams, where all is pure and bright.
35 For him the scenes of old renown possess
Romantic[2] charms, all veil'd from other eyes;
There every form of nature's loveliness
Wakes in his breast a thousand sympathies;
As music's voice, in some lone mountain-dell,
40 From rocks and caves around calls forth each echo's swell.

V.

For him Italia's brilliant skies illume
The bard's lone haunts, the warrior's combat-plains,
And the wild-rose yet lives to breathe and bloom,
Round Doric Pæstum's[3] solitary fanes.[4]
45 But most, fair Greece! on thy majestic shore,
He feels the fervors of his spirit rise;
Thou birth-place of the Muse! whose voice, of yore,
Breathed in thy groves immortal harmonies;
And lingers still around the well-known coast,
50 Murmuring a wild farewell to fame and freedom lost. [...]

---

1 meaner] lower or less worthy.

2 Romantic] here and throughout in the predominant sense in Hemans's day: charac-
teristic of the literature of medieval and renaissance romances, i.e., fantastical,
extravagant, imaginary, or idealized.

3 Pæstum] ancient Greek settlement on the Italian coast south of Naples; its major
temples ("fanes" here) were in the Doric style, or simplest system of Greek archi-
tectural decoration.

4 *Round Doric Pæstum's solitary fanes*. "The Pæstan rose, from its peculiar fragrance and
the singularity of blowing twice a year, is often mentioned by the classic poets. The
wild rose, which now shoots up among the ruins, is of the small single damask kind,
with a very high perfume; as a farmer assured me on the spot, it flowers both in
spring and autumn." —Swinburne's Travels in the two Sicilies. [Hemans's endnote,
quoting from Henry Swinburne, *Travels in the Two Sicilies ... In the Years 1777, 1778,
1779, and 1780* (2 vols, London, 1783-1785), vol. 2, pp. 131-32].

XXV.

He, thought-entranced, may wander where of old
From Delphi's chasm[1] the mystic vapour rose,
And trembling nations heard their doom foretold,
By the dread spirit throned midst rocks and snows.
Though its rich fanes be blended with the dust,   245
And silence now the hallow'd haunt possess,
Still is the scene of ancient rites august,
Magnificent in mountain loneliness;
Still Inspiration hovers o'er the ground,
Where Greece her councils held,[2] her Pythian victors crown'd.   250

XXVI.

Or let his steps the rude[3] grey cliffs explore
Of that wild pass,[4] once dyed with Spartan blood,
When by the waves that break on Œta's shore,
The few, the fearless, the devoted, stood!
Or rove where, shadowing Mantinea's plain,   255
Bloom the wild laurels o'er the warlike dead,[5]

---

1 chasm] Delphi: important religious and ceremonial centre of ancient Greece, home
   of Apollo's oracle, where the Pythia or prophetess answered questions while in a
   trance induced by vapours from a chasm.
2 *Where Greece her councils held, her Pythian victors crown'd.* The Amphictyonic council
   was convened in spring and autumn at Delphi or Thermopylæ, and presided at the
   Pythian games, which were celebrated at Delphi every fifth year. [Hemans's end-
   note]
3 rude] here, rough or rugged.
4 pass] the following lines refer to sites of famous battles: the mountain pass of Ther-
   mopylae, where in 480 BC a small army of Greeks held off a much larger Persian
   army until they were betrayed; Œta, a mountain where Thermopylæ is located and
   where the mythic hero Hercules died; Mantinea, where the Spartans defeated the
   city-state of Mantinea in 418 BC and were defeated in 362 BC; Platæa, a town in
   southern Boeotia where the Greeks defeated a Persian army in 479 BC.
5 *Bloom the wild laurels o'er the warlike dead.* "This spot (the field of Mantinea) on
   which so many brave men were laid to rest, is now covered with rosemary and lau-
   rels." —Pouqueville's Travels in the Morea. [Hemans's endnote, slightly misquoting
   from François Charles Hugues Laurent Pouqueville (1770–1838), *Travels through the
   Morea, Albania, and Several Other Parts of the Ottoman Empire, to Constantinople; During
   the Years 1798, 1799, 1800, and 1801* (translated London, 1806), p. 31; Pouqueville
   trained in medicine, accompanied Napoleon's expedition to Egypt as artistic and

Or lone Platæa's ruins yet remain,
To mark the battle-field of ages fled;
Still o'er such scenes presides a sacred power,
Though Fiction's[1] gods have fled from fountain, grot,[2] and
    bower. [...]

XXXII.

Still, where that column of the mosque aspires,[3]
Landmark of slavery, towering o'er the waste,
There Science[4] droops, the Muses hush their lyres,
And o'er the blooms of fancy and of taste
315   Spreads the chill blight—as in that orient isle,
Where the dark upas taints the gale around,[5]
Within its precincts not a flower may smile,
Nor dew nor sunshine fertilize the ground;
Nor wild birds' music float on zephyr's breath,
320 But all is silence round, and solitude, and death.

XXXIII.

Far other influence pour'd the Crescent's light,[6]
O'er conquer'd realms, in ages past away;

---

scientific consultant, was captured by pirates on his way back to France, escaped, was seized by the Turks, and spent two years in Greece and Constantinople; publication of his travels led to posting as consul to Ali Pasha in Albania; on return to France he published a great deal on Greece, stressing Turkish oppression of the Greeks.]

1 Fiction's] myth's.

2 grot] common poeticism for grotto, a cave or retreat.

3 aspires] towers or soars.

4 Science] knowledge or learning in general.

5 *Where the dark upas taints the gale around.* For the accounts of the upas or poison-tree of Java, now generally believed to be fabulous, or greatly exaggerated, see the notes to Darwin's Botanic Garden. [Hemans's endnote, referring to Erasmus Darwin (1731-1802), *The Botanic Garden, Part II; containing The Loves of the Plants, a Poem* (1789), l. 238 and note, and pp. 167-73; Darwin was a physician, leader of the English Midlands Enlightenment, and grandfather of Charles Darwin the theorist of evolution; *The Botanic Garden* allegorizes botany in heroic couplets, with copious scientific notes.]

6 light] the crescent moon was an emblem used by Muslim rulers; reference here is to Muslims' preservation of remains of ancient Greek and Roman learning during the "dark ages" after collapse of the Western Roman empire.

Full and alone it beam'd, intensely bright,
While distant climes in midnight darkness lay.
Then rose th' Alhambra,¹ with its founts and shades,   325
Fair marble halls, alcoves, and orange bowers:
Its sculptured lions,² richly wrought arcades,
Aërial pillars, and enchanted towers;
Light, splendid, wild, as some Arabian tale
Would picture fairy domes, that fleet before the gale.   330

XXXIV.

Then foster'd genius lent each Caliph's throne³
Lustre barbaric pomp could ne'er attain;
And stars unnumber'd o'er the orient shone,
Bright as that Pleïad, sphered in Mecca's fane.⁴

1   Alhambra] building complex in Granada, a cultural centre of Muslim Spain.

2   *Its sculptured lions, richly wrought arcades.* "The court most to be admired of the
     Alhambra is that called the court of the Lions; it is ornamented with sixty elegant
     pillars of an architecture which bears not the least resemblance to any of the known
     orders, and might be called the Arabian order. —— But its principal ornament, and
     that from which it took its name, is an alabaster cup six feet in diameter, supported
     by twelve lions, which is said to have been made in imitation of the Brazen Sea of
     Solomon's temple."—Bourgoanne's Travels in Spain. [Hemans's endnote, quoting
     from Jean François, Baron de Bourgoing (1748-1811), *Nouveau voyage en Espagne*
     (1789), translated as *Modern State of Spain* ... (4 vols, London, 1808), with *Essays on
     Spain by M. Peyron; and the Book of Post Roads* as volume 4; the passages are from
     Peyron, vol. 4, pp. 171, 172.]

3   throne] caliph: chief Muslim religious and civil ruler, ostensibly the successor (Ara-
     bic "khalifah") of Mohammed, founder of Islam; Hemans acknowledges the artistic
     and scientific achievements of medieval Muslim civilization, though implying that
     these appropriate and orientalize Greek and Roman culture in regions the Arabs
     conquered, from the east (Syria, Bagdat, or Baghdad) to the west (Andalusia, in
     southern Spain).

4   *Bright as that Pleïad, sphered in Mecca's fane.* "Sept des plus fameux parmi les anciens
     poëtes Arabiques, sont designés par les ecrivains orientaux sous le nom de *Pleïade
     Arabique*, et leurs ouvrages etaient suspendus autour de la Caaba, ou Mosque de la
     Mecque."—Sismondi Litterature du Midi. [Hemans's endnote, quoting from J.C.L.
     Sismondi, *La Littérature du Midi de l'Europe* (3rd edition, 4 vols, Paris, 1829), vol. 1,
     ch. 2, translated: "Seven of the most famous of these ancient poets have been cele-
     brated by the Oriental writers under the title of the Arabian Pleiades: and their
     works were suspended around the Caaba, or Temple of Mecca" (Sismondi, *Historical
     View of the Literature of the South of Europe*, translated by Thomas Roscoe, 2 vols,
     London, 1823, vol. 1, p. 53); the Pleiades are a constellation of seven stars, in differ-
     ent mythologies representing various figures, and in literature representing a group
     of brilliant writers.]

335   From Bagdat's palaces the choral strains
       Rose and re-echoed to the desert's bound,
       And Science, wooed on Egypt's burning plains,
       Rear'd her majestic head with glory crown'd;
       And the wild Muses breathed romantic lore,
340 From Syria's palmy groves to Andalusia's shore.

XXXV.

       Those years have past in radiance — they have past,
       As sinks the day-star in the tropic main;
       His parting beams no soft reflection cast,
       They burn — are quench'd — and deepest shadows reign.
345   And Fame and Science have not left a trace,
       In the vast regions of the Moslem's power, —
       Regions, to intellect a desert space,
       A wild without a fountain or a flower,
       Where towers oppression midst the deepening glooms,
350 As dark and lone ascends the cypress midst the tombs.

XXXVI.

       Alas for thee, fair Greece! when Asia pour'd
       Her fierce fanatics to Byzantium's[1] wall,
       When Europe sheathed, in apathy, her sword,
       And heard unmoved the fated city's call,
355   No bold crusaders ranged their serried line
       Of spears and banners round a falling throne;
       And thou, O last and noblest Constantine![2]
       Didst meet the storm unshrinking and alone.

---

1 Byzantium, or Constantinople (modern Istanbul), was capital of the christian East-
   ern Roman empire, captured by Turks in AD 1453.
2 *And thou, O last and noblest Constantine!* "The distress and fall of the last Constantine
   are more glorious than the long prosperity of the Byzantine Cæsars." — Gibbon's
   Decline and Fall, &c. vol. xii. p. 226. [Hemans's endnote, quoting from Edward
   Gibbon (1737-94), *Decline and Fall of the Roman Empire* (1776-88), ch. 68 (vol. 3, p.
   770 in New York, Modern Library edition); the "last Constantine" or ruler of
   Byzantium was Constantine Palæologus, celebrated in Joanna Baillie's play of that
   title.]

Oh! blest to die in freedom, though in vain,
Thine empire's proud exchange the grave, and not the
    chain. [...]   360

XLVI.

Yet if thy light, fair Freedom, rested there,
How rich in charms were that romantic clime,
With streams, and woods, and pastoral valleys fair,
And walled with mountains, haughtily sublime.
Heights, that might well be deem'd the Muses' reign,   455
Since, claiming proud alliance with the skies,
They lose in loftier spheres their wild domain.
Meet home for those retired divinities
That love, where nought of earth may e'er intrude,
Brightly to dwell on high, in lonely sanctitude. [...]   460

XLVIII.

Those savage cliffs and solitudes might seem
The chosen haunts where Freedom's foot would roam;
She loves to dwell by glen and torrent-stream,
And make the rocky fastnesses her home.
And in the rushing of the mountain-flood,   475
In the wild eagle's solitary cry,
In sweeping winds that peal through cave and wood,
There is a voice of stern sublimity,
That swells her spirit to a loftier mood
Of solemn joy severe, of power, of fortitude.[1]   [...]   480

LIX.

Oh! thus it is with man — a tree, a flower,
While nations perish, still renews its race,

---

1   lines 478-80 echo Wordsworth's representation of the moral effects of sublime
    nature, though the effect of the mountain sublime here is explicitly political: land-
    scape shapes the moral character of its human inhabitants and thus the political
    character of their society.

And o'er the fallen records of his power
Spreads in wild pomp, or smiles in fairy grace.
585   The laurel shoots when those have past away
Once rivals for its crown, the brave, the free;
The rose is flourishing o'er beauty's clay,
The myrtle[1] blows when love hath ceased to be;
Green waves the bay[2] when song and bard are fled,
590 And all that round us blooms, is blooming o'er the dead. [...]

LXX.

But thou, fair Attica![3] whose rocky bound
All art and nature's richest gifts enshrined,
Thou little sphere, whose soul-illumined round
Concentrated each sunbeam of the mind;
695   Who, as the summit of some Alpine height
Glows earliest, latest, with the blush of day,
Didst first imbibe the splendours of the light,
And smile the longest in its lingering ray;[4]
Oh! let us gaze on thee, and fondly deem
700 The past awhile restored, the present but a dream. [...]

LXXVII.

Bright age of Pericles![5] let fancy still
Through time's deep shadows all thy splendour trace,
And in each work of art's consummate skill
Hail the free spirit of thy lofty race.
765   That spirit, roused by every proud reward

---

1   myrtle] shrub associated in myth with Venus, and hence with love.
2   bay (or laurel) leaves were used in wreaths to crown poets.
3   Attica] region of Greece around Athens.
4   *And smile the longest in its lingering ray.* "We are assured by Thucydides that Attica was the province of Greece in which population first became settled, and where the earliest progress was made toward civilization."—Mitford's Greece, vol. i. p. 35. [Hemans's endnote, slightly misquoting from Mitford, *History of Greece*, ch. 1, section 3.]
5   Pericles (*c.* 490-429 BC) was military and political leader of Athens during its golden age of culture, wealth, and power.

That hope could picture, glory could bestow,
Foster'd by all the sculptor and the bard
Could give of immortality below.
Thus were thy heroes form'd, and o'er their name
Thus did thy genius shed imperishable fame. [...] 770

LXXX.

City of Theseus!¹ bursting on the mind,
Thus dost thou rise, in all thy glory fled!
Thus guarded by the mighty of mankind,
Thus hallow'd by the memory of the dead:
Alone in beauty and renown—a scene 795
Whose tints are drawn from freedom's loveliest ray.
'Tis but a vision now—yet thou hast been
More than the brightest vision might pourtray;
And every stone, with but a vestige fraught
Of thee, hath latent power to wake some lofty thought. 800

LXXXI.

Fall'n are thy fabrics, that so oft have rung
To choral melodies, and tragic lore;²
Now is the lyre of Sophocles unstrung,
The song that hail'd Harmodius³ peals no more.
Thy proud Piræus⁴ is a desart strand, 805
Thy stately shrines are mouldering on their hill,
Closed are the triumphs of the sculptor's hand,
The magic voice of eloquence is still;

---

1 Theseus] legendary Athenian hero and ruler.
2 lore] in classical Greek literature, odes ("choral melodies") and the tragedies of such
   writers as Sophocles (495-406 BC) were associated with Athenian "democracy"
   through reference to poems about Harmodius, who led an attempt to overthrow
   the tyrants Hippias and Hipparchus in the late 6th century BC.
3 Harmodius] an Athenian who, with his friend Aristogeiton, was killed after they
   slew the younger brother of the tyrant Hippias during the Panathenaic festival of
   514 BC; when Hippias was later expelled from Athens, the friends became popular
   heroes, celebrated in songs and depicted in sculpture.
4 Piræus] the port of Athens

Minerva's veil is rent[1]—her image gone,
810 Silent the sage's bower—the warrior's tomb o'erthrown.

LXXXII.

Yet in decay thine exquisite remains
Wondering we view, and silently revere,
As traces left on earth's forsaken plains
By vanish'd beings of a nobler sphere!
815 Not all the old magnificence of Rome,
All that dominion there hath left to time,
Proud Coliseum, or commanding dome,
Triumphal arch, or obelisk sublime,[2]
Can bid such reverence o'er the spirit steal,
820 As aught by thee imprest with beauty's plastic[3] seal.

LXXXIII.

Though still the empress of the sun-burnt waste,
Palmyra rises, desolately grand—
Though with rich gold[4] and massy sculpture graced,

---

1 *Minerva's veil is rent — her image gone.* The peplus, which is supposed to have been
suspended as an awning over the statue of Minerva, in the Parthenon, was a princi-
pal ornament of the Panathenaic festival; it was embroidered with various colours,
representing the battle of the Gods and Titans, and the exploits of Athenian heroes.
When the festival was celebrated, the peplus was brought from the Acropolis, and
suspended as a sail to the vessel, which on that day was conducted through the
Ceramicus and principal streets of Athens, till it had made the circuit of the Acrop-
olis. The peplus was then carried to the Parthenon, and consecrated to Minerva. —
See Chandler's Travels, Stuart's Athens, &c. [Hemans's endnote, referring to
Richard Chandler (1738-1810), *Travels in Asia Minor* (1775), *Travels in Greece* (1776);
James Stuart (1713-88), *The Antiquities of Athens* (1762, 1789); Minerva was the
Roman name for Athena, the presiding deity of Athens.]
2 ll. 817-18 refer to the Coliseum, an arena for games; the dome of the Pantheon, a
large temple; triumphal arches erected by various military victors and emperors;
and obelisks (tall tapering pillars) brought to Rome from Egypt as symbols of
imperial conquest.
3 plastic] here, capable of shaping.
4 *Though with rich gold and massy sculpture graced.* The gilding amidst the ruins of
Persepolis is still, according to Winckelmann, in high preservation. [Hemans's end-
note, refering to J.J. Winckelmann, *Geschichte der Kunst des Altertums* (1764), book 7,
chapter 2, section 10.]

Commanding still, Persepolis may stand
In haughty solitude — though sacred Nile   825
The first-born temples of the world surveys,
And many an awful and stupendous pile
Thebes of the hundred gates e'en yet displays;[1]
City of Pericles! oh, who like thee
Can teach how fair the works of mortal hand may be?   830

LXXXIV.

Thou led'st the way to that illumined sphere
Where sovereign beauty dwells; and thence didst bear,
Oh, still triumphant in that high career!
Bright archetypes of all the grand and fair.
And still to thee th' enlightened mind hath flown,   835
As to her country;—thou hast been to earth
A cynosure;[2]—and, e'en from victory's throne,
Imperial Rome gave homage to thy worth;
And nations rising to their fame afar,
Still to thy model turn, as seamen to their star.   840

LXXXV.

Glory to those whose relics thus arrest
The gaze of ages! Glory to the free!
For they, they only, could have thus imprest
Their mighty image on the years to be!
Empires and cities in oblivion lie,   845
Grandeur may vanish, conquest be forgot: —
To leave on earth renown that cannot die,
Of high-soul'd genius is th' unrivall'd lot.
Honour to thee, O Athens! thou hast shewn
What mortals may attain, and seized the palm[3] alone.   850

---

1   ll. 822-28 refer to famous cities of classical antiquity, "oriental" in location and cul-
    ture and, unlike Athens, supposedly leaving no legacy to the West: Palmyra, princi-
    pal city of a state north-east of present-day Damascus; Persepolis, capital of the Per-
    sian empire; and Thebes, major city and religious centre of Egypt.
2   cynosure] originally, the pole star, and thus a guide, as in l. 840.
3   palm] palm branches were used to symbolize victory.

LXXXVI.

Oh! live there those who view with scornful eyes
All that attests the brightness of thy prime?[1]
Yes; they who dwell beneath thy lovely skies,
And breathe th' inspiring ether[2] of thy clime!
855 Their path is o'er the mightiest of the dead,
Their homes are midst the works of noblest arts;
Yet all around their gaze, beneath their tread,
Not one proud thrill of loftier thought imparts.
Such are the conquerors of Minerva's land,
860 Where Genius first reveal'd the triumphs of his hand!

LXXXVII.

For them in vain the glowing light may smile
O'er the pale marble, colouring's warmth to shed,
And in chaste beauty many a sculptured pile
Still o'er the dust of heroes lift its head.
865 No patriot feeling binds them to the soil,
Whose tombs and shrines their fathers have not rear'd,
Their glance is cold indifference, and their toil
But to destroy what ages have revered,
As if exulting sternly to erase
870 Whate'er might prove *that* land had nurs'd a nobler race.[3]

LXXXVIII.

And who may grieve that, rescued from their hands,
Spoilers of excellence and foes to art,

---

1 prime] lines 851-52 refer to the Turks who live amongst the ruins of Athens but undervalue them, implicitly like those British critics who undervalue the Elgin marbles, through lack of taste and disregard for the political liberty that inspires great art.

2 ether] clear sky, upper regions of the atmosphere.

3 race] it was often claimed that the Turks deliberately vandalized ancient Greek monuments so that modern Greeks might not be inspired to revolt by these visible reminders of their past liberty and power; thus Lord Elgin claimed to have saved the Parthenon sculptures by removing them to England.

Thy relics, Athens! borne to other lands,
Claim homage still to thee from every heart?
Though now no more th' exploring stranger's sight,   875
Fix'd in deep reverence on Minerva's fane,
Shall hail, beneath their native heaven of light,
All that remain'd of forms adored in vain;
A few short years—and, vanish'd from the scene,
To blend with classic dust their proudest lot had been.   880

LXXXIX.

Fair Parthenon! yet still must fancy weep
For thee, thou work of nobler spirits flown.
Bright, as of old, the sunbeams o'er thee sleep
In all their beauty still—and thine is gone!
Empires have sunk since thou wert first revered,   885
And varying rites¹ have sanctified thy shrine.
The dust is round thee of the race that rear'd
Thy walls; and thou—their fate must soon be thine!
But when shall earth again exult to see
Visions divine like theirs renew'd in aught like thee?   890

XC.

Lone are thy pillars now—each passing gale
Sighs o'er them as a spirit's voice, which moan'd
That loneliness, and told the plaintive tale
Of the bright synod² once above them throned.
Mourn, graceful ruin! on thy sacred hill,   895
Thy gods, thy rites, a kindred fate have shared:
Yet art thou honour'd in each fragment³ still,
That wasting years and barbarous hands had spared;

---

1   rites] over the centuries the Parthenon was used as a temple or church by various
    religions as Athens and Greece were occupied by various imperial powers.
2   synod] assembly or council, here referring to the statues of Greek gods that deco-
    rated the Parthenon, surviving fragments of which were removed by Lord Elgin.
3   fragment] critics of the Elgin marbles argued that the collection comprised mere
    fragments; supporters such as Benjamin Robert Haydon and John Keats argued that
    the fragments still had great artistic value.

Each hallow'd stone, from rapine's fury borne,
900　Shall wake bright dreams of thee in ages yet unborn.

XCI.

Yes; in those fragments, though by time defaced,
And rude[1] insensate conquerors, yet remains
All that may charm th' enlighten'd eye of taste,
On shores where still inspiring freedom reigns.
905　As vital fragrance breathes from every part
Of the crush'd myrtle, or the bruised rose,
E'en thus th' essential energy of art,
There in each wreck imperishably glows![2]
The soul of Athens lives in every line,
910　Pervading brightly still the ruins of her shrine.

XCII.

Mark — on the storied frieze[3] the graceful train,
The holy festival's triumphal throng,
In fair procession, to Minerva's fane,
With many a sacred symbol move along.
915　There every shade of bright existence trace,
The fire of youth, the dignity of age;
The matron's calm austerity of grace,
The ardent warrior, the benignant sage;
The nymph's light symmetry, the chief's proud mien,
920　Each ray of beauty caught and mingled in the scene.

1　rude] here, rough in the sense of ignorant and uncivilized.

2　*There in each wreck imperishably glows.* "In the most broken fragment the same great principle of life can be proved to exist, as in the most perfect figure," is one of the observations of Mr. Haydon on the Elgin Marbles. [Hemans's endnote, quoting from Benjamin Robert Haydon (1786-1846), *The Judgment of Connoisseurs upon Works of Art Compared with that of Professional Men; in Reference More Particularly to the Elgin Marbles; First Published in the Examiner and the Champion* (London, 1816, p. 6), an attack on disparagers of the artistic quality of the Elgin marbles; Haydon was a historical painter, art critic, and friend of Keats, and helped get the marbles placed in the British Museum.]

3　frieze] decorative strip of sculpture in low relief depicting the procession of the Panathenaic festival, around the top of the *cella*, or inner chamber of the Parthenon.

XCIII.

Art unobtrusive there ennobles form,[1]
Each pure chaste outline exquisitely flows;
There e'en the steed, with bold expression warm,[2]
Is clothed with majesty, with being glows.
One mighty mind hath harmonized the whole;   925
Those varied groups the same bright impress bear;
One beam and essence of exalting soul
Lives in the grand, the delicate, the fair;
And well that pageant of the glorious dead
Blends us with nobler days, and loftier spirits fled. [...]   930

XCIX.

And who can tell how pure, how bright a flame,
Caught from these models, may illume the west?
What British Angelo may rise to fame,[3]
On the free isle what beams of art may rest?

---

1   *Art unobtrusive there ennobles form.* "Every thing here breathes life, with a veracity,
    with an exquisite knowledge of art, but without the least ostentation or parade of
    it, which is concealed by consummate and masterly skill." — Canova's Letter to the
    Earl of Elgin. [Hemans's endnote, quoting from Canova's letter, dated London, 10
    November 1815, as translated and published in the *Report from the Select Committee
    of the House of Commons on the Earl of Elgin's Collection of Sculptured Marbles; &c.*
    (London, 1816), Appendix, p. xxiii.]

2   *There e'en the steed, with bold expression warm.* Mr. West, after expressing his admira-
    tion of the horse's head in Lord Elgin's collection of Athenian sculpture, thus pro-
    ceeds: "We feel the same when we view the young equestrian Athenians, and in
    observing them we are insensibly carried on with the impression, that they and
    their horses actually existed, as we see them, at the instant when they were convert-
    ed into marble." — West's Second Letter to Lord Elgin. [Hemans's endnote, quot-
    ing from letter by Benjamin West (1738-1820) dated 20 March 1811, in *Memoran-
    dum on the Subject of the Earl of Elgin's Pursuits in Greece*, 2nd edition, corrected (Lon-
    don, 1815), p. 54; West was an American painter who worked in England and suc-
    ceeded Sir Joshua Reynolds as president of the Royal Academy in 1792.]

3   *What British Angelo may rise to fame.* "Let us suppose a young man at this time in
    London, endowed with powers such as enabled Michael Angelo to advance the
    arts, as he did, by the aid of one mutilated specimen of Grecian excellence in sculp-
    ture; to what an eminence might not such a genius carry art, by the opportunity of
    studying those sculptures in the aggregate, which adorned the temple of Minerva at
    Athens?" — West's Second Letter to Lord Elgin. [Hemans's endnote, citing a pas-
    sage from West's testimony in *Memorandum on the Subject of the Earl of Elgin's Pursuits*

985   Deem not, O England! that by climes confined,
       Genius and taste diffuse a partial ray;[1]
       Deem not th' eternal energies of mind
       Sway'd by that sun whose doom is but decay!
       Shall thought be foster'd but by skies serene?
990   No! thou hast power to be what Athens e'er[2] hath been.

C.

       But thine are treasures oft unprized, unknown,
       And cold neglect hath blighted many a mind,
       O'er whose young ardors, had thy smile but shone,
       Their soaring flight had left a world behind!
995   And many a gifted hand, that might have wrought
       To Grecian excellence the breathing stone,
       Or each pure grace of Raphael's[3] pencil caught,
       Leaving no record of its power, is gone!
       While thou hast fondly sought, on distant coast,[4]
1000 Gems far less rich than those, thus precious, and thus lost.

---

     in Greece, p. 55; the Italian painter, architect, and sculptor Michelangelo (1475-1564)
     followed models from classical antiquity and was regarded as the greatest artist of
     renaissance Europe.]

1   *Genius and taste diffuse a partial ray*. In allusion to the theories of Du Bos, Winckle-
     mann, Montesquieu, &c. with regard to the inherent obstacles in the climate of
     England to the progress of genius and the arts. —See Hoare's Epochs of the Arts,
     page 84, 5. [Hemans's endnote; referring to Prince Hoare (1755-1834), *Epochs of the
     Arts: Including Hints on the Use and Progress of Painting and Sculpture in Great Britain*
     (London, 1813), pp. 84, 85; Hoare argues that the main use of the arts "is, the *celebra-
     tion of the essential virtue*, or *fundamental strength*, of the individual in which they are
     cultivated" (p. 324); in England's case these strengths were "our pure religion," "the
     wisdom of EQUAL LAWS, constituting what is denominated the *Freedom of the
     English Constitution*," and "the extent of our COMMERCE, maintaining and sup-
     porting our political eminence under the influence of" the English constitution
     (pp. 326-27); Hemans follows this line in her poem, though Hoare attacked Elgin
     and opposed the state's acquisition of the marbles.]

2   e'er] contraction for "ever," but Hemans here may intend "ere," meaning "earlier"
     or "formerly."

3   Raphael] Raffaello Sanzio (1483-1520) was one of the most important Italian
     renaissance painters, and considered the leading exponent of the artistic ideals of
     classical antiquity.

4   coast] a reference to British quest for mere commercial wealth from colonies on
     "distant coasts," such as India, famous for its gems (referred to in the next line);
     "fondly": in the earlier sense of "foolishly."

CI.

Yet rise, O Land in all but Art alone,[1]
Bid the sole wreath that is not thine be won!
Fame dwells around thee — Genius is thine own;
Call his rich blooms to life — be Thou their Sun!
So, should dark ages[2] o'er thy glory sweep,   1005
Should *thine* e'er be as now are Grecian plains,
Nations unborn shall track thine own blue deep,
To hail thy shore, to worship thy remains;
Thy mighty monuments with reverence trace,
And cry, "This ancient soil hath nurs'd a glorious race!"   1010

---

1   alone] Britain was the sole superpower after the fall of Napoleon.
2   ages] Anna Lætitia Barbauld's controversial *Eighteen Hundred and Eleven: A Poem*
    (1812) imagines a distant age when Britain, too, will have become a land of past
    glories and ruins of empire, visited by the descendants of its former colonies.

FROM *TRANSLATIONS FROM CAMOENS, AND OTHER POETS, WITH ORIGINAL POETRY* (1818)[1]

FROM "TRANSLATIONS FROM CAMOENS AND OTHER POETS":[2]

CAMOENS.[3]

SONNET 282.

From Psalm CXXXVII.
Na ribeira do Euprates assentado.

WRAPT in sad musings, by Euphrates' stream[4]
I sat, retracing days for ever flown,
While rose thine image on the exile's dream,
O much-loved Salem![5] and thy glories' gone.

---

1 possibly completed as early as 1813; see letter 7 in this edition; if so, the translations would have been written not when FH's husband had left for Italy but before they were allowed to marry; the book's epigraph, from Lodovico Vittorio Savioli (1729-1804), reads: "Siamo nati veramente in un secolo in cui gl'ingegni e gli studj degli uomini sono rivolti all'utilità. L'Agricoltura, le Arti, il Commercio acquistano tutto di novi lumi dalle ricerche de' Saggi; e il voler farsi un nome *tentando di dilettare*, quand' altri v'aspira con più di giustizia giovando, sembra impresa dura e difficile." ("Truly we have been born in a century in which men's ingenuity and studies have turned to utility. Agriculture, the Arts, Commerce all acquire new illumination from the researches of the learned; and the wish to make oneself a name by trying to please, when others with more justice aspire to it by being useful, seems a hard and difficult undertaking.")

2 for context and commentary, see Introduction, pp. 25-6.

3 Camoens] Luis de Camões (*c.* 1524-80), the major Portuguese poet, wrote the epic *Os Lusiadas*, plays, and other poems; he was a soldier and adventurer, like the English renaissance poet Sir Philip Sidney, regarded in the late 18th and early 19th century as an exemplary figure for the nation; British interest in Spanish and Portuguese writers was quickened by the Peninsular War; Romantic writers took up Renaissance romance and love poetry as early expressions of their own interest in subjective experience and its trials in an often hostile world.

4 Euphrates] major river of ancient Babylon, biblical place of captivity of the Jews before returned to Palestine by divine intervention.

5 Jerusalem, main city of ancient Palestine.

When they, who caused the ceaseless tears I shed,   5
Thus to their captive spoke,—"Why sleep thy lays?
Sing of thy treasures lost, thy splendor fled,
And all thy triumphs in departed days!

Know'st thou not, Harmony's resistless charm
Can soothe each passion, and each grief disarm?   10
Sing then, and tears will vanish from thine eye."
With sighs I answered,—When the cup of woe
Is filled, till misery's bitter draught o'erflow,
The mourner's cure is not to sing,—but die.

VINCENZO DA FILICAJA.[1]

Italia, Italia! O tu cui diè la sorte.

ITALIA! thou, by lavish Nature graced
With ill-starr'd beauty, which to thee hath been
A fatal dowry, whose effects are traced
In the deep sorrows graven on thy mien;

Oh! that more strength, or fewer charms were thine,   5
That those might fear thee more, or love thee less,
Who seem to worship at thy beauty's shrine,
Then leave thee to the death-pang's bitterness!

Not then the herds of Gaul[2] would drain the tide
Of that Eridanus[3] thy blood hath dyed;   10
Nor from the Alps would legions, still renew'd,
Pour down; nor wouldst thou wield a foreign brand,
Nor fight thy battles with the stranger's hand,
Still doomed to serve, subduing or subdued![4]

---

1   or Filicaia (1641-1707), Italian administrator who wrote sonnets and odes on moral,
religious, and civic subjects; his patriotic poems against foreign domination of Italy
were taken up by European Romantic poets who supported liberal nationalism; an
altered version of this translation was published in FH's *Poetical Remains* (1836).
2   Gaul] ancient name for France.
3   Eridanus] in myth a river later identified with the Po in northern Italy.
4   ll. 11-14 refer to Italy's long history of invasion by foreign powers and of Italian
states inviting foreign rulers to their aid.

FROM "ORIGINAL POETRY":

GUERILLA SONG,

Founded on the story related of the Spanish Patriot, Mina.[1]

OH! forget not the hour, when through forest and vale,
We returned with our chief to his dear native halls;
Through the woody Sierra[2] there sighed not a gale,
And the moonbeam was bright on his battlement-walls;
5   And nature lay sleeping, in calmness and light,
Round the home of the valiant, that rose on our sight.

We entered that home—all was loneliness round,
The stillness, the darkness, the peace of the grave;
Not a voice, not a step, bade its echoes resound,
10   Ah! such was the welcome that waited the brave!
For the spoilers had passed, like the poison-wind's breath,
And the loved of his bosom lay silent in death.

Oh! forget not that hour—let its image be near,
In the light of our mirth, in the dreams of our rest,
15   Let its tale awake feelings too deep for a tear,
And rouse into vengeance each arm and each breast,
Till cloudless the dayspring of liberty shine
O'er the plains of the olive, and hills of the vine.

---

1   Mina] Francisco Espoz y Mina (1781-1836), Spanish guerilla leader and military commander during the Peninsular War, serving under Wellington; he fell into disfavour at the restoration of the reactionary king Ferdinand but led several liberal revolts and eventually helped achieve a liberal constitution; the poem refers to the bloody reprisals of the French against Spanish opponents, their families, and towns; patriotic nationalist leaders, past and present, were often represented as motivated by violation of their domestic and local relations, as in Jane Porter's novel *The Scottish Chiefs* (1810), which FH read.

2   mountains, here, of northern Spain, from which the guerillas operated.

FROM *TALES, AND HISTORIC SCENES, IN VERSE* (1819)[1]

THE WIDOW OF CRESCENTIUS.[2]

"L'orage peut briser en un moment les fleurs qui tiennent encore la tête levée."

MAD. DE STAEL.[3]

ADVERTISMENT.

"IN the reign of Otho III., Emperor of Germany, the Romans, excited by their Consul, Crescentius, who ardently desired to restore the ancient glory of the republic, made a bold attempt to shake off the Saxon yoke, and the authority of the Popes, whose vices rendered them objects of universal contempt. The Consul was besieged by Otho in the Mole of Hadrian,[4] which, long afterwards, continued to be called the Tower of Crescen-

---

1 text from 1st edn; Hemans's endnotes are extensive and so have been left in place at the end of each poem and indicated in the text by capital letters; for context and commentary, see Introduction, pp. 26-31.

2 the events, described in Hemans's "Advertisement," occurred in the late 10th century AD, during the long struggle for control of Rome between the German Holy Roman Emperor, the Papacy, and the city's populace; in Hemans's day, Rome, like other Italian states, was again caught in internal and international conflict when French Revolutionary and Napoleonic armies invaded Italy; after the fall of Napoleon, the European powers restored the reactionary Papal government, "protected" by Austria; liberals conspired for reform and national independence, idealizing figures like Crescentius as forerunners; he is still such a symbol: in present-day Rome Via Crescenzio runs through a quarter (north of Castel Sant'Angelo) where streets have been named for heroes of classical republicanism.

3 Stael] Anne Louise Germaine Necker, Baronne de Staël-Holstein (1766-1817), the most famous woman writer during the Romantic period, published fiction, criticism, and cultural studies; the sentence is spoken by Corinne to her beloved, Oswald, in *Corinne; ou, l'Italie* (3 vols, London, 1807, vol.1, p. 155; book 4, ch. 2): "... the storm may in a moment dash down flowers that still hold their heads upright."

4 the mausoleum of the Emperor Hadrian (ruled 117 to 138AD), from Latin for a massive structure, especially of stone; Hadrian's tomb was later fortified as the Castel Sant'Angelo.

tius. Otho, after many unavailing attacks upon this fortress, at last entered into negotiations; and pledging his imperial word to respect the life of Crescentius, and the rights of the Roman citizens, the unfortunate leader was betrayed into his power, and immediately beheaded with many of his partisans. Stephania, his widow, concealing her affliction and her resentment for the insults to which she had been exposed, secretly resolved to revenge her husband and herself. On the return of Otho from a pilgrimage to Mount Gargano, which, perhaps, a feeling of remorse had induced him to undertake, she found means to be introduced to him, and to gain his confidence, and a poison administered by her was soon afterwards the cause of his painful death." —*See Sismondi, History of the Italian Republics*, vol. i.[1]

MIDST Tivoli's [2] luxuriant glades,
Bright-foaming falls, and olive shades,
Where dwelt, in days departed long,
The sons of battle and of song,
No tree, no shrub its foliage rears,
But o'er the wrecks of other years,
Temples and domes, which long have been
The soil of that enchanted scene.

There the wild fig-tree and the vine
O'er Hadrian's mouldering villa twine;^A
The cypress, in funereal grace,
Usurps the vanish'd column's place;
O'er fallen shrine, and ruin'd frieze,

---

1 passage from Jean Charles Léonard de Sismondi (1773-1842), *Histoire des Républiques Italiennes du moyen age*, (16 vols, Paris, 1809-18); not translated into English until 1832; the translation here, presumably Hemans's, conflates passages from vol. 1, ch. 3, pp. 163-70; Sismondi was a Swiss-born economist and historian; he accompanied Staël to Italy on the trip that inspired *Corinne*; his widely read *Histoire* promotes a broad liberalism, and inspired many Romantic writers besides Hemans, including Mary Shelley (e.g., *Valperga*, 1823).
2 Tivoli] town south of Rome and site of the celebrated Renaissance Villa d'Este and of the ruins of the vast villa of the Roman emperor Hadrian (described in the following lines), where the emperor had built replicas of buildings from several parts of his empire.

The wall-flower rustles in the breeze;
Acanthus-leaves[1] the marble hide,   15
They once adorn'd, in sculptured pride,
And nature hath resumed her throne
O'er the vast works of ages flown.

Was it for this that many a pile,[2]
Pride of Ilissus and of Nile,   20
To Anio's banks the image lent
Of each imperial monument?[B]
Now Athens weeps her shatter'd fanes,
Thy temples, Egypt, strew thy plains;
And the proud fabrics Hadrian rear'd,   25
From Tibur's vale have disappear'd.
We need no prescient sybil[3] there
The doom of grandeur to declare;
Each stone, where weeds and ivy climb,
Reveals some oracle of Time;   30
Each relic utters Fate's decree,
The future as the past shall be.

Halls of the dead! in Tibur's vale,
Who now shall tell your lofty tale?
Who trace the high patrician's dome,   35
The bard's retreat, the hero's home?
When moss-clad wrecks alone record
There dwelt the world's departed lord!
In scenes where verdure's rich array
Still sheds young beauty o'er decay,   40

---

1   Acanthus] a herbaceous plant common in Mediterranean regions; stylized forms of
    its leaves were carved on the capitals of columns, especially in the Corinthian order,
    the most ornate of the ancient styles of architectural decoration and thus associated
    by later writers with excessive luxury and decadence which supposedly caused the
    downfall of the Roman empire; see l. 46.
2   in ll. 19-42 Hemans uses a well known literary figure of loss, in a view of history as
    cyclical, signalled by the phrase "Was it for this," used by poets since ancient times;
    the poet refers to buildings ("piles") and temples ("fanes") of antiquity, now in
    ruins, associated with rivers: the Ilissus near Athens in Greece, the Nile in Egypt,
    and the Anio and Tibur (not the Tiber that flows through Rome) near Tivoli.
3   sybil] or sibyl, in ancient Roman myth a woman of prophetic powers.

And sunshine on each glowing hill,
Midst ruins finds a dwelling still.

Sunk is thy palace, but thy tomb,
Hadrian! hath shared a prouder doom,^C
Though vanish'd with the days of old
Its pillars of Corinthian mould;
And the fair forms by sculpture wrought,
Each bodying some immortal thought,
Which o'er that temple of the dead,
Serene, but solemn beauty shed,
Have found, like glory's self, a grave
In time's abyss, or Tiber's wave:^D
Yet dreams more lofty, and more fair,
Than art's bold hand hath imaged e'er,
High thoughts of many a mighty mind,
Expanding when all else declined,
In twilight years, when only they
Recalled the radiance passed away,
Have made that ancient pile their home,
Fortress of freedom and of Rome.

There he, who strove in evil days,
Again to kindle glory's rays,
Whose spirit sought a path of light,
For those dim ages far too bright,
Crescentius, long maintain'd the strife,
Which closed but with its martyr's life,
And left th' imperial tomb a name,
A heritage of holier fame.
There closed De Brescia's[1] mission high,
From thence the patriot came to die;^E
And thou, whose Roman soul the last,
Spoke with the voice of ages past,^F
Whose thoughts so long from earth had fled,
To mingle with the glorious dead,

---

1 see Hemans's endnote to the next line.

That midst the world's degenerate race 75
They vainly sought a dwelling-place,
Within that house of death didst brood
O'er visions to thy ruin woo'd.
Yet, worthy of a brighter lot,
Rienzi![1] be thy faults forgot! 80
For thou, when all around thee lay
Chain'd in the slumbers of decay;
So sunk each heart, that mortal eye
Had scarce a *tear* for liberty;
Alone, amidst the darkness there, 85
Couldst gaze on Rome — yet not despair![G]

'Tis morn, and Nature's richest dyes
Are floating o'er Italian skies;
Tints of transparent lustre shine
Along the snow-clad Apennine;[2] 90
The clouds have left Soracte's height,[3]
And yellow Tiber winds in light,
Where tombs and fallen fanes have strew'd
The wide Campagna's[4] solitude.
'Tis sad amidst that scene to trace 95
Those relics of a vanish'd race;
Yet o'er the ravaged path of time,
Such glory sheds that brilliant clime,
Where nature still, though empires fall,
Holds her triumphant festival; 100
E'en Desolation wears a smile,
Where skies and sunbeams laugh the while;
And Heaven's own light, Earth's richest bloom,
Array the ruin and the tomb.

---

1 Rienzi] Cola (or Nicolà) di Rienzi (*c.* 1313-54 AD) aimed to restore Rome's
   ancient liberties, moral probity, and power, and to unite Italian states against Ger-
   man interference, but he was killed in a riot; during the 18th and 19th centuries he
   became a symbol of democratic revolution, represented in poetry, fiction, and
   music.
2 Apennine] the central mountain range running down the Italian peninsula.
3 Soracte] mountain near Rome, often mentioned in classical literature.
4 Campagna] countryside around Rome, site of many ancient tombs.

But she, who from yon convent tower
Breathes the pure freshness of the hour;
She, whose rich flow of raven hair
Streams wildly on the morning air;
Heeds not how fair the scene below,
Robed in Italia's brightest glow.
Though throned midst Latium's[1] classic plains,
Th' Eternal City's towers and fanes,
And they, the Pleiades[2] of earth,
The seven proud hills of Empire's birth,
Lie spread beneath: not now her glance
Roves o'er that vast sublime expanse;
Inspired, and bright with hope, 'tis thrown
On Adrian's massy tomb alone;
There, from the storm, when Freedom fled,
His faithful few Crescentius led;
While she, his anxious bride, who now
Bends o'er the scene her youthful brow,
Sought refuge in the hallow'd fane,
Which then could shelter, not in vain.[3]
But now the lofty strife is o'er,
And Liberty shall weep no more.
At length imperial Otho's voice
Bids her devoted[4] sons rejoice;
And he, who battled to restore
The glories and the rights of yore,
Whose accents, like the clarion's sound,
Could burst the dead repose around,
Again his native Rome shall see,
The sceptred city of the free!
And young Stephania waits the hour
When leaves her lord his fortress-tower,

---

1 Latium] Latin name for the region in which Rome is situtated, the modern Lazio;
   Rome was called the "Eternal City" (l. 112) because it had been continuously
   occupied over many centuries.
2 Pleiades] group of seven stars in the constellation Taurus, here compared to the
   seven hills on which ancient Rome was built.
3 churches were supposed to be safe refuges.
4 devoted] here, perhaps both "doomed" and "dedicated."

Her ardent heart with joy elate,
That seems beyond the reach of fate;
Her mien, like creature from above,
All vivified with hope and love.   140

Fair is her form, and in her eye
Lives all the soul of Italy!
A meaning lofty and inspired,
As by her native day-star[1] fired;
Such wild and high expression, fraught   145
With glances of impassion'd thought,
As fancy sheds in visions bright,
O'er priestess of the God of Light![2]
And the dark locks that lend her face
A youthful and luxuriant grace,   150
Wave o'er a cheek, whose kindling dyes
Seem from the fire within to rise;[3]
But deepen'd by the burning heaven
To her own land of sunbeams given.
Italian art[4] that fervid glow   155
Would o'er ideal beauty throw,
And with such ardent life express
Her high-wrought dreams of loveliness;—
Dreams which, surviving Empire's fall,
The shade of glory still recal.   160

But see,—the banner of the brave
O'er Adrian's tomb hath ceased to wave.
'Tis lower'd—and now Stephania's eye
Can well the martial train descry,
Who, issuing from that ancient dome,   165

---

1 day-star] Italian sun, standing for the climate and landscape of Italy, supposedly
   forming the soul of a patriot.
2 God of Light] Apollo, at whose temple at Delphi, in Greece, a priestess would go
   into a trance and answer questions about the future on his behalf.
3 Susan Wolfson suggests a parallel to P.B. Shelley's description of the veiled visionary
   dream maid in *Alastor* (1816): "the solemn mood / Of her pure mind kindled
   through all her frame / A permeating fire." (161-3)
4 in Hemans's day Italian art was thought to be characterized by an idealizing quality.

Pour through the crowded streets of Rome.
Now from her watch-tower on the height,
With step as fabled wood-nymph's light,
She flies — and swift her way pursues,
170 Through the lone convent's avenues.
Dark cypress groves, and fields o'erspread
With records of the conquering dead,
And paths which track a glowing waste,
She traverses in breathless haste;
175 And by the tombs where dust is shrined,
Once tenanted by loftiest mind,
Still passing on, hath reach'd the gate
Of Rome, the proud, the desolate!
Throng'd are the streets, and, still renew'd,
180 Rush on the gathering multitude.

Is it their high-soul'd chief to greet
That thus the Roman thousands meet?
With names that bid their thoughts ascend,
Crescentius, thine in song to blend;
185 And of triumphal days gone by
Recall th' inspiring pageantry?
— There is an air of breathless dread,
An eager glance, a hurrying tread;
And now a fearful silence round,
190 And now a fitful murmuring sound,
Midst the pale crowds, that almost seem
Phantoms of some tumultuous dream.
Quick is each step, and wild each mien,
Portentous of some awful[1] scene.
195 Bride of Crescentius! as the throng
Bore thee with whelming force along,
How did thine anxious heart beat high,
Till rose suspense to agony!
Too brief suspense, that soon shall close,
200 And leave thy heart to deeper woes.

---

1   awful] here and throughout, inspiring awe, the usual sense in Hemans's day.

Who midst yon guarded precinct stands,
With fearless mien, but fetter'd hands?
The ministers of death are nigh,
Yet a calm grandeur lights his eye;
And in his glance there lives a mind,   205
Which was not form'd for chains to bind,
But cast in such heroic mould
As theirs, th' ascendant ones of old.
Crescentius! freedom's daring son,
Is this the guerdon[1] thou has won?   210
O worthy to have lived and died
In the bright days of Latium's pride!
Thus must the beam of glory close
O'er the seven hills again that rose,
When at thy voice, to burst the yoke,   215
The soul of Rome indignant woke?
Vain dream! the sacred shields are gone,[H]
Sunk is the crowning city's throne:[I]
Th' illusions, that around her cast
Their guardian spells, have long been past.[J]   220
Thy life hath been a shot-star's ray,[2]
Shed o'er her midnight of decay;
Thy death at freedom's ruin'd shrine
Must rivet every chain — but thine.

Calm is his aspect, and his eye   225
Now fix'd upon the deep-blue sky,
Now on those wrecks of ages fled,
Around in desolation spread;
Arch, temple, column, worn and grey,
Recording triumphs pass'd away;   230
Works of the mighty and the free,
Whose steps on earth no more shall be,
Though their bright course hath left a trace
Nor years nor sorrows can efface.

---

1   guerdon] reward or recompense, a mainly literary usage.
2   shot-star] shooting star or meteor.

235   Why changes now the patriot's mien,
        Erewhile so loftily serene?
        Thus can approaching death control
        The might of that commanding soul?
        No!—Heard ye not that thrilling cry
240   Which told of bitterest agony?
        He heard it, and, at once subdued,
        Hath sunk the hero's fortitude.
        He heard it, and his heart too well
        Whence rose that voice of woe can tell;
245   And midst the gazing throngs around
        One well-known form his glance hath found;
        One fondly loving and beloved,
        In grief, in peril, faithful proved.
        Yes, in the wildness of despair,
250   She, his devoted[1] bride, is there.
        Pale, breathless, through the crowd she flies,
        The light of frenzy in her eyes:
        But ere her arms can clasp the form,
        Which life ere long must cease to warm;
255   Ere on his agonizing breast
        Her heart can heave, her head can rest;
        Check'd in her course by ruthless hands,
        Mute, motionless, at once she stands;
        With bloodless cheek and vacant glance,
260   Frozen and fix'd in horror's trance;
        Spell-bound, as every sense were fled,
        And thought o'erwhelm'd, and feeling dead.
        And the light waving of her hair,
        And veil, far floating on the air,
265   Alone, in that dread moment, show
        She is no sculptured form of woe.

        The scene of grief and death is o'er,
        The patriot's heart shall throb no more:
        But *hers*—so vainly form'd to prove

---

1   devoted] here, both "loyal" and "doomed."

The pure devotedness of love,   270
And draw from fond affection's eye
All thought sublime, all feeling high;
When consciousness again shall wake,
Hath now no refuge—but to break.
The spirit long inured to pain   275
May smile at fate in calm disdain;
Survive its darkest hour, and rise
In more majestic energies.
But in the glow of vernal pride,
If each warm hope *at once* hath died,   280
Then sinks the mind, a blighted flower,
Dead to the sunbeam and the shower;
A broken gem, whose inborn light
Is scatter'd—ne'er to re-unite.

PART II.

HAST thou a scene that is not spread
With records of thy glory fled?
A monument that doth not tell
The tale of liberty's farewell?
Italia! thou art but a grave   5
Where flowers luxuriate o'er the brave,
And nature gives her treasures birth
O'er all that hath been great on earth.
Yet smile thy heavens as once they smiled,
When thou wert freedom's favour'd child:[1]   10
Tho' fane and tomb alike are low,
Time hath not dimm'd thy sunbeam's glow;
And robed in that exulting ray,
Thou seem'st to triumph o'er decay;
O yet, though by thy sorrows bent,   15
In nature's pomp magnificent;
What marvel if, when all was lost,
Still on thy bright, enchanted coast,

---

1 referring to ancient republican Rome.

Though many an omen warn'd him thence,
20 Linger'd the lord of eloquence?^K
Still gazing on the lovely sky,
Whose radiance woo'd him — but to die:
Like him *who* would not linger there,
Where heaven, earth, ocean, all are fair?
25 Who midst thy glowing scenes could dwell,
Nor bid awhile his griefs farewell?
Hath not thy pure and genial air
Balm for all sadness but despair?^L
No! there are pangs, whose deep-worn trace
30 Not all *thy* magic can efface!
Hearts, by unkindness wrung, may learn
The world and all its gifts to spurn;
Time may steal on with silent tread,
And dry the tear that mourns the dead;
35 May change fond love, subdue regret,
And teach e'en vengeance to forget:
But thou, Remorse! there is no charm,
Thy sting, avenger, to disarm!
Vain are bright suns and laughing skies,
40 To sooth thy victim's agonies:
The heart once made thy burning throne,
Still, while it beats, is thine alone.

In vain for Otho's joyless eye
Smile the fair scenes of Italy,
45 As through her landscapes' rich array
Th' imperial pilgrim bends his way.
Thy form, Crescentius, on his sight
Rises when nature laughs in light,
Glides round him at the midnight hour,
50 Is present in his festal bower,
With awful voice and frowning mien,
By all but him unheard, unseen.
Oh! thus to shadows of the grave
Be every tyrant still a slave!

Where through Gargano's woody dells,   55
O'er bending oaks the north-wind swells,^M
A sainted hermit's lowly tomb
Is bosom'd in umbrageous gloom,
In shades that saw him live and die
Beneath their waving canopy.   60
'Twas his, as legends tell, to share
The converse of immortals there;
Around that dweller of the wild
There "bright appearances" have smiled,^N
And angel-wings, at eve, have been   65
Gleaming the shadowy boughs between.
And oft from that secluded bower
Hath breathed, at midnight's calmer hour,
A swell of viewless[1] harps, a sound
Of warbled anthems pealing round.   70
Oh, none but voices of the sky
Might wake that thrilling harmony,
Whose tones, whose very echos[2] made
An Eden[3] of the lonely shade!

Years have gone by; the hermit sleeps   75
Amidst Gargano's woods and steeps;
Ivy and flowers have half o'ergrown,
And veil'd his low, sepulchral stone:
Yet still the spot is holy, still
Celestial footsteps haunt the hill;   80
And oft the awe-struck mountaineer
Aërial vesper-hymns may hear,
Around those forest-precincts float,
Soft, solemn, clear,—but still remote.
Oft will Affliction breathe her plaint   85
To that rude shrine's departed saint,

---

1   viewless] invisible, a common poeticism.
2   echos] in Hemans's day an accepted spelling for the more usual "echoes."
3   Eden] in the Bible, Eden is a paradisal garden created by God for Adam and Eve
    before their disobedience and expulsion into time, toil, and mortality.

And deem that spirits of the blest
There shed sweet influence o'er her breast.

And thither Otho now repairs,
To sooth his soul with vows and prayers;
And if for him, on holy ground,
The lost-one, Peace, may yet be found,
Midst rocks and forests, by the bed,
Where calmly sleep the sainted dead,
She dwells, remote from heedless eye,
With Nature's lonely majesty.

Vain, vain the search — his troubled breast
Nor vow nor penance lulls to rest;
The weary pilgrimage is o'er,
The hopes that cheer'd it are no more.
Then sinks his soul, and day by day,
Youth's buoyant energies decay.
The light of health his eye hath flown,
The glow that tinged his cheek is gone.
Joyless as one on whom is laid
Some baleful spell that bids him fade,
Extending its mysterious power
O'er every scene, o'er every hour;
E'en thus *he* withers; and to him,
Italia's brilliant skies are dim.
He withers — in that glorious clime
Where Nature laughs in scorn of Time;
And suns, that shed on all below
Their full and vivifying glow,
From him alone their power withhold,
And leave his heart in darkness cold.
Earth blooms around him, heaven is fair,
He only seems to perish there.

Yet sometimes will a transient smile
Play o'er his faded cheek awhile,

When breathes his minstrel-boy a strain
Of power to lull all earthly pain;
So wildly sweet, its notes might seem
Th' ethereal music of a dream,
A spirit's voice from worlds unknown,   125
Deep thrilling power in every tone!
Sweet is that lay,[1] and yet its flow
Hath language only given to woe;
And if at times its wakening swell
Some tale of glory seems to tell,   130
Soon the proud notes of triumph die,
Lost in a dirge's harmony:
Oh! many a pang the heart hath proved,
Hath deeply suffer'd, fondly loved,
Ere the sad strain could catch from thence   135
Such deep impassion'd eloquence! —
Yes! gaze on him, that minstrel boy —
He is no child of hope and joy;
Though few his years, yet have they been
Such as leave traces on the mien,   140
And o'er the roses of our prime
Breathe other blights than those of time.

Yet, seems his spirit wild and proud,
By grief unsoften'd and unbow'd.
Oh! there are sorrows which impart   145
A sternness foreign to the heart,
And rushing with an earthquake's power,
That makes a desert in an hour;
Rouse the dread passions in their course,
As tempests wake the billows' force! —   150
'Tis sad, on youthful Guido's face,
The stamp of woes like these to trace.
Oh! where can ruins awe mankind,
Dark as the ruins of the mind?

---

1   lay] poeticism for song, typically a ballad.

His mien is lofty, but his gaze
Too well a wandering soul betrays:
His full dark eye at times is bright
With strange and momentary light,
Whose quick uncertain flashes throw
O'er his pale cheek a hectic[1] glow:
And oft his features and his air
A shade of troubled mystery wear,
A glance of hurried wildness, fraught
With some unfathomable thought.
Whate'er that thought, still, unexpress'd,
Dwells the sad secret in his breast;
The pride his haughty brow reveals,
All other passion well conceals.
He breathes each wounded feeling's tone,
In music's eloquence alone;
His soul's deep voice is only pour'd
Through his full song and swelling chord.

He seeks no friend, but shuns the train
Of courtiers with a proud disdain;
And, save when Otho bids his lay
Its half unearthly power essay,
In hall or bower the heart to thrill,
His haunts are wild and lonely still.
Far distant from the heedless throng,
He roves old Tiber's banks along,
Where Empire's desolate remains
Lie scatter'd o'er the silent plains:
Or, lingering midst each ruin'd shrine
That strews the desert Palatine,[2]
With mournful, yet commanding mien,
Like the sad genius[3] of the scene,
Entranced in awful thought appears
To commune with departed years.

1 hectic] feverish; the usual sense in Hemans's day.
2 Palatine] one of ancient Rome's seven hills, site of the emperor's palace.
3 genius] presiding spirit.

Or at the dead of night, when Rome
Seems of heroic shades[1] the home;
When Tiber's murmuring voice recalls
The mighty to their ancient halls;
When hush'd is every meaner sound,
And the deep moonlight-calm around
Leaves to the solemn scene alone   195
The majesty of ages flown;
A pilgrim to each hero's tomb,
He wanders through the sacred gloom;
And, midst those dwellings of decay,
At times will breathe so sad a lay,   200
So wild a grandeur in each tone,
'Tis like a dirge for empires gone!

Awake thy pealing harp again,
But breathe a more exulting strain,
Young Guido! for awhile forgot   205
Be the dark secrets of thy lot,
And rouse th' inspiring soul of song
To speed the banquet's hour along! —
The feast is spread; and music's call
Is echoing through the royal hall,   210
And banners wave, and trophies[2] shine,
O'er stately guests in glittering line;
And Otho seeks awhile to chase
The thoughts he never can erase,
And bid the voice, whose murmurs deep   215
Rise like a spirit on his sleep,
The still small voice[3] of conscience die,
Lost in the din of revelry.

On his pale brow dejection lowers,[4]
But that shall yield to festal hours: 220

---

1 shades] ghosts or spirits.
2 trophies] here, weapons and other spoils of battle.
3 in the Bible, first book of Kings, God addresses the prophet Elijah in a "still small
   voice" (19.12).
4 lowers] less common form of "lours": frowns or looks dark and threatening.

A gloom is in his faded eye,
But that from music's power shall fly:
His wasted cheek is wan with care,
But mirth shall spread fresh crimson there.
225   Wake, Guido! wake thy numbers high,
Strike the bold chord exultingly!
And pour upon th' enraptured ear
Such strains as warriors love to hear!
Let the rich mantling[1] goblet flow,
230   And banish all resembling woe;
And, if a thought intrude, of power
To mar the bright convivial hour,
Still must its influence lurk unseen,
And cloud the heart—but not the mien!
235

Away, vain dream!—on Otho's brow,
Still darker lower[2] the shadows now;
Changed are his features, now o'erspread
With the cold paleness of the dead;
Now crimson'd with a hectic dye,
240   The burning flush of agony!
His lip is quivering, and his breast
Heaves with convulsive pangs oppress'd;
Now his dim eye seems fix'd and glazed,
And now to heaven in anguish raised;
245   And as, with unavailing aid,
Around him throng his guests dismay'd,
He sinks—while scarce his struggling breath
Hath power to falter—"This is death!"

Then rush'd that haughty child of song,
250   Dark Guido, through the awe-struck throng;
Fill'd with a strange delirious light,
His kindling eye shone wildly bright,
And on the sufferer's mien awhile
Gazing with stern vindictive smile,

---

1   mantling] foaming with bubbles from the wine.
2   lower] lour.

A feverish glow of triumph dyed   255
His burning cheek, while thus he cried: —
"Yes! these are death-pangs — on thy brow
Is set the seal of vengeance now!
Oh! well was mix'd the deadly draught,
And long and deeply hast thou quaff'd;   260
And bitter as thy pangs may be,
They are but guerdons meet[1] from me!
Yet, these are but a moment's throes,
Howe'er intense, they soon shall close.
Soon shalt thou yield thy fleeting breath,   265
My life hath been a lingering death;
Since one dark hour of woe and crime,
A blood-spot on the page of time!

"Deem'st thou my mind of reason void?
It is not phrensied, — but destroy'd!   270
Aye! view the wreck with shuddering thought, —
That work of ruin thou hast wrought!

"The secret of thy doom to tell,
My name alone suffices well!
Stephania! — once a hero's bride!   275
Otho! thou know'st the rest — *he died.*
Yes! trusting to a monarch's word,
The Roman fell, untried, unheard!
And thou, whose every pledge was vain,
How couldst *thou* trust in aught again?   280

"He died, and I was changed — my soul,
A lonely wanderer, spurn'd control.
From peace, and light, and glory hurl'd,
The outcast of a purer world,[2]
I saw each brighter hope o'erthrown,   285
And lived for one dread task alone.
The task is closed — fulfill'd the vow,

---

1 meet] appropriate.
2 ll. 283-4 recall the plight of the rebel angels in Milton's *Paradise Lost.*

The hand of death is on thee now.
Betrayer! in thy turn betray'd,
290   The debt of blood shall soon be paid!
Thine hour is come — the time hath been
My heart had shrunk from such a scene;
That feeling long is past — my fate
Hath made me stern as desolate.

295   "Ye that around me shuddering stand,
Ye chiefs and princes of the land!
Mourn ye a guilty monarch's doom?
— Ye wept not o'er the patriot's tomb!
He sleeps unhonour'd — yet be mine
300   To share his low, neglected shrine.
His soul with freedom finds a home,
His grave is that of glory — Rome!
Are not the great of old with her,
That city of the sepulchre?
305   Lead me to death! and let me share
The slumbers of the mighty there!"

The day departs — that fearful day
Fades in calm loveliness away:
From purple heavens its lingering beam
310   Seems melting into Tiber's stream,
And softly tints each Roman hill
With glowing light, as clear and still,
As if, unstain'd by crime or woe,
Its hours had pass'd in silent flow.
315   The day sets calmly — it hath been
Mark'd with a strange and awful scene:
One guilty bosom throbs no more,
And Otho's pangs and life are o'er.
And thou, ere yet another sun
320   His burning race hath brightly run,
Released from anguish by thy foes,
Daughter of Rome! shalt find repose. —
Yes! on thy country's lovely sky

Fix yet once more thy parting eye!
A few short hours — and all shall be   325
The silent and the past for thee.

Oh! thus with tempests of a day
We struggle, and we pass away,
Like the wild billows as they sweep,
Leaving no vestige on the deep!   330
And o'er thy dark and lowly bed
The sons of future days shall tread,
The pangs, the conflicts, of thy lot,
By them unknown, by thee forgot.

[HEMANS'S] NOTES.

A   *O'er Hadrian's mouldering villa twine.* (part 1, line 10)
"J'etais allé passer quelques jours seuls à Tivoli. Je parcourus
les environs, et surtout celles de la Villa Adriana. Surpris par la
pluie au milieu de ma course, je me réfugiai dans les Salles des
Thermes voisins du *Pécile* (monumens de la villa), sous un figuier
qui avait renversé le pau d'un mur en s'élevant. Dans un petit
salon octogone, ouvert devant moi, une vigne vierge avait
percé la voûte de l'édifice, et son gros cep lisse, rouge, et
tortueux, montait le long du mur comme un serpent. Autour
de moi, à travers les arcades des ruines, s'ouvraient des points de
vue sur la Campagne Romaine. Des buissons de sureau rem-
plissaient les salles désertes où venaient se refugier quelques
merles solitaires. Les fragmens de maçonnerie étaient tapissées
de feuilles de scolopendre, dont la verdure satinée se dessinait
comme un travail en mosaïque sur la blancheur des marbres: çà
et là de hauts cyprès remplaçaient les colonnes tombées dans
ces palais de la Mort; l'acanthe sauvage rampait à leurs pieds, sur
des débris, comme si la nature s'était plu à reproduire sur ces
chefs d'œuvre mutilés d'architecture, l'ornement de leur beauté
passée."[1]—*Chateaubriand, Souvenirs d'Italie.*

---

1   slightly misquoted from François René, Vicomte de Chateaubriand (1768-1848),
    *Souvenirs d'Italie, d'Angleterre et d'Amérique, suivi de morceaux divers de morale et de lit-
    térature* (2 vols, London, 1815), 1.19-20; translated as *Recollections of Italy, England and*

B   *Of each imperial monument?* (1.22)

The gardens and buildings of Hadrian's villa were copies of the most celebrated scenes and edifices in his dominions; the Lycæum, the Academia, the Prytaneum of Athens, the Temple of Serapis at Alexandria, the Vale of Tempe,[1] &c.

C   *Sunk is thy palace, but thy tomb,*
         Hadrian! hath shared a prouder doom. (1.43-4)

The mausoleum of Hadrian, now the castle of St. Angelo, was first converted into a citadel by Belisarius,[2] in his successful defence of Rome against the Goths. "The lover of the arts," says Gibbon, "must read with a sigh that the works of Praxiteles and Lysippus were torn from their lofty pedestals, and hurled into the ditch on the heads of the besiegers."[3] He adds, in a note, that the celebrated sleeping Faun of the Barberini palace

---

America, with Essays on Various Subjects, in Morals and Literature (2 vols, London, 1815, 1.19-20): "... I passed some days alone at Tivoli. I traversed the ruins in its environs, and particularly those of Villa Adriana. Being overtaken by a shower of rain in the midst of my excursion, I took refuge in the halls of Thermes near Pécile under a fig-tree, which had thrown down a wall by its growth. In a small octagonal saloon, which was open before me, a vine had penetrated through fissures in the arched roof, while its smooth and red crooked stem mounted along the wall like a serpent. Round me, across the arcades, the Roman country was seen in different points of view. Large elder trees filled the deserted apartments, where some solitary black-birds found a retreat. The fragments of masonry were garnished with leaves of scolopendra, the satin verdure of which appeared like mosaic work upon the white marble. Here and there lofty cypresses replaced the columns, which had fallen into these palaces of death. The wild acanthus crept at their feet on the ruins, as if nature had taken pleasure in reproducing, upon these mutilated *chefs-d'œuvre* of architecture, the ornament of their past beauty."

1   Tempe] Tempe: valley in northern Thessaly, Greece, famous for its beauty and favoured by Apollo; Lyceum: complex of buildings and gardens dedicated to Apollo at Athens where young men pursued sports and philosophical discussion; Prytaneum: building where hospitality was offered to visiting dignitaries and distinguished Athenians; the temple of Serapis honoured Osiris, Egyptian god of the underworld.

2   Belisarius] a general (*c*. AD 505-565) sent by the emperor Justinian I to reconquer Italy from the Goths, resulting in destruction of important classical buildings and art works, which had in fact been collected by the Romans themselves as the loot of empire.

3   besiegers] the passage is from Edward Gibbon, *The Decline and Fall of the Roman Empire* (1776-88), ch. 41 (2.566 and note in Modern Library Edition, New York); Praxiteles and Lyssipus (4th century BC) were the most famous sculptors of ancient Greece, and the Romans made numerous copies of their works.

was found, in a mutilated state, when the ditch of St. Angelo was cleansed under Urban VIII.[1] In the middle ages, the moles Hadriani was made a permanent fortress by the Roman government, and bastions, outworks, &c. were added to the original edifice, which had been stripped of its marble covering, its Corinthian pillars, and the brazen cone which crowned its summit.

D   *Have found, like glory's self, a grave*
     In time's abyss, or Tiber's wave. (1.51-2)
"Les plus beaux monumens des arts, les plus admirables statues ont étés jetées dans le Tibre, et sont cachées sous ses flots. Qui sait si, pour les chercher, on ne le détournera pas un jour de son lit? Mais quand on songe que les chef d'œuvres du génie humain sont peut-être là devant nous, et qu'un œil plus perçant les verrait à travers les ondes, l'on éprouve je ne sais quelle émotion qui renait à Rome sans cesse sous diverses formes, et fait trouver une societé pour la pensée dans les objets physiques, muets partout ailleurs."[2]—*Mad. de Staël.*

E   *There closed De Brescia's mission high;*
     From thence the patriot came to die. (1.69-70)
Arnold de Brescia, the undaunted and eloquent champion of Roman liberty, after unremitting efforts to restore the ancient constitution of the republic, was put to death in the year 1155 by Adrian IV. This event is thus described by Sismondi, Histoire des Republiques Italiennes, Vol. II. pages 68 and 69. "Le préfect demeura dans le château Saint Ange avec son prisonnier; il le fit transporter un matin sur la place des-

---

1 Urban VIII] Pope from 1623 to 1644, he involved the Papacy in European military and political affairs, and fortified Rome, turning the former tomb of Hadrian into a fortress known as the Castel Sant-Angelo.

2 ailleurs] from de Staël, *Corinne* (3 vols, London, 1807, 1.237; book 5, ch. 2); translated by Isabel Hill as: "The finest statues and other works of art were thrown into the Tiber, and are hidden beneath its tides. Who knows but that, in search of them, the river may at last be driven from its bed? But, while we muse on efforts of human genius that lie, perhaps, beneath us, and that some eye, more piercing than our own, may yet see through these waves, we feel that awe which, in Rome, is constantly reviving in various forms, and giving the mind companions in those physical objects which are elsewhere dumb." (*Corinne*, London, 1833, p. 81)

tinée aux exécutions, devant la porte du peuple. Arnaud de Brescia, élevé sur un bûcher, fut attaché à un poteau, en face du Corso. Il pouvoit mesurer des yeux les trois longues rues qui aboutissoient devant son echafaud; elles font presqu'une moitié de Rome. C'est là qu'habitoient les hommes qu'il avoit si souvent appelés à la liberté. Ils reposoient encore en paix, ignorant le danger de leur legislateur. Le tumulte de l'execution et la flamme du bûcher réveillèrent les Romains; ils s'armèrent, ils accoururent, mais trop tard; et les cohortes du pape repoussèrent, avec leurs lances, ceux qui, n'ayant pu sauver Arnaud, vouloient du moins recueillir ses cendres comme de précieuses reliques."[1]

F   *Spoke with the voice of ages past.* (1.72)

"Posterity will compare the virtues and failings of this extraordinary man; but in a long period of anarchy and servitude, the name of Rienzi has often been celebrated as the deliverer of his country, and the last of the Roman patriots." — *Gibbon's Decline and Fall, &c.* vol. xii. page 362.[2]

G   *Couldst gaze on Rome—yet not despair!* (1.86)

"Le consul Terentius Varron avoit fui honteusement jusqu'à Venouse: cet homme de la plus basse naissance, n'avoit été élevé au consulat que pour mortifier la noblesse: mais le sénat ne voulut pas jouir de ce malheureux triomphe; il vit

---

1   from Sismondi, *Histoire des Républiques Italiennes du moyen age*, vol. 2 (1809), 68–69: "The prefect remained in the Castel Sant'Angelo with his prisoner; he had him transported one morning to the square where executions took place, before the Porta del Popolo. Arnaud de Brescia was placed upon the pyre and tied to the stake, opposite the Corso. From there he could look down the three long streets that led to his scaffold; they extend through almost half of Rome. There lived the men he had so often called to freedom. They still reposed in peace, unaware of the danger to their ruler. The tumult of the execution and the flames of the pyre woke up the Romans; they took up arms and ran to the spot, but too late; and the cohorts of the Pope used their lances to force back those who, having failed to save Arnaud, at least wanted to gather his ashes as precious relics." Arnaldo da Brescia (?1100–55): Italian reformer, angered by corruption in the clergy, led a popular revolt against the Bishop of Brescia; exiled by the Second Lateran Council, he was betrayed by Frederick I and burned at the stake in Rome.

2   from ch. 70 (3.842 in Modern Library Edition, New York).

combien il étoit nécessaire qu'il s'attirât dans cette occasion la confiance du peuple, il alla au-devant Varron, et le remercia de ce *qu'il n'avoit pas désespéré de la republique.*" —*Montesquieu's Grandeur et Decadence des Romains.*[1]

H   *Vain dream! the sacred shields are gone.* (1.217)

Of the sacred bucklers, or ancilia of Rome, which were kept in the temple of Mars, Plutarch gives the following account. "In the eighth year of Numa's reign a pestilence prevailed in Italy; Rome also felt its ravages. While the people were greatly dejected, we are told that a brazen buckler fell from heaven into the hands of Numa. Of this he gave a very wonderful account, received from Egeria and the Muses: that the buckler was sent down for the preservation of the city, and should be kept with great care: that eleven others should be made as like it as possible in size and fashion, in order that if any person were disposed to steal it, he might not be able to distinguish that which fell from heaven from the rest. He further declared, that the place, and the meadows about it, where he frequently conversed with the Muses, should be consecrated to those divinities; and that the spring which watered the ground should be sacred to the use of the Vestal Virgins,[2] daily to sprinkle and purify their temple. The immediate cessation of the pestilence is said to have confirmed the truth of this account." —*Life of Numa.*[3]

---

1   from Charles Louis de Secondat, Baron de la Brede et de Montesquieu (1689-1755), *Considérations sur les causes de la grandeur et de la décadence des Romains* (1734), ch. 4, Hemans's emphasis; the book is a major essay in the philosophy of history, and, like Gibbon's *Decline and Fall of the Roman Empire*, is an oblique critique of 18th-century European court monarchies; translated:"... Terentius Varro the consul had fled ignominiously as far as Venusia: this man, whose extraction was very mean, had been raised to the consulship merely to mortify the nobles. However the Senate would not enjoy the unhappy triumph: they saw how necessary it was for them to gain the confidence of the people on this occasion; they therefore went out to meet Varro, and returned him thanks for not despairing of the safety of the commonwealth." (*Reflections on the Causes of the Rise and Fall of the Roman Empire*, Oxford, 1825)

2   Virgins] attendants of Vesta, Roman goddess of hearth and home.

3   from the translation by John and William Langhorne (London, 1770, vol. 1, 170-71) of the life of Numa in *Parallel Lives* by Plutarch (*c.* AD 46-120), a Greek teacher and biographer whose work was widely read over the centuries as ethical philosophy,

I   *Sunk is the crowning city's throne.* (1.218)

"Who hath taken this counsel against Tyre, the *crowning city,* whose merchants are princes, whose traffickers are the honourable of the earth?" —*Isaiah*, chap. 23.[1]

J   *Their guardian spells, have long been past.* (1.220)

"Un mélange bizarre de grandeur d'ame, et de foiblesse entroit dès cette époque, (l'onzième siècle) dans le caractère des Romains. —Un mouvement généreux vers les grandes choses faisoit place tout-à-coup à l'abattement; ils passoient de la liberté la plus orageuse, à la servitude la plus avilissante. On auroit dit que les ruines et les portiques déserts de la capitale du monde, entretenoient ses habitans dans le sentiment de leur impuissance; au milieu de ces monumens de leur domination passée, les citoyens éprouvoient d'une manière trop décourageante leur propre nullité. Le nom des Romains qu'ils portoient ranimoit fréquemment leur enthousiasme, comme il le ranime encore aujourd'hui; mais bientôt la vue de Rome, du forum désert, des sept collines de nouveau rendues au pâturage des troupeaux, des temples désolés, des monumens tombant en ruine, les ramenoit à sentir qu'ils n'étoient plus les Romains d'autrefois." —*Sismondi, Histoire des Républiques Italiennes,* vol. I. p. 172.[2]

---

statesman's manual, and source of classical republicanism; Numa Pompilius (715-672 BC) was a legendary elected king of Rome, credited with founding many of Rome's religious and political institutions.

1 from the Bible, book of Isaiah (23.8), where the prophet foretells the fall of the commercial empire of Tyre, a city on the east coast of the Mediterranean; Hemans's emphasis.

2 translated: "A strange mixture of greatness of soul and of weakness entered the Roman character from that era [the 11th century]. A generous urge towards great things would suddenly give way to dejection; they went from the most tempestuous freedom to the most degrading servitude. It was as if the deserted ruins and gateways of the world's capital city kept alive within its inhabitants the sense of their own impotence; in the middle of these monuments to their former dominance, the citizens were too dispiritingly aware of their own worthlessness. The fact that they bore the name of Romans often revived their enthusiasm, as it still does today, but soon the sight of Rome, of the deserted forum, of the seven hills returned again to grazing land for the herds, of the abandoned temples, of the monuments falling into ruin, brought back the feeling that they were no longer the Romans of yesteryear."

K   *Linger'd the lord of eloquence?* (2.20)

"As for Cicero, he was carried to Astyra, where, finding a vessel, he immediately went on board, and coasted along to Circæum with a favourable wind. The pilots were preparing immediately to sail from thence, but whether it was that he feared the sea, or had not yet given up all his hopes in Cæsar, he disembarked, and travelled a hundred furlongs on foot, as if Rome had been the place of his destination. Repenting, however, afterwards, he left that road, and made again for the sea. He passed the night in the most perplexing and horrid thoughts; insomuch, that he was sometimes inclined to go privately into Cæsar's house and stab himself upon the altar of his domestic gods, to bring the divine vengeance upon his betrayer. But he was deterred from this by the fear of torture. Other alternatives, equally distressful, presented themselves. At last, he put himself in the hands of his servants, and ordered them to carry him by sea to Cajeta, where he had a delightful retreat in the summer, when the Etesian winds set in. There was a temple of Apollo on that coast, from which a flight of crows came with great noise towards Cicero's vessel as it was making land. They perched on both sides the sail-yard, where some sat croaking, and others pecking the ends of the ropes. All looked upon this as an ill omen; yet Cicero went on shore, and, entering his house, lay down to repose himself. In the mean time a number of the crows settled in the chamber-window, and croaked in the most doleful manner. One of them even entered it, and alighting on the bed, attempted, with its beak, to draw off the clothes with which he had covered his face. On sight of this, the servants began to reproach themselves. 'Shall we,' said they, 'remain to be spectators of our master's murder? Shall we not protect him, so innocent and so great a sufferer as he is, when the brute creatures give him marks of their care and attention?' Then partly by entreaty, partly by force, they got him into his litter, and carried him towards the sea." —*Plutarch. Life of Cicero.*[1]

---

1   from the Langhornes' translation of Plutarch's *Parallel Lives* (5.324-25); Marcus Tullius Cicero (106-43 BC) was an orator and ethical philosopher of late republican Rome and one of the most influential Latin writers in western European culture.

L   *Balm for all sadness but despair?* (2.28)
       "Now purer air
      Meets his approach, and to the heart inspires
      Vernal delight and joy, able to drive
      All sadness but despair." —*Milton*.[1]

M   *O'er bending oaks the north-wind swells.* (2.56)
     Mount Gargano. "This ridge of mountains forms a very
large promontory advancing into the Adriatic, and separated
from the Apennines on the west by the plains of Lucera and
San Severo. We took a ride into the heart of the mountains
through shady dells and noble woods, which brought to our
minds the venerable groves, that in ancient times bent with the
loud winds sweeping along the rugged sides of Garganus.
        'Aquilonibus
        Querceta Gargani laborant
        Et foliis viduantur orni.' —*Horace*.[2]

    "There is still a respectable forest of evergreen and common
oak, pine, hornbeam, chesnut,[3] and manna-ash. The sheltered
valleys are industriously cultivated, and seem to be blest with
luxuriant vegetation." —*Swinburne's Travels*.[4]

N   *There "bright appearances" have smiled.* (2.64)

    "In yonder nether world where shall I seek
    His bright appearances, or footstep trace?"
                          —*Milton*.[5]

---

1   from *Paradise Lost*, 4.153-156, describing Satan's feelings approaching Eden.

2   Quintus Horatius Flaccus (65-8 BC), major Roman lyrical and satirical poet; the
    verse is from his *Carmen* (*Odes*), book 2, number 9 ("To Valgius"), line 6, translated
    by Lord Lytton: "Nor on lofty Garganus the loud-groaning oaks / Wrestle, rocked
    to and fro with the blasts of the north, / Nor the ash-trees droop widowed of
    leaves."

3   chesnut] the usual spelling for "chestnut" until about 1820

4   from Henry Swinburne, *Travels in the Two Sicilies … in the Years 1777, 1778, 1779, and
    1780*, 2 vols (London, 1785), 1.155-56.

5   *Paradise Lost*, ll.328-29; after his expulsion from Eden into a fallen world, Adam
    laments to the archangel Michael that he will be unable to show Eden to his chil-
    dren, as the place where God had visited him, or to find God's traces in the world.

THE WIFE OF ASDRUBAL.[1]

"This governor, who had braved death when it was at a distance, and protested that the sun should never see him survive Carthage, this fierce Asdrubal, was so mean-spirited, as to come alone, and privately throw himself at the conqueror's feet. The general, pleased to see his proud rival humbled, granted his life, and kept him to grace his triumph.[2] The Carthaginians in the citadel no sooner understood that their commander had abandoned the place, than they threw open the gates, and put the proconsul in possession of Byrsa. The Romans had now no enemy to contend with but the nine hundred deserters, who, being reduced to despair, retired into the temple of Esculapius, which was a second citadel within the first: there the proconsul attacked them; and these unhappy wretches, finding there was no way to escape, set fire to the temple. As the flames spread, they retreated from one part to another, till they got to the roof of the building: there Asdrubal's wife appeared in her best apparel, as if the day of her death had been a day of triumph; and after having uttered the most bitter imprecations against her husband, whom she saw standing below with Emilianus,— 'Base Coward!' said she, 'the mean things thou hast done to save thy life shall not avail thee; thou shalt die this instant, at least in thy two children.' Having thus spoken, she drew out a dagger, stabbed them both, and while they were yet struggling for life, threw them from the top of the temple, and leaped down after them into the flames."

—*Ancient Universal History.*[3]

---

1   set during the Punic wars of the 3rd and 2nd centuries BC between Rome and Carthage for dominance of the Mediterranean; in the final siege of Carthage in 146 BC, its leader Hasdrubal held the fortified temple of Eshmun (Esculapius), but surrendered to the Roman general, Scipio Æmilianus, to save himself; after the city's fall, surviving Carthaginians were enslaved and the Romans obliterated all trace of their former rival; Hasdrubal lived comfortably as a state prisoner in Italy.

2   triumph] victorious Roman generals could be awarded a triumph, or victory parade through Rome, displaying enemy prisoners and spoils.

3   Hemans's preface; passage from *An Universal History, from the Earliest Account of Time to the Present ...; The Ancient Part* (7 vols, London, 1736-44), vol. 4 (1739), p. 778.

THE sun sets brightly — but a ruddier glow
O'er Afric's heaven the flames of Carthage throw;
Her walls have sunk, and pyramids of fire
In lurid splendor from her domes aspire;
5   Sway'd by the wind, they wave — while glares the sky
As when the desert's red Simoom[1] is nigh;
The sculptured altar, and the pillar'd hall,
Shine out in dreadful brightness ere they fall;
Far o'er the seas the light of ruin streams,
10   Rock, wave, and isle, are crimson'd by its beams;
While captive thousands, bound in Roman chains,
Gaze in mute horror on their burning fanes;[2]
And shouts of triumph, echoing far around,
Swell from the victor's tents with ivy crown'd.[3]
15   But mark! from yon fair temple's loftiest height
What towering form bursts wildly on the sight,
All regal in magnificent attire,
And sternly beauteous in terrific[4] ire?
She might be deem'd a Pythia[5] in the hour
20   Of dread communion and delirious power;
A being more than earthly, in whose eye
There dwells a strange and fierce ascendancy.
The flames are gathering round — intensely bright,
Full on her features glares their meteor-light,
25   But a wild courage sits triumphant there,
The stormy grandeur of a proud despair;
A daring spirit, in its woes elate,
Mightier than death, untameable by fate.
The dark profusion of her locks unbound,
30   Waves like a warrior's floating plumage round;
Flush'd is her cheek, inspired her haughty mien,
She seems th' avenging goddess of the scene.

---

1   Simoom] a hot dry wind from Africa.
2   fanes] temples, a common poeticism.
3   It was a Roman custom to adorn the tents of victors with ivy. [Hemans's footnote]
4   terrific] here, inspiring terror, the usual sense in Hemans's day.
5   priestess at the oracle of the god Apollo at Delphi in Greece; she would go into a
    trance and answer questions about the future by communing with the oracle, or
    spirit of the god.

Are those *her* infants, that with suppliant-cry
Cling round her, shrinking as the flame draws nigh,
Clasp with their feeble hands her gorgeous[1] vest,   35
And fain would rush for shelter to her breast?
Is that a mother's glance, where stern disdain,
And passion awfully[2] vindictive, reign?

Fix'd is her eye on Asdrubal, who stands,
Ignobly safe, amidst the conquering bands;   40
On him, who left her to that burning tomb,
Alone to share her children's martyrdom;
Who when his country perish'd, fled the strife,
And knelt to win the worthless boon of life.
"Live, traitor, live!" she cries, "since dear to thee,   45
E'en in thy fetters, can existence be!
Scorn'd and dishonour'd, live! — with blasted name,
The Roman's triumph not to grace, but shame.
O slave in spirit! bitter be thy chain
With tenfold anguish to avenge my pain!   50
Still may the manès[3] of thy children rise
To chase calm slumber from thy wearied eyes;
Still may their voices on the haunted air
In fearful whispers tell thee to despair,
Till vain remorse thy wither'd heart consume,   55
Scourged by relentless shadows of the tomb!
E'en now my sons shall die—and thou, their sire,
In bondage safe, shalt yet in them expire.
Think'st thou I love them not?—'Twas thine to fly—
'Tis mine with these to suffer and to die.   60
Behold their fate!—the arms that cannot save
Have been their cradle, and shall be their grave."
Bright in her hand the lifted dagger gleams,
Swift from her children's hearts the life-blood streams;

---

1 gorgeous] here, richly and colourfully adorned, perhaps meant to indicate that she
   belongs to a non-Roman, non-European, "exotic" race.
2 awfully] here, awe-inspiringly.
3 manès] normally the deified souls of ancestors, supposed to protect their living rel-
   atives.

65   With frantic laugh she clasps them to the breast
    Whose woes and passions soon shall be at rest;
    Lifts one appealing, frenzied glance on high,
    Then deep midst rolling flames is lost to mortal eye.

FROM *A SELECTION OF WELSH AIRS*
(1822)

THE ROCK OF CADER-IDRIS.[1]

A i r —*"The Ash Grove."*[2]

I.

I lay on that rock where the storms have their dwelling,
The birth-place of phantoms, the home of the cloud;
Around it for ever deep music is swelling,
The voice of the mountain-wind, solemn and loud.
'Twas a midnight of shadows all fitfully streaming,   5
Of wild waves and breezes,[3] that mingled their moan,
Of dim shrouded stars, at brief intervals gleaming,
And I felt, midst a world of dread grandeur, alone![4]

II.

I lay there in silence—a spirit came o'er me,
Man's tongue hath no language to speak what I saw!   10
Things glorious, unearthly, pass'd floating before me,
And my heart almost fainted with rapture and awe!
I view'd the dread beings, around us that hover,
Tho' veil'd by the mists of Mortality's breath,
I call'd upon Darkness the vision to cover,   15
For a strife was within me of madness and Death![5]

---

1   later republished in the *New Monthly Magazine* 40 (1834), with slight differences in
    punctuation and some substantive changes; for context and commentary, see Intro-
    duction, pp. 32-3.
2   omitted in *NMM*.
3   waves and breezes] *NMM*: gusts and torrents
4   in *NMM* the line reads: And my strife with stern nature was darksome and lone.
5   in *NMM* the line reads: For within me was battling of madness and death!

III.

I saw them—the powers of the wind and ocean,[1]
The rush of whose pinion bears onward the storms;[2]
Like a sweep of the proud-crested[3] wave was their motion,
20   I felt their deep[4] presence—but knew not their forms![5]
I saw them—the mighty of ages departed,
The dead were around me that night on the hill;
From their eyes, as they pass'd, a cold radiance they darted,
—There was light on my soul, but my heart's blood was chill!

IV.

25   I saw what man looks on, and dies!—but my spirit
Was strong, and triumphantly liv'd thro' that hour!
And as from the grave, I awoke to inherit
A flame all immortal, a voice and a power!
Day burst on that rock with the purple cloud crested,
30   And high Cader-Idris rejoic'd in the sun;
But, oh! what new glory all nature invested,
When the sense, which gives *soul* to her beauty, was won![6]

There is a popular Welsh tradition, that on the summit of Cader-Idris, one of the highest mountains in North Wales, is an excavation in the rock resembling a couch, and that who-ever should pass a night in that seat, would be found in the morning either dead, raving mad, or endowed with supernatur-al genius. —*See* DAVIS's *Celtic Researches.*[7]

---

1   ocean] *NMM*: the Ocean
2   storms] *NMM*: storm
3   a sweep of the proud-crested] *NMM*: the sweep of the white-rolling
4   deep] *NMM*: dread
5   forms!] *NMM*: form.
6   One of the Welsh poetical Triads thus describes the attributes of Genius: – "The three primary requisites of genius: an eye that can see nature, a heart that can feel nature, and boldness that dares follow nature." [Hemans's footnote]
7   Edward Davies (1756-1831), *Celtic Researches, on the Origin, Traditions and Language, of the Ancient Britons; with some Introductory Sketches, on Primitive Society* (1804); in the *NMM* text the postscript is worded slightly differently and placed as a headnote, and lacks the reference to Davies.

FROM *THE SIEGE OF VALENCIA:*
A DRAMATIC POEM;
THE LAST CONSTANTINE:
WITH OTHER POEMS (1823)

FROM "THE SIEGE OF VALENCIA: A DRAMATIC POEM":[1]

FROM SCENE I:

[Gonzalez, governor of Valencia, has learned that the besieging Moors have captured his sons and will execute them unless he surrenders the city; he speaks to his wife Elmina and daughter Ximena]

ELMINA.
Gonzalez, *who* must die?

GONZALEZ (*hurriedly*).
They on whose lives a fearful price is set,
But to be paid by treason! — Is't enough?
Or must I yet seek words?

ELMINA.
That look saith more!
Thou canst not mean——

GONZALEZ.   235
I do! why dwells there not
Power in a glance to speak it? — They must die!
They — must their names be told — *Our sons* must die
Unless I yield the city!

---

1 in her prefatory "Advertisement" Hemans associates the drama with the historical Moorish siege of Valencia, ruled by "El Cid," in the 1090s, and she uses names from the literature of El Cid; see notes to "Songs of the Cid"; for context and commentary, see Introduction, pp. 33-5.

XIMENA.

Oh I look up!
240   My mother, sink not thus!—Until the grave
Shut from our sight its victims, there is hope.

ELMINA (*in a low voice*).

Whose knell was in the breeze?—No, no, not *theirs!*
Whose was the blessed voice that spoke of hope?
—And there *is* hope!—I will not be subdued—
245   I will not hear a whisper of despair!
For Nature is all-powerful, and her breath
Moves like a quickening spirit o'er the depths
Within a father's heart.—Thou too, Gonzalez,
Wilt tell me there is hope!

GONZALEZ (*solemnly*).

Hope but in Him
250   Who bade the patriarch lay his fair young son
Bound on the shrine of sacrifice, and when
The bright steel quiver'd in the father's hand
Just raised to strike, sent forth his awful voice
Through the still clouds, and on the breathless air,
255   Commanding to withhold![1]—Earth has no hope,
It rests with Him.

ELMINA.

Thou canst not tell me this!
Thou father of my sons, within whose hands
Doth lie thy children's fate.

GONZALEZ.

If there have been
Men in whose bosoms Nature's voice hath made
260   Its accents as the solitary sound
Of an o'erpowering torrent, silencing

---

1   in the Bible, God commands the patriarch Abraham to sacrifice his son instead of a
sheep, to test Abraham's faith, but revokes the command at the last moment (Gene-
sis ch. 22).

Th' austere and yet divine remonstrances
Whisper'd by faith and honour, lift thy hands,
And, to that Heaven, which arms the brave with strength,
Pray, that the father of thy sons may ne'er   265
Be thus found wanting!

ELMINA.
                    Then their doom is seal'd!
Thou wilt not save thy children?

GONZALEZ.
                    Hast thou cause,
Wife of my youth! to deem it lies within
The bounds of possible things, that I should link
My name to that word—*traitor?*—They that sleep   270
On their proud battle-fields, thy sires and mine,
Died not for this!

ELMINA.
                    Oh, cold and hard of heart!
Thou shouldst be born for empire, since thy soul
Thus lightly from all human bonds can free
Its haughty flight!—Men! men! too much is yours   275
Of vantage; ye, that with a sound, a breath,
A shadow, thus can fill the desolate space
Of rooted up affections, o'er whose void
Our yearning hearts must wither!—So it is,
Dominion must be won!—Nay, leave me not—   280
My heart is bursting, and I *must* be heard!
Heaven hath given power to mortal agony
As to the elements in their hour of might
And mastery o'er creation!—Who shall dare
To mock that fearful strength?—I *must* be heard!   285
Give me my sons!

GONZALEZ.
                    That they may live to hide
With covering hands th' indignant flush of shame
On their young brows, when men shall speak of him

They call'd their father! — Was the oath, whereby,
290 On th' altar of my faith, I bound myself,
With an unswerving spirit to maintain
This free and christian city for my God,
And for my king, a writing traced on sand?
That passionate tears should wash it from the earth,
295 Or e'en the life-drops of a bleeding heart
Efface it, as a billow sweeps away
The last light vessel's wake? — Then never more
Let man's deep vows be trusted! — though enforced
By all th' appeals of high remembrances,
300 And silent claims o' th' sepulchres, wherein
His fathers with their stainless glory sleep,
On their good swords! Thinkst thou *I* feel no pangs?
He that hath given me sons, doth know the heart
Whose treasure she recalls. — Of this no more.
305 'Tis vain. I tell thee that th' inviolate cross
Still, from our ancient temples, must look up
Through the blue heavens of Spain, though at its foot
I perish, with my race.[1] Thou *darest* not ask
That I, the son of warriors — men who died
310 To fix it on that proud supremacy —
Should tear the sign of our victorious faith,
From its high place of sunbeams, for the Moor
In impious joy to trample!

ELMINA.
                              Scorn me not
In mine extreme of misery! — Thou art strong —
315 Thy heart is not as mine. — My brain grows wild;
I know not what I ask! — And yet 'twere but
Anticipating fate — since it must fall,
That cross *must* fall at last! There is no power,
No hope within this city of the grave,
320 To keep its place on high. Her sultry air
Breathes heavily of death, her warriors sink
Beneath their ancient banners, ere the Moor

---

1 race] here, family in an extended sense.

Hath bent his bow against them; for the shaft
Of pestilence flies more swiftly to its mark,
Than the arrow of the desert. Ev'n the skies   325
O'erhang the desolate splendour of her domes
With an ill omen's aspect, shaping forth,
From the dull clouds, wild menacing forms and signs
Foreboding ruin. *Man* might be withstood,
But who shall cope with famine and disease,   330
When leagued with armed foes? — Where now the aid,
Where the long-promised lances of Castile?[1]
— We are forsaken, in our utmost need,
By heaven and earth forsaken!

GONZALEZ.

                              If this be,
(And yet I will not deem it) we must fall   335
As men that in severe devotedness
Have chosen their part, and bound themselves to death,
Through high conviction that their suffering land,
By the free blood of martyrdom alone,
Shall call deliverance down.

ELMINA.

                              Oh! I have stood   340
Beside thee through the beating storms of life,
With the true heart of unrepining love,
As the poor peasant's mate doth cheerily,
In the parch'd vineyard, or the harvest-field,
Bearing her part, sustain with him the heat   345
And burden of the day;—But now the hour,
The heavy hour is come, when human strength
Sinks down, a toil-worn pilgrim, in the dust,
Owning that woe is mightier! —Spare me yet
This bitter cup, my husband! —Let not her,   350
The mother of the lovely, sit and mourn
In her unpeopled home, a broken stem,
O'er its fall'n roses dying!

---

1 Castile] kingdom in north-west Spain that led the long campaign of Christian
   forces to expel the Moors, completed in 1492.

GONZALEZ.

Urge me not,
Thou that through all sharp conflicts hast been found
Worthy a brave man's love, oh! urge me not
To guilt, which through the midst of blinding tears,
In its own hues thou seest not! — Death may scarce
Bring aught like this!

ELMINA.

All, all thy gentle race,
The beautiful beings that around thee grew,
Creatures of sunshine! Wilt thou doom them all?
— She too, thy daughter — doth her smile unmark'd
Pass from thee, with its radiance, day by day?
Shadows are gathering round her — seest thou not?
The misty dimness of the spoiler's breath
Hangs o'er her beauty, and the face which made
The summer of our hearts, now doth but send,
With every glance, deep bodings through the soul,
Telling of early fate.

GONZALEZ.

I see a change
Far nobler on her brow! — She is as one,
Who, at the trumpet's sudden call, hath risen
From the gay banquet, and in scorn cast down
The wine-cup, and the garland, and the lute
Of festal hours, for the good spear and helm,
Beseeming sterner tasks. — Her eye hath lost
The beam which laugh'd upon th' awakening heart,
E'en as morn breaks o'er earth. But far within
Its full dark orb, a light hath sprung, whose source
Lies deeper in the soul. — And let the torch
Which but illumed the glittering pageant, fade!
The altar-flame, i' th' sanctuary's recess,
Burns quenchless, being of heaven! — She hath put on
Courage, and faith, and generous constancy,
Ev'n as a breastplate. — Aye, men look on her,
As she goes forth serenely to her tasks,

Binding the warrior's wounds, and bearing fresh   385
Cool draughts to fever'd lips; they look on her,
Thus moving in her beautiful array
Of gentle fortitude, and bless the fair
Majestic vision, and unmurmuring turn
Unto their heavy toils.

ELMINA.
                    And seest thou not   390
In that high faith and strong collectedness,
A fearful inspiration?—*They* have cause
To tremble, who behold th' unearthly light
Of high, and, it may be, prophetic thought,
Investing youth with grandeur!—From the grave   395
It rises, on whose shadowy brink thy child
Waits but a father's hand to snatch her back
Into the laughing sunshine.—Kneel with me,
Ximena, kneel beside me, and implore
That which a deeper, more prevailing voice   400
Than ours doth ask, and will not be denied;
—His children's lives!

XIMENA.
                    Alas! this may not be,
Mother!—I cannot.   [*Exit* XIMENA.

GONZALEZ.
                    My heroic child!
—A terrible sacrifice thou claim'st, O God!
From creatures in whose agonizing hearts   405
Nature is strong as death!

ELMINA.
                    Is't thus in thine?
Away!—what time is given thee to resolve
On?—what I cannot utter!—Speak! thou know'st
Too well what I would say.

GONZALEZ.
                    Until—ask not!
The time is brief.

ELMINA.
                    Thou saidst—I heard not right—

GONZALEZ.
The time is brief.

ELMINA.
                    What! must we burst all ties
Wherewith the thrilling chords of life are twined;
And, for this task's fulfilment, can it be
That man, in his cold heartlessness, hath dared
To number and to mete[1] us forth the sands
Of hours, nay, moments?—Why, the sentenced wretch,
He on whose soul there rests a brother's blood
Pour'd forth in slumber, is allow'd more time
To wean his turbulent passions from the world
His presence doth pollute!—It is not thus!
We must have Time to school us.

GONZALEZ.
                              We have but
To bow the head in silence, when Heaven's voice
Calls back the things we love.

ELMINA.
Love! love!—there are soft smiles and gentle words,
And there are faces, skilful to put on
The look we trust in—and 'tis mockery all!
—A faithless mist, a desert-vapour, wearing
The brightness of clear waters, thus to cheat
The thirst that semblance kindled!—There is none,
In all this cold and hollow world, no fount

---

1   mete] measure.

Of deep, strong, deathless love, save that within
A mother's heart. — It is but pride, wherewith
To his fair son the father's eye doth turn,
Watching his growth. Aye, on the boy he looks,
The bright glad creature springing in his path,   435
But as the heir of his great name, the young
And stately tree, whose rising strength ere long
Shall bear his trophies[1] well. — And this is love!
This is *man's* love! — What marvel? —*you* ne'er made
Your breast the pillow of his infancy,   440
While to the fulness of your heart's glad heavings
His fair cheek rose and fell; and his bright hair
Waved softly to your breath! —*You* ne'er kept watch
Beside him, till the last pale star had set,
And morn, all dazzling, as in triumph, broke   445
On your dim weary eye; not *yours* the face
Which, early faded thro' fond care for him,
Hung o'er his sleep, and, duly as Heaven's light,
Was there to greet his wakening! *You* ne'er smooth'd
His couch, ne'er sung him to his rosy rest,   450
Caught his least whisper, when his voice from yours
Had learn'd soft utterance; press'd your lip to his,
When fever parch'd it; hush'd his wayward cries,
With patient, vigilant, never-wearied love!
No! these are *woman's* tasks! — In these her youth,   455
And bloom of cheek, and buoyancy of heart,
Steal from her all unmark'd! — My boys! my boys!
Hath vain affection borne with all for this?
— Why were ye given me?

                    GONZALEZ.
                              Is there strength in man
Thus to endure? — That thou couldst read, thro' all   460
Its depths of silent agony, the heart
Thy voice of woe doth rend!

---

1   trophies] here, weaponry, banners, etc. taken in battle.

ELMINA.

Thy heart!—*thy* heart!—Away! it feels not *now*!
But an hour comes to tame the mighty man
465 Unto the infant's weakness; nor shall Heaven
Spare you that bitter chastening!—May you live
To be alone, when loneliness doth seem
Most heavy to sustain!—For me, my voice
Of prayer and fruitless weeping shall be soon
470 With all forgotten sounds; my quiet place
Low with my lovely ones, and we shall sleep,
Tho' kings lead armies o'er us, we shall sleep,
Wrapt in earth's covering mantle!—you the while
Shall sit within your vast, forsaken halls,
475 And hear the wild and melancholy winds
Moan thro' their drooping banners, never more
To wave above your race. Aye, then call up
Shadows—dim phantoms from ancestral tombs,
But all—all *glorious*—conquerors, chieftains, kings—
480 To people that cold void!—And when the strength
From your right arm hath melted, when the blast
Of the shrill clarion gives your heart no more
A fiery wakening; if at last you pine
For the glad voices, and the bounding steps,
485 Once thro' your home re-echoing, and the clasp
Of twining arms, and all the joyous light
Of eyes that laugh'd with youth, and made your board
A place of sunshine;—When those days are come,
Then, in your utter desolation, turn
490 To the cold world, the smiling, faithless world,
Which hath swept past you long, and bid it quench
Your soul's deep thirst with *fame!* immortal *fame!*
Fame to the sick of heart!—a gorgeous robe,
A crown of victory, unto him that dies
I' th' burning waste, for water!

GONZALEZ.

495   This from *thee!*
Now the last drop of bitterness is pour'd.

Elmina—I forgive thee!   [*Exit* ELMINA.
                    Aid me, Heaven!
From whom alone is power!—Oh! thou hast set
Duties, so stern of aspect, in my path,
They almost, to my startled gaze, assume   500
The hue of things less hallow'd! Men have sunk
Unblamed beneath such trials!—Doth not He
Who made us know the limits of our strength?
My wife! my sons!—Away! I must not pause
To give my heart one moment's mastery thus! [*Exit*
    GONZALEZ.

FROM SCENE 6:

[the citizens of Valencia have met to discuss bargaining with
the besieging Moors to have their city spared; Ximena, daugh-
ter of the city's governor, Alvar Gonzalez, appears.]

XIMENA *enters, with Attendants carrying a Banner.*

XIMENA.
Men of Valencia! in an hour like this,
What do ye here?

A CITIZEN.
We die!

XIMENA.
                    Brave men die *now*
Girt for the toil, as travellers suddenly   60
By the dark night o'ertaken on their way!
These days require such death!—It is too much
Of luxury for our wild and angry times,
To fold the mantle round us, and to sink
From life, as flowers that shut up silently,   65
When the sun's heat doth scorch them!—Hear ye not?

A CITIZEN.

Lady! what wouldst thou with us?

XIMENA.

Rise and arm!
E'en now the children of your chief are led
Forth by the Moor[1] to perish! — Shall this be,
70   Shall the high sound of such a name be hush'd,
I' th' land to which for ages it hath been
A battle-word, as 'twere some passing note
Of shepherd-music? — Must this work be done,
And ye lie pining here, as men in whom
75   The pulse which God hath made for noble thought
Can so be thrill'd no longer?

A CITIZEN.

'Tis even so!
Sickness, and toil, and grief, have breath'd upon us,
Our hearts beat faint and low.

XIMENA.

Are ye so poor
Of soul, my countrymen! that ye can draw
80   Strength from no deeper source than that which sends
The red blood mantling[2] through the joyous veins,
And gives the fleet step wings? — Why, how have age
And sensitive womanhood ere now endured,
Through pangs of searching fire, in some proud cause,
85   Blessing that agony? — Think ye the Power
Which bore them nobly up, as if to teach
The torturer where eternal Heaven had set
Bounds to his sway, was earthy, of this earth,
This dull mortality? — Nay, then look on me!
90   Death's touch hath mark'd me, and I stand amongst you,
As one whose place, i' th' sunshine of your world,

---

1   Moor] general term for a Muslim north African, though Moors had inhabited and
    ruled parts of Spain for centuries.
2   mantling] here, causing to blush, as from drinking wine.

Shall soon be left to fill!—I say, the breath
Of th' incense, floating through yon fane,[1] shall scarce
Pass from your path before me! But even now,
I have that within me, kindling through the dust,   95
Which from all time hath made high deeds its voice
And token to the nations;—Look on me!
Why hath Heaven pour'd forth courage, as a flame
Wasting the womanish heart, which must be still'd
Yet sooner for its swift consuming brightness,   100
If not to shame your doubt, and your despair,
And your soul's torpor?—yet, arise and arm!
It may not be too late.

A CITIZEN.

                        Why, what are we,
To cope with hosts?—Thus faint, and worn, and few,
O'ernumber'd and forsaken, is't for us   105
To stand against the mighty?

XIMENA.

                        And for whom
Hath He, who shakes the mighty with a breath
From their high places, made the fearfulness,
And ever-wakeful presence of his power,
To the pale startled earth most manifest,   110
But for the weak?—Was't for the helm'd[2] and crown'd
That suns were stay'd at noonday?—Stormy seas
As a rill parted?—Mail'd archangels sent
To wither up the strength of kings with death?[3]
—I tell you, if these marvels have been done,   115
'Twas for the wearied and th' oppress'd of men,
They needed such!—And generous faith hath power
By her prevailing spirit, e'en yet to work
Deliverances, whose tale shall live with those

---

1   church.
2   helm'd] helmeted.
3   ll. 55-8 refer to God's interventions on behalf of his chosen people, the Israelites,
    described in the Bible, and including the parting of the waters of the Red Sea so
    that the Israelites could escape from their bondage in Egypt (Exodus ch. 14).

Of the great elder time! — Be of good heart!
120   *Who* is forsaken? — He that gives the thought
A place within his breast! — 'Tis not for you.
— Know ye this banner?

CITIZENS (*murmuring to each other*).
                    Is she not inspired?
Doth not Heaven call us by her fervent voice?

XIMENA.
Know ye this banner?

CITIZENS.
                    'Tis the Cid's.[1]

XIMENA.
125   The Cid's!
Who breathes that name but in th' exulting tone
Which the heart rings to? — Why, the very wind
As it swells out the noble standard's fold
Hath a triumphant sound! — The Cid's! — it moved
130   Even as a sign of victory through the land,
From the free skies ne'er stooping to a foe!

OLD CITIZENS.
Can ye still pause, my brethren? — Oh! that youth
Through this worn frame were kindling once again!

XIMENA.
Ye linger still? — Upon this very air,
135   He that was born in happy hour for Spain[2]
Pour'd forth his conquering spirit! — 'Twas the breeze
From your own mountains which came down to wave

---

1   for El Cid see note to title of Hemans's "Songs of the Cid"; Ximena goes on to
     remind the citizens of his legendary ghostly interventions in the long struggle
     between Christian Spaniards and Moorish kingdoms and invaders of Spain.
2   "El que en buen hora nasco;" he that was born in happy hour. An appellation
     given to the Cid in the ancient chronicles. [Hemans's endnote]

The banner of his battles, as it droop'd
Above the champion's death-bed. Nor even then
Its tale of glory closed. — They made no moan   140
O'er the dead hero, and no dirge was sung,[1]
But the deep tambour and shrill horn of war
Told when the mighty pass'd! — They wrapped him not
With the pale shroud, but braced the warrior's form
In war-array, and on his barbed steed,   145
As for a triumph, rear'd him; marching forth
In the hush'd midnight from Valencia's walls,
Beleaguer'd then, as now. All silently
The stately funeral moved: — but who was he
That follow'd, charging on the tall white horse,   150
And with the solemn standard, broad and pale,
Waving in sheets of snow-light? — And the cross,
The bloody cross, far-blazing from his shield,
And the fierce meteor-sword? — They fled, they fled!
The kings of Afric, with their countless hosts,   155
Were dust in his red path! — The scimetar
Was shiver'd as a reed! — for in that hour
The warrior-saint that keeps the watch for Spain,
Was arm'd betimes! — And o'er that fiery field
The Cid's high banner stream'd all joyously,   160
For still its lord was there!

      CITIZENS (*rising tumultuously*).
                    Even unto death
Again it shall be follow'd!

      XIMENA.
                Will he see
The noble stem hewn down, the beacon-light
Which his house for ages o'er the land
Hath shone through cloud and storm, thus quench'd
      at once?   165
Will he not aid his children in the hour

---

1 For this, and the subsequent allusions to Spanish legends, see *The Romances and Chronicles of the Cid*. [Hemans's endnote]

Of this their uttermost peril? — Awful power
Is with the holy dead, and there are times
When the tomb hath no chain they cannot burst?
170 — Is it a thing forgotten, how he woke
From the deep rest of old, remembering
Spain In her great danger? — At the night's mid-watch
How Leon[1] started, when the sound was heard
That shook her dark and hollow-echoing streets,
175 As with the heavy tramp of steel-clad men,
By thousands marching through! — For he had risen!
The Campeador[2] was on his march again,
And in his arms, and follow'd by his hosts
Of shadowy spearmen! — He had left the world
180 From which we are dimly parted, and gone forth,
And call'd his buried warriors from their sleep,
Gathering them round him to deliver Spain;
For Afric was upon her! — Morning broke —
Day rush'd through clouds of battle; — but at eve
185 Our God had triumph'd, and the rescued land
Sent up a shout of victory from the field,
That rock'd her ancient mountains.

THE CITIZENS.

Arm! to arms!
On to our chief! — We have strength within us yet
To die with our blood roused! — Now, be the word,
For the Cid's house!
[*They begin to arm themselves.*

XIMENA.
190 Ye know his battle-song?
The old rude strain wherewith his bands went forth
To strike down Paynim[3] swords!

(*She sings*)

---

1 Leon] capital of the feudal kingdom of the same name in north-west Spain, where
   El Cid was re-buried and where he (and even his horse) was venerated.
2 Campeador] El Cid.
3 Paynim] non-Christian, especially Muslim; a term from medieval romance.

The Moor is on his way!
With the tambour-peal and the tecbir-shout,[1]
And the horn o'er the blue seas ringing out,   195
   He hath marshall'd his dark array!

Shout through the vine-clad land!
That her sons on all their hills may hear,
And sharpen the point of the red wolf spear,
   And the sword for the brave man's hand!   200

(*The* CITIZENS *join in the song, while they continue arming themselves*).

Banners are in the field!
The chief must rise from his joyous board,
And turn from the feast ere the wine be pour'd,
   And take up his father's shield!

The Moor is on his way!   205
Let the peasant leave his olive-ground,
And the goats roam wild through the pine-woods round!
   —There is nobler work to-day!

Send forth the trumpet's call!
Till the bridegroom cast the goblet down,   210
And the marriage-robe and the flowery crown,
   And arm in the banquet-hall!

And stay the funeral-train!
Bid the chanted mass be hush'd awhile,
And the bier laid down in the holy aile,   215
   And the mourners girt for Spain!

(*They take up the banner, and follow* XIMENA *out*.

---

1   tecbir] a battle-cry glorifying Allah.

Their voices are heard gradually dying away
at a distance).

Ere night, must swords be red!
It is not an hour for knells and tears,
But for helmets braced, and serried spears!
    To-morrow for the dead!

The Cid is in array!
His steed is barbed, his plume waves high,
His banner is up in the sunny sky,
Now, joy for the Cross to-day!

FROM "OTHER POEMS":

SONGS OF THE CID.[1]

The following ballads are not translations from the Spanish, but are founded upon some of the "wild and wonderful" traditions preserved in the romances of that language, and the ancient poem of the Cid.[2]

---

1 Originally published in the *New Monthly Magazine*. [Hemans's footnote; text here from first book-form publication in *The Siege of Valencia ...* (1823); significant changes from magazine versions are noted; Hemans's misnumbering of her endnotes is corrected here and they are placed as footnotes and indicated as hers; El Cid (from an Arabic word meaning "leader") was a nickname of Rodrigo (or Ruy) Díaz de Vivar (*c.* 1043-), a Spanish feudal chief, also known as "Campeador" (l.2, from the Latin *campi doctor*, meaning "teacher of the battlefield," or "champion"); he fought as a freelance for christian and muslim rulers of different kingdoms in Spain and eventually seized Valencia for himself in 1094 and defended it against a new wave of muslim invaders from North Africa; he died in 1099 but his widow Jimena (or Ximena) held the city for a time before withdrawing to the family estates in north-west Spain, where he was re-buried; thereafter El Cid was made a legendary figure for christian and united Spain, celebrated in chronicles as well as popular ballads and romances; he entered wider European literature through Pierre Corneille's play *Le Cid* (1636), and by the late 18th and early 19th century he was made a figure for patriotic heroism, especially during the Peninsular War; for further context and commentary, see Introduction, pp. 36-8].

2 Hemans's prefatory note, referring to the *Poema de mio Cid*; earlier literature about El Cid was revived in the late 18th and early 19th century, in response to political

THE CID'S DEPARTURE INTO EXILE.[1]

WITH sixty knights in his gallant train,
Went forth the Campeador of Spain;
For wild sierras and plains afar,
He left the lands of his own Bivar.[2]

To march o'er field, and to watch in tent,   5
From his home in good Castile he went;
To the wasting siege and the battle's van,
— For the noble Cid was a banish'd man!

Through his olive-woods the morn-breeze play'd,
And his native streams wild music made,   10
And clear in the sunshine his vineyards lay,
When for march and combat he took his way.

With a thoughtful spirit his way he took,
And he turn'd his steed for a parting look,
For a parting look at his own fair towers;   15
— Oh! the Exile's heart hath weary hours!

The pennons were spread, and the band array'd,
But the Cid at the threshold a moment stay'd;

---

and social changes described in the editor's Introduction; the manuscript of the *Poema de mio Cid* (also known as the *Cantar de mio Cid*), a major early work, was first published in 1779, then redacted, amalgamated with other relevant works, and translated by Robert Southey in his *Chronicle of the Cid* (1808); a selection of Juan de Escobar's early collection, *Romancero e historia del muy valeroso cavallero el Cid* (1661), was republished in 1818, and early Cid material was translated by Johann Gottfried von Herder in *Der Cid: ... nach spanischen romanzen* (1805); the early Spanish *Romancero general*, or ballad anthology, contained *romances* about El Cid and was edited and arranged by the German writer Georg Bernhard Depping in 1817; this in turn was selected and freely translated by John Gibson Lockhart in *Ancient Spanish Ballads Historical and Romantic* (1823); in form and style, Hemans's "Songs of the Cid" resembles Lockhart's translations.

1 referring to an incident early in the *Poema de mio Cid*; supposedly as a result of court intrigue, the Cid was banished by King Alfonso of León, whom he had served as military leader.

2 BIVAR, the supposed birth-place of the Cid, was a castle, about two leagues from Burgos. [Hemans's endnote]

It *was* but a moment—the halls were lone,
And the gates of his dwelling all open thrown.

There was not a steed in the empty stall,
Nor a spear nor a cloak on the naked wall,
Nor a hawk on the perch, nor a seat at the door,
Nor the sound of a step on the hollow floor.[1]

25 Then a dim tear swell'd to the warrior's eye,
As the voice of his native groves went by;
And he said—"My foemen their wish have won—
—Now the will of God be in all things done!"

But the trumpet blew, with its note of cheer,
30 And the winds of the morning swept off the tear,
And the fields of his glory lay distant far,
—He is gone from the towers of his own Bivar!

THE CID'S DEATH BED.[2]

IT was an hour of grief and fear
Within Valencia's walls,

---

1   Tornaba la cabeza, e estabalos catando:
              Vio puertas abiertas, e uzos sin cañados,
              Alcandaras vacias, sin pielles e sin mantos:
              E sin falcones, e sin adtores mudados.
              Sospirò mio Cid.

                                    Poem of the Cid.

[Hemans's endnote; passage from beginning of surviving text of the *Poema de mio Cid*, describing the Cid's departure into exile: "... he turned his head and stood looking at them. He saw doors left open and gates unlocked, empty pegs without fur tunics or cloaks, perches without falcons or moulted hawks. The Cid sighed…"; *The Poem of the Cid*, ed. Ian Michael, translated by Rita Hamilton and Janet Perry, 1975, p. 23.]

2 first published with title "The Cid's Death-bed: a Ballad" in *New Monthly Magazine* 7 (April 1823): 307-8, with slight differences in punctuation and spelling; the poem parallels Southey's *Chronicle of the Cid* (1808), book 11, section 5, and resembles romance 95 in *Romancero e historia del muy valeroso cavallero El Cid Ruy Diaz de Vibar, en lenguage antiguo*, compiled by Juan de Escobar (Cadiz, 1702); both works were studied by Hemans.

When the blue spring-heaven lay still and clear
　　Above her marble halls.

There were pale cheeks and troubled eyes,　　　　　　5
　　And steps of hurrying feet,
Where the Zambra's[1] notes were wont to rise,
　　Along the sunny street.

It was an hour of fear and grief,
　　On bright Valencia's shore,　　　　　　　　　　10
For Death was busy with her chief,
　　The noble Campeador.

The Moor-king's barks were on the deep,
　　With sounds and signs of war,
For the Cid was passing to his sleep,　　　　　　　15
　　In the silent Alcazar.[2]

No moan was heard through the towers of state,
　　No weeper's aspect seen,
But by the couch Ximena sate,[3]
　　With pale, yet stedfast mien.[4]　　　　　　　　20

Stillness was round the leader's[5] bed,
　　Warriors stood mournful nigh,
And banners, o'er his glorious head,
　　Were drooping heavily.

1　The zambra, a Moorish dance. When Valencia was taken by the Cid, many of the
　　Moorish families chose to remain there, and reside under his government.
　　[Hemans's endnote; in *NMM* the footnote reads simply, "Zambra, a Moorish
　　dance." In fact, El Cid's rule of Valencia seems to have been harsh; with some
　　exceptions, religious persecution by either Muslims or Christians was not a promi-
　　nent characteristic of his period.]
2　Alcazar] a fortified palace.
3　sate] archaic spelling of sat.
4　The calm fortitude of Ximena is frequently alluded to in the romances. [Hemans's
　　endnote]
5　leader's] *NMM*: conqueror's

　　And feeble grew the conquering[1] hand,
　　　　And cold the valiant breast;
　　— He had fought the battles of the land,
　　　　And his hour was come to rest.

　　What said the Ruler[2] of the field?
　　　　— His voice is faint and low;
　　The breeze that creeps o'er his lance and shield
　　　　Hath louder accents now.

　　"Raise ye no cry, and let no moan
　　　　Be made when I depart;
　　The Moor must hear no dirge's tone,
　　　　Be ye of mighty[3] heart!

　　"Let the cymbal-clash and the trumpet-strain
　　　　From your walls ring far and shrill,
　　And fear ye not, for the saints of Spain
　　　　Shall grant you victory still.

　　"And gird my form with mail-array,
　　　　And set me on my steed,
　　So go ye forth on your funeral-way,
　　　　And God shall give you speed.[4]

　　"Go with the dead in the front of war,
　　　　All armed with sword and helm,
　　And march by the camp of King Bucar,[5]
　　　　For the good Castilian realm.

　　"And let me slumber in the soil
　　　　Which gave my fathers birth;

1　conquering] *NMM*: mighty
2　Ruler] *NMM*: leader
3　mighty] *NMM*: dauntless
4　speed] here, success
5　Bucar] possibly the Almoravide governor of Seville and Moorish general Ibn Abu Bekr, or Abu Bekr ibn Abd al-Aziz, emir of Valencia.

I have closed my day of battle-toil,
    And my course is done on earth."

—Now wave, ye glorious[1] banners, wave![2]
    Through the lattice a wind sweeps by,
And the arms, o'er the death-bed of the brave,   55
    Send forth a hollow sigh.

Now wave, ye banners of many a fight!
    As the fresh wind o'er you sweeps;
The wind and the banners fall hush'd as night,
    The Campeador—he sleeps!   60

Sound the battle-horn on the breeze of morn,
    And swell out the trumpet's blast,
Till the notes prevail o'er the voice of wail,
    For the noble Cid hath pass'd!

THE CID'S FUNERAL PROCESSION.[3]

THE Moor had beleaguer'd Valencia's towers,
And lances gleam'd up through her citron-bowers,[4]
And the tents of the desert had girt her plain,
And camels were trampling the vines of Spain;
    For the Cid was gone to rest.   5

---

1   glorious] *NMM*: stately.

2   Banderas antiguas, tristes.
                      De victorias un tiempo amadas,
                      Tremolando estan al viento
                      Y lloran aunque no hablan, &c.
    Herder's translation of these romances (Der Cid, nach Spanischen Romanzen besungen) are remarkable for their spirit and scrupulous fidelity. [Hemans's endnote; the passage translates: "Banners ancient and sad / from [a time of] once dear victories, / are fluttering in the wind, / and they grieve without speaking ..."; in *NMM* the footnote reads, "See the Spanish Ballad, "*Banderas antiguas, tristes, &c.*"]

3   first published in the *New Monthly Magazine* 7 (April 1823): 376-78, with slight differences in punctuation and spelling, and with a footnote to the title: "See the Legends recorded in Southey's Chronicle of the Cid." Hemans's poem parallels material in Southey's *Chronicle of the Cid*, book 11, sections 6-9, and is similar to romance 98 in Escobar's *Romancero*.

4   citron-bowers] citron formerly included lemon and lime, and is used often by Hemans to represent southern (non-English) landscape.

There were men from wilds where the death-wind sweeps,
There were spears from hills where the lion sleeps,
There were bows from sands where the ostrich runs,
For the shrill horn of Afric had call'd her sons
10   To the battles of the West.

The midnight bell, o'er the dim seas heard,
Like the roar of waters, the air had stirr'd;
The stars were shining o'er tower and wave,
And the camp lay hush'd, as a wizard's cave;
15   But the Christians woke[1] that night.

They rear'd the Cid on his barbed steed,
Like a warrior mail'd[2] for the hour of need,
And they fix'd the sword in the cold right hand,
Which had fought so well for his father's land,
20   And the shield from his neck hung bright.

There was arming heard in Valencia's halls,
There was vigil kept on the rampart walls;
Stars had not faded, nor clouds turn'd red,
When the knights had girded the noble dead,
25   And the burial-train moved out.

With a measured pace, as the pace of one,
Was the still death-march of the host begun;
With a silent step went the cuirass'd[3] bands,
Like a lion's tread on the burning sands,
30   And they gave no battle-shout.

When the first went forth, it was midnight deep,
In heaven was the moon, in the camp was sleep.
When the last through the city's gates had gone,
O'er tent and rampart the bright day shone,
35   With a sun-burst from the sea.[4]

---

1   woke] stayed awake, kept vigil.
2   mail'd] dressed in armour of chain-mail.
3   cuirass: body armour originally made of leather (French *cuir*).
4   sea.] *NMM*: sea!

There were knights five hundred went arm'd before,
And Bermudez[1] the Cid's green standard bore;[2]
To its last fair field, with the break of morn,
Was the glorious banner in silence borne,
    On the glad wind streaming free.   40

And the Campeador came stately then,
Like a leader circled with steel-clad men!
The helmet was down o'er the face of the dead,
But his steed went proud, by a warrior led,
    For he knew that the Cid was there.   45

He was there, the Cid, with his own good sword,
And Ximena following her noble lord;
Her eye was solemn, her step was slow,
But there rose not a sound of war or woe,
    Not a whisper on the air.   50

The halls in Valencia were still and lone,
The churches were empty, the masses done;
There was not a voice through the wide streets far,
Nor a foot-fall heard in the Alcazar,
    —So the burial-train moved out.   55

With a measured pace, as the pace of one,
Was the still[3] death-march of the host begun;
With a silent step went the cuirass'd bands,
Like a lion's tread on the burning sands;
    —And they gave no battle-shout.   60

But the deep hills peal'd with a cry ere long,
When the Christians burst on the Paynim throng!

---

1 Bermudez] Pedro Bermúdez, a historical person, portrayed in *Poema de mio Cid* as
   El Cid's nephew and standard-bearer.
2 "And while they stood there they saw the Cid Ruy Diez coming up with three
   hundred knights; for he had not been in the battle, and they knew his *green pennon*."
   – *Southey's Chronicle of the Cid*. [Hemans's endnote; passage from Southey, book 2,
   section 11; Hemans's emphasis]
3 still] *NMM*: slow

—With a sudden flash of the lance and spear,
And a charge of the war-steed in full career,
It was Alvar Fañez came!¹

He that was wrapt with no funeral shroud,
Had pass'd before, like a threatening cloud!
And the storm rush'd down on the tented plain,
And the Archer-Queen,² with her bands lay slain,
For the Cid upheld his fame.

Then a terror fell on the King Bucar,
And the Libyan kings who had join'd his war;
And their hearts grew heavy, and died away,
And their hands could not wield an assagay,³
For the dreadful things they saw!

For it seem'd where Minaya⁴ his onset made,
There were seventy thousand knights array'd,
All white as the snow on Nevada's steep,⁵

65

70

75

---

1   Alvar Fañez Minaya, one of the Cid's most distinguished warriors.
    [Hemans's endnote (footnote in *NMM*, worded slightly differently); in the *Poema de
    mio Cid* he is El Cid's nephew and faithful companion.]

2   ——*The archer queen*——
    A Moorish Amazon, who, with a band of female warriors, accompanied King
    Bucar from Africa. Her arrows were so unerring, that she obtained the name of the
    Star of archers.

                        Una Mora muy gallarda,
                        Gran maestra en el tirar,
                        Con Saetas del Aljava,
                        De los arcos de Turquia
                        Estrella era nombrada,
                        Por la destreza que avia
                        En el herir de la Xára.

    [Hemans's endnote; an Amazon is a female warrior, here supposedly a Moorish
    queen, skilled in archery, who allied herself to king Bucar and brought a force of
    archers to take Valencia from El Cid; the quotation that follows is from romance 98
    in Escobar's *Romancero e historia del muy valeroso cavallero El Cid Ruy Diaz de Vibar*,
    and translates: "A very valiant Moor, / Great master in shooting / with arrows from
    her quiver, / with Turkish bows – she was renowned as the Star [of archers] / for
    the skill she had / in piercing with the dart."]

3   assagay] a slender spear or lance used by the Moors.

4   Minaya] a title meaning "my brother," applied to Alvar Fañez in the romances
    about El Cid.

5   steep] the Sierra Nevada mountains.

And they came like the foam of a roaring deep;
  —'Twas a sight of fear and awe!   80

And the crested form of a warrior tall,
With a sword of fire,[1] went before them all;
With a sword of fire, and a banner pale,
And a blood-red cross[2] on his shadowy mail,
  He rode in the battle's van!   85

There was fear in the path of his dim white horse,
There was death in the Giant-warrior's course!
Where his banner stream'd with its ghostly light,
Where his sword blazed out, there was hurrying flight,
  For it seem'd not the sword of man!   90

The field and the river grew darkly red,
As the kings and leaders of Afric fled;
There was work for the men of the Cid that day!
  —They were weary at eve, when they ceased to slay,
  As reapers whose task is done!   95

The kings and the leaders of Afric fled!
The sails of their galleys in haste were spread;
But the sea had its share of the Paynim-slain,[3]
And the bow of the desert was broke in Spain;
  —So the Cid to his grave pass'd on!   100

THE CID'S RISING.[4]

'Twas the deep mid-watch of the silent night,
    And Leon[5] in slumber lay,
  When a sound went forth, in rushing might,[6]

---

1 El Cid's famous sword, called Tizón ("fire-brand"), originally taken from a Moor.
2 cross] symbol of Christian Spain.
3 Paynim-slain] the terrified Moors fled into the sea, where many drowned.
4 first published *New Monthly Magazine* 7 (April 1823): 378; the poem parallels
   Southey's *Chronicle of the Cid*, book 11, section 21.
5 Leon] town and kingdom in northern Spain.
6 might] text in *The Siege of Valencia* volume has "night," which subsequent editions
   restore to the *NMM* reading, "might."

Like an army on its way![1]
In the stillness of the hour,
When the dreams of sleep have power,
And men forget the day.

Through the dark and lonely streets it went,
Till the slumberers[2] woke in dread;—
The sound of a passing armament,
With the charger's stony tread.[3]
There was heard no trumpet's peal,
But the heavy tramp of steel,
As a host's, to combat led.

Through the dark and lonely streets it pass'd,
And the hollow pavement rang,
And the towers, as with a sweeping blast,
Rock'd to the stormy clang!
But the march of the viewless[4] train
Went on to a royal fane,[5]
Where a priest his night-hymn sang.

There was knocking that shook the marble floor,
And a voice at the gate, which said—
"That the Cid Ruy Diez, the Campeador,
Was there in his arms array'd;
And that with him, from the tomb,
Had the Count Gonzalez[6] come,
With a host, uprisen to aid!

---

1 See Southey's *Chronicle of the Cid*, p. 352. [Hemans's endnote, footnote to l. 3 in *NMM*]
2 slumberers] *NMM*: sleepers
3 tread.] *NMM*: tread!
4 viewless] invisible, but also unseeing.
5 fane] church of San Isidro, burial place of Fernando 1 of León (ruled 1035-65), who united Castile and Galicia to his kingdom, and thus prefigured the final unification of Spain in 1492
6 Gonzalez] probably Count Fernán González, military leader under Ferdinand I of León and hero of another medieval Spanish romance; also the name of the governor of Valencia in Hemans's "The Siege of Valencia."

"And they came for the buried king that lay
    At rest in that ancient fane;   30
For he must be arm'd on the battle-day,
    With them, to deliver Spain!"
    — Then the march went sounding on,
    And the Moors, by noontide sun,
    Were dust on Tolosa's plain.[1]

FROM "OTHER POEMS":

FROM "GREEK SONGS":

III.

THE VOICE OF SCIO.[2]

A VOICE from Scio's isle,
A voice of song, a voice of old,
Swept far as cloud or billow roll'd,
    And earth was hush'd the while.

The souls of nations woke!   5
Where lies the land whose hills among,
That voice of Victory hath not rung,
    As if a trumpet spoke?

---

1 plain] site of the battle of Navas de Tolosa in 1212, where a Christian army led by
   Alfonso VIII of Castile defeated the Almoravide Moors and thereby secured the
   future of the Christian kingdoms in Spain.

2 first published *New Monthly Magazine* 7 (April 1823): 352, with minor differences in
   spelling and punctuation; substantive differences are noted; Scio, or Chios, is an
   island in the Aegean, where in June 1821, during the Greek War of Independence,
   the Greek forces obtained a victory famous throughout Europe when they steered
   a fireship into the Turkish fleet, causing great havoc; in 1822 the Greeks of Scio
   rebelled against the Turks; the ensuing massacre by Turkish forces aroused wide-
   spread European support for the Greek cause, though the Greeks also inflicted
   atrocities on the Turks and fought among themselves.

To sky, and sea, and shore
10   Of those whose blood, on Ilion's plain,[1]
Swept[2] from the rivers to the main,
    A glorious tale it bore.[3]

    Still, by our sun-bright deep,
With all the fame that fiery lay
15   Threw round them, in its rushing way,
    The sons of battle sleep.

    And kings their turf have crown'd!
And pilgrims o'er the foaming wave
Brought garlands there: so rest the brave,
20   Who thus their bard have found!

    A voice from Scio's isle,
A voice as deep hath risen again!
As far shall peal its thrilling strain,
    Where'er our sun may smile!

25   Let not its tones expire!
Such power to waken earth and heaven,
And might and vengeance ne'er was given
    To mortal song or lyre![4]

    Know ye not whence it comes?
30   — From ruin'd hearths, from burning fanes,[5]
From kindred blood on yon red plains,
    From desolated homes!

    'Tis with us through the night!
'Tis on our hills, 'tis in our sky —

---

1   Ilion] alternative name for the ancient city of Troy, site of the famous Greek siege
     recounted in Homer's epic poem the Iliad, the "glorious tale" in l. 12.
2   Swept] NMM: Flowed
3   bore.] NMM: bore!
4   lyre!] NMM: lyre.
5   fanes] a common poeticism for temples or churches; here, perhaps both, thereby
     merging the Greeks' ancient pagan religion with their modern Christianity.

—Hear it, ye heavens![1] when swords flash high,[2]
O'er the mid-waves of fight!

IV.

THE SPARTANS'S MARCH.[3]

"The Spartans used not the trumpet in their march into battle, says
Thucydides, because they wished not to excite the rage of their war-
riors. Their charging-step was made to the 'Dorian mood of flutes and
soft recorders.' The valour of a Spartan was too highly tempered to
require a stunning or rousing impulse. His spirit was like a steed too
proud for the spur."

— CAMPBELL *on the Elegiac Poetry of the Greeks.*[4]

'TWAS morn upon the Grecian hills,
    Where peasants dress'd the vines,
Sunlight was on Cithæron's[5] rills,
    Arcadia's[6] rocks and pines.

---

1   ye heavens] *NMM*: thou Heaven
2   high] *NMM*: nigh
3   Originally published in the Edinburgh Magazine. [Hemans's note, referring to the
    Edinburgh Magazine and Literary Miscellany 10 (june 1822): 755; slight differences in
    spelling and punctuation; substantive differences noted; Sparta was in ancient times
    the chief city of the Peloponnesus region in southern Greece, and was known for
    its independent and martial culture; the poem seems to refer to the battle of Ther-
    mopylae in 480 BC, when a Greek army led by Spartans was exterminated by an
    invading Persian army in a heroic defensive action; Hemans's poem may revise a
    militantly nationalistic poem by Jane West, "The Spartan Mother."]
4   epigraph in *EM*: "'It was at once a delightful and terrible sight,' says Plutarch, 'to see
    them (the Spartans) marching on to the tunes of their flutes, without ever troubling
    their order, or confounding their ranks; their music leading them into danger with
    a deliberate hope and assurance, as if some Divinity had sensibly assisted them.[']
    See Campbell on the Elegiac Poetry of the Greeks." Thomas Campbell's comments on
    Greek poetry were contained in his lectures on poetry, published during the early
    1820s in the *New Monthly Magazine.*
5   Cithæron] a mountain range in east-central Greece.
6   Arcadia] a region of the central Peloponnesus in Greece, enclosed by mountains
    and in classical times supposed to be characterized by simple pastoral life; the Pelo-
    ponnesus was the scene of active revolt against the Turks during the Greek war of
    independence.

And brightly, through his reeds and flowers,
    Eurotas¹ wander'd by,
When a sound arose from Sparta's towers
    Of solemn harmony.

Was it the hunters'² choral strain
    To the woodland-goddess pour'd?
Did virgin-hands in Pallas'³ fane
    Strike the full-sounding chord?⁴

But helms were glancing on the stream,
    Spears ranged in close array,
And shields flung back a⁵ glorious beam
    To the morn of a fearful day!

And the mountain-echoes of the land
    Swell'd through the deep-blue sky,
While to soft strains moved forth a band
    Of men that moved to die.

They march'd not with the trumpet's blast,
    Nor bade the horn peal out,
And the laurel-groves,⁶ as on they pass'd,
    Rung with no battle-shout!

They ask'd no clarion's voice to fire
    Their souls with an impulse high;
But the Dorian reed and the Spartan lyre
    For the sons of liberty!

---

1   river of Laconia in the Peloponnesus, of which Sparta was the capital.

2   hunters'] *EM*: shepherds'

3   Pallas] or Athene, in ancient Greek mythology the goddess of war and practical reason, and protectress of the city-state Athens.

4   ll. 10-12] *EM*: That hymn'd the forest-god? / Or the virgins, as to Pallas' fane / With their full-ton'd lyres they trod?

5   a] *EM*: its

6   laurel-groves] *EM*: laurel-woods

And still sweet flutes, their path around,
    Sent forth Eolian breath;[1]   30
They needed not a sterner sound
    To marshal them for death!

So moved they calmly to their field,
    Thence never to return,
Save bearing back the Spartan shield,   35
    Or on it proudly borne![2]

THE TOMBS OF PLATÆA.[3]

FROM A PAINTING BY WILLIAMS.[4]

AND there they sleep! — the men who stood
In arms before th' exulting sun,
And bathed their spears in Persian blood,
And taught the earth how freedom might be won.

They sleep! — th' Olympic[5] wreaths are dead,   5
Th' Athenian lyres are hush'd and gone;
    The Dorian[6] voice of song is fled—
—Slumber, ye mighty! slumber deeply on!

---

1   Eolian] Eolus, or Æolus, was the ancient Greek god of winds.

2   lines 35-6 refer to a widely believed anecdote from ancient history in which a Spartan mother gave her son a shield as he went off to battle and enjoined him to return with it or on it, i.e., victorious or dead, because soldiers fleeing from battle would throw away their shields.

3   Platæa] ancient city in Greek region of Boeotia and site of a Greek victory over the Persians in 479 BC.

4   Williams] Hugh William Williams (1773-1829), Scottish painter of Welsh descent, influenced by the Arcadian paintings of Poussin and Claude, and known as "Grecian" Williams from his *Travels in Italy, Greece, and the Ionian Islands* (2 vols, 1820), his successful exhibition at Edinburgh in 1822 of views taken during his tour, and his *Select Views of Greece, with Classical Illustrations* (2 vols, 1829).

5   Olympic] the ancient Greeks celebrated their gods and engaged in competitive games at the shrine of Olympus.

6   Dorian] Doris was a region in central Greece and Doric culture was supposedly characterized by virtuous rustic simplicity, perhaps in contrast to the culture of Athens (previous line), known for its classical magnificence.

They sleep, and seems not all around
10　　　As hallow'd unto glory's tomb?
Silence is on the battle ground,
The heavens are loaded with a breathless gloom.

And stars are watching on their height,
But dimly seen through mist and cloud,
15　　　And still and solemn is the light
Which folds the plain, as with a glimmering shroud.

And thou, pale night-queen! here thy beams
Are not as those the shepherd loves,
Nor look they down on shining streams,
20　　　By Naiads[1] haunted, in their laurel[2] groves:

Thou seest no pastoral hamlet sleep,
In shadowy quiet, midst its vines;
No temple gleaming from the steep,
Midst the grey olives, or the mountain pines:

25　　　But o'er a dim and boundless waste,
Thy rays, e'en like a tomb-lamp's, brood,
Where man's departed steps are traced
But by his dust, amidst the solitude.

And be it thus! — What slave shall tread
30　　　O'er freedom's ancient battle-plains?[3]
Let deserts wrap the glorious dead,
When their bright land sits weeping o'er her chains:

Here, where the Persian clarion rung,
And where the Spartan sword flash'd high,

1　water nymphs in classical mythology.

2　laurel] or bay, the leaves of which were used to weave victors' garlands in ancient times.

3　in fact, battlefields of the Revolutionary and Napoleonic wars (especially Waterloo) became favourite tourist spots after 1815, inspiring many verse and prose meditations.

And where the Pæan[1] strains were sung,   35
From year to year swell'd on by liberty!

Here should no voice, no sound, be heard,
Until the bonds of Greece be riven,
Save of the leader's charging word,
Or the shrill trumpet, pealing up through heaven!   40

Rest in your silent homes, ye brave!
No vines festoon your lonely tree![2]
No harvest o'er your war-field wave,
Till rushing winds proclaim — the land is free!

ENGLAND'S DEAD.

SON of the ocean isle!
Where sleep your mighty dead?
Show me what high and stately pile
Is rear'd o'er Glory's bed.

Go, stranger! track the deep,   5
Free, free, the white sail spread!
Wave may not foam, nor wild wind sweep,
Where rest not England's dead.

On Egypt's[3] burning plains,
By the pyramid o'ersway'd,   10
With fearful power the noon-day reigns,
And the palm-trees yield no shade.

But let the angry sun
From heaven look fiercely red,
Unfelt by those whose task is done!   15
There slumber England's dead.

---

1 Pæan] ancient Greek song of praise or triumph.
2 A single tree appears in Mr. Williams's impressive picture. [Hemans's note]
3 Egypt was the scene of notable British victories over Napoleon.

The hurricane hath might
Along the Indian shore,
And far, by Ganges'[1] banks at night,
Is heard the tiger's roar.

20

But let the sound roll on!
It hath no tone of dread,
For those that from their toils are gone;
—*There* slumber England's dead[.]

25

Loud rush the torrent-floods
The western wilds among,
And free, in green Columbia's[2] woods,
The hunter's bow is strung.

But let the floods rush on!
Let the arrow's flight be sped!
30

Why should *they* reck whose task is done?
There slumber England's dead!

The mountain-storms rise high
In the snowy Pyrenees,
And toss the pine-boughs through the sky,
35

Like rose-leaves on the breeze.

But let the storm rage on!
Let the forest-wreaths be shed!
For the Roncesvalles' field[3] is won,
40

There slumber England's dead.

On the frozen deep's repose
'Tis a dark and dreadful hour,

---

1 Ganges] principal river of northern India, one of Britain's major colonies.
2 Columbia is a river on the border of what are now Canada and the United States,
   but here the name probably refers to North America, or perhaps the New World in
   general, "discovered" by Christopher Columbus in 1492.
3 valley in northern Spain famous in medieval romance for a heroic rearguard action
   by Roland and his knights protecting the withdrawal of their king, Charlemagne, and
   in Hemans's day site of a British victory over the French during the Peninsular War.

When round the ship the ice-fields close,
To chain her with their power.[1]

But let the ice drift on!   45
Let the cold-blue desert spread!
Their course with mast and flag is done,
There slumber England's dead.

The warlike of the isles,
The men of field and wave![2]   50
Are not the rocks their funeral piles,
The seas and shores their grave?

Go, stranger![3] track the deep,
Free, free the white sail spread!
Wave may not foam, nor wild wind sweep,   55
Where rest not England's dead.

THE VOICE OF SPRING.[4]

I COME, I come! ye have call'd me long,
I come o'er the mountains with light and song!
Ye may trace my step o'er the wakening earth,
By the winds which tell of the violet's birth,
By the primrose-stars in the shadowy grass,   5
By the green leaves, opening, as I pass.

I have breathed on the south, and the chesnut[5] flowers

---

1 reference to arduous and near-disastrous voyages in search of a north-west passage
   through the Arctic Ocean from Europe to Asia, led by John Franklin, William
   Parry, and others in the late 1810s and early 1820s; Parry published accounts in 1818
   and 1821, and Franklin in 1823.
2 lines 49-50 probably refer to Scots from the Highlands and islands who formed
   crack regiments during the Napoleonic wars and who also settled in British
   colonies around the world, especially in Canada.
3 a common invocation on grave-stones.
4 Originally published in the *New Monthly Magazine* [7 (May 1823): 439-
   40]. [Hemans's footnote; text from first book-form publication in *The Siege of
   Valencia*, which differs somewhat from the *NMM* text, mostly in spelling and punc-
   tuation; substantive differences noted here.]
5 chesnut] common spelling of chestnut into the early 19th century.

By thousands have burst from the forest-bowers,
And the ancient graves, and the fallen fanes,
10   Are veil'd with wreaths on Italian plains;
—But it is not for me, in my hour of bloom,
To speak of the ruin or the tomb!

I have look'd[1] o'er the hills of the stormy north,
And the larch has hung all his tassels forth,
15   The fisher is out on the sunny sea,
And the rein-deer bounds o'er the pastures[2] free,
And the pine has a fringe of softer green,
And the moss looks bright, where my foot[3] hath been.

I have sent through the wood-paths a glowing[4] sigh,
20   And call'd out each voice of the deep blue sky;
From the night-bird's lay through the starry time,
In the groves of the soft Hesperian[5] clime,
To the swan's wild note, by the Iceland lakes,
When the dark fir-branch[6] into verdure breaks.

25   From the streams and founts I have loosed the chain,
They are sweeping on to the silvery main,
They are flashing down from the mountain brows,
They are flinging spray o'er[7] the forest-boughs,

They are bursting fresh from their sparry caves,
30   And the earth resounds with the joy of waves!

Come forth, O ye children of gladness, come!
Where the violets lie may be now your home.
Ye of the rose lip[8] and dew-bright eye,

---

1   look'd] *NMM*: pass'd
2   o'er the pastures] *NMM*: through the pasture
3   foot] *NMM*: step
4   glowing] *NMM*: gentle
5   Hesperian] western, or paradisal; from Hesperus, the evening star which sets in the
    west, or from the Hesperides, nymphs who guarded a paradise in the west.
6   fir-branch] *NMM*: fir-bough
7   o'er] *NMM*: on
8   rose lip] *NMM*: rose-cheek

And the bounding footstep, to meet me fly![1]
With the lyre, and the wreath, and the joyous lay   35
Come forth to the sunshine, I may not stay.

Away from the dwellings of care-worn men,
The waters are sparkling in grove and glen![2]
Away from the chamber and sullen[3] hearth,
The young leaves are dancing in breezy mirth![4]   40
Their light stems thrill to the wild-wood strains,
And youth is abroad in my green domains.

But ye! — ye are changed since ye met me last![5]
There is something bright from your features pass'd,[6]
There is that come over your brow and eye,   45
Which speaks of a world where the flowers must die!
— Ye smile! but your smile hath a dimness yet —
Oh! what have ye look'd on since last we met?

Ye are changed, ye are changed! — and I see not here
All whom I saw in the vanish'd year!   50
There were graceful heads, with their ringlets bright,
Which toss'd in the breeze with a play of light,
There were eyes, in whose glistening laughter lay
No faint remembrance of dull decay!

There were steps that flew o'er the cowslip's head,   55
As if for a banquet all earth were spread;
There were voices that rung through the sapphire sky,
And had not a sound of mortality!
Are they gone? is their mirth from the mountains[7] pass'd?
— Ye have look'd on death since ye met me last!   60

---

1   fly!] *NMM*: fly,
2   glen!] *NMM*: glen,
3   sullen] *NMM*: dusky
4   mirth!] *NMM*: mirth,
5   last!] *NMM*: last;
6   in *NMM* the line reads: A shade of earth has been round you cast!
7   mountains] *NMM*: green hills

I know whence the shadow comes o'er you[1] now,
Ye have strewn the dust on the sunny brow!
Ye have given the lovely to[2] earth's embrace,
She hath taken the fairest of beauty's race,[3]
65 With their laughing eyes and their festal crown,
They are gone from amongst you in silence down![4]

They are gone from amongst you, the young[5] and fair,
Ye have lost the gleam of their shining hair!
—But I know of a land[6] where there falls no blight,
70 I shall find them there, with their eyes of light!
Where Death midst the blooms of the morn may dwell,
I tarry no longer—farewell, farewell!

The summer is coming,[7] on soft winds borne,
Ye may press the grape, ye may bind the corn![8]
75 For me, I depart to a brighter shore,
Ye are mark'd by care, ye are mine no more.
I go where the loved who have left you dwell,
And the flowers are not death's—fare ye well, farewell!

---

1 you] *NMM*: ye
2 to] *NMM*: to the
3 race,] *NMM*: race!
4 down!] *NMM*: down.
5 young] *NMM*: bright
6 land] *NMM*: world
7 coming] *NMM*: hastening
8 corn] then the common term for cereal grain, specifically wheat.

FROM *THE VESPERS OF PALERMO:*
A TRAGEDY (1823)[1]

FROM ACT 2, SCENE 4:

Entrance of a Cave, surrounded by Rocks and Forests. A rude Cross seen amongst the Rocks.

[...]

PROCIDA. I knew a young Sicilian, one whose heart   45
Should be all fire. On that most guilty day,
When, with our martyr'd Conradin, the flower
Of the land's knighthood perish'd; he, of whom
I speak, a weeping boy, whose innocent tears
Melted a thousand hearts that dared not aid,   50
Stood by the scaffold, with extended arms,
Calling upon his father, whose last look
Turn'd full on him its parting agony.
That father's blood gush'd o'er him!—and the boy
Then dried his tears, and, with a kindling eye,   55
And a proud flush on his young cheek, look'd up
To the bright heaven.—Doth he remember still
That bitter hour?
    2 SICILIAN.   He bears a sheathless sword!
—Call on the orphan when revenge is nigh.
    PROCIDA. Our band shows gallantly—but there are men   60
Who should be with us now, had they not dared
In some wild moment of festivity
To give their hearts full way, and breathe a wish
For freedom!—and some traitor—it might be
A breeze perchance—bore the forbidden sound
To Eribert:—so they must die—unless   65
Fate, (who at times is wayward) should select
Some other victim first!—But have they not
Brothers or sons amongst us?

---

1   based on a historical event known as the Sicilian Vespers, a popular uprising of Sicilians against the oppressive rule of the French king Charles I of Anjou, who had seized Naples and Sicily by force from its German Hohenstaufen ruler, Conradin (see l. 48; that episode was treated in Hemans's "The Death of Conradin," in *Tales, and Historic Scenes*); for context and commentary, see Introduction, p. 35.

GUIDO.   Look on me!

70 I have a brother, a young high-soul'd boy,
And beautiful as a sculptor's dream, with brow
That wears, amidst its dark rich curls, the stamp
Of inborn nobleness. In truth, he is
A glorious creature! — But his doom is seal'd
75 With their's[1] of whom you spoke; and I have knelt —
— Ay, scorn me not! 'twas for his life — I knelt
E'en at the viceroy's feet, and he put on
That heartless laugh of cold malignity
We know so well, and spurn'd me. — But the stain
80 Of shame like this, takes blood to wash it off,
And *thus* it shall be cancell'd! — Call on me,
When the stern moment of revenge is nigh.
      PROCIDA. I call upon thee *now!* The land's high soul
Is roused, and moving onward, like a breeze
85 Or a swift sunbeam, kindling nature's hues
To deeper life before it. In his chains,
The peasant dreams of freedom! — ay, 'tis thus
Oppression fans th' imperishable flame
With most unconscious hands. — No praise be her's
90 For what she blindly works! — When slavery's cup
O'erflows its bounds, the creeping poison, meant
To dull our senses, thro' each burning vein
Pours fever, lending a delirious strength
To burst man's fetters — and they *shall* be burst!
95 I have hoped, when hope seemed frenzy; but a power
Abides in human will, when bent with strong
Unswerving energy on one great aim,
To make and rule its fortunes! — I have been
A wanderer in the fulness of my years,
100 A restless pilgrim of the earth and seas,
Gathering the generous thoughts of other lands,
To aid our holy cause. And aid is near:
But we must give the signal. Now, before
The majesty of yon pure heaven, whose eye

---

1   their's] for "theirs"; like "her's" in l. 89, at that time a common though increasingly
non-standard usage.

Is on our hearts, whose righteous arm befriends   105
The arm that strikes for freedom; speak! decree
The fate of our oppressors.
    MONTALBA.   Let them fall
When dreaming least of peril! — When the heart,
Basking in sunny pleasure, doth forget
That hate may smile, but sleeps not. — Hide the sword   110
With a thick veil of myrtle,[1] and in halls
Of banquetting, where the full wine-cup shines
Red in the festal torch-light; meet we there,
And bid them welcome to the feast of death.
    PROCIDA. Thy voice is low and broken, and thy words   115
Scarce meet our ears.
    MONTALBA.   Why, then, I thus repeat
Their import. Let th' avenging sword burst forth
In some free festal hour, and woe to him
Who first shall spare.
    RAIMOND.   Must innocence and guilt
Perish alike?
    MONTALBA.   Who talks of innocence?   120
When hath *their* hand been stay'd for innocence?
Let them all perish! — Heaven will chuse its own.
Why should *their* children live? — The earthquake[2] whelms
Its undistinguish'd thousands, making graves
Of peopled cities in its path — and this   125
Is Heaven's dread justice — ay, and it is well!
Why then should *we* be tender, when the skies
Deal thus with man? — What, if the infant bleed?
Is there not power to hush the mother's pangs?
What, if the youthful bride perchance should fall   130
In her triumphant beauty? — Should we pause?
As if death were not mercy to the pangs
Which make our lives the records of our foes?
Let them all perish! — And if one be found

---

1   myrtle] flowering shrub associated in myth with Venus, and thus with love and
     pleasure.
2   earthquakes and other natural disasters were common symbols for violent revolu-
     tion, and also instances of apparently futile and meaningless mass death and human
     suffering that seem incompatible with the idea of a benevolent god.

135 Amidst our band, to stay th' avenging steel
For pity, or remorse, or boyish love,
Then be his doom as theirs!   [*A pause.*

                    Why gaze ye thus?
Brethren, what means your silence?
          SICILIANS.   Be it so!
If one amongst us stay th' avenging steel
140 For love or pity, be his doom as theirs!
Pledge we our faith to this!
          RAIMOND. (*Rushing forward indignantly.*)
                         Our faith to *this!*
No! I but *dreamt* I heard it! — Can it be?
My countrymen, my father! — Is it thus
That freedom should be won? — Awake! Awake
145 To loftier thoughts! — Lift up, exultingly,
On the crown'd heights, and to the sweeping winds,
Your glorious banner! — Let your trumpet's blast
Make the tombs thrill with echoes! Call aloud,
Proclaim from all your hills, the land shall bear
150 The stranger's yoke no longer! — What is he
Who carries on his practised lip a smile,
Beneath his vest a dagger, which but waits
Till the heart bounds with joy, to still its beatings?
That which our nature's instinct doth recoil from,
155 And our blood curdle at — Ay, yours and mine —
A murderer! — Heard ye? — Shall that name with ours
Go down to after days? — Oh, friends! a cause
Like that for which we rise, hath made bright names
Of the elder time as rallying-words to men,
And shall not ours be such?
160   MONTALBA.   Fond dreamer, peace!
Fame! What is fame? — Will our unconscious dust
Start into thrilling rapture from the grave,
At the vain breath of praise? — I tell thee, youth,
Our souls are parch'd with agonizing thirst,
165 Which must be quench'd tho' death were in the draught:
We must have vengeance, for our foes have left
No other joy unblighted.

PROCIDA.   Oh! my son,
The time is past for such high dreams as thine.
Thou know'st not whom we deal with. Knightly faith,
And chivalrous honour, are but things whereon   170
They cast disdainful pity. We must meet
Falsehood with wiles, and insult with revenge.
And, for our names—whate'er the deeds, by which
We burst our bondage—is it not enough
That in the chronicle of days to come,   175
We, thro' a bright "For Ever," shall be call'd
The men who saved their country?
        RAIMOND.   Many a land
Hath bow'd beneath the yoke, and then arisen,
As a strong lion rending silken bonds,
And on the open field, before high heaven,   180
Won such majestic vengeance, as hath made
Its name a power on earth.—Ay, nations own
It is enough of glory to be call'd
The children of the mighty, who redeem'd
Their native soil—but not by means like these.   185
        MONTALBA. I have no children.—Of Montalba's blood
Not one red drop doth circle thro' the veins
Of aught that breathes!—Why, what have *I* to do
With far futurity?—My spirit lives
But in the past.—Away! when thou dost stand   190
On this fair earth, as doth a blasted tree
Which the warm sun revives not, *then* return,
Strong in thy desolation: but, till then,
Thou art not for our purpose; we have need
Of more unshrinking hearts.
        RAIMOND.   Montalba, know,   195
I shrink from crime alone. Oh! if my voice
Might yet have power amongst you, I would say,
Associates, leaders, *be* avenged! but yet
As knights, as warriors!
        MONTALBA.   Peace! have we not borne
Th' indelible taint of contumely and chains?   200
We *are not* knights and warriors.—Our bright crests

Have been defiled and trampled to the earth.
Boy! we are slaves — and our revenge shall be
Deep as a slave's disgrace.

    RAIMOND.   Why, then, farewell:
205 I leave you to your councils. He that still
Would hold his lofty nature undebased,
And his name pure, were but a loiterer here.

    PROCIDA. And is it thus indeed? — dost *thou* forsake
Our cause, my son?

    RAIMOND.   Oh, father! what proud hopes
210 This hour hath blighted! — yet, whate'er betide
It is a noble privilege to look up
Fearless in heaven's bright face — and this is mine,
And shall be still. —   [*Exit* Raimond.

    PROCIDA.   He's gone! — Why, let it be!
I trust our Sicily hath many a son
215 Valiant as mine. — Associates! —'tis decreed
Our foes shall perish. We have but to name
The hour, the scene, the signal.

    MONTALBA.   It should be
In the full city, when some festival
Hath gathered throngs, and lull'd infatuate hearts
220 To brief security. Hark! is there not
A sound of hurrying footsteps on the breeze?
We are betray'd. — Who art thou?

                    Vittoria *enters.*

    PROCIDA.   *One* alone
Should be thus daring. Lady, lift the veil
That shades thy noble brow.

    (*She raises her veil, the Sicilians draw back with respect.*)

    SICILIANS.   Th' affianced bride
Of our lost King!

225   PROCIDA. And more, Montalba; know
Within this form there dwells a soul as high,
As warriors in their battles e'er have proved,
Or patriots on the scaffold.

    VITTORIA.   Valiant men!
I come to ask your aid. Ye see me, one
230 Whose widow'd youth hath all been consecrate

To a proud sorrow, and whose life is held
In token and memorial of the dead.
Say, is it meet that, lingering thus on earth,
But to behold one great atonement made,
And keep one name from fading in men's hearts,   235
A tyrant's will should force me to profane
Heaven's altar with unhallow'd vows — and live
Stung by the keen, unutterable scorn
Of my own bosom, live — another's bride?
    SICILIANS. Never, oh never! — fear not, noble lady!   240
Worthy of Conradin!
    VITTORIA.   Yet hear me still.
His bride, that Eribert's, who notes our tears
With his insulting eye of cold derision,
And, could he pierce the depths where feeling works,
Would number e'en our agonies as crimes.   245
— Say, is this meet?
    GUIDO.   We deem'd these nuptials, lady,
Thy willing choice; but 'tis a joy to find
Thou art noble still. Fear not; by all our wrongs
This shall not be.
    PROCIDA.   Vittoria, thou art come
To ask *our* aid, but we have need of thine.   250
Know, the completion of our high designs
Requires — a festival; and it must be
Thy bridal!
    VITTORIA.   Procida!
    PROCIDA.   Nay, start not thus.
'Tis no hard task to bind your raven hair
With festal garlands, and to bid the song   255
Rise, and the wine-cup mantle. No — nor yet
To meet your suitor at the glittering shrine,
Where death, not love, awaits him!
    VITTORIA.   Can my soul
Dissemble thus?
    PROCIDA.   We have no other means
Of winning our great birthright back from those   260
Who have usurp'd it, than so lulling them
Into vain confidence, that they may deem

All wrongs forgot; and this may best be done
By what I ask of thee.
    MONTALBA.   Then will we mix
265 With the flush'd revellers, making their gay feast
The harvest of the grave.
    VITTORIA.   A bridal day!
— Must it be so? — Then, chiefs of Sicily,
I bid you to my nuptials! but be there
With your bright swords unsheath'd, for thus alone
My guests should be adorn'd.
270   PROCIDA.   And let thy banquet
Be soon announced, for there are noble men
Sentenced to die, for whom we fain would purchase
Reprieve with other blood.
    VITTORIA.   Be it then the day
Preceding that appointed for their doom.
275   GUIDO. My brother, thou shalt live! — Oppression boasts
No gift of prophecy! — It but remains
To name our signal, chiefs!
    MONTALBA.   The Vesper-bell.
    PROCIDA. Even so, the vesper-bell, whose deep-toned peal
Is heard o'er land and wave. Part of our band,
280 Wearing the guise of antic revelry,
Shall enter, as in some fantastic pageant,
The halls of Eribert; and at the hour
Devoted to the sword's tremendous task,
I follow with the rest. — The vesper-bell!
285 That sound shall wake th' avenger; for 'tis come,
The time when power is in a voice, a breath,
To burst the spell which bound us. — But the night
Is waning, with her stars, which, one by one,
Warn us to part. Friends, to your homes! — your *homes?*
290 *That* name is yet to win. — Away, prepare
For our next meeting in Palermo's walls.
The Vesper-bell! Remember!
    SICILIANS.   Fear us not.
The Vesper-bell!   *[Exeunt omnes.*

END OF ACT THE SECOND.

FROM *THE FOREST SANCTUARY; AND OTHER POEMS* (1825), AND *THE FOREST SANCTUARY: WITH OTHER POEMS*, 2ND EDITION (1829)

THE FOREST SANCTUARY.[1]

Ihr Plätze aller meiner stillen freuden,
Euch lass' ich hinter mir auf immerdar!

.   .   .   .   .   .

So ist des geistes ruf an mich ergangen,
Mich treibt nicht eitles, irdisches verlangen.[2]

Die Jungfrau von Orleans.

Long time against oppression have I fought,
And for the native liberty of faith
Have bled and suffer'd bonds.[3]

Remorse, a Tragedy.

---

1   text: 1st edition; numerous minor changes were introduced in 2nd (1829) and 3rd edition (1835), almost all in punctuation; significant substantive variants are noted, including some from Hemans's manuscript in the Liverpool Public Library Record Office (here designated "Liverpool MS"); Hemans's endnotes are often lengthy and so have been retained in their original position and indicated in the text by capital letters, moved from the beginning of the annotated passage to its end, as in editions after the 1st; in the Liverpool MS there is a crossed out title, "The Forest of Refuge," and the title on the manuscipt is "The Forest-Sanctuary"; for other significant differences between the printed and the manuscript text, see selections from manuscript poems on my website; for context and commentary, see Introduction, pp. 38-44.

2   passage slightly misquoted from *Die Jungfrau von Orleans* (1801), a play about Joan of Arc by Friedrich Schiller (1759-1805); lines spoken by Joan:

> Ye scenes where all my tranquil joys I knew,
> For ever now I leave you far behind!
> …
> Such is to me the Spirit's high behest;
> No earthly vain ambition fires my breast.

(Prologue, scene 4) *The Maid of Orleans*, in *The Works of Frederick Schiller: Historical Dramas*, translated by Joseph Mellish (London: 1872), p. 340.

3   passage from *Remorse, A Tragedy* (act 2, scene 2, lines 6-8), by Samuel Taylor Coleridge (1772-1834), produced at Drury Lane theatre, London, in 1813 and pub-

The following Poem is intended to describe the mental con-
flicts, as well as outward sufferings, of a Spaniard, who, flying
from the religious persecutions of his own country in the 16th
century, takes refuge with his child in a North American Forest.
The story is supposed to be related by himself amidst the
wilderness which has afforded him an asylum.[1]

I.

THE voices of my home! — I hear them still!
They have been with me through the dreamy night —
The blessed household voices, wont to fill
My heart's clear depths with unalloy'd delight!
I hear them still, unchang'd: — though some from earth
Are music parted, and the tones of mirth —
Wild, silvery tones, that rang through days more bright!
Have died in others, — yet to me they come,
Singing of boyhood back — the voices of my home!

II.

They call me through this hush of woods, reposing
In the grey stillness of the summer morn,
They wander by when heavy flowers are closing,

---

lished the same year; the play is set in the Spain of Philip 11 and the Inquisition's
campaign against non-Christians and Protestants; the lines are spoken by Alvar, a
Protestant, who has returned from exile and imprisonment to confront the brother
who betrayed him.

1 Liverpool MS: last sentence reads, "The story is supposed to be narrated by himself
in the Wilderness which has afforded him an Asylum, and is intended more as the
record of a Mind, than as a tale abounding with romantic and extraordinary inci-
dent." By tales "abounding with romantic and extraordinary incident" Hemans
means narrative poems which resemble romance in having action, adventure, and
improbable or extravagant incidents, written by contemporaries such as Walter
Scott and Byron; the poem's narrator is a former Spanish conquistador who
recounts, from his exile somewhere in eastern North America during the mid-16th
century, how he came to flee his native country because of religious persecution; in
Hemans's day, reforms introduced in Spain by Napoleon and supported by many
"liberales" were replaced in 1815 by a reactionary and repressive government and
official religious intolerance, leading to a liberal revolt (1820-24) suppressed by
reactionary European powers.

And thoughts grow deep, and winds and stars are born;
Ev'n as a fount's remember'd gushings burst
On the parch'd traveller in his hour of thirst,   15
E'en thus they haunt me with sweet sounds, till worn
By quenchless longings, to my soul I say —
Oh! for the dove's swift wings, that I might flee away,[1]

III.

And find mine ark![2] — yet whither? — I must bear
A yearning heart within me to the grave.   20
I am of those o'er whom a breath of air —
Just darkening in its course the lake's bright wave,
And sighing through the feathery canes[A] — hath power
To call up shadows, in the silent hour,
From the dim past, as from a wizard's cave! —   25
So must it be! — These skies above me spread,
Are they my own soft skies? — Ye rest not here, my dead!

IV.

Ye far amidst the southern flowers lie sleeping,
Your graves all smiling in the sunshine clear,
Save one! — a blue, lone, distant main is sweeping   30
High o'er *one* gentle head — ye rest not here! —
'Tis not the olive, with a whisper swaying,
Not thy low ripplings, glassy water, playing
Through my own chesnut[3] groves, which fill mine ear;
But the faint echoes in my breast that dwell,   35
And for their birth-place moan, as moans the ocean-shell.[B]

---

1   away] echo of Psalm 55 (line 6) in the Bible: "Oh that I had wings like a dove! for
    then would I fly away, and be at rest."

2   ark] the book of Genesis in the Bible (ch. 7-9) recounts how God advised Noah to
    build an ark to save his family and animals from a universal flood to be inflicted on
    humanity for their sins; Noah would know the flood was receding when a dove
    released from the ark returned with an olive branch; dove and olive branch came to
    symbolize reconciliation between God and humanity.

3   chesnut] the predominant spelling until about 1820; "chestnut" in 2nd and 3rd edi-
    tions.

V.

Peace!—I will dash these fond regrets to earth,
Ev'n as an eagle shakes the cumbering rain
From his strong pinion. Thou that gav'st me birth,
And lineage, and once home,—my native Spain!
My own bright land—my father's land—my child's!
What hath thy son brought from thee to the wilds?
He hath brought marks of torture and the chain,
Traces of things which pass not as a breeze,
A blighted name, dark thoughts, wrath, woe—thy gifts are
these.

40

45

VI.

A blighted name!—I hear the winds of morn—
Their sounds are not of this!—I hear the shiver
Of the green reeds, and all the rustlings, borne
From the high forest, when the light leaves quiver:
Their sounds are not of this!—the cedars, waving,
Lend it no tone: His wide savannahs laving,[1]
It is not murmur'd by the joyous river!
What part hath mortal name, where God alone
Speaks to the mighty waste, and through its heart is known?

50

VII.

Is it not much that I may worship Him,
With nought my spirit's breathings to control,
And feel His presence in the vast, and dim,
And whispery woods, where dying thunders roll
From the far cataracts?—Shall I not rejoice
That I have learn'd at last to know *His* voice
From man's?—I will rejoice!—my soaring soul
Now hath redeem'd her birth-right of the day,
And won, through clouds, to Him, her own unfetter'd way!

55

60

---

1   laving] washing or running alongside, a poeticism; savannahs: grassy treeless plains,
especially in tropical or sub-tropical America.

VIII.

And thou, my boy! that silent at my knee
Dost lift to mine thy soft, dark, earnest eyes,   65
Fill'd with the love of childhood, which I see
Pure through its depths, a thing without disguise;
Thou that hast breath'd in slumber on my breast,
When I have check'd its throbs to give thee rest,
Mine own! whose young thoughts fresh before me rise!   70
    Is it not much that I may guide thy prayer,
And circle thy glad soul with free and healthful air?

IX.

Why should I weep on thy bright head, my boy?
Within thy fathers' halls thou wilt not dwell,
Nor lift their banner, with a warrior's joy,   75
Amidst the sons of mountain chiefs,[1] who fell
For Spain of old. — Yet what if rolling waves
Have borne us far from our ancestral graves?
Thou shalt not feel thy bursting heart rebel
As mine hath done; nor bear what I have borne,   80
    Casting in falsehood's mould th' indignant brow of scorn.

X.

This shall not be thy lot, my blessed child!
I have not sorrow'd, struggled, liv'd in vain —
Hear me! magnificent and ancient wild;
And mighty rivers, ye that meet the main,   85
As deep meets deep; and forests, whose dim shade
The flood's voice, and the wind's, by swells pervade;
Hear me! —'tis well to die, and not complain,
    Yet there are hours when the charg'd heart must speak,
Ev'n in the desert's ear to pour itself, or break!   90

---

1   chiefs] the narrator's family traces its lineage to the Christian Visigoths who, several
    centuries earlier, sought refuge from invading Moors by retreating to the mountains
    of north-east Spain.

XI.

I see an oak before me,[c] it hath been
The crown'd one of the woods; and might have flung
Its hundred arms to Heaven, still freshly green,
But a wild vine around the stem hath clung,
From branch to branch close wreaths of bondage
90   throwing,
Till the proud tree, before no tempest bowing,
Hath shrunk and died, those serpent-folds among.[1]
Alas! alas! — what is it that I see?
An image of man's mind, land of my sires, with thee!

XII.

100 Yet art thou lovely! — Song is on thy hills —
Oh sweet and mournful melodies of Spain,
That lull'd my boyhood, how your memory thrills
The exile's heart with sudden-wakening pain! —
Your sounds are on the rocks — that I might hear
105 Once more the music of the mountaineer! —
And from the sunny vales the shepherd's strain
Floats out, and fills the solitary place
With the old tuneful names of Spain's heroic race.

XIII.

But there was silence one bright, golden day,
Through my own pine-hung mountains. Clear, yet
110   lone,
In the rich autumn light the vineyards lay,
And from the fields the peasant's voice was gone;
And the red grapes untrodden strew'd the ground,
And the free flocks untended roam'd around:
115 Where was the pastor? — where the pipe's wild tone?

---

1 liberals and reformists considered that the energy and glory of Spain had been
sapped by parasitic institutions of church and state, as the parasitic vine saps the
energy of its host plant.

Music and mirth were hush'd the hills among,
While to the city's gates each hamlet pour'd its throng.[1]

XIV.

Silence upon the mountains! — But within
The city's gates a rush — a press — a swell
Of multitudes their torrent way to win;   120
And heavy boomings of a dull deep bell,
A dead pause following each — like that which parts
The dash of billows, holding breathless hearts
Fast in the hush of fear — knell after knell;
And sounds of thickening steps, like thunder-rain,   125
That plashes on the roof of some vast echoing fane![2]

XV.

What pageant's hour approach'd? — The sullen gate
Of a strong ancient prison-house was thrown
Back to the day. And who, in mournful state,
Came forth, led slowly o'er its threshold-stone?   130
They that had learn'd, in cells of secret gloom,
How sunshine is forgotten! — They, to whom
The very features of mankind were grown
Things that bewilder'd! — O'er their dazzled sight,
They lifted their wan hands, and cower'd before the light! 135

XVI.

To this man brings his brother! — Some were there,
Who with their desolation had entwin'd
Fierce strength, and girt the sternness of despair
Fast round their bosoms, ev'n as warriors bind
The breast-plate on for fight: but brow and cheek   140
Seem'd *theirs* a torturing panoply to speak!

---

1   ll. 115-17 parallel John Keats's description of a similar scene in his "Ode on a Gre-
    cian Urn" (1820), though there is no direct evidence that Hemans read Keats.
2   fane] church, a common poeticism.

And there were some, from whom the very mind
Had been wrung out: they smil'd—oh! startling smile
Whence man's high soul is fled!—where doth it sleep the
    while?

XVII.

145 But onward moved the melancholy train,
For their false creeds in fiery pangs to die.
This was the solemn sacrifice of Spain—
Heaven's offering from the land of chivalry!
Through thousands, thousands of their race they mov'd—
150 Oh! how unlike all others!—the belov'd,
The free, the proud, the beautiful! whose eye
Grew fix'd before them, while a people's breath
Was hush'd, and its one soul bound in the thought of death!

XVIII.

It might be that amidst the countless throng,
155 There swell'd some heart with Pity's weight oppress'd,
For the wide stream of human love is strong;
And woman, on whose fond and faithful breast
Childhood is rear'd, and at whose knee the sigh
Of its first prayer is breath'd, she, too, was nigh.
160 —But life is dear, and the free footstep bless'd,
And home a sunny place, where each may fill
Some eye with glistening smiles,—and therefore all were
    still—

XIX.

All still—youth, courage, strength!—a winter laid,
A chain of palsy, cast on might and mind!
165 Still, as at noon a southern forest's shade,
They stood, those breathless masses of mankind;
Still, as a frozen torrent!—but the wave
Soon leaps to foaming freedom—they, the brave,

Endur'd — they saw the martyr's place assign'd
In the red flames — whence is the withering spell   170
That numbs each human pulse? — they saw, and thought it
    well.

XX.

And I, too, thought it well! That very morn
From a far land I came, yet round me clung
The spirit of my own. No hand had torn
With a strong grasp away the veil which hung   175
Between mine eyes and truth. I gaz'd, I saw,
Dimly, as through a glass.[1] In silent awe
I watch'd the fearful rites; and if there sprung
One rebel feeling from its deep founts up,
Shuddering, I flung it back, as guilt's own poison-cup.   180

XXI.

But I was waken'd as the dreamers waken
Whom the shrill trumpet and the shriek of dread
Rouse up at midnight, when their walls are taken,
And they must battle till their blood is shed
On their own threshold-floor. A path for light   185
Through my torn breast was shatter'd by the might
Of the swift thunder-stroke — and Freedom's tread
Came in through ruins, late, yet not in vain,
Making the blighted place all green with life again.

XXII.

Still darkly, slowly, as a sullen mass   190
Of cloud, o'ersweeping, without wind, the sky,
Dream-like I saw the sad procession pass,
And mark'd its victims with a tearless eye.

---

1   echo of the Bible: "For now [before spiritual redemption] we see through a glass,
    darkly; but then [after redemption] face to face: now I know in part; but then shall I
    know even as I am known" (1 Corinthians 13.12).

They mov'd before me but as pictures, wrought
195　Each to reveal some secret of man's thought,
On the sharp edge of sad mortality,
Till in his place came one—oh! could it be?
—My friend, my heart's first friend!—and did I gaze on thee?

XXIII.

On thee! with whom in boyhood I had play'd,
200　At the grape-gatherings, by my native streams;
And to whose eye my youthful soul had laid
Bare, as to Heaven's, its glowing world of dreams;
And by whose side midst warriors I had stood,
And in whose helm[1] was brought—oh! earn'd with
blood!—
205　The fresh wave[2] to my lips, when tropic beams
Smote on my fever'd brow!—Ay, years had pass'd,
Severing our paths, brave friend!—and *thus* we met at last!

XXIV.

I see it still—the lofty mien thou borest—
On thy pale forehead sat a sense of power!
210　The very look that once thou brightly worest,
Cheering me onward through a fearful hour,
When we were girt by Indian bow and spear,
Midst the white Andes[3]—ev'n as mountain deer,
Hemm'd in our camp—but thro' the javelin shower
215　We rent[4] our way, a tempest of despair!
—And thou—hadst thou but died with thy true brethren
there!

1　helm] here, helmet, a common poeticism.
2　wave] water.
3　the narrator and Alvar were comrades-in-arms in Peru, after the Inca empire was
overthrown by Francisco Pizarro in 1532-33, and during the period of civil wars
and Inca revolts; an independent state of Peru was established in 1822-24.
4　rent] tore, in the sense of tore apart or split asunder; by Hemans's day a literary
usage.

XXV.

I call the fond wish back — for thou hast perish'd
More nobly far, my Alvar![1] — making known
The might of truth;[D] and be thy memory cherish'd
With theirs, the thousands, that around her throne   220
Have pour'd their lives out smiling, in that doom
Finding a triumph, if denied a tomb!
— Ay, with their ashes hath the wind been sown,
And with the wind their spirit shall be spread,
Filling man's heart and home with records of the dead.   225

XXVI.

Thou Searcher[2] of the Soul! in whose dread sight
Not the bold guilt alone, that mocks the skies,
But the scarce-own'd, unwhisper'd thought of night,
As a thing written with the sunbeam lies;
Thou know'st — whose eye through shade and depth
    can see,   230
That this man's crime was but to worship thee,
Like those that made their hearts thy sacrifice,
The call'd of yore; wont by the Saviour's side,
On the dim Olive-Mount[3] to pray at eventide.

XXVII.

For the strong spirit will at times awake,   235
Piercing the mists that wrap her clay-abode;[4]

---

1 Alvar] recalls Alvar in Coleridge's play *Remorse* (see above), and also Alvar Fañez,
  nicknamed "Minaya" or brother, close companion of El Cid, a medieval Christian
  warlord, long celebrated in popular ballads, who was made into a symbol of Spanish
  patriotic resistance during the Napoleonic occupation of Spain.
2 Searcher] God as "true" Inquisitor, in contrast to the human institution of the
  Inquisition.
3 Olive-Mount] hill in Jerusalem where Christ went to pray with his disciples, and
  where he was betrayed by Judas to be arrested and crucified (e.g., gospels of
  Matthew ch. 26, Mark ch. 14, Luke ch. 22).
4 clay-abode] body is the mortal part as distinct from the immortal spirit; in the
  Bible, God created Adam, the first man, from clay, and in Greek myth Prometheus
  fashioned man from clay.

And, born of thee, she may not always take
Earth's accents for the oracles of God;
And ev'n for this — O dust, whose mask is power!
240   Reed, that wouldst be a scourge thy little hour!
Spark,[1] whereon yet the mighty hath not trod,
And therefore thou destroyest! — where were flown
Our hope, if man were left to man's decree[2] alone?

XXVIII.

But this I felt not yet. I could but gaze
245   On him, my friend; while that swift moment threw
A sudden freshness back on vanish'd days,
Like water-drops on some dim picture's hue;
Calling the proud time up, when first I stood
Where banners floated, and my heart's quick blood
250   Sprang to a torrent as the clarion blew,
And he — his sword was like a brother's worn,
That watches through the field his mother's youngest born.

XXIX.

But a lance met me in that day's career,
Senseless I lay amidst th' o'ersweeping fight,
255   Wakening at last — how full, how strangely clear,
That scene on memory flash'd! — the shivery light,
Moonlight, on broken shields — the plain of slaughter,
The fountain-side — the low sweet sound of water —
And Alvar bending o'er me — from the night
260   Covering me with his mantle! — all the past
Flow'd back — my soul's far chords all answer'd to the blast.

---

1   Spark] with "dust" and "reed" echoes Biblical language indicating the frail and tran-
    sient nature of humanity in contrast to divine power.

2   decree] human as distinct from divine command; government by decree, or arbi-
    trary edict, was also thought to be characteristic of absolute monarchies and the
    Revolutionary and Napoleonic regimes; the decree, or *pronunciamiento*, was widely
    used by different factions in Spain during the political turmoils of the early nine-
    teenth century.

XXX.

Till, in that rush of visions, I became
As one that by the bands of slumber wound,
Lies with a powerless, but all-thrilling frame,
Intense in consciousness of sight and sound,   265
Yet buried in a wildering dream which brings
Lov'd faces round him, girt with fearful things!
Troubled ev'n thus I stood, but chain'd and bound
On that familiar form mine eye to keep—
—Alas! I might not fall upon his neck and weep![1]   270

XXXI.

He pass'd me—and what next?—I look'd on two,
Following his footsteps to the same dread place,
For the same guilt—his sisters!E—Well I knew
The beauty on those brows, though each young face
Was chang'd—so deeply chang'd!—a dungeon's air   275
Is hard for lov'd and lovely things to bear,
And ye, O daughters of a lofty race,
Queen-like Theresa! radiant Inez![2]—flowers
So cherish'd! were ye then but rear'd for those dark hours?

XXXII.

A mournful home, young sisters! had ye left,   280
With your lutes hanging hush'd upon the wall,
And silence round the aged man, bereft
Of each glad voice, once answering to his call.

---

1 weep] the passage echoes biblical images of fraternal love in the book of Genesis: Esau weeps on his brother Jacob's neck (33.4), and Joseph weeps on his brother Benjamin's neck (45.14).

2 Theresa ... Inez] well known names in Spanish history: St Theresa (1515-82) was a mystic, church reformer, and the most famous female saint of Spain; Inez de Castro (died 1355) was the mistress and possibly wife of Prince Pedro of Portugal; she was murdered in a court intrigue and then treated romantically in European literature as a victim of conflicting love and politics, as in Hemans's "The Coronation of Inez de Castro" (*Songs of the Affections*, 1830).

Alas, that lonely father! doom'd to pine
285   For sounds departed in his life's decline,
And, midst the shadowing banners of his hall,
With his white hair to sit, and deem the name
A hundred chiefs had borne, cast down by you to shame!^F

XXXIII.

And woe for you, midst looks and words of love,
290   And gentle hearts and faces, nurs'd so long!
How had I seen you in your beauty move,
Wearing the wreath, and listening to the song!
— Yet sat, ev'n then, what seem'd the crowd to shun,
Half veil'd upon the clear pale brow of one,
295   And deeper thoughts than oft to youth belong,
Thoughts, such as wake to evening's whispery sway,
Within the drooping shade of her sweet eyelids lay.

XXXIV.

And if she mingled with the festive train,
It was but as some melancholy star
300   Beholds the dance of shepherds on the plain,
In its bright stillness present, though afar.
Yet would she smile — and that, too, hath its smile —
Circled with joy which reach'd her not the while,
And bearing a lone spirit, not at war
305   With earthly things, but o'er their form and hue
Shedding too clear a light, too sorrowfully true.

XXXV.

But the dark hours wring forth the hidden might
Which hath lain bedded in the silent soul,
A treasure all undreamt of;—as the night
310   Calls out the harmonies of streams that roll
Unheard by day. It seem'd as if her breast
Had hoarded energies, till then suppress'd

Almost with pain, and bursting from control,
And finding first that hour their pathway free:
— Could a rose brave the storm, such might her emblem be!   315

XXXVI.

For the soft gloom whose shadow still had hung
On her fair brow, beneath its garlands worn,
Was fled; and fire, like prophecy's had sprung
Clear to her kindled eye. It might be scorn —
Pride — sense of wrong — ay, the frail heart is bound   320
By these at times, ev'n as with adamant round,
Kept so from breaking! — yet not *thus* upborne
She mov'd, though some sustaining passion's wave
Lifted her fervent soul — a sister for the brave!

XXXVII.

And yet, alas! to see the strength which clings   325
Round woman in such hours! — a mournful sight,
Though lovely! — an o'erflowing of the springs,
The full springs of affection, deep as bright!
And she, because her life is ever twin'd
With other lives, and by no stormy wind   330
May thence be shaken, and because the light
Of tenderness is round her, and her eye
Doth weep such passionate tears — therefore she thus can die.

XXXVIII.

Therefore didst *thou*, through that heart-shaking scene,
As through a triumph[1] move; and cast aside   335
Thine own sweet thoughtfulness for victory's mien,
O faithful sister! cheering thus the guide,
And friend, and brother of thy sainted youth,
Whose hand had led thee to the source of truth,

---

1 triumph] spectacle or pageant; also parade of a victor's spoils and captives of war.

340   Where thy glad soul from earth was purified;
　　　 Nor wouldst thou, following him through all the past,
　　　 That he should see thy step grow tremulous at last.

XXXIX.

　　　 For thou hadst made no deeper love a guest
　　　 Midst thy young spirit's dreams, than that which grows
345   Between the nurtur'd of the same fond breast,
　　　 The shelter'd of one roof; and thus it rose
　　　 Twin'd in with life. — How is it, that the hours
　　　 Of the same sport, the gathering early flowers
　　　 Round the same tree, the sharing one repose,
350   And mingling one first prayer in murmurs soft,
　　 From the heart's memory fade, in this world's breath, so oft?

XL.

　　　 But thee that breath had touch'd not; thee, nor him,
　　　 The true in all things found! — and thou wert blest
　　　 Ev'n then, that no remember'd change could dim
355   The perfect image of affection, press'd
　　　 Like armour to thy bosom! — thou hadst kept
　　　 Watch by that brother's couch of pain, and wept,
　　　 Thy sweet face covering with thy robe, when rest
　　　 Fled from the sufferer; thou hadst bound his faith
360   Unto thy soul—one light, one hope ye chose—one death.

XLI.

　　　 So didst thou pass on brightly! — but for her,
　　　 Next in that path, how may *her* doom be spoken!
　　　 — All-merciful! to think that such things were,
　　　 And *are*, and seen by men with hearts unbroken!
365   To think of that fair girl, whose path had been
　　　 So strew'd with rose-leaves, all one fairy scene!

And whose quick glance came ever as a token
Of hope to drooping thought, and her glad voice
As a free bird's in spring, that makes the woods rejoice!

XLII.

And she to die! — she lov'd the laughing earth   370
With such deep joy in its fresh leaves and flowers!
— Was not her smile even as the sudden birth
Of a young rainbow, colouring vernal showers?
Yes! but to meet her fawn-like step, to hear
The gushes of wild song, so silvery clear,   375
Which, oft unconsciously, in happier hours
Flow'd from her lips, was to forget the sway
Of Time and Death below,—blight, shadow, dull decay!

XLIII.

Could this change be? — the hour, the scene, where last
I saw that form, came floating o'er my mind: 380
— A golden vintage-eve;— the heats were pass'd,
And, in the freshness of the fanning wind,
Her father sat, where gleam'd the first faint star
Through the lime-boughs;[1] and with her light guitar,
She, on the greensward at his feet reclin'd,   385
In his calm face laugh'd up; some shepherd-lay[2]
Singing, as childhood sings on the lone hills at play.

XLIV.

And now — oh God! — the bitter fear of death,
The sore amaze, the faint o'ershadowing dread,
Had grasp'd her! — panting in her quick-drawn breath,   390
And in her white lips quivering;— onward led,
She look'd up with her dim bewilder'd eyes,

---

1 lime] here an ornamental garden tree rather than the tropical fruit tree.
2 shepherd-lay] folksong or perhaps artificial pastoral song popular in European
   upper-class literature of the 16th century.

And there smil'd out her own soft brilliant skies,
Far in their sultry southern azure spread,
395   Glowing with joy, but silent! — still they smil'd,
Yet sent down no reprieve for earth's poor trembling child.

XLV.

Alas! that earth had all too strong a hold,
Too fast, sweet Inez! on thy heart, whose bloom
Was given to early love, nor knew how cold
400   The hours which follow. There was one, with whom,
Young as thou wert, and gentle, and untried,
Thou might'st, perchance, unshrinkingly have died;
But he was far away;—and with thy doom
Thus gathering, life grew so intensely dear,
405 That all thy slight frame shook with its cold mortal fear!

XLVI.

No aid! — thou too didst pass! — and all had pass'd,
The fearful — and the desperate — and the strong!
Some like the bark that rushes with the blast,[1]
Some like the leaf swept shiveringly along,
410   And some as men, that have but one more field
To fight, and then may slumber on their shield,
Therefore they arm in hope. But now the throng
Roll'd on, and bore me with their living tide,
Ev'n as a bark wherein is left no power to guide.

XLVII.

415   Wave swept on wave. We reach'd a stately square,
Deck'd for the rites. An altar stood on high,
And gorgeous, in the midst. A place for prayer,
And praise, and offering. Could the earth supply

---

1   blast] strong wind, a poeticism; bark: any small sailboat, also a recurring image of
the fragility of human life and happiness in Percy Shelley's poem *Alastor* (1816) and
Mary Shelley's novel *The Last Man* (1826).

No fruits, no flowers for sacrifice, of all
Which on her sunny lap unheeded fall? 420
No fair young firstling of the flock to die,
As when before their God the Patriarchs[1] stood?
—Look down! man brings thee, Heaven! his brother's guiltless
blood!

XLVIII.

Hear its voice, hear!—a cry goes up to thee,
From the stain'd sod;—make thou thy judgment known 425
On him, the shedder!—let his portion be
The fear that walks at midnight—give the moan
In the wind haunting him a power to say
"Where is thy brother?"[2]—and the stars a ray
To search and shake his spirit, when alone 430
With the dread splendor of their burning eyes!
—So shall earth own thy will—mercy, not sacrifice!

XLIX.

Sounds of triumphant praise!—the mass was sung—
—Voices that die not might have pour'd such strains!
Thro' Salem's[3] towers might that proud chant have rung, 435
When the Most High, on Syria's palmy plains,
Had quell'd her foes![4]—so full it swept, a sea
Of loud waves jubilant, and rolling free!

---

1 in the Old Testament of the Bible, patriarchs, or male tribal elders, sacrificed a lamb
   to God in a ritual of collective worship; in Genesis (ch. 22) God commanded the
   patriarch Abraham to sacrifice his son as a test of faith; when Abraham was about to
   do so, God substituted a ram in the son's place, indicating his rejection of the
   human sacrifice demanded in other religions; in the New Testament Christ is called
   "the lamb of God" because he sacrificed himself to absolve humanity of their sins.
2 in the Bible, when Cain murders his brother Abel, God "said unto Cain, Where is
   Abel, thy brother? And he said, I know not: Am I my brother's keeper?" (Genesis
   4.9)
3 Salem is Jerusalem, chief city of ancient Israel and religious centre of the Jews.
4 foes] in the Bible, 2 Kings 18-19, an angel sent by God destroys an Assyrian army
   besieging Jerusalem (late 8th century BC); Hemans may be recalling Byron's poem
   on this subject, "The Destruction of Sennacherib" (*Hebrew Melodies*, 1815).

—Oft when the wind, as thro' resounding fanes,
440   Hath fill'd the choral forests with its power,
Some deep tone brings me back the music of that hour.

L.

It died away;—the incense-cloud was driven
Before the breeze—the words of doom were said;
And the sun faded mournfully from Heaven,
445   —He faded mournfully! and dimly red,
Parting in clouds from those that look'd their last,
And sigh'd—"farewell, thou sun!"—Eve glow'd and
          pass'd—
Night—midnight and the moon—came forth and shed
Sleep, even as dew, on glen, wood, peopled spot—
450   Save one—a place of death—and there men slumber'd not.

LI.

'Twas not within the city^G—but in sight
Of the snow-crown'd sierras,[1] freely sweeping,
With many an eagle's eyrie on the height,
And hunter's cabin, by the torrent peeping
455   Far off: and vales between, and vineyards lay,
With sound and gleam of waters on their way,
And chesnut-woods, that girt the happy sleeping,
In many a peasant-home!—the midnight sky
Brought softly that rich world round those who came to die.

LII.

460   The darkly-glorious midnight sky of Spain,
Burning with stars!—What had the torches' glare
To do beneath that Temple, and profane
Its holy radiance?—By their wavering flare,
I saw beside the pyres—I see thee *now*,

---

1   sierras] mountain ranges of Spain.

O bright Theresa! with thy lifted brow,   465
And thy clasp'd hands, and dark eyes fill'd with prayer!
And thee, sad Inez! bowing thy fair head,
And mantling¹ up thy face, all colourless with dread!

LIII.

And Alvar, Alvar! — I beheld thee too,
Pale, stedfast,² kingly; till thy clear glance fell   470
On that young sister; then perturb'd it grew,
And all thy labouring bosom seem'd to swell
With painful tenderness. Why came I there,
That troubled image of my friend to bear,
Thence, for my after-years? — a thing to dwell   475
In my heart's core, and on the darkness rise,
Disquieting my dreams with its bright mournful eyes?

LIV.

Why came I? oh! the heart's deep mystery! — Why
In man's last hour doth vain affection's gaze
Fix itself down on struggling agony,   480
To the dimm'd eye-balls freezing, as they glaze?
It might be — yet the power to will seem'd o'er —
That my soul yearn'd to hear his voice once more!
But mine was fetter'd! — mute in strong amaze,
I watch'd his features as the night-wind blew,   485
And torch-light or the moon's pass'd o'er their marble hue.

LV.

The trampling of a steed! — a tall white steed,
Rending his fiery way the crowds among —
A storm's way through a forest — came at speed,
And a wild voice cried "Inez!" Swift she flung   490

---

1   mantling] here, cloaking.
2   stedfast] changed to the usual modern spelling "steadfast" in the 2nd edition, but
    back to "stedfast" in the 3rd edition.

The mantle from her face, and gaz'd around,
With a faint shriek at that familiar sound,
And from his seat a breathless rider sprung,
And dash'd off fiercely those who came to part,
495 And rush'd to that pale girl, and clasp'd her to his heart.

LVI.

And for a moment all around gave way
To that full burst of passion! — on his breast,
Like a bird panting yet from fear she lay,
But blest — in misery's very lap — yet blest! —
500 Oh love, love, strong as death! — from such an hour
Pressing out joy by thine immortal power,
Holy and fervent love! had earth but rest
For thee and thine, this world were all too fair!
How could we thence be wean'd to die without despair?

LVII.

505 But she — as falls a willow from the storm,
O'er its own river streaming — thus reclin'd
On the youth's bosom hung her fragile form,
And clasping arms, so passionately twin'd
Around his neck — with such a trusting fold,
510 A full deep sense of safety in their hold,
As if nought earthly might th' embrace unbind!
Alas! a child's fond faith, believing still
Its mother's breast beyond the lightning's reach to kill!

LVIII.

Brief rest! upon the turning billow's height,
515 A strange sweet moment of some heavenly strain,
Floating between the savage gusts of night,
That sweep the seas to foam! Soon dark again
The hour — the scene — th' intensely present, rush'd
Back on her spirit, and her large tears gush'd
520 Like blood-drops from a victim; with swift rain

Bathing the bosom where she lean'd that hour,
As if her life would melt into th' o'erswelling shower.

LIX.

But he, whose arm sustain'd her!—oh! I knew
'Twas vain, and yet he hop'd!—he fondly strove
Back from her faith her sinking soul to woo,   525
As life might yet be hers!—A dream of love
Which could not look upon so fair a thing,
Remembering how like hope, like joy, like spring,
Her smile was wont to glance, her step to move,
And deem that men indeed, in very truth,   530
Could mean the sting of death for her soft flowering youth!

LX.

He woo'd her back to life.—"Sweet Inez, live!
My blessed Inez!—visions have beguil'd
Thy heart—abjure them!—thou wert form'd to give,
And to find, joy; and hath not sunshine smil'd   535
Around thee ever? Leave me not, mine own!
Or earth will grow too dark!—for thee alone,
Thee have I lov'd, thou gentlest! from a child,
And borne thine image with me o'er the sea,
Thy soft voice in my soul—speak!—Oh! yet live for me!"   540

LXI.

She look'd up wildly; these were anxious eyes
Waiting that look—sad eyes of troubled thought,
Alvar's—Theresa's!—Did her childhood rise,
With all its pure and home-affections fraught,
In the brief glance?—She clasp'd her hands—the strife   545
Of love, faith, fear, and that vain dream of life,
Within her woman's breast so deeply wrought,
It seem'd as if a reed so slight and weak
Must, in the rending storm not quiver only—break!

LXII.

550   And thus it was—the young cheek flush'd and faded,
    As the swift blood in currents came and went,
    And hues of death the marble brow o'ershaded,
    And the sunk eye a watery lustre sent
    Thro' its white fluttering lids. Then tremblings pass'd
555   O'er the frail form, that shook it, as the blast
    Shakes the sere leaf, until the spirit rent
    Its way to peace—the fearful way unknown—
Pale in love's arms she lay —*she*! — what had lov'd was gone!

LXIII.

    Joy for thee, trembler! — thou redeem'd one, joy!
560   Young dove set free! earth, ashes, soulless clay,
    Remain'd for baffled vengeance to destroy;
    —*Thy* chain[1] was riven! — nor hadst thou cast away
    Thy hope in thy last hour! — though love was there
    Striving to wring thy troubled soul from prayer,
565   And life seem'd robed in beautiful array,
    Too fair to leave! — but this might be forgiven,
Thou wert so richly crown'd with precious gifts of Heaven!

LXIV.

    But woe for him who felt the heart grow still,
    Which, with its weight of agony, had lain
570   Breaking on his! — Scarce could the mortal chill
    Of the hush'd bosom, ne'er to heave again,
    And all the silence curdling round the eye,
    Bring home the stern belief that she could die,
    That she indeed could die! — for wild and vain
575   As hope might be—his soul *had* hoped—'twas o'er—
    —Slowly his failing arms dropp'd from the form they bore.

---

1   chain] prisoner's chain, and also tie to mortal life.

LXV.

They forc'd him from that spot. — It might be well,
That the fierce, reckless words by anguish wrung
From his torn breast, all aimless as they fell,
Like spray-drops from the strife of torrents flung, 580
Were mark'd as guilt. — There are, who note these things
Against the smitten heart; its breaking strings
—On whose low thrills once gentle music hung—
With a rude hand of touch unholy trying,
And numbering then as crimes, the deep, strange tones
replying.¹ 585

LXVI.

But ye in solemn joy, O faithful pair!
Stood gazing on your parted sister's dust;
I saw your features by the torch's glare,
And they were brightening with a heavenward trust!
I saw the doubt, the anguish, the dismay, 590
Melt from my Alvar's glorious mien away,
And peace was there—the calmness of the just!
And, bending down the slumberer's brow to kiss,
"Thy rest is won," he said;—"sweet sister! praise for this!"

LXVII.

I started as from sleep;—yes! he had spoken— 595
A breeze had troubled memory's hidden source!
At once the torpor of my soul was broken—
Thought, feeling, passion, woke in tenfold force.
—There are soft breathings in the southern wind,
That so your ice-chains, O ye streams! unbind, 600

---

1   the passage refers to the Inquisition's use of spies to report any expressions that
    could be construed as heresy and punished; spies were similarly used in Britain and
    elsewhere during the French Revolution and its aftermath; Henry Blanco White's
    Letters of Don Leucadio Doblado (1822), which partly inspired Hemans's poem,
    blames the Inquisition's use of spies for undermining social and familial bonds.

And free the foaming swiftness of your course!
　—I burst from those that held me back, and fell
Ev'n on his neck, and cried—"Friend, brother! fare thee
　　　well!"

LXVIII.

Did *he* not say "Farewell?"—Alas! no breath
605　Came to mine ear. Hoarse murmurs from the throng
Told that the mysteries[1] in the face of death
Had from their eager sight been veil'd too long.
And we were parted as the surge might part
Those that would die together, true of heart.
610　—*His* hour was come—but in mine anguish strong,
Like a fierce swimmer through the midnight sea,[2]
Blindly I rush'd away from that which was to be.

LXIX.

Away—away I rush'd;—but swift and high
The arrowy pillars of the firelight grew,
615　Till the transparent darkness of the sky
Flush'd to a blood-red mantle in their hue;
And, phantom-like, the kindling city seem'd
To spread, float, wave, as on the wind they stream'd,
With their wild splendour chasing me!—I knew
620　The death-work was begun—I veil'd mine eyes,
Yet stopp'd in spell-bound fear to catch the victims' cries.

LXX.

What heard I then?—a ringing shriek of pain,
Such as for ever haunts the tortur'd ear?

1　mysteries] sacred rites, though usually the term applies to the Christian sacraments, not executions.
2　in classical myth and literature, Leander swam across the Hellespont for nightly trysts with Hero, a priestess, guided by her lamp, but when it failed one night he drowned, and she killed herself in grief.

—I heard a sweet and solemn-breathing strain
Piercing the flames, untremulous and clear!   625
—The rich, triumphal tones!—I knew them well,
As they came floating with a breezy swell!
Man's voice was there—a clarion voice to cheer
In the mid-battle—ay, to turn the flying—
Woman's—that might have sung of Heaven beside the dying!   630

LXXI.

It was a fearful, yet a glorious thing,
To hear that hymn of martyrdom, and know
That its glad stream of melody could spring
Up from th' unsounded gulfs of human woe!
Alvar! Theresa!—what is deep? what strong?   635
—God's breath within the soul!—It fill'd that song
From your victorious voices!—but the glow
On the hot air and lurid skies increas'd—
—Faint grew the sounds—more faint—I listen'd—they had
        ceas'd!

LXXII.

And thou indeed hadst perish'd, my soul's friend!   640
I might form other ties—but thou alone
Couldst with a glance the veil of dimness rend,
By other years o'er boyhood's memory thrown!
Others might aid me onward:—Thou and I
Had mingled the fresh thoughts that early die,   645
Once flowering—never more!—And thou wert gone!
Who could give back my youth, my spirit free,
Or be in aught again what thou hadst been to me?

LXXIII.

And yet I wept thee not, thou true and brave!
I could not weep!—there gather'd round thy name   650

Too deep a passion! —*thou* denied a grave![1]
Thou, with the blight flung on thy soldier's fame!
Had I not known thy heart from childhood's time?
Thy heart of hearts? —and couldst thou die for crime?
655 —No! had all earth decreed that death of shame,
I would have set, against all earth's decree,
Th' inalienable trust of my firm soul in thee!

LXXIV.

There are swift hours in life —strong, rushing hours,
That do the work of tempests in their might!
660 They shake down things that stood as rocks and towers
Unto th' undoubting mind;—they pour in light
Where it but startles —like a burst of day
For which th' uprooting of an oak makes way;—
They sweep the colouring mists from off our sight,
665 They touch with fire, thought's graven page, the roll
Stamp'd with past years —and lo! it shrivels as a scroll!

LXXV.

And this was of such hours! —the sudden flow
Of my soul's tide seem'd whelming me; the glare
Of the red flames, yet rocking to and fro,
670 Scorch'd up my heart with breathless thirst for air,
And solitude, and freedom. It had been
Well with me then, in some vast desert scene,
To pour my voice out, for the winds to bear
On with them, wildly questioning the sky,
675 Fiercely th' untroubled stars, of man's dim destiny.

LXXVI.

I would have call'd, adjuring the dark cloud;
To the most ancient Heavens I would have said

---

1 heretics were denied burial in consecrated ground.

—"Speak to me! show me truth!"[H]—through night aloud
I would have cried to him, the newly dead,
"Come back! and show me truth!"—My spirit seem'd   680
Grasping for some free burst, its darkness teem'd
With such pent storms of thought!—again I fled—
I fled, a refuge from man's face to gain,
Scarce conscious when I paus'd, entering a lonely fane.

LXXVII.

A mighty minster,[1] dim, and proud, and vast!   685
Silence was round the sleepers, whom its floor
Shut in the grave;[2] a shadow of the past,
A memory of the sainted steps that wore
Erewhile its gorgeous pavement, seem'd to brood
Like mist upon the stately solitude,   690
A halo of sad fame to mantle o'er
Its white sepulchral forms of mail-clad men,
And all was hush'd as night in some deep Alpine[3] glen.

LXXVIII.

More hush'd, far more!—for there the wind sweeps by,
Or the woods tremble to the streams' loud play!   695
Here a strange echo made my very sigh
Seem for the place too much a sound of day!
Too much my footstep broke the moonlight, fading,
Yet arch through arch in one soft flow pervading;
And I stood still:—prayer, chant, had died away,   700
Yet past me floated a funereal breath
Of incense.—I stood still—as before God and death!

---

1 minster] large church or cathedral.
2 the dead, especially the wealthy and powerful, were buried beneath the church
   floors.
3 Alpine] here, of mountains in general, rather than the Alps of central Europe.

LXXIX.

For thick ye girt me round, ye long-departed![1]
Dust — imaged form — with cross, and shield, and crest;
It seem'd as if your ashes would have started,
Had a wild voice burst forth above your rest!
Yet ne'er, perchance, did worshipper of yore
Bear to your thrilling presence what *I* bore
Of wrath — doubt — anguish — battling in the breast!
I could have pour'd out words, on that pale air,
To make your proud tombs ring: — no, no! I could not *there!*

LXXX.

Not midst those aisles, through which a thousand years
Mutely as clouds and reverently had swept;
Not by those shrines, which yet the trace of tears
And kneeling votaries on their marble kept!
Ye were too mighty in your pomp of gloom
And trophied age, O temple, altar, tomb!
And you, ye dead! — for in that faith ye slept,
Whose weight had grown a mountain's on my heart,
Which could not *there* be loos'd. — I turn'd me to depart.

LXXXI.

I turn'd — what glimmer'd faintly on my sight,
Faintly, yet brightening, as a wreath of snow
Seen through dissolving haze? — The moon, the night,
Had waned, and dawn pour'd in; — grey, shadowy, slow,
Yet day-spring[1] still! — a solemn hue it caught,
Piercing the storied windows,[2] darkly fraught
With stoles and draperies of imperial glow;
And soft, and sad, that colouring gleam was thrown,
Where, pale, a pictur'd form above the altar shone.[3]

705
710

715
720

725

---

1 day-spring] dawn, a usage from the Bible.
2 stained glass windows in churches often depict stories from the Bible and saints' lives.
3 the following stanzas describe a picture illustrating the story of one of Christ's

LXXXII.

Thy form, thou[1] Son of God! — a wrathful deep,   730
With foam, and cloud, and tempest, round thee spread,
And such a weight of night! — a night, when sleep
From the fierce rocking of the billows fled.
A bark show'd dim beyond thee, with its mast
Bow'd, and its rent sail shivering to the blast;   735
But, like a spirit in thy gliding tread,
Thou, as o'er glass, didst walk that stormy sea
Through rushing winds, which left a silent path for thee.[2]

LXXXIII.

So still thy white robes fell! — no breath of air
Within their long and slumberous folds had sway!   740
So still the waves of parted, shadowy hair
From thy clear brow flow'd droopingly away!
Dark were the Heavens above thee, Saviour! — dark
The gulfs, Deliverer! round the straining bark!
But thou! — o'er all thine aspect and array   745
Was pour'd one stream of pale, broad, silvery light —
— Thou wert the single star of that all-shrouding night!

LXXXIV.

Aid for one sinking! — Thy lone brightness gleam'd
On his wild face, just lifted o'er the wave,
With its worn, fearful, *human* look that seem'd   750
To cry through surge and blast — "I perish — save!"
Not to the winds — not vainly! — thou wert nigh,

---

miracles, recounted in the Bible (Mark, 6.45-52, and corresponding passages in Matthew and Luke), when Christ walked on the waters of the sea at night during a storm, calming the waves and reassuring his fishermen-disciples; the incident was frequently illustrated in the visual arts.

1 thou] here and elsewhere in these stanzas the first letter of the pronouns "thee" and "thou" are capitalized in the 2nd and 3rd editions in accord with pious usage for pronouns referring to God or Jesus.

2 period added in 2nd edition.

Thy hand was stretch'd to fainting agony,
Even in the portals of th' unquiet grave!
755   O thou that art the life! and yet didst bear
Too much of mortal woe to turn from mortal prayer![1]

LXXXV.

But was it not a thing to rise on death,
With its remember'd light, that face of thine,
Redeemer! dimm'd by this world's misty breath,
760   Yet mournfully, mysteriously divine?
—Oh! that calm, sorrowful, prophetic eye,
With its dark depths of grief, love, majesty!
And the pale glory of the brow!—a shrine
Where Power sat veil'd, yet shedding softly round
765 What told that *thou* couldst be but for a time uncrown'd![2]

LXXXVI.

And more than all, the Heaven of that sad smile!
The lip of mercy, our immortal trust!
Did not that look, that very look, erewhile,
Pour its o'ershadow'd beauty on the dust?
Wert thou not such when earth's dark cloud hung o'er
770   thee?
—Surely thou wert!—my heart grew hush'd before thee,
Sinking with all its passions, as the gust
Sank at thy voice, along its billowy way: —
—What had I there to do, but kneel, and weep, and pray?

LXXXVII.

775   Amidst the stillness rose my spirit's cry
Amidst the dead—"By that full cup of woe,

---

1   the line refers to the Christian belief that Jesus Christ assumed human form to
     suffer and die as a mortal and thereby redeem humanity from their sins.
2   in becoming mortal to redeem humanity, Christ temporarily set aside his "crown"
     of divinity as the son of God.

Press'd from the fruitage[1] of mortality,
Saviour! for thee—give light! that I may know
If by *thy* will, in thine all-healing name,
Men cast down human hearts to blighting shame,   780
And early death—and say, if this be so,
Where then is mercy?—whither shall we flee,
So unallied to hope, save by our hold on thee?

LXXXVIII.

"But didst thou not, the deep sea brightly treading,
Lift from despair that struggler with the wave?   785
And wert thou not, sad tears, yet awful, shedding,
Beheld, a weeper at a mortal's grave?[2]
And is this weight of anguish, which they bind
On life, this searing to the quick of mind,
That but to God its own free path would crave,   790
This crushing out of hope, and love, and youth,
Thy will indeed?—Give light! that I may know the truth![3]

LXXXIX.

"For my sick soul is darken'd unto death,
With shadows from the suffering it hath seen
The strong foundations of mine ancient faith   795
Sink from beneath me—whereon shall I lean?
—Oh! if from thy pure lips was wrung the sigh
Of the dust's anguish! if like man to die,
—And earth round *him* shuts heavily—hath been

---

1   fruitage] here, the fruit of experience ("mortality") producing "woe," which may
    however be morally and spiritually instructive and chastening, as pressed grapes
    produce the juice made into wine, which may be used to ameliorate human life; a
    common biblical image and one used in referring to the human misery produced
    by the conflicts of the Revolutionary and Napoleonic eras.
2   in the Bible, "Jesus wept" at the graveside of Lazarus before raising him from the
    dead (John, 11.35).
3   the passage refers to theodicy, or the problem of evil, much debated in the 18th
    century, and especially during the French Revolution and Napoleonic wars; the
    problem was to reconcile belief in a benevolent God with the historical reality of
    widespread misery and suffering.

800　　　Even to *thee* bitter, aid me! — guide me! — turn
　　　My wild and wandering thoughts back from their starless
　　　　　　　bourne!"

XC.

　　　And calm'd I rose: — but how the while had risen
　　　Morn's orient sun, dissolving mist and shade!
　　　— Could there indeed be wrong, or chain, or prison,
805　　In the bright world such radiance might pervade?
　　　It fill'd the fane, it mantled[1] the pale form
　　　Which rose before me through the pictured storm,
　　　Even the grey tombs it kindled, and array'd
　　　With life! — how hard to see thy race begun,
810　And think man wakes to grief, wakening to *thee*, O sun![2]

XCI.

　　　I sought my home again: — and thou, my child,
　　　There at thy play beneath yon ancient pine,
　　　With eyes, whose lightning laughter[J] hath beguil'd
　　　A thousand pangs, thence flashing joy to mine;
815　　Thou in thy mother's arms, a babe, didst meet
　　　My coming with young smiles, which yet, though sweet,
　　　Seem'd on my soul all mournfully to shine,
　　　And ask a happier heritage for thee,
　　　Than but in turn the blight of human hope to see.

XCII.

820　　Now sport, for thou are free — the bright birds chasing,
　　　Whose wings waft star-like gleams from tree to tree;
　　　Or with the fawn, thy swift wood-playmate racing,
　　　Sport on, my joyous child! for thou art free!
　　　Yes, on that day I took thee to my heart,

1　mantled] here, covered with a blush-red.
2　sun] familiar pun on "son," i.e., Christ as the son of God, but also as the light of rev-
　　elation and truth.

And inly vow'd, for thee a better part 825
To choose; that so thy sunny bursts of glee
Should wake no more dim thoughts of far-seen woe,
But, gladdening fearless eyes, flow on—as now they flow.

XCIII.

Thou hast a rich world round thee: —Mighty shades
Weaving their gorgeous tracery o'er thy head, 830
With the light melting through their high arcades,
As through a pillar'd cloister's:ᴷ but the dead
Sleep not beneath; nor doth the sunbeam pass
To marble shrines through rainbow-tinted glass;
Yet thou, by fount and forest-murmur led 835
To worship, thou art blest! —to thee is shown
Earth in her holy pomp, deck'd for her God alone.

THE FOREST SANCTUARY.
PART SECOND.

Wie diese treue liebe seele
Von ihrem Glauben Voll,
Der ganz allein
Ihr selig machend ist, sich heilig quäle,
Das sie den liebsten Mann verloren halten soll!

FAUST.[1]

---

1   from *Faust* (part 1, 1808, lines 3529-33, scene 18), a play by the German writer
    Johann Wolfgang von Goethe (1749-1832) in which a scholar sells his soul to the
    Devil in exchange for transcendental knowledge; the lines are spoken by Faust
    about his lover, Margarete:

    How a true loving soul like this,
    Full of the faith she doth believe
    To be the pledge of endless bliss,
    Must mourn, her soul with anguish tossed,
    Thinking the man she loves forever lost.

(*Dramatic Works of Goethe*, translated by Anna Swanwick, London, 1873).

I never shall smile more—but all my days
Walk with still footsteps and with humble eyes,
An everlasting hymn within my soul.

WILSON.[1]

I.

BRING me the sounding of the torrent-water,
With yet a nearer swell—fresh breeze, awake![L]
And river, darkening ne'er with hues of slaughter
Thy wave's pure silvery green,—and shining lake,
5 Spread far before my cabin, with thy zone
Of ancient woods, ye chainless things and lone!
Send voices through the forest aisles, and make
Glad music round me, that my soul may dare,
Cheer'd by such tones, to look back on a dungeon's air!

II.

10 Oh, Indian hunter[2] of the desert's race!
That with the spear at times, or bended bow,
Dost cross my footsteps in thy fiery chase
Of the swift elk or blue hill's flying roe;
Thou that beside the red night-fire thou heapest,
15 Beneath the cedars and the star-light sleepest,
Thou know'st not, wanderer—never may'st thou know!—
Of the dark holds[3] wherewith man cumbers earth,
To shut from human eyes the dancing seasons' mirth.

---

1 from the last scene of *The Convict* (1816), a verse drama by John Wilson (1785-1854), Scottish poet, novelist, and critic for *Blackwood's Magazine*, where Hemans first published many of her poems; the speaker is the convict's Wife, who has learned that her husband, falsely accused of murder, has been released by the timely confession of the actual murderer; Hemans alters the meaning of the passage in the original by leaving out its last words: "… within my soul, / To the great God of Mercy."

2 hunter] the supposedly innocent or "noble savage," here an American aborigine, was a familiar figure in reformist criticism of European decadence and corruption.

3 holds] prison cells, typically supposed to be in a "hold," or fortress.

III.

There, fetter'd down from day, to think the while
How bright in Heaven the festal sun is glowing,   20
Making earth's loneliest places, with his smile,
Flush like the rose; and how the streams are flowing
With sudden sparkles through the shadowy grass,
And water-flowers, all trembling as they pass;
And how the rich dark summer-trees are bowing   25
With their full foliage;— this to know, and pine
Bound unto midnight's heart, seems a stern lot —'twas mine.

IV.

Wherefore was this? — Because my soul had drawn
Light from the book[1] whose words are grav'd in light!
There, at its well-head, had I found the dawn,   30
And day, and noon of freedom: — but too bright
It shines on that which man to man hath given,
And call'd the truth—the very truth, from Heaven!
And therefore seeks he, in his brother's sight,
To cast the mote;[2] and therefore strives to bind   35
With his strong chains to earth, what is not earth's —the
        mind!

V.

It is a weary and a bitter task
Back from the lip the burning word to keep,
And to shut out Heaven's air with falsehood's mask,
And in the dark urn of the soul to heap   40
Indignant feelings — making even of thought

---

1 book] the Christian Bible; many Protestants claimed that, unlike Roman Catholics,
   they drew their religious beliefs directly from the Bible rather than from the
   authority of a worldly church.
2 mote] speck; reference to a passage from Christ's Sermon on the Mount in the
   Bible, in which he rebukes his listeners for engaging in criticism of others: "And
   why beholdest thou the mote that is in thy brother's eye, but perceivest not the
   beam that is in thine own eye?" (Luke, 6.41; also Matthew, 7.3)

A buried treasure, which may but be sought
When shadows are abroad—and night—and sleep.
I might not brook it long—and thus was thrown
45   Into that grave-like cell, to wither there alone.

VI.

And I a child of danger, whose delights
Were on dark hills and many-sounding seas—
I, that amidst the Cordillera heights[1]
Had given Castilian banners to the breeze,[2]
50   And the full circle of the rainbow seen
There, on the snows;[M] and in my country been
A mountain wanderer, from the Pyrenees
To the Morena crags[3]—how left I not
Life, or the soul's life quench'd, on that sepulchral spot?

VII.

55   Because *Thou* didst not leave me, oh, my God!
Thou wert with those that bore the truth of old
Into the deserts from the oppressor's rod,
And made the caverns of the rock their fold,
And in the hidden chambers of the dead,[4]
60   Our guiding lamp with fire immortal fed,
And met when stars met, by their beams to hold
The free heart's communing with Thee,—and Thou
Wert in the midst, felt, own'd—the strengthener then as now!

---

1   heights] here, Andes mountains.
2   Castile, one of the kingdoms of medieval Christian Spain, led the unification of
    Spain and expulsion of the Moors and monopolized conquest and management of
    the Spanish empire in the New World.
3   the Sierra Morena is a mountain range in southern Spain, the Pyrenees a range
    forming Spain's northern frontier with France.
4   when persecuted by the Roman government, early Christians would worship
    secretly in desert places, caves, and catacombs (underground caverns where bodies
    of the dead were kept).

VIII.

Yet once I sank. Alas! man's wavering mind!
Wherefore and whence the gusts that o'er it blow?   65
How they bear with them, floating uncombin'd,
The shadows of the past, that come and go,
As o'er the deep the old long-buried things,
Which a storm's working to the surface brings!
Is the reed shaken, and must *we* be so,   70
With every wind?[1]—So, Father! must we be,
Till we can fix undimm'd our stedfast[2] eyes on Thee.

IX.

Once my soul died within me. What had thrown
That sickness o'er it?—Even a passing thought
Of a clear spring, whose side, with flowers o'ergrown,   75
Fondly and oft my boyish steps had sought!
Perchance the damp roof's water-drops, that fell
Just then, low tinkling through my vaulted cell,
Intensely heard amidst the stillness, caught
Some tone from memory, of the music, welling   80
Ever with that fresh rill, from its deep rocky dwelling.

X.

But so my spirit's fever'd longings wrought,
Wakening, it might be, to the faint sad sound,
That from the darkness of the walls they brought
A lov'd scene round me, visibly around.[N]   85
Yes! kindling, spreading, brightening, hue by hue,
Like stars from midnight, through the gloom it grew,
That haunt of youth, hope, manhood! — till the bound

---

1   in the Bible, Jesus asks a doubting multitude who had gone to see the prophet and ascetic John the Baptist if they went only in order to see "a reed shaken with the wind" (Matthew, 11.7), i.e., a morally frail impostor or hypocrite shaken by temptation.

2   stedfast] altered to the usual modern "steadfast" in the 2nd and 3rd editions.

Of my shut cavern seem'd dissolv'd, and I
90 Girt by the solemn hills and burning pomp of sky.

XI.

I look'd—and lo! the clear broad river flowing,
Past the old Moorish ruin[1] on the steep,
The lone tower dark against a Heaven all glowing,
Like seas of glass and fire!—I saw the sweep
95 Of glorious woods far down the mountain side,
And their still shadows in the gleaming tide,
And the red evening on its waves asleep;
And midst the scene—oh! more than all—there smil'd
My child's fair face, and hers, the mother of my child!

XII.

100 With their soft eyes of love and gladness rais'd
Up to the flushing sky, as when we stood
Last by that river, and in silence gaz'd
On the rich world of sunset:—but a flood
Of sudden tenderness my soul oppress'd,
105 And I rush'd forward with a yearning breast,
To clasp—alas! a vision!—Wave and wood,
And gentle faces, lifted in the light
Of day's last hectic blush, all melted from my sight.

XIII.

Then darkness!—oh! th' unutterable gloom
110 That seem'd as narrowing round me, making less
And less my dungeon, when, with all its bloom,
That bright dream vanish'd from my loneliness!
It floated off, the beautiful!—yet left
Such deep thirst in my soul, that thus bereft,

---

1 ruin] the Moors, a coalition of Muslim Berbers and other tribes from North Africa,
   seized parts of the Iberian peninsula in the 8th century AD and ruled parts of it until
   1492.

I lay down, sick with passion's vain excess,   115
And pray'd to die. — How oft would sorrow weep
Her weariness to death, if he might come like sleep!

XIV.

But I was rous'd — and how? — It is no tale
Even midst *thy* shades, thou wilderness, to tell!
I would not have my boy's young cheek made pale,   120
Nor haunt his sunny rest with what befel
In that drear prison-house. — His eyes must grow
More dark with thought, more earnest his fair brow,
More high his heart in youthful strength must swell;
So shall it fitly burn when all is told: —   125
Let childhood's radiant mist the free child yet enfold!

XV.

It is enough that through such heavy hours,
As wring us by our fellowship of clay,
I liv'd, and undegraded. We have powers
To snatch th' oppressor's bitter joy away!   130
Shall the wild Indian, for his savage fame,
Laugh and expire,[1] and shall not truth's high name
Bear up her martyrs with all-conquering sway?
It is enough that Torture may be vain —
I had seen Alvar die — the strife was won from Pain.   135

XVI.

And faint not, heart of man! though years wane slow![2]
There have been those that from the deepest caves,
And cells of night, and fastnesses, below

---

1 reference to the supposed use of ritual torture by some eastern North American
   aboriginal tribes; war captives were tortured to death, and the victim who with-
   stood the pain without complaint was supposed to have increased his and his tribe's
   prestige.
2 exclamation mark omitted in 3rd edition.

The stormy dashing of the ocean-waves,
140 Down, farther down than gold lies hid, have nurs'd
A quenchless hope, and watch'd their time, and burst
On the bright day, like wakeners from the graves![1]
I was of such at last! — unchain'd I trod
This green earth, taking back my freedom from my God!

XVII.

145 That was an hour to send its fadeless trace
Down life's far sweeping tide! — A dim, wild night,
Like sorrow, hung upon the soft moon's face,
Yet how my heart leap'd in her blessed light!
The shepherd's light — the sailor's on the sea —
150 The hunter's homeward from the mountains free,
Where its lone smile makes tremulously bright
The thousand streams! — I could but gaze through tears —
Oh! what a sight is Heaven, thus first beheld for years!

XVIII.

The rolling clouds! — they have the whole blue space
155 Above to sail in — all the dome of sky!
My soul shot with them in their breezy race
O'er star and gloom! — but I had yet to fly,
As flies the hunted wolf. A secret spot,
And strange, I knew — the sunbeam knew it not;—
160 Wildest of all the savage glens that lie
In far sierras, hiding their deep springs,
And travers'd but by storms, or sounding eagles' wings.

XIX.

Ay, and I met the storm there! — I had gain'd
The covert's heart with swift and stealthy tread:
165 A moan went past me, and the dark trees rain'd

---

1   according to the Bible, at the end of human history God will resurrect the dead and take those who deserve salvation to eternal life in heaven.

Their autumn foliage rustling on my head;
A moan—a hollow gust—and there I stood
Girt with majestic night, and ancient wood,
And foaming water. — Thither might have fled
The mountain Christian with his faith of yore,   170
When Afric's tambour¹ shook the ringing western shore!

XX.

But through the black ravine the storm came swelling—
Mighty thou art amidst the hills, thou blast!
In thy lone course the kingly cedars felling,
Like plumes upon the path of battle cast!   175
A rent oak thunder'd down beside my cave—
Booming it rush'd, as booms a deep sea-wave;
A falcon soar'd; a startled wild-deer pass'd;
A far-off bell toll'd faintly through the roar—
How my glad spirit swept forth with the winds once more!   180

XXI.

And with the arrowy lightnings!—for they flash'd,
Smiting the branches in their fitful play,
And brightly shivering where the torrents dash'd
Up, even to crag and eagle's nest, their spray!
And there to stand amidst the pealing strife,   185
The strong pines groaning with tempestuous life,
And all the mountain-voices on their way,—
Was it not joy?—'twas joy in rushing might,
After those years that wove but one long dead of night!

XXII.

There came a softer hour, a lovelier moon,   190
And lit me to my home of youth again,
Through the dim chesnut shade, where oft at noon,

---

1   tambour] bass drum; when the Moors invaded Spain from north Africa, the Chris-
tians fled into the northern mountains.

By the fount's flashing burst, my head had lain,
In gentle sleep: but now I pass'd as one
195   That may not pause where wood-streams whispering run,
Or light sprays[1] tremble to a bird's wild strain,
Because th' avenger's voice is in the wind,
The foe's quick rustling step close on the leaves behind.

XXIII.

My home of youth! — oh! if indeed to part
200   With the soul's lov'd ones be a mournful thing,
When we go forth in buoyancy of heart,
And bearing all the glories of our spring
For life to breathe on, — is it less to meet,
When these are faded? — who shall call it sweet?
205   — Even though love's mingling tears may haply bring
Balm as they fall, too well their heavy showers
Teach us how much is lost of all that once was ours!

XXIV.

Not by the sunshine, with its golden glow,
Nor the green earth, nor yet the laughing sky,
210   Nor the faint flower-scents,° as they come and go
In the soft air, like music wandering by;
— Oh! not by these, th' unfailing, are we taught
How time and sorrow on our frames have wrought,
But by the sadden'd eye, the darken'd brow,
215   Of kindred aspects, and the long dim gaze,
Which tells us *we* are chang'd, — how chang'd from other days!

XXV.

Before my father — in my place of birth,
I stood an alien. On the very floor
Which oft had trembled to my boyish mirth,

---

1   sprays] branches.

The love that rear'd me, knew my face no more! 220
There hung the antique armour, helm and crest,
Whose every stain woke childhood in my breast,
There droop'd the banner, with the marks it bore
Of Paynim[1] spears; and I, the worn in frame
And heart, what there was I?—another and the same! 225

XXVI.

Then bounded in a boy, with clear dark eye—
—How should *he* know his father?—when we parted,
From the soft cloud which mantles infancy,
His soul, just wakening into wonder, darted
Its first looks round. Him follow'd one, the bride 230
Of my young days, the wife how lov'd and tried!
Her glance met mine—I could not speak—she started
With a bewilder'd gaze;—until there came
Tears to my burning eyes, and from my lips her name.

XXVII.

She knew me then!—I murmur'd "*Leonor!*" 235
And her heart answer'd!—oh! the voice is known
First from all else, and swiftest to restore
Love's buried images with one low tone,
That strikes like lightning, when the cheek is faded,
And the brow heavily with thought o'ershaded, 240
And all the brightness from the aspect gone!
—Upon my breast she sunk, when doubt was fled,
Weeping as those may weep, that meet in woe and dread.

XXVIII.

For there we might not rest. Alas! to leave
Those native towers, and know that they must fall 245

---

1 Paynim] a common poeticism, cognate with "pagan," for a non-Christian, especial-
ly a Muslim; here a reference to the wars of the Christian kingdoms of Spain to
expel the Moors.

By slow decay, and none remain to grieve
When the weeds cluster'd on the lonely wall!
We were the last—my boy and I—the last
Of a long line which brightly thence had pass'd!
250 My father bless'd me as I left his hall—
—With his deep tones and sweet, tho' full of years,
He bless'd me there, and bath'd my child's young head with
tears.

XXIX.

I had brought sorrow on his grey hairs down,
And cast the darkness of my branded name
255 (For so *he* deem'd it) on the clear renown,
My own ancestral heritage of fame.
And yet he bless'd me!—Father! if the dust
Lie on those lips benign, my spirit's trust
Is to behold thee yet, where grief and shame
260 Dim the bright day no more; and thou wilt know
That not thro' guilt thy son thus bow'd thine age with woe!

XXX.

And thou, my Leonor! that unrepining,
If sad in soul, didst quit all else for me,
When stars—the stars that earliest rise—are shining,
265 How their soft glance unseals each thought of thee!
For on our flight they smil'd;—their dewy rays,
Thro' the last olives, lit thy tearful gaze
Back to the home we never more might see;
So pass'd we on, like earth's first exiles, turning
270 Fond looks where hung the sword above their Eden burning.[1]

---

1 reference to Milton's recasting (*Paradise Lost* 12.624-49) of the Bible's account
(Genesis, 3.24) of the destruction of Eden, or paradise created by God for Adam
and Eve, the first man and woman; God sends a sword-bearing angel to expel them
("earth's first exiles") from the garden for disobeying his prohibition against eating
fruit from the Tree of Knowledge of good and evil; thereafter, humanity was con-
demned to time, mortality, and labour until God should command the end of time
and the gathering of the righteous to eternal life in heaven.

XXXI.

It was a woe to say — "Farewell, my Spain!
The sunny and the vintage land, farewell!"
— I could have died upon the battle plain
For thee, my country! but I might not dwell
In thy sweet vales, at peace. — The voice of song   275
Breathes, with the myrtle[1] scent, thy hills along;
The citron's[2] glow is caught from shade and dell;
But what are these? — upon thy flowery sod
I might not kneel, and pour my free thoughts out to God!

XXXII.

O'er the blue deep I fled, the chainless deep!   280
— Strange heart of man! that ev'n midst woe swells high,
When thro' the foam he sees his proud bark sweep,
Flinging out joyous gleams to wave and sky!
Yes! it swells high, whate'er he leaves behind;
His spirit rises with the rising wind;   285
For, wedded to the far futurity,
On, on, it bears him ever, and the main
Seems rushing, like his hope, some happier shore to gain.

XXXIII.

Not thus is woman. Closely *her* still heart
Doth twine itself with ev'n each lifeless thing,   290
Which, long remember'd, seem'd to bear its part
In her calm joys. For ever would she cling,
A brooding dove, to that sole spot of earth
Where she hath loved, and given her children birth,
And heard their first sweet voices.[3] There may Spring   295

---

1 myrtle] a shrub with shiny evergreen leaves and white sweet-smelling flowers, associated in myth and literature with the goddess Venus and love.

2 citron is a tree-fruit, larger than the lemon, formerly including the lemon and the lime.

3 Susan Wolfson suggests that the description of Leonor echoes that of Margaret, loyal wife and mother in Wordsworth's *The Excursion* (1814, 1.953-55; 910-12 in 1850 text).

Array no path, renew no flower, no leaf,
But hath its breath of home, its claim to farewell grief.

XXXIV.

I look'd on Leonor, and if there seem'd
A cloud of more than pensiveness to rise,
300   In the faint smiles that o'er her features gleam'd,
And the soft darkness of her serious eyes,
Misty with tender gloom; I call'd it nought
But the fond exile's pang, a lingering thought
Of her own vale, with all its melodies
305   And living light of streams. Her soul would rest
Beneath your shades, I said, bowers of the gorgeous west![1]

XXXV.

Oh! could we live in visions! could we hold
Delusion faster, longer, to our breast,
When it shuts from us, with its mantle's fold,
310   That which we see not, and are therefore blest!
But they, our lov'd and loving, they to whom
We have spread out our souls in joy and gloom,
Their looks and accents, unto ours address'd,
Have been a language of familiar tone
315 Too long to breathe, at last, dark sayings and unknown.

XXXVI.

I told my heart 'twas but the exile's woe
Which press'd on that sweet bosom;—I deceiv'd
My heart but half: —a whisper faint and low,
Haunting it ever, and at times believ'd,
320   Spoke of some deeper cause. How oft we seem
Like those that dream, and *know* the while[2] they dream,

---

1   the "west," or New World, is "gorgeous" (richly and brilliantly coloured) because of
    its association with sunset.

2   the while] poetic ellipsis for "all the while."

Midst the soft falls of airy voices griev'd,
And troubled, while bright phantoms round them play,
By a dim sense that all will float and fade away!

XXXVII.

Yet, as if chasing joy, I woo'd the breeze,   325
To speed me onward with the wings of morn.
—Oh! far amidst the solitary seas,
Which were not made for man, what man hath borne,
Answering their moan with his!—what *thou* didst bear,
My lost and loveliest! while that secret care   330
Grew terror, and thy gentle spirit, worn
By its dull brooding weight, gave way at last,
Beholding me as one from hope for ever cast![1]

XXXVIII.

For unto thee, as thro' all change, reveal'd
Mine inward being lay. In other eyes   335
I had to bow me yet, and make a shield,
To fence my burning bosom, of disguise;
By the still hope sustain'd, ere long to win
Some sanctuary, whose green retreats within,
My thoughts unfetter'd to their source might rise,   340
Like songs and scents of morn. —But thou didst look
Thro' all my soul, and thine even unto fainting shook.

XXXIX.

Fall'n, fall'n, I seem'd—yet, oh! not less belov'd,
Tho' from thy love was pluck'd the early pride,
And harshly, by a gloomy faith reproved,   345
And sear'd with shame!—tho' each young flower had died,
There was the root,—strong, living, not the less
That all it yielded now was bitterness;

---

1   a heretic is "for ever cast" beyond hope of salvation in the afterlife, where otherwise
the narrator and his wife might be re-united.

Yet still such love as quits not misery's side,
350   Nor drops from guilt its ivy-like embrace,[1]
Nor turns away from death's its pale heroic face.

XL.

Yes! thou hadst follow'd me thro' fear and flight;
Thou wouldst have follow'd had my pathway led
Even to the scaffold; had the flashing light
355   Of the rais'd axe made strong men shrink with dread,
Thou, midst the hush of thousands, wouldst have been
With thy clasp'd hands beside me kneeling seen,
And meekly bowing to the shame thy head—
— The shame!—oh! making beautiful to view
360   The might of human love—fair thing! so bravely true!

XLI.

There was thine agony—to love so well
Where fear made love life's chastener.—Heretofore
Whate'er of earth's disquiet round thee fell,
Thy soul, o'erpassing its dim bounds, could soar
365   Away to sunshine, and thy clear eye speak
Most of the skies when grief most touch'd thy cheek.
Now, that far brightness faded! never more
Couldst thou lift heavenwards for its hope thy heart,
Since at Heaven's gate[2] it seem'd that thou and I must part.

XLII.

370   Alas! and life hath moments when a glance
(If thought to sudden watchfulness be stirr'd,)
A flush—a fading of the cheek perchance,
A word—less, less—the *cadence* of a word,
Lets in our gaze the mind's dim veil beneath,
375   Thence to bring haply knowledge fraught with death!

---

1   ivy is a clinging plant but also parasitic, killing its host.
2   where the saved enter but the damned are excluded.

—Even thus, what never from thy lip was heard
Broke on my soul. —I knew that in thy sight
I stood—howe'er belov'd—a recreant[1] from the light!

XLIII.

Thy sad sweet hymn, at eve, the seas along,—
—Oh! the deep soul it breath'd!—the love, the woe,   380
The fervor, pour'd in that full gush of song,
As it went floating through the fiery glow
Of the rich sunset!—bringing thoughts of Spain,
With all her vesper-voices,[2] o'er the main,
Which seem'd responsive in its murmuring flow.   385
—"*Ave sanctissima!*"[3]—how oft that lay
Hath melted from my heart the martyr-strength away!

    Ave, sanctissima!
    'Tis night-fall on the sea;
      Ora pro nobis![4]   390
    Our souls rise to thee!

    Watch us, while shadows lie
    O'er the dim water spread;
    Hear the heart's lonely sigh,
      —*Thine*, too, hath bled!   395

    Thou that hast look'd on death,
    Aid us when death is near!
    Whisper of Heaven to faith;
    Sweet mother, hear!

    Ora pro nobis!   400
    The wave must rock our sleep,

---

1 recreant] apostate, one who has abandoned the true faith ("the light").
2 vesper-voices] voices heard at evening (vesper: evening star), or during evening religious service (vespers).
3 *Ave sanctissima*] hail, most holy.
4 Ora pro nobis] pray for us.

Ora, mater,[1] ora!
Thou star of the deep!

XLIV.

"*Ora pro nobis, mater!*" — What a spell
405   Was in those notes, with day's last glory dying
On the flush'd waters! — seem'd they not to swell
From the far dust, wherein my sires were lying
With crucifix and sword? — Oh! yet how clear
Comes their reproachful sweetness to mine ear!
410   "*Ora!*" — with all the purple waves replying,
All my youth's visions rising in the strain —
— And I had thought it much to bear the rack and chain!

XLV.

Torture! — the sorrow of affection's eye,
Fixing its meekness on the spirit's core,
415   Deeper, and teaching more of agony,
May pierce than many swords! — and this I bore
With a mute pang. Since I had vainly striven
From its free springs to pour the truth of Heaven
Into thy trembling soul, my Leonor!
420   Silence rose up where hearts no hope could share:
— Alas! for those that love, and may not blend in prayer!

XLVI.

We could not pray together midst the deep,
Which, like a floor of sapphire, round us lay,
Through days of splendour, nights too bright for sleep,
425   Soft, solemn, holy! — We were on our way
Unto the mighty Cordillera-land,[2]

---

1   mater] mother, i.e., Mary, mother of Jesus, particularly venerated in the Roman Catholic church.
2   Cordillera-land] Peru, dominated by the "cordillera," or mountains, of the Andes.

With men whom tales of that world's golden strand¹
Had lur'd to leave their vines.²—Oh! who shall say
What thoughts rose in us, when the tropic sky
Touch'd all its molten seas with sunset's alchemy?³   430

XLVII.

Thoughts no more mingled!—Then came night—th'
    intense
Dark blue—the burning stars!—I saw *thee* shine
Once more, in thy serene magnificence,
O Southern Cross!ᴾ as when thy radiant sign
First drew my gaze of youth.—No, not as then;   435
I had been stricken by the darts of men
Since those fresh days, and now thy light divine
Look'd on mine anguish, while within me strove
The still small voice⁴ against the might of suffering love.

XLVIII.

But thou, the clear, the glorious! thou wert pouring   440
Brilliance and joy upon the crystal wave,
While she that met thy ray with eyes adoring,
Stood in the lengthening shadow of the grave!
—Alas! I watch'd her dark religious glance,
As it still sought thee through the Heaven's expanse,   445
Bright Cross!—and knew not that I watch'd what gave
But passing lustre—shrouded soon to be—
A soft light found no more—no more on earth or sea!

---

1 strand] "shore," which is "golden" because conquerors and colonizers were attracted
    to the New World by stories of gold there.
2 vines] vineyards, symbolizing homelands.
3 alchemy] suggesting that the New World's real wealth is not mineral gold but nat-
    ural beauty: alchemy was supposed to enable transmutation of base metals into
    gold; the poetic representation of the New World here resembles that in *Voyage aux*
    régions équinoctiales du Nouveau Continent (1807) by Friedrich Heinrich Alexander
    von Humboldt (1769-1859), used as a source by Hemans (see her note P).
4 in the Bible, God speaks to the prophet Elijah in a "still small voice" (1 Kings,
    19.12).

XLIX.

450
I knew not all — yet something of unrest
Sat on my heart. Wake, ocean-wind! I said;
Waft us to land, in leafy freshness drest,
Where through rich clouds of foliage o'er her head,
Sweet day may steal, and rills unseen go by,
455
Like singing voices, and the green earth lie
Starry with flowers, beneath her graceful tread!
— But the calm bound us midst the glassy main;[1]
Ne'er was her step to bend earth's living flowers again.

L.

Yes! as if Heaven upon the waves were sleeping,
Vexing my soul with quiet, there they lay,
460
All moveless through their blue transparence keeping,
The shadows of our sails, from day to day;
While she — oh! strongest is the strong heart's woe —
And yet I live! I feel the sunshine's glow —
And I am he that look'd, and saw decay
465
Steal o'er the fair of earth, th' ador'd too much!
— It is a fearful thing to love what death may touch.

LI.

A fearful thing that love and death may dwell
In the same world! — She faded on — and I —
Blind to the last, there needed death to tell
470
My trusting soul that she *could* fade to die!
Yet, ere she parted, I had mark'd a change,
— But it breath'd hope — 'twas beautiful, though strange:
Something of gladness in the melody
Of her low voice, and in her words a flight

---

1 this incident may parallel the central episode Coleridge's "The Rime of the Ancient Mariner" (1798), where a ship is becalmed after the Mariner trangresses against nature, and is only released by fresh winds after symbolically sacrificial deaths have occurred.

Of airy thought—alas! too perilously bright!

LII.

And a clear sparkle in her glance, yet wild,
And quick, and eager, like the flashing gaze
Of some all wondering and awakening child,
That first the glories of the earth surveys.
—How could it thus deceive me?—she had worn   480
Around her, like the dewy mists of morn,
A pensive tenderness through happiest days,
And a soft world of dreams had seem'd to lie
Still in her dark, and deep, and spiritual eye.

LIII.

And I could hope in that strange fire!—she died,   485
She died, with all its lustre on her mien!
—The day was melting from the waters wide,
And through its long bright hours her thoughts had been,
It seem'd, with restless and unwonted yearning,
To Spain's blue skies and dark sierras turning;   490
For her fond words were all of vintage-scene,
And flowering myrtle, and sweet citron's breath—
—Oh! with what vivid hues life comes back oft on death!

LIV.

And from her lips the mountain-songs of old,
In wild faint snatches, fitfully had sprung;   495
Songs of the orange bower, the Moorish hold,
The "*Rio verde*,"ᴼ on her soul that hung,
And thence flow'd forth.—But now the sun was low,
And watching by my side its last red glow,
That ever stills the heart, once more she sung   500
Her own soft "*Ora, mater!*"—and the sound
Was even like love's farewell—so mournfully profound.

LV.

The boy had dropp'd to slumber at our feet;—
—"And I have lull'd him to his smiling rest
Once more!" she said:—I rais'd him—it was sweet,
Yet sad, to see the perfect calm which bless'd
His look that hour;—for now her voice grew weak;
And on the flowery crimson of his cheek,
With her white lips a long, long kiss she press'd,
Yet light, to wake him not.—Then sank her head
Against my bursting heart—What did I clasp?—the dead!

LVI.

I call'd—to call what answers not our cries—
By that we lov'd to stand unseen, unheard,
With the loud passion of our tears and sighs
To see but some cold glistering ringlet stirr'd,
And in the quench'd eye's fixedness to gaze,
All vainly searching for the parted rays;
This is what waits us!—Dead!—with that chill word
To link our bosom-names!—For this we pour
Our souls upon the dust—nor tremble to adore!

LVII.

But the true parting came!—I look'd my last
On the sad beauty of that slumbering face;
How could I think the lovely spirit pass'd,
Which there had left so tenderly its trace?
Yet a dim awfulness was on the brow—
No! not like sleep to look upon art Thou,
Death, death!—She lay, a thing for earth's embrace,
To cover with spring-wreaths.—For earth's?—the wave
That gives the bier no flowers—makes moan above her grave!

LVIII.

On the mid-seas a knell!—for man was there,   530
Anguish and love—the mourner with his dead!
A long low-rolling knell—a voice of prayer—
Dark glassy waters, like a desert spread,—
And the pale-shining Southern Cross on high,
Its faint stars fading from a solemn sky,   535
Where mighty clouds before the dawn grew red;—
Were these things round me?—Such o'er memory sweep
Wildly when aught brings back that burial of the deep.

LIX.

Then the broad lonely sunrise!—and the plash
Into the sounding waves!ᴿ—around her head   540
They parted, with a glancing moment's flash,
Then shut—and all was still. And now thy bed
Is of their secrets, gentlest Leonor!
Once fairest of young brides!—and never more,
Lov'd as thou wert, may human tear be shed   545
Above thy rest!—No mark the proud seas keep,
To show where he that wept may pause again to weep.

LX.

So the depths took thee!—Oh! the sullen sense
Of desolation in that hour compress'd!
Dust going down, a speck, amidst th' immense   550
And gloomy waters, leaving on their breast
The trace a weed might leave there!—Dust!—the thing
Which to the heart was as a living spring
Of joy, with fearfulness of love possess'd,
Thus sinking!—Love, joy, fear, all crush'd to this—   555
And the wide Heaven so far—so fathomless th' abyss!

LXI.

Where the line sounds not,[1] where the wrecks lie low,
What shall wake thence the dead? — Blest, blest are they
That earth to earth[2] entrust; for they may know
560 And tend the dwelling whence the slumberer's clay
Shall rise at last, and bid the young flowers bloom,
That waft a breath of hope around the tomb,
And kneel upon the dewy turf to pray!
But thou, what cave hath dimly chamber'd *thee?*
565 Vain dreams! — oh! art thou not where there is no more sea?[s]

LXII.

The wind rose free and singing: — when for ever,
O'er that sole spot of all the watery plain,
I could have bent my sight with fond endeavour
Down, where its treasure was, its glance to strain;
570 Then rose the reckless[3] wind! — Before our prow
The white foam flash'd — ay, joyously — and thou
Wert left with all the solitary main
Around thee — and thy beauty in my heart,
And thy meek sorrowing love — oh! where could *that* depart?

LXIII.

575 I will not speak of woe; I may not tell —
Friend tells not such to friend — the thoughts which rent
My fainting spirit, when its wild farewell
Across the billows to thy grave was sent,
Thou, there most lonely! — He that sits above,
580 In his calm glory, will forgive the love
His creatures bear each other, ev'n if blent

---

1 water's depth is measured in fathoms when the weighted end of a rope thrown overboard "sounds," or touches bottom; if it cannot do so, the depth is immeasurable, or "fathomless," which also means "incomprehensible."
2 dead body buried, echoing words of the church's funeral service.
3 reckless] uncaring as well as heedless of consequences.

With a vain worship;[1] for its close is dim
Ever with grief, which leads the wrung soul back to Him!

LXIV.

And with a milder pang if now I bear
To think of thee in thy forsaken rest,   585
If from my heart be lifted the despair,
The sharp remorse with healing influence press'd,
If the soft eyes that visit me in sleep
Look not reproach, though still they seem to weep;
It is that He my sacrifice hath bless'd,   590
And fill'd my bosom, through its inmost cell,
With a deep chastening sense that all at last is well.

LXV.

Yes! thou art now — Oh! wherefore doth the thought
Of the wave dashing o'er thy long bright hair,
The sea-weed into its dark tresses wrought,   595
The sand thy pillow — thou that wert so fair!
Come o'er me still? — Earth, earth! — it is the hold
Earth ever keeps on that of earthy[2] mould!
But *thou* art breathing now in purer air,
I well believe, and freed from all of error,   600
Which blighted here the root of thy sweet life with terror.

LXVI.

And if the love which here was passing light
Went with what died not — Oh! that *this* we knew,
But this! — that through the silence of the night,
Some voice, of all the lost ones and the true,   605
Would speak, and say, if in their far repose,

---

1   many Christians believed that excessive love for another human transgressed on the
love due to God, and would be punished by loss of the beloved; blent is a poeticism
for blended or mingled.

2   earthy] "earthly" in 2nd and 3rd editions.

We are yet aught of what we were to those
We call the dead! — their passionate adieu,
Was it but breath, to perish? — Holier trust
610   Be mine! — thy love *is* there, but purified from dust!¹

LXVII.

A thing all heavenly! — clear'd from that which hung
As a dim cloud between us, heart and mind!
Loos'd from the fear, the grief, whose tendrils flung
A chain, so darkly with its growth entwin'd.
615   This is my hope! — though when the sunset fades,
When forests rock the midnight on their shades,
When tones of wail are in the rising wind,
Across my spirit some faint doubt may sigh;
For the strong hours *will* sway this frail mortality!

LXVIII.

620   We have been wanderers since those days of woe,
Thy boy and I! — As wild birds tend their young,
So have I tended him — my bounding roe!²
The high Peruvian solitudes among;
And o'er the Andes-torrents borne his form,
625   Where our frail bridge hath quiver'd midst the storm.ᵀ
— But there the war-notes³ of my country rung,
And, smitten deep of⁴ Heaven and man, I fled
To hide in shades unpierc'd a mark'd and weary head.

---

1   dust] here, the desires of the mortal self, or body.
2   the image may echo Wordsworth's description of himself as a boy in "Tintern
     Abbey" (1798), "... when like a roe / I bounded o'er the mountains, by the sides /
     Of the deep rivers, and the lonely streams, / Wherever nature led ..." (69-72 in
     1798 text)
3   war-notes] a reference to the civil wars among the Spanish conquerors of Peru, or
     to the Spanish campaigns of extermination against the native Peruvians.
4   of] by.

LXIX.

But he went on in gladness — that fair child!
Save when at times his bright eye seem'd to dream,   630
And his young lips, which then no longer smil'd,
Ask'd of his mother! — that was but a gleam
Of Memory, fleeting fast; and then his play
Through the wide Llanos^U cheer'd again our way,
And by the mighty Oronoco stream,¹   635
On whose lone margin we have heard at morn,
From the mysterious rocks, the sunrise-music borne.^V

LXX.

So like a spirit's voice! a harping² tone,
Lovely, yet ominous to mortal ear,
Such as might reach us from a world unknown,   640
Troubling man's heart with thrills of joy and fear!
'Twas sweet! — yet those deep southern shades oppress'd
My soul with stillness,^W like the calms that rest
On melancholy waves: I sigh'd to hear
Once more earth's breezy sounds, her foliage fann'd,   645
And turn'd to seek the wilds of the red³ hunter's land.

LXXI.

And we have won a bower of refuge now,
In this fresh waste, the breath of whose repose
Hath cool'd, like dew, the fever of my brow,
And whose green oaks and cedars round me close,   650
As temple-walls and pillars, that exclude
Earth's haunted dreams from their free solitude;
All, save the image and the thought of those
Before us gone; our lov'd of early years,
Gone where affection's cup hath lost the taste of tears.   655

---

1   principal river of Venezuela and the Caribbean coast of South America.
2   harping] here, like a harp.
3   Europeans perceived the skin colour of aboriginal North Americans as red.

LXXII.

I see a star — eve's first-born! — in whose train
Past scenes, words, looks, come back. The arrowy spire
Of the lone cypress, as of wood-girt fane,
Rests dark and still amidst a heaven of fire;
660   The pine gives forth its odours, and the lake
Gleams like one ruby, and the soft winds wake,
Till every string of nature's solemn lyre
Is touch'd to answer; its most secret tone
Drawn from each tree, for each hath whispers all its own.

LXXIII.

665   And hark! another murmur on the air,
Not of the hidden rills, or quivering shades!
— That is the cataract's, which the breezes bear,
Filling the leafy twilight of the glades
With hollow surge-like sounds, as from the bed
670   Of the blue mournful seas, that keep the dead:
But *they* are far! — the low sun here pervades
Dim forest-arches, bathing with red gold
Their stems, till each is made a marvel to behold,

LXXIV.

Gorgeous, yet full of gloom! — In such an hour,
675   The vesper-melody of dying bells
Wanders through Spain, from each grey convent's tower
O'er shining rivers pour'd, and olive-dells,
By every peasant heard, and muleteer,
And hamlet, round my home: — and I am here,
680   Living again through all my life's farewells,
In these vast woods, where farewell ne'er was spoken,
And sole I lift to Heaven a sad heart — yet unbroken!

LXXV.

In such an hour are told the hermit's beads;[1]
With the white sail the seaman's hymn floats by:
Peace be with all! whate'er their varying creeds,   685
With all that send up holy thoughts on high!
Come to me, boy!—by Guadalquivir's[2] vines,
By every stream of Spain, as day declines,
Man's prayers are mingled in the rosy sky.
—We, too, will pray; nor yet unheard, my child!   690
Of Him whose voice *we* hear at eve amidst the wild.

LXXVI.

At eve?—oh! through all hours!—From dark dreams oft
Awakening, I look forth, and learn the might
Of solitude, while thou art breathing soft,
And low, my lov'd one! on the breast of night: 695
I look forth on the stars—the shadowy sleep
Of forests—and the lake, whose gloomy deep
Sends up red sparkles to the fire-flies' light.
A lonely world!—ev'n fearful to man's thought,
But for His presence felt, whom here my soul hath sought.[3]   700

---

1   in Roman Catholic practice, to tell one's beads is to recite a number of prayers,
    keeping count by the beads on a string, or rosary.
2   the Guadalquivir is an important river in southern Spain.
3   the Liverpool manuscript of the poem has a different ending, with an additional
    stanza:

> —Again that Sound, as of the rolling Wave!—
> Night-fall hath given it power, - and yet again -
> —What! shall my Spirit, that o'erswept the Grave,
> Sink if a touch press Memory into pain?
> —There is a wild Song haunts me with that moan,
> A wild low Song, and mournful! - yet a tone
> Of Hope, thro' all the sadness of the strain,
> Breathes up to Heaven; - Strange! - twas the sweet Voice fled
> Ev'n Leonor's, that sang - "Thou Sea, restore the Dead!"

This stanza is followed in the Liverpool manuscript by the poem published sepa-
rately as "The Treasures of the Deep" (included in this edition).

[HEMANS'S] NOTES.

A   *And sighing through the feathery canes, &c.*
       [part 1, line 23]
The canes in some parts of the American forests form a thick
undergrowth for many hundred miles. — See Hodgson's Let-
ters from North America, vol. i. p. 242.[1]

B   *And for their birth-place moan, as moans the ocean-shell.*
       [1.36]
     Such a shell as Wordsworth has beautifully described.

> "I have seen
> A curious child, who dwelt upon a tract
> Of inland ground, applying to his ear
> The convolutions of a smooth-lipp'd shell;
> To which, in silence hush'd, his very soul
> Listen'd intently, and his countenance soon
> Brightened with joy; for murmurings from within
> Were heard — sonorous cadences! whereby,
> To his belief, the monitor express'd
> Mysterious union with its native sea.
> — Even such a shell the universe itself
> Is to the ear of Faith." — The Excursion.[2]

C   *I see an oak before me, &c.* [1.91]
     "I recollect hearing a traveller, of poetical temperament,
expressing the kind of horror which he felt on beholding, on
the banks of the Missouri, an oak of prodigious size, which had

---

1   Adam Hodgson, *Letters from North America, Written During a Tour in the United States
     and Canada* (London, 1824), 1.242 note; Hodgson was a Liverpool merchant and
     the letters, originally published in a periodical, were intended to encourage greater
     understanding between Britain and the United States; the letters were republished
     in the United States without his permission and with alterations and additions as
     *Remarks During a Journey through North America in the Years 1819, 1820, and 1821, in
     a Series of Letters, with an Appendix Containing an Account of Several of the Indian Tribes
     and the Principal Missionary Stations, &c.* (New York, 1823).
2   slightly misquoted from Wordsworth, *The Excursion* (1814, book 4, "Despondency
     Corrected," 1149-57; 1132-42 in 1850 text).

been in a manner overpowered by an enormous wild grape-vine. The vine had clasped its huge folds round the trunk, and from thence had wound about every branch and twig, until the mighty tree had withered in its embrace. It seemed like Lao-coon[1] struggling ineffectually in the hideous coils of the mon-ster Python." —Bracebridge Hall. Chapter on Forest Trees.[2]

D   *Thou hast perish'd*
       More nobly far, my Alvar!—making known
       The might of truth. [1.217-9]
For a most interesting account of the Spanish Protestants, and the heroic devotion with which they met the spirit of per-secution in the sixteenth century, see the Quarterly Review, No. 57, art. Quin's Visit to Spain.[3]

E   *I look'd on two,*
       Following his footsteps to the same dread place,
       For the same guilt—his sisters!—[1.271-3]
"A priest, named Gonzalez, had, among other proselytes, gained over two young females, his sisters, to the protestant faith. All three were confined in the dungeons of the Inquisi-tion. The torture, repeatedly applied, could not draw from them the least evidence against their religious associates. Every artifice was employed to obtain a recantation from the two sis-ters, since the constancy and learning of Gonzalez precluded all hopes of a theological victory. Their answer, if not exactly log-ical, is wonderfully simple and affecting. 'We will die in the faith of our brother: he is too wise[4] to be wrong, and too good to deceive us.'—The three stakes on which they died were

---

1 Laocoon] in ancient Greek myth, Laocoon and his sons were destroyed by serpents because Laocoon profaned the temple of Apollo; a well known ancient sculpture depicting this event was housed in the Vatican museum in Rome, referred to in Hemans's *The Restoration of the Works of Art to Italy.*

2 *Hall] Bracebridge Hall; or, The Humourists: A Medley* (2 vols, 1822), by "Geoffrey Crayon," the American writer James Fenimore Cooper (1789-1851).

3 Michael Joseph Quin, *A Visit to Spain* … (London, 1823), reviewed in the *Quarterly Review*, vol. 29 (April 1823), 240-76; the passage referred to here is on 246-56 of the review.

4 wise] substituted for "clever" by Hemans.

near each other. The priest had been gagged till the moment of lighting up the wood. The few minutes that he was allowed to speak he employed in comforting his sisters, with whom he sung the 109th Psalm,[1] till the flames smothered their voices." — Ibid.[2]

F   *And deem the name*
        A hundred chiefs had borne, cast down by you to shame.
        [1.287-8]
The names, not only of the immediate victims of the Inquisition, were devoted to infamy, but those of all their relations were branded with the same indelible stain, which was likewise to descend as an inheritance to their latest posterity.

G   *'Twas not within the city—but in sight*
        Of the snow-crown'd sierras. [1.451-2]
The piles erected for these executions were without the towns, and the final scene of an Auto da Fe was sometimes, from the length of the preceding ceremonies, delayed till midnight.

H   *I would have call'd, adjuring the dark cloud:*
        To the most ancient Heavens I would have said,
        "Speak to me! show me truth!" [1.676-8]
For one of the most powerful and impressive pictures perhaps ever drawn, of a young mind struggling against habit and superstition in its first aspirations after truth, see the admirable Letters from Spain by Don Leucadio Doblado.[3]

---

1   Psalm] Psalm 109 in the Bible is attributed to king David and calls on God for aid and to punish his enemies.

2   from Quin, *A Visit to Spain*, as quoted in the *Quarterly Review* 255-56.

3   Joseph Blanco White (1775-1841), *Letters from Spain by Don Leucadio Doblado* (London, 1822); according to Hemans, a passage in this book gave her the idea for her poem (Chorley, 1.105; Hughes, 81); Blanco White was born in Seville, of Irish Catholic descent, and was destined for the family business; to escape, he trained for the priesthood; reading Enlightenment writers made him doubt the church, and he welcomed French intervention in Spain as a step to national reform, but he then became a patriot and escaped to England, where he produced anti-French propaganda for the government, though associated with liberal political circles; later he converted to Anglicanism and became an anti-Catholic campaigner.

I   *For thick ye girt me round, ye long-departed!*
        Dust—imaged form—with cross, and shield, and crest.
        [1.703-4]

"You walk from end to end over a floor of tombstones, inlaid in brass with the forms of the departed, mitres, and croziers, and spears, and shields, and helmets, all mingled together—all worn into glass-like smoothness by the feet and the knees of long-departed worshippers. Around, on every side, each in their separate chapel, sleep undisturbed from age to age the venerable ashes of the holiest or the loftiest that of old came thither to worship—their images and their dying prayers sculptured among the resting-places of their remains." —From a beautiful description of ancient Spanish Cathedrals, in Peter's Letters to his Kinsfolk.[1]

J   *With eyes, whose lightning laughter hath beguil'd*
        A thousand pangs. [1.813]
        "E'l *lampeggiar* de l'angelico riso." —Petrarch.[2]

K   *Mighty shades*
        Weaving their gorgeous tracery o'er thy head,
        With the light melting through their high arcades,
        As through a pillar'd cloister's. [1.829-32]

"Sometimes their discourse was held in the deep shades of moss-grown forests, whose gloom and interlaced boughs first suggested that Gothic architecture, beneath whose pointed arches, where they had studied and prayed, the parti-coloured windows shed a tinged light; scenes, which the gleams of sunshine, penetrating the deep foliage, and flickering on the variegated turf below, might have recalled to their memory." — Webster's Oration on the Landing of the Pilgrim Fathers in New England.[3]—See Hodgson's Letters from North America, vol. ii. p. 305

---

1   by John Gibson Lockhart (3 vols, 1819), 3.158-59.
2   from the 14th-century Italian poet Francesco Petrarca, *Rime*, 292, line 6: "and the lightning of the angelic smile."
3   from Daniel Webster's bicentenary oration, in Hodgson, *Letters from North America*, 2.304-5; Hemans's poem on the landing of the Pilgrims was one of her most famous, especially in the United States.

L   *Bring me the sounding of the torrent-water,*
       With yet a nearer swell—fresh breeze, awake! [2.1-2]

The varying sounds of waterfalls are thus alluded to in an interesting work of Mrs. Grant's. "On the opposite side the view was bounded by steep hills, covered with lofty pines, from which a waterfall descended, which not only gave animation to the sylvan scene, but was the best barometer imaginable; foretelling by its varied and intelligible sounds every approaching change, not only of the weather but of the wind." —Memoirs of an American Lady, vol. i. p. 143.[1]

M   *And the full circle of the rainbow seen*
       There, on the snows. [2.50-1]

The circular rainbows, occasionally seen amongst the Andes, are described by Ulloa.[2]

N   *But so my spirit's fever'd longings wrought,*
       Wakening, it might be, to the faint sad sound,
       That from the darkness of the walls they brought
       A lov'd scene round me, visibly around. [2.82-5]

Many striking instances of the vividness with which the mind, when strongly excited, has been known to renovate past impressions, and embody them into visible imagery, are noticed and accounted for in Dr. Hibbert's Philosophy of Apparitions.[3] The following illustrative passage is quoted in the same work, from the writings of the late Dr. Ferriar. "I remember that, about the age of fourteen, it was a source of great amusement to myself, if I had been viewing any interesting object in the course of the day, such as a romantic ruin, a fine seat,[4] or a

---

1 by Anne Macvicar Grant (2 vols, London, 1808), celebrating the domestic life of Grant's friend and tracing the progress of the new American society "from virtuous simplicity, to the dangerous 'knowledge of good and evil'" (vol. 1, p. v)—a reference to the biblical tree of the knowledge of good and evil in the Garden of Eden (Genesis 2.16-17).

2 Antonio de Ulloa (1716-95), *Relacion historica del viage a la America meridional* (1748), translated as *A Voyage to South America* (London, 1758; another edition, 1806); the reference here is to book 6, ch. 9.

3 Samuel Hibbert-Ward (1782-1848), *Sketches of the Philosophy of Apparitions; or, An Attempt to Trace Such Illusions to Their Physical Causes* (1824; 2nd edition, 1825), 322-23.

4 seat] country residence or manor house.

review of a body of troops, as soon as evening came on, if I had occasion to go into a dark room, the whole scene was brought before my eyes with a brilliancy equal to what it had possessed in daylight, and remained visible for several minutes. I have no doubt that dismal and frightful images have been thus presented to young persons after scenes of domestic affliction or public horror."[1]

The following passage from the "Alcazar of Seville," a tale, or historical sketch, by the author of Doblado's letters, affords a further illustration of this subject. "When, descending fast into the vale of years, I strongly fix my mind's eye on those narrow, shady, silent streets, where I breathed the scented air which came rustling through the surrounding groves; where the footsteps re-echoed from the clean watered porches of the houses, and where every object spoke of quiet and contentment; ... the objects around me begin to fade into a mere delusion, and not only the thoughts, but the external sensations, which I then experience, revive with a reality that almost makes me shudder—it has so much the character of a trance, or vision."[2]

O   *Nor the faint flower-scents, as they come and go*
       In the soft air, like music wandering by. [2.210-11]

"For because the breath of flowers is farre sweeter in the aire (where it comes and goes like the warbling of musick) than in the hand, therefore nothing is more fit for that delight than to know what be the flowers and plants which doe best perfume the aire." —Lord Bacon's Essay on Gardens.[3]

---

1   from John Ferriar, *An Essay towards a Theory of Apparitions* (1813).

2   slightly misquoted from pp. 32-33 of Joseph Blanco White's "The Alcazar of Seville, and the Tale of the Green Taper," in the *Forget Me Not: A Christmas and New Year's Present for 1825* (pp. 3-54), a literary annual in which Hemans published several poems from 1826 to 1829; White's piece is a critique of both the historic monarchic regime of Spain, including the Inquisition, and the French regime that supplanted it under Napoleon.

3   Francis Bacon (1561-1626), Baron Verulam and Viscount St. Alban's, English jurist, politician, and philosopher; his *Essays; or, Counsels, Civill and Morall* (1597; expanded 1612; expanded again 1625) was widely read in the centuries after his death.

P   *I saw* thee *shine*
Once more, in thy serene magnificence,
O Southern Cross! [2.432-4]

"The pleasure we felt on discovering the Southern Cross was warmly shared by such of the crew as had lived in the colonies. In the solitude of the seas, we hail a star as a friend from whom we have long been separated. Among the Portugueze and the Spaniards, peculiar motives seem to increase this feeling; a religious sentiment attaches them to a constellation, the form of which recals the sign of the faith planted by their ancestors in the deserts of the New World.... It has been observed at what hour of the night, in different seasons, the Cross of the South is erect or inclined. It is a time-piece that advances very regularly near four minutes a day, and no other group of stars exhibits to the naked eye an observation of time so easily made. How often have we heard our guides exclaim, in the savannahs of Venezuela, or in the desert extending from Lima to Truxillo,[1] 'Midnight is past, the cross begins to bend!' How often these words reminded us of that affecting scene where Paul and Virginia,[2] seated near the source of the river of Lataniers, conversed together for the last time, and where the old man, at the sight of the Southern Cross, warns them that it is time to separate!" — De Humboldt's Travels.[3]

Q   *Songs of the orange bower, the Moorish hold,*
The "Rio Verde." [2.496-7]

"Rio verde, rio verde," the popular Spanish Romance, known to the English reader in Percy's translation.[4]

---

1   Truxillo] in Peru.

2   title characters of *Paul et Virginie* (1787), one of the most widely read novels of the literature of Sensibility, by French philosopher Jacques Henri Bernardin de St. Pierre (1737-1814).

3   *Voyage aux régions équinoctiales du Nouveau Continent* (1807) by Friedrich Heinrich Alexander von Humboldt (1769-1859), German naturalist and travel writer; the passage is from his friend Helen Maria Williams's translation (1814), 2.21-22; the work is a factual yet lyrical account of von Humboldt's scientific travels in the New World with his lover, French botanist Aimé Bonpland; Williams presents von Humboldt as a hero of peaceful and beneficial adventure, in implied contrast to Napoleon as a "hero" of destructive military adventure.

4   Thomas Percy (1729-1811), antiquarian and bishop of Dromore in Ireland; this translation appeared in his collection of popular songs and ballads, *Reliques of*

"Gentle river, gentle river,
Lo, thy streams are stain'd with gore!
Many a brave and noble captain
Floats along thy willow'd shore," &c. &c.

R   *Then the broad lonely sun-rise!—and the plash*
         Into the sounding waves!—[2.539-40]
De Humboldt, in describing the burial of a young Asturian
at sea, mentions the entreaty of the officiating priest, that the
body, which had been brought upon deck during the night,
might not be committed to the waves until after sun-rise, in
order to pay it the last rites according to the usage of the
Romish church.

S   *Oh art thou not where there is no more sea?* [2.565]
"And there was no more sea." —Rev. chap. xxi. v. 1.[1]

T   *And o'er the Andes-torrents borne his form,*
         Where our frail bridge hath quiver'd midst the storm.
         [2.624-5]
The bridges over many deep chasms amongst the Andes are
pendulous, and formed only of the fibres of equinoctial plants.
Their tremulous motion has afforded a striking image to one of
the stanzas in "Gertrude of Wyoming."[2]
    "Anon some wilder portraiture he draws,
    Of nature's savage glories he would speak;

Ancient English Poetry (1765), a major influence on the imitation and appropriation
of folksong in Britain and Europe during the Romantic period.

1 from the Bible, book of Revelation, which is St. John's vision of the end of time;
   the full verse reads, "And I saw a new heaven and a new earth: for the first heaven
   and the first earth were passed away; and there was no more sea"; Revelation was
   much read at the end of the Napoleonic era as a possible prophecy of imminent
   apocalypse.

2 from *Gertrude of Wyoming; or, The Pennsylvanian Cottage* (1809), part 2, stanza 16, by
   the Scottish writer Thomas Campbell (1777-1844); the young hero is recounting
   his travels in South America; the poem is based on a historical incident in the
   American Revolutionary war, when a party of Indians fighting for the British
   destroyed what Campbell represents as a paradisal settlement of European refugees
   from tyranny; Hemans's poem resembles Campbell's in Spenserian stanza form,
   length, layout, certain themes, and supporting apparatus of notes.

The loneliness of earth, that overawes,
Where, resting by the tomb of old Cacique,
The lama-driver, on Peruvia's peak,
Nor voice nor living motion marks around,
But storks that to the boundless forest shriek,
Or wild-cane arch, high flung o'er gulf profound,
That fluctuates when the storms of El Dorado sound."[1]

U   *And then his play*
        Through the wide Llanos cheer'd again our way.
        [2.633-4]
Llanos, or savannas, the great plains in South America.

V   *And by the mighty Oronoco stream,*
        On whose lone margin we have heard at morn,
        From the mysterious rocks, the sunrise-music borne.
        [2.635-7]
De Humboldt speaks of these rocks on the shores of the
Oronoco. Travellers have heard from time to time subterrane-
ous sounds proceed from them at sun-rise, resembling those of
an organ. He believes in the existence of this mysterious music,
although not fortunate enough to have heard it himself, and
thinks that it may be produced by currents of air issuing
through the crevices.

W   *Yet those deep southern shades oppress'd*
        My soul with stillness.[2] [2.642-3]
The same distinguished traveller[3] frequently alludes to the
extreme stillness of the air in the equatorial regions of the new
continent, and particularly on the thickly wooded shores of the
Oronoco. "In this neighbourhood," he says, "no breath of wind
ever agitates the foliage."

---

1   sound] no closing quotation marks in 1st edition.
2   stillness] 2nd and 3rd editions expand the quotation to "melancholy waves."
3   traveller] von Humboldt.

FROM "MISCELLANEOUS PIECES":

THE TREASURES OF THE DEEP.[1]

WHAT hid'st thou in thy treasure-caves and cells?
Thou hollow-sounding and mysterious main!
—Pale glistening pearls, and rainbow-colour'd shells,
Bright things which gleam unreck'd-of, and in vain!
—Keep, keep thy riches, melancholy sea!   5
   We ask not such from thee.

Yet more, the depths have more!—what wealth untold,
Far down, and shining through their stillness lies!
Thou hast the starry gems, the burning gold,
Won from ten thousand royal Argosies![2]   10
—Sweep o'er thy spoils, thou wild and wrathful main!
   Earth claims not *these*[3] again.

Yet more, the depths have more!—thy waves have roll'd
Above the cities of a world gone by![4]
Sand hath fill'd up the palaces of old,   15
Sea-weed o'ergrown the halls of revelry.
—Dash o'er them, ocean! in thy scornful play!
   Man yields them to decay.

Yet more! the billows and the depths have more!
High hearts and brave are gather'd to thy breast!   20
They hear not now the booming waters roar,

---

1 first published in the *New Monthly Magazine* 8 (Aug. 1823): 160; text here from first book-form publication in 1st edn of *The Forest Sanctuary; and Other Poems* (1825), which differs in minor matters of spelling (e.g., less capitalization of nouns); minor variations in 2nd edn in book form (1829); in the Liverpool Public Records Library manuscript of "The Forest Sanctuary," "The Treasures of the Deep" is a continuation of the ending of that poem.

2 Argosies!] *NMM*: Argosies. Argosies are treasure ships or, more generally, merchant vessels, from a corrupted version of Ragusa, a port on the Adriatic Sea, but erroneously associated with the Argo, in Greek mythology the ship used by Jason and his companions in their quest for the golden fleece.

3 *these* again.] *NMM*: these again!

4 lines 13-14 probably refer to Atlantis, a mythical ancient city supposedly sunk beneath the sea.

The battle-thunders will not break their rest.
—Keep thy red gold and gems, thou stormy grave!
        Give back the true and brave!

25 Give back the lost and lovely! — those for whom
The place was kept at board and hearth so long,
The prayer went up through midnight's breathless gloom,
And the vain yearning woke 'midst festal song!
Hold fast thy buried Isles, thy towers o'erthrown—
30   But all is not thine own.¹

To thee the love of woman hath gone down,
Dark flow thy tides o'er manhood's noble head,
O'er youth's bright locks, and beauty's flowery crown,
—Yet must thou hear a voice—restore the dead!
35 Earth shall reclaim her precious things from thee!—²
        —Restore the dead, thou sea!

CASABIANCA.³

THE boy stood on the burning deck
        Whence all but he had fled;
The flame that lit the battle's wreck,
        Shone round him o'er the dead.

5   Yet beautiful and bright he stood,
        As born to rule the storm;
A creature of heroic blood,
        A proud, though child-like form.

---

1 own.] *NMM*: own!
2 thee!—] *NMM*: thee,
3 Young Casabianca, a boy about thirteen years old, son to the Admiral of the Ori-
   ent, remained at his post (in the Battle of the Nile) after the ship had taken fire, and
   all the guns had been abandoned; and perished in the explosion of the vessel, when
   the flames had reached the powder. [Hemans's note; Louis de Casabianca (1762-
   98), a Corsican nobleman, commanded the "Orient," which was the flagship of the
   French admiral F. P. Brueys at the battle of the Nile in 1798, when Horatio Nel-
   son's victory thwarted Napoleon's plan to use Egypt, which he had just seized, as
   the gateway to Britain's empire in India; text first published in and taken from 2nd
   edn (1829).

The flames rolled on — he would not go,
   Without his Father's word;   10
That Father, faint in death below,
   His voice no longer heard.

He called aloud: — "Say, Father, say
   If yet my task is done?"
He knew not that the chieftain lay   15
   Unconscious of his son.

"Speak, Father!" once again he cried,
   "If I may yet be gone!
And" — but the booming shots replied,
   And fast the flames rolled on.   20

Upon his brow he felt their breath,
   And in his waving hair,
And looked from that lone post of death,
   In still, yet brave despair.

And shouted but once more aloud,   25
   "My Father! must I stay?"
While o'er him fast, through sail and shroud,
   The wreathing fires made way.

They wrapt the ship in splendour wild,
   They caught the flag on high,   30
And streamed above the gallant child,
   Like banners in the sky.

There came a burst of thunder sound —
   The boy — oh! where was he?
Ask of the winds that far around   35
   With fragments strewed the sea! —

With mast, and helm, and pennon fair,
   That well had borne their part —
But the noblest thing which perished there
   Was that young faithful heart!   40

EVENING PRAYER,
AT A GIRLS' SCHOOL.[1]

Now in thy youth, beseech of Him
Who giveth, upbraiding not;
That his light in thy heart become not dim,
And his love be unforgot;
And thy God, in the darkest of days, will be,
Greenness, and beauty, and strength to thee.

BERNARD BARTON.[2]

HUSH! 'tis a holy hour — the quiet room
　　Seems like a temple, while yon soft lamp sheds
A faint and starry radiance, through the gloom
　　And the sweet stillness, down on fair young heads,
5　With all their clust'ring locks, untouched by care,
And bowed, as flowers are bowed with night, in prayer.

Gaze on — 'tis lovely! — Childhood's lip and cheek,
　　Mantling[3] beneath its earnest brow of thought —
Gaze — yet what seest thou in those fair, and meek,
10　　And fragile things, as but for sunshine wrought? —
Thou seest what Grief must nurture for the sky,
What Death must fashion for Eternity!

Oh! joyous creatures! that will sink to rest,
　　Lightly, when those pure orisons are done,
15　As birds with slumber's honey-dew opprest,
　　'Midst the dim folded leaves, at set of sun —
Lift up your hearts! though yet no sorrow lies
Dark in the summer-heaven of those clear eyes.

1　first published in *The Forget Me Not* (1826), a literary annual; text from first book-
　form publication in 2nd edn of *The Forest Sanctuary* (1829), which differs slightly in
　punctuation and spelling; substantive differences are noted here.
2　from "The Ivy: Addressed to a Young Friend," ll. 43-8; Barton also published fre-
　quently in the literary annuals.
3　here, blushing.

Though fresh within your breasts th' untroubled springs
    Of Hope make melody where'er ye tread,   20
And o'er your sleep bright shadows, from the wings
    Of spirits visiting but youth, be spread —
Yet in those flute-like voices, mingling low,
Is woman's tenderness — how soon her wo!

Her look[1] is on you — silent tears to weep,   25
    And patient smiles to wear through suffering's hour,
And sumless riches, from affection's deep,
    To pour on broken reeds — a wasted shower!
And to make idols, and to find them clay,
And to bewail that worship — therefore pray!   30

Her lot is on you — to be found untir'd,
    Watching the stars out by the bed of pain,
With a pale cheek, and yet a brow inspir'd,
    And a true heart of hope, though hope be vain;
Meekly to bear with wrong, to cheer decay,   35
And, oh! to love through all things — therefore pray!

And take the thought of this calm vesper time,
    With its low murmuring sounds and silvery light,
On through the dark days fading from their prime,
    As a sweet dew to keep your souls from blight!   40
Earth will forsake — oh! happy to have given
Th' unbroken heart's first fragrance unto Heaven.

---

1   look] *Forget Me Not*: lot

THE LOST PLEIAD.[1]

"Like the lost Pleiad seen no more below."—BYRON.[2]

AND is there glory from the heavens departed?—
  Oh! void unmark'd!—thy sisters of the sky
    Still hold their place on high,
  Though from its rank thine orb so long hath started,
5   Thou, that no more art seen of mortal eye!

Hath the night lost a gem, the regal night?
  She wears her crown of old magnificence,
    Though thou art exil'd thence—[3]
  No desert seems to part those urns of light,
10   'Midst the far depths of purple gloom intense.

They rise in joy, the starry myriads burning—
  The shepherd greets them on his mountains free;
    And from the silvery sea
  To them the sailor's wakeful eye is turning—
15   Unchang'd they rise, they have not mourn'd for thee.

Couldst thou be shaken from thy radiant place,
  Ev'n as a dew-drop from the myrtle spray,
    Swept by the wind away?
  Wert thou not peopled by some glorious race,
20   And was there power to smite them with decay?

---

1 first published in the *New Monthly Magazine* 8 (Dec. 1823): 526; text from first
   book-form publication in 2nd edn of *The Forest Sanctuary* (1829), which differs
   slightly in spelling and punctuation (e.g., less capitalization of nouns and fewer
   dashes); in Greek mythology the Pleiades were the 7 daughters of Atlas and
   Pleione; they were turned into stars—depending on the myth—at grief over
   sufferings of their father, or at death of other sisters, or to escape the amorous
   hunter Orion; the Pleiades star cluster is in the constellation Taurus, and one star is
   always dim or invisible, supposedly as Electra mourning the fall of Troy or as
   Merope ashamed of having wedded the mortal, Sisyphus.
2 *Beppo*, l. 112.
3 thence—] *NMM*: thence!

Why, who shall talk of thrones, of sceptres riven? —
Bow'd be our hearts[1] to think on what *we* are,
When from its height afar
A world sinks thus — and yon majestic heaven
Shines not the less for that one vanish'd star!   25

THE BREEZE FROM SHORE.[2]

Poetry reveals to us the loveliness of nature, brings back the
freshness of youthful feeling, revives the relish of simple plea-
sures, keeps unquenched the enthusiasm which warmed the
spring-time of our being, refines youthful love, strengthens our
interest in human nature, by vivid delineations of its tenderest
and loftiest feelings, and, through the brightness of its prophetic
visions, helps faith to lay hold on the future life.

—CHANNING.[3]

JOY is upon the lonely seas
When Indian forests pour
Forth to the billow and the breeze
Their odours from the shore;
Joy, when the soft air's fanning sigh   5
Bears on the breath of Araby.

Oh! welcome are the winds that tell
A wanderer of the deep,
Where, far away, the jasmines dwell,
And where the myrrh-trees weep!   10
Blest, on the sounding surge and foam,
Are tidings of the citron's home!

---

1 Bowed be our hearts] *NMM:* — It is too sad
2 text first published in *The Literary Souvenir; or, Cabinet of Poetry and Romance* (1826),
   a literary annual edited by Alaric Watts; text here taken from first book-form pub-
   lication, in 2nd edn of *The Forest Sanctuary* (1829).
3 William Ellery Channing (1780-1842), American clergyman, proponent of unitari-
   anism, pacifist, prohibitionist, and anti-slavery campaigner, promoter of improve-
   ment in the condition of the working classes, and advocate of a moralistic national
   literature; he corresponded with FH and promoted her work in the United States;
   the passage is from *Remarks on the Character and Writings of Milton* (1826).

The sailor at the helm they greet,
    And hope his bosom stirs,
15   Upspringing, midst the waves, to greet
    The fair earth's messengers,
That woo him, from the moaning main,
Back to her glorious bowers again.

They woo him, whispering lovely tales
20   Of many a flowering glade,
    And fount's bright gleam in island vales
    Of golden-fruited shade;
Across his lone ship's wake they bring
A vision and a glow of spring.

25   And oh! ye masters of the lay,
    Come not ev'n thus your songs
That meet us on life's weary way,
    Amidst her telling throngs?
Yes! o'er the spirit thus they bear
30 A current of celestial air.

Their power is from the brighter clime
    That in our birth hath part;
Their tones are of the world, which time
    Sears not within the heart;
35 They tell us of the living light
In its green places ever bright.

They call us, with a voice divine,
    Back to our early love,—
Our vows of youth at many a shrine,
40   Whence far and fast we rove: —
Welcome high thought and holy strain
That makes us Truth's and Heaven's again!

FROM *RECORDS OF WOMAN: WITH OTHER POEMS* (1828):[1]

FROM "RECORDS OF WOMAN":[2]

ARABELLA STUART.[3]

"THE LADY ARABELLA," as she has been frequently entitled, was descended from Margaret, eldest daughter of Henry VII. and consequently allied by birth to Elizabeth, as well as James I. This affinity to the throne proved the misfortune of her life, as the jealousies which it constantly excited in her royal relatives, who were anxious to prevent her marrying, shut her out from the enjoyment of that domestic happiness which her heart appears to have so fervently desired. By a secret, but early discovered union with William Seymour, son of Lord Beauchamp, she alarmed the cabinet of James, and the wedded lovers were immediately placed in separate confinement. From this they found means to concert a romantic plan of escape; and having won over a female attendant, by whose assistance she was disguised in male attire, Arabella, though faint from recent sickness and suffering, stole out in the night, and at last reached an appointed spot, where a boat and servants were in waiting. She embarked; and, at break of day, a French vessel, engaged to receive her, was discovered and gained. As Seymour, however

---

1 all texts from the 1st edition; there were slight changes in punctuation and spelling in the 2nd edition; for fully annotated text of the entire volume, with illustrations, see Paula R. Feldman's edition (Lexington: University Press of Kentucky, 1999), to which I am indebted here.

2 Hemans's endnotes to "Records of Woman" are not as extensive as in some of her earlier works and so have been placed as footnotes here and indicated as hers; for context and commentary on the group of poems as a whole, see Introduction, pp. 45-8.

3 Arabella—properly Arbella—Stuart (1575-1615) was of royal blood and a possible claimant to the throne; consequently her marriageability was closely supervised by two successive monarchs—Elizabeth 1 and James 1—who were her relations, and her marriage without royal permission led to her imprisonment and perhaps her death, in the circumstances described in Hemans's preface here; for context and commentary on this poem, see Introduction, pp. 48-50.

had not yet arrived, she was desirous that the vessel should lie at anchor for him; but this wish was overruled by her companions, who, contrary to her entreaties, hoisted sail, "which," says D'Israeli, "occasioned so fatal a termination to this romantic adventure. Seymour, indeed, had escaped from the Tower;—he reached the wharf, and found his confidential man waiting with a boat, and arrived at Lee. The time passed; the waves were rising; Arabella was not there; but in the distance he descried a vessel. Hiring a fisherman to take him on board, he discovered, to his grief, on hailing it, that it was not the French ship charged with his Arabella; in despair and confusion he found another ship from Newcastle, which for a large sum altered its course, and landed him in Flanders." — Arabella, meantime, whilst imploring her attendants to linger, and earnestly looking out for the expected boat of her husband, was overtaken in Calais Roads by a vessel in the King's service, and brought back to a captivity, under the suffering of which her mind and constitution gradually sank. — "What passed in that dreadful imprisonment, cannot perhaps be recovered for authentic history,—but enough is known; that her mind grew impaired, that she finally lost her reason, and, if the duration of her imprisonment was short, that it was only terminated by her death. Some effusions, often begun and never ended, written and erased, incoherent and rational, yet remain among her papers." — D'Israeli's *Curiosities of Literature*.[1]—— The following poem, meant as some record of her fate, and the imagined fluctuations of her thoughts and feelings, is supposed to commence during the time of her first imprisonment, whilst her mind was yet buoyed up by the consciousness of Seymour's affection, and the cherished hope of eventual deliverance.[2]

---

1 the passages, with some deletions and minor variations, are from "The Loves of 'The lady Arabella'" in Isaac D'Israeli, *A Second Series of Curiosities of Literature: Consisting of Researches in Literary, Biographical, and Political History; of Critical and Philosophical Inquiries; and of Secret History*, 3 vols, (London: John Murray, 1823), 1.256-92; pp. 284-5, 288).

2 Hemans's preface.

And is not love in vain,
Torture enough without a living tomb?

BYRON.[1]

Fermossi al fin il cor che balzò tanto.

PINDEMONTE.[2]

I.

'TWAS but a dream! — I saw the stag leap free,
  Under the boughs where early birds were singing,
I stood, o'ershadowed by the greenwood tree,
  And heard, it seemed, a sudden bugle ringing
Far thro' a royal forest: then the fawn   5
Shot, like a gleam of light, from grassy lawn
To secret covert; and the smooth turf shook,
And lilies quiver'd by the glade's lone brook,
And young leaves trembled, as, in fleet career,
A princely band, with horn, and hound, and spear,   10
Like a rich masque swept forth. I saw the dance
Of their white plumes, that bore a silvery glance
Into the deep wood's heart; and all pass'd by,
Save one — I met the smile of *one* clear eye,
Flashing out joy to mine. — Yes, *thou* wert there,   15
Seymour! a soft wind blew the clustering hair
Back from thy gallant brow, as thou didst rein
Thy courser, turning from that gorgeous train,
And fling, methought, thy hunting-spear away,
And, lightly graceful in thy green array,   20

---

1   from "The Prophecy of Dante" (1819), 3.147-48.

2   variation of line from "Clizia" by Ippolito Pindemonte (1753-1828), quoted in this
    form by the heroine of Germaine de Staël's novel *Corinne; ou, l'Italie* (1807; end of
    book 18, ch. 5): "This heart which beat so fast has stopped at last"; according to
    Henry Chorley, one of Hemans's friends considered the line an apt epitaph for her
    (*Memorials of Mrs. Hemans ...*, 2nd edn, 2 vols, London, 1837, 2.299n); Pindemonte's
    poem adapts a legend from Ovid's *Metamorphoses* (book 4), in which the nymph
    Clytie causes the death of a rival in love for the sun-god but is spurned as a conse-
    quence, pines away, and metamorphoses into a heliotrope, a flower that always faces
    the sun.

Bound to my side; and we, that met and parted,
  Ever in dread of some dark watchful power,
Won back to childhood's trust, and, fearless-hearted,
  Blent the glad fulness of our thoughts that hour,
25 Ev'n like the mingling of sweet streams, beneath
Dim woven leaves, and midst the floating breath
Of hidden forest flowers.

II.

                    'Tis past! — I wake,
  A captive, and alone, and far from thee,
My love and friend! Yet fostering, for thy sake,
30   A quenchless hope of happiness to be;
And feeling still my woman's spirit strong,
In the deep faith which lifts from earthly wrong
A heavenward glance. I know, I know our love
Shall yet call gentle angels from above,
35 By its undying fervour; and prevail,
Sending a breath, as of the spring's first gale,
Thro' hearts now cold; and, raising its bright face,
With a free gush of sunny tears erase
The characters of anguish. In this trust,
40 I bear, I strive, I bow not to the dust,
That I may bring thee back no faded form,
No bosom chill'd and blighted by the storm.
But all my youth's first treasures, when we meet,
Making past sorrow, by communion, sweet.

III.

45 And thou too art in bonds! — yet droop thou not,
Oh, my belov'd! — there is *one* hopeless lot,
But one, and that not ours. Beside the dead
There sits the grief that mantles up its head,
Loathing the laughter and proud pomp of light,
50 When darkness, from the vainly-doting sight,

Covers its beautiful!¹ If thou wert gone
   To the grave's bosom, with thy radiant brow,—
If thy deep-thrilling voice, with that low tone
   Of earnest tenderness, which now, ev'n now,
Seems floating thro' my soul, were music taken   55
For ever from this world,—oh! thus forsaken,
Could I bear on?—thou liv'st, thou liv'st, thou'rt mine!
With this glad thought I make my heart a shrine,
And by the lamp which quenchless there shall burn,
Sit, a lone watcher for the day's return.   60

IV.

And lo! the joy that cometh with the morning,
   Brightly victorious o'er the hours of care!
I have not watch'd in vain, serenely scorning
   The wild and busy whispers of despair!
Thou hast sent tidings, as of heaven.—I wait   65
   The hour, the sign, for blessed flight to thee.
Oh! for the skylark's wing that seeks its mate
   As a star shoots!—but on the breezy sea
We shall meet soon.—To think of such an hour!
   Will not my heart, o'erburden'd by its bliss,   70
Faint and give way within me, as a flower
   Borne down and perishing by noontide's kiss?
Yet shall I *fear* that lot?—the perfect rest,
The full deep joy of dying on thy breast,
After long-suffering won? So rich a close   75
Too seldom crowns with peace affection's woes.

---

1   *When darkness, from the vainly-doting sight,*
    Covers its beautiful!
    "Wheresoever you are, or in what state soever you be, it sufficeth me you are mine.
    Rachel wept, and would not be comforted, because her children were no more. And that,
    indeed, is the remediless sorrow, and none else!"—From a letter of Arabella Stuart's
    to her husband.—See Curiosities of Literature. [Hemans's endnote; passage slight-
    ly misquoted from D'Israeli, *A Second Series of Curiosities of Literature*, 1.274.]

V.

Sunset! — I tell each moment — from the skies
    The last red splendour floats along my wall,
Like a king's banner! — Now it melts, it dies!
80   I see one star — I hear — 'twas not the call,
Th' expected voice; my quick heart throbb'd too soon.
I must keep vigil till yon rising moon
Shower down less golden light. Beneath her beam
Thro' my lone lattice pour'd, I sit and dream
85 Of summer-lands afar, where holy love,
Under the vine, or in the citron-grove,
May breathe from terror.
    Now the night grows deep,
And silent as its clouds, and full of sleep.
90 I hear my veins beat. — Hark! a bell's slow chime.
My heart strikes with it. — Yet again — 'tis time!
A step! — a voice! — or but a rising breeze?
— Hark! — haste! — I come, to meet thee on the seas.

    ✳   ✳   ✳   ✳   ✳   ✳   ✳   ✳

VI.

Now never more, oh! never, in the worth
Of its pure cause, let sorrowing love on earth
95 Trust fondly — never more! — the hope is crush'd
That lit my life, the voice within me hush'd
That spoke sweet oracles; and I return
To lay my youth, as in a burial-urn,
Where sunshine may not find it. — All is lost!
100 No tempest met our barks — no billow toss'd;
Yet were they sever'd, ev'n as we must be,
That so have lov'd, so striven our hearts to free
From their close-coiling fate! In vain — in vain!
The dark links meet, and clasp themselves again,
105 And press out life. — Upon the deck I stood,
And a white sail came gliding o'er the flood,
Like some proud bird of ocean; then mine eye
Strained out, one moment earlier to descry

The form it ached for, and the bark's career
Seem'd slow to that fond yearning: It drew near,   110
Fraught with our foes! — What boots it to recall
The strife, the tears? Once more a prison-wall
Shuts the green hills and woodlands from my sight,
And joyous glance of waters to the light,
And thee, my Seymour, thee!

                           I will not sink!   115
  Thou, *thou* hast rent the heavy chain that bound thee;
And this shall be my strength — the joy to think
  That thou mayst wander with heaven's breath around thee,
And all the laughing sky! This thought shall yet
Shine o'er my heart, a radiant amulet,   120
Guarding it from despair. Thy bonds are broken,
And unto me, I know, thy true love's token
Shall one day be deliverance, tho' the years
Lie dim between, o'erhung with mists of tears.

VII.

My friend, my friend! where art thou? Day by day,   125
Gliding, like some dark mournful stream, away,
My silent youth flows from me. Spring, the while,
  Comes and rains beauty on the kindling boughs
Round hall and hamlet; Summer, with her smile,
  Fills the green forest;— young hearts breathe their vows;   130
Brothers long parted meet; fair children rise
Round the glad board; Hope laughs from loving eyes;
All this is in the world! — These joys lie sown,
The dew of every path — On *one* alone
Their freshness may not fall — the stricken deer,   135
Dying of thirst with all the waters near.

VIII.

Ye are from dingle and fresh glade, ye flowers!
  By some kind hand to cheer my dungeon sent;
O'er you the oak shed down the summer showers,

140 And the lark's nest was where your bright cups bent,
     Quivering to breeze and rain-drop, like the sheen
     Of twilight stars. On you Heaven's eye hath been,
     Thro' the leaves, pouring its dark sultry blue
     Into your glowing hearts; the bee to you
145 Hath murmur'd, and the rill. —My soul grows faint
     With passionate yearning, as its quick dreams paint
     Your haunts by dell and stream,—the green, the free,
     The full of all sweet sound,—the shut from me!

IX.

     There went a swift bird singing past my cell—
150   O Love and Freedom! ye are lovely things!
     With you the peasant on the hills may dwell,
         And by the streams; but I—the blood of kings,
     A proud unmingling river, thro' my veins
     Flows in lone brightness,—and its gifts are chains!
155 Kings! —I had silent visions of deep bliss,
     Leaving their thrones far distant, and for this
     I am cast under their triumphal car,[1]
     An insect to be crush'd. —Oh! Heaven is far,—
     Earth pitiless!

160 Dost thou forget me, Seymour? I am prov'd[2]
     So long, so sternly! Seymour, my belov'd!
     There are such tales of holy marvels done
     By strong affection, of deliverance won
     Thro' its prevailing power! Are these things told
165 Till the young weep with rapture, and the old
     Wonder, yet dare not doubt,—and thou, oh! thou,
         Dost thou forget me in my hope's decay?—
     Thou canst not! —thro' the silent night, ev'n now,
         I, that need prayer so much, awake and pray
170 Still first for thee. —Oh! gentle, gentle friend!
     How shall I bear this anguish to the end?

---

1 triumphal car] chariot in a triumph, or parade in honour of a victor.
2 prov'd] tested.

Aid! — comes there yet no aid? — the voice of blood
Passes Heaven's gate, ev'n ere the crimson flood
Sinks thro' the greensward![1] — is there not a cry
From the wrung heart, of power, thro' agony,   175
To pierce the clouds? Hear, Mercy! hear me! None
That bleed and weep beneath the smiling sun,
Have heavier cause! — yet hear! — my soul grows dark —
Who hears the last shriek from the sinking bark,
On the mid seas, and with the storm alone,   180
And bearing to th' abyss, unseen, unknown,
Its freight of human hearts? — th' o'ermastering wave!
Who shall tell how it rush'd — and none to save?

Thou hast forsaken me! I feel, I know,
There would be rescue if this were not so.   185
Thou'rt at the chase, thou'rt at the festive board,
Thou'rt where the red wine free and high is pour'd,
Thou'rt where the dancers meet! — a magic glass
Is set within my soul, and proud shapes pass,
Flushing it o'er with pomp from bower and hall;—   190
I see one shadow, stateliest there of all,—
Thine! — What dost *thou* amidst the bright and fair,
Whispering light words, and mocking my despair?
It is not well of thee! — my love was more
Than fiery song may breathe, deep thought explore;   195
And there thou smilest, while my heart is dying,
With all its blighted hopes around it lying;
Ev'n thou, on whom they hung their last green leaf—
Yet smile, smile on! too bright art thou for grief.

Death! — what, is death a lock'd and treasur'd thing,   200
Guarded by swords of fire?[2] a hidden spring,

---

1 the last prayer of the executed reaches heaven before her or his blood has time to
   soak the ground at the place of execution: at the notorious Tower of London, state
   prisoners were beheaded on Tower Hill during this period.
2 *Death!—what, is death a lock'd and treasur'd thing,*
   Guarded by swords of fire?
   "And if you remember of old, *I dare die. —— * Consider what the world would con-
   ceive, if I should be violently enforced to do it."—*Fragments of her Letters.*

A fabled fruit, that I should thus endure,
As if the world within me held no cure?
Wherefore not spread free wings — Heaven, Heaven! controul
205 These thoughts — they rush — I look into my soul
As down a gulph, and tremble at th' array
Of fierce forms crowding it! Give strength to pray,
So shall their dark host pass.

                    The storm is still'd.
Father in Heaven! Thou, only thou, canst sound[1]
210 The heart's great deep, with floods of anguish fill'd,
For human line too fearfully profound.
Therefore, forgive, my Father! if Thy child,
Rock'd on its heaving darkness, hath grown wild,
And sinn'd in her despair! It well may be,
215 That Thou wouldst lead my spirit back to Thee,
By the crush'd hope too long on this world pour'd,
The stricken love which hath perchance ador'd
A mortal in Thy place![2] Now let me strive
With Thy strong arm no more! Forgive, forgive!
Take me to peace!

220   And peace at last is nigh.
A sign is on my brow, a token sent
Th' o'erwearied dust, from home:[3] no breeze flits by,
But calls me with a strange sweet whisper, blent
Of many mysteries.

            Hark! the warning tone
225 Deepens — its word is *Death*. Alone, alone,

[Hemans's endnote; the quotation conflates two passages in D'Israeli, *A Second Series of Curiosities of Literature*, the one before the dash from a letter to Lord Fenton (1.289), and the one after the dash to an unnamed person (1. 290).]

1 sound] measure depth, as of water at sea, using a weighted line of rope (l. 211), but here perhaps also using lines of poetry.

2 a common form of Christian consolation was the idea that God caused loss of a loved one as a lesson not to let love for another human exceed love for the divine.

3 home] the Christian heaven; dust: a common term in the Bible (and in literature) for the mortal body.

And sad in youth, but chasten'd, I depart,
Bowing to heaven. Yet, yet my woman's heart
Shall wake a spirit and a power to bless,
Ev'n in this hour's o'ershadowing fearfulness,
Thee, its first love!—oh! tender still, and true!   230
Be it forgotten if mine anguish threw
Drops from its bitter fountain on thy name,
Tho' but a moment.

               Now, with fainting frame,
With soul just lingering on the flight begun,
To bind for thee its last dim thoughts in one,   235
I bless thee! Peace be on thy noble head,
Years of bright fame, when I am with the dead!
I bid this prayer survive me, and retain
Its might, again to bless thee, and again!
Thou hast been gather'd into my dark fate   240
Too much; too long, for my sake, desolate
Hath been thine exiled youth; but now take back,
From dying hands, thy freedom, and re-track
(After a few kind tears for her whose days
Went out in dreams of thee) the sunny ways   245
Of hope, and find thou happiness! Yet send,
Ev'n then, in silent hours a thought, dear friend!
Down to my voiceless chamber; for thy love
Hath been to me all gifts of earth above,
Tho' bought with burning tears! It is the sting   250
Of death to leave that vainly-precious thing
In this cold world! What were it then, if thou,
With thy fond eyes, wert gazing on me now?
Too keen a pang!—Farewell! and yet once more,
Farewell!—the passion of long years I pour   255
Into that word: thou hears't not,—but the wo
And fervour of its tones may one day flow
To thy heart's holy place; there let them dwell—
We shall o'ersweep the grave to meet—Farewell!

THE SWITZER'S WIFE.[1]

Werner Stauffacher, one of the three confederates of the field of
Grutli, had been alarmed by the envy with which the Austrian
Bailiff, Landenberg, had noticed the appearance of wealth and
comfort which distinguished his dwelling. It was not, however,
until roused by the entreaties of his wife, a woman who seems
to have been of an heroic spirit, that he was induced to deliber-
ate with his friends upon the measures by which Switzerland
was finally delivered.[2]

> Nor look nor tone revealeth aught
> Save woman's quietness of thought;
> And yet around her is a light
> Of inward majesty and might.
>
> M.J.J.[3]

❋   ❋   ❋   ❋   ❋

> Wer solch ein herz an seinen Busen drückt,
> Der kann für herd und hof mit freuden fechten.
>
> WILLHOLM TELL.[4]

IT was the time when children bound to meet
  Their father's homeward step from field or hill,

---

1 first published in the *New Monthly Magazine* 16 (Jan. 1826): 23-25, with slight diff-
   erences in punctuation and spelling; substantive variants noted here; for context and
   commentary on this poem, see Introduction, pp. 50-51.
2 Hemans's prefatory note, a footnote in *NMM*; the poem is based on act 1, scene 2
   of Friedrich Schiller's play *Willhelm Tell* (1804), in which Gertrud Stauffacher urges
   her husband, a well-to-do Swiss farmer, to resist rather than placate oppression by
   the foreign Austrian ruler; Hemans reinforces the domestic sentiment of Schiller's
   scene by adding the small boy and inserting an oblique reference to the possibility
   of Gertrud's rape by the vengeful Austrians (l. 59).
3 M.J.J.] passage from "Arria" (ll. 5-8), one of the "Historical Sketches" published in
   Phantasmagoria; or, Sketches of Life and Literature (2 vols, 1825; 1.122-4) by Maria Jane
   Jewsbury (1800-33), Hemans's friend and correspondent; Arria was a woman of
   ancient Roman who showed her patriotic but unjustly imprisoned husband that it
   was easier to commit suicide than be ignobly executed.
4 Willholm TELL] i.e., *Wilhelm Tell* by Friedrich Schiller (1.2.148-49): "If a man can
   hold a heart like yours to his, then he will fight for hearth and home rejoicing ..."

And when the herd's returning bells are sweet
   In the Swiss valleys, and the lakes grow still,
And the last note of that wild horn swells by,   5
Which haunts the exile's heart with melody.

And lovely smil'd full many an Alpine home,
   Touch'd with the crimson of the dying hour,
Which lit its low roof by the torrent's foam,
   And pierced its lattice thro' the vine-hung bower;   10
But one, the loveliest o'er the land that rose,
Then first look'd mournful in its green repose.

For Werner sat beneath the linden-tree,
   That sent its lulling whispers through his door,
Ev'n as man sits whose heart alone would be   15
   With some deep care, and thus can find no more
Th' accustom'd joy in all which evening brings,
Gathering a household with her quiet wings.

His wife stood hush'd before him,—sad, yet mild
   In her beseeching mien;—he mark'd it not.   20
The silvery laughter of his bright-hair'd child
   Rang from the greensward round the shelter'd spot,
But seem'd unheard; until at last the boy
Rais'd from his heap'd-up flowers a glance of joy,

And met his father's face: but then a change   25
   Pass'd swiftly o'er the brow of infant glee,
And a quick sense of something dimly strange
   Brought him from play to stand beside the knee
So often climb'd, and lift his loving eyes
That shone through clouds of sorrowful surprise.   30

Then the proud bosom of the strong man shook;
   But tenderly his babe's fair mother laid
Her hand on his, and with a pleading look,

(translation by John Prudhoe, Manchester: Manchester University Press; New York: Barnes and Noble, 1970); this epigraph is not in *NMM*.

Thro' tears half quivering, o'er him bent, and said,
35   "What grief, dear friend, hath made thy heart its prey,[1]
That thou shouldst turn thee from our love away ?

"It is too sad to see thee thus, my friend!
Mark'st thou the wonder on thy boy's fair brow,
Missing the smile from thine? Oh![2] cheer thee! bend
40   To his soft arms, unseal thy thoughts e'en now!
Thou dost not kindly to withhold the share
Of tried affection in thy secret care."

He looked up into that sweet earnest face,
But sternly, mournfully: not yet the band
45 Was loosen'd from his soul; its inmost place
Not yet unveil'd by love's o'emastering hand.
"Speak low!" he cried, and pointed where on high
The white Alps glitter'd thro' the solemn sky:

"We must speak low amidst our ancient hills
50   And their free torrents; for the days are come
When tyranny lies couch'd by forest-rills,
And meets the shepherd in his mountain-home.
Go, pour the wine of our own grapes in fear,
Keep silence by the hearth! its foes are near.

55   "The envy of th' oppressor's eye hath been
Upon my heritage. I sit to-night
Under my household tree,[3] if not serene,
Yet with the faces best-belov'd in sight:
To-morrow eve may find me chain'd, and thee—
60   How can I bear the boy's young smiles to see?"

---

1   *Hemans's footnote in NMM*: See the beautiful scene between Stauffacher and his wife
    in Schiller's Wilhelm Tell—"So ernst, mein freiund? Ich kenne dich nicht mehr,"
    &c.
2   Oh!] *NMM*: Oh.
3   household tree,] *NMM*: household-tree! —

The bright blood left that youthful mother's cheek;
   Back on the linden-stem she lean'd her form,
And her lip trembled, as it strove to speak,
   Like a frail[1] harp-string, shaken by the storm.
'Twas but a moment, and the faintness pass'd,   65
And the free Alpine spirit woke at last.

And she, that ever thro' her home had mov'd
   With the meek thoughtfulness and quiet smile
Of woman, calmly loving and belov'd,
   And timid in her happiness the while,   70
Stood brightly forth, and stedfastly, that hour,
Her clear glance kindling into sudden power.

Ay, pale she stood, but with an eye of light,
   And took her fair child to her holy breast,
And lifted her soft voice, that gathered might   75
   As it found language: — "Are we thus oppress'd?
Then must we rise upon our mountain-sod,
And man must arm, and woman call on God!

"I know what thou wouldst do,—and be it done!
   Thy soul is darken'd with its fears for me.   80
Trust me to Heaven, my husband! — this, thy son,
   The babe whom I have born[2] thee, must be free!
And the sweet memory of our pleasant hearth
May well give strength—if aught be strong on earth.

"Thou hast been brooding o'er the silent dread   85
   Of my desponding tears; now lift once more,
My hunter of the hills![3] thy stately head,
   And let thine eagle glance my joy restore!
I can bear all, but seeing *thee* subdued,—
Take to thee back thine own undaunted mood.   90

---

1 frail] *NMM*: wild
2 born] *NMM*: borne (the usual form)
3 hills!] *NMM*: Hills,

"Go forth beside the waters, and along
   The chamois-paths, and thro' the forests go;[1]
And tell, in burning words, thy tale of wrong
   To the brave hearts that midst the hamlets glow.
95   God shall be with thee, my belov'd![2]—Away!
Bless but thy child, and leave me,—I can pray!"

He sprang up like a warrior-youth awaking
   To clarion-sounds upon the ringing air;
He caught her to his breast, while proud tears breaking
100   From his dark eyes, fell o'er her braided hair,—
And "Worthy art thou," was his joyous cry,
"That man for thee should gird himself to die.[3]

"My bride, my wife, the mother of my child!
   Now shall thy name be armour to my heart;
105   And this our land, by chains no more defiled,
   Be taught of thee to choose the better part!
I go — thy spirit on my words shall dwell,
Thy gentle voice shall stir the Alps — Farewell!"

And thus they parted, by the quiet lake,
110   In the clear starlight: he, the strength to rouse
Of the free[4] hills; she, thoughtful for his sake,
   To rock her child beneath the whispering boughs,
Singing its blue, half-curtain'd eyes to sleep,
With a low hymn, amidst the stillness deep.

---

1   go; *NMM*: go!
2   belov'd! *NMM*: beloved.
3   die. *NMM*: die!
4   free] *NMM*: deep

PROPERZIA ROSSI.[1]

Properzia Rossi, a celebrated female sculptor of Bologna, possessed also of talents for poetry and music, died in consequence of an unrequited attachment. — A painting by Ducis, represents her showing her last work, a basso-relievo of Ariadne, to a Roman Knight, the object of her affection, who regards it with indifference.[2]

> —— Tell me no more, no more
> Of my soul's lofty gifts! Are they not vain
> To quench its haunting thirst for happiness?
> Have I not lov'd, and striven, and fail'd to bind
> One true heart unto me, whereon my own
> Might find a resting-place, a home for all
> Its burden of affections? I depart,
> Unknown, tho' Fame goes with me; I must leave
> The earth unknown. Yet it may be that death
> Shall give my name a power to win such tears
> As would have made life precious.[3]

I.

ONE dream of passion and of beauty more!
And in its bright fulfilment let me pour
My soul away! Let earth retain a trace
Of that which lit my being, tho' its race
Might have been loftier far. — Yet one more dream!   5

---

1 Properzia de'Rossi (*c.* 1490-1530), from Bologna, the only woman artist in the 1st edition of *Le Vite de' più eccelenti pittori, scultori et architettori* (1550; known in English as *The Lives of the Artists*) by Giorgio Vasari (1511-74), who represents de'Rossi as victim of a transgressive erotic passion that impeded her artistic career; for context and commentary on this poem, see Introduction, pp. 51-2.

2 Hemans's preface; the painting by Jean-Louis Ducis (1775-1847) is one of a set of four entitled *Arts under the Empire of Love*, exhibited at the Paris Salon of 1822; the arts are poetry, painting, sculpture, and music, and de'Rossi is shown with a bas-relief of Ariadne who, in classical myth, helped save Theseus's life and loyally loved him, though he later abandoned her.

3 the epigraph is probably by Hemans herself, a practice she used increasingly in her later work, inviting the reader to identify author with subject of the poem.

From my deep spirit one victorious gleam
Ere I depart! For thee alone, for thee!
May this last work, this farewell triumph be,
Thou, lov'd so vainly! I would leave enshrined
10   Something immortal of my heart and mind,
That yet may speak to thee when I am gone,
Shaking thine inmost bosom with a tone
Of lost affection;—something that may prove
What she hath been, whose melancholy love
15   On thee was lavish'd; silent pang and tear,
And fervent song, that gush'd when none were near,
And dream by night, and weary thought by day,
Stealing the brightness from her life away,—
While thou——Awake! not yet within me die,
20   Under the burden and the agony
Of this vain tenderness,—my spirit, wake!
Ev'n for thy sorrowful affection's sake,
Live! in thy work breathe out!—that he may yet,
Feeling sad mastery there, perchance regret
Thine unrequited gift.

II.

25   It comes,—the power
Within me born, flows back; my fruitless dower
That could not win me love. Yet once again
I greet it proudly, with its rushing train
Of glorious images: —they throng—they press—
30   A sudden joy lights up my loneliness,—
I shall not perish all!
                    The bright work grows
Beneath my hand, unfolding, as a rose,
Leaf after leaf, to beauty; line by line,
I fix my thought, heart, soul, to burn, to shine,
35   Thro' the pale marble's veins. It grows—and now
I give my own life's history to thy brow,
Forsaken Ariadne! thou shalt wear
My form, my lineaments; but oh! more fair,

Touch'd into lovelier being by the glow
    Which in me dwells, as by the summer-light   40
All things are glorified. From thee my wo
    Shall yet look beautiful to meet his sight,
When I am pass'd away. Thou art the mould
Wherein I pour the fervent thoughts, th' untold,
The self-consuming! Speak to him of me,   45
Thou, the deserted by the lonely sea,
With the soft sadness of thine earnest eye,
Speak to him, lorn one! deeply, mournfully,
Of all my love and grief! Oh! could I throw
Into thy frame a voice, a sweet, and low,   50
And thrilling voice of song! when he came nigh,
To send the passion of its melody
Thro' his pierc'd bosom—on its tones to bear
My life's deep feeling, as the southern air
Wafts the faint myrtle's[1] breath,—to rise, to swell,   55
To sink away in accents of farewell,
Winning but one, *one* gush of tears, whose flow
Surely my parted spirit yet might know,
If love be strong as death!

III.

        Now fair thou art,
Thou form, whose life is of my burning heart!   60
Yet all the vision that within me wrought,
    I cannot make thee! Oh! I might have given
Birth to creations of far nobler thought,
    I might have kindled, with the fire of heaven,
Things not of such as die! But I have been   65
Too much alone; a heart, whereon to lean,
With all these deep affections that o'erflow
My aching soul, and find no shore below;
An eye to be my star, a voice to bring
Hope o'er my path, like sounds that breathe of spring,   70

---

1   myrtle] in classical myth and literature associated with Venus and love.

These are denied me — dreamt of still in vain, —
Therefore my brief aspirings from the chain,
Are ever but as some wild fitful song,
Rising triumphantly, to die ere long
In dirge-like echoes.

IV.

75   Yet the world will see
Little of this, my parting work, in thee,
   Thou shalt have fame! Oh, mockery! give the reed
From storms a shelter, — give the drooping vine
Something round which its tendrils may entwine, —
80   Give the parch'd flower a rain-drop, and the meed
Of love's kind words to woman! Worthless fame!
That in *his* bosom wins not for my name
Th' abiding place it asked! Yet how my heart,
In its own fairy world of song and art,
85 Once beat for praise! — Are those high longings o'er?
That which I have been can I be no more?
Never, oh! never more; tho' still thy sky
Be blue as then, my glorious Italy!
And tho' the music, whose rich breathings fill
90 Thine air with soul, be wandering past me still,
And tho' the mantle of thy sunlight streams
Unchang'd on forms instinct with poet-dreams;
Never, oh! never more! Where'er I move,
The shadow of this broken-hearted love
95 Is on me and around! Too well *they* know,
   Whose life is all within, too soon and well,
When there the blight hath settled; — but I go
   Under the silent wings of peace to dwell;
From the slow wasting, from the lonely pain,
100 The inward burning of those words — *"in vain,"*
   Sear'd on the heart — I go. 'Twill soon be past.
Sunshine, and song, and bright Italian heaven,
   And thou, oh! thou, on whom my spirit cast
Unvalued wealth, — who know'st not what was given

In that devotedness,—the sad, and deep,   105
And unrepaid—farewell! If I could weep
Once, only once, belov'd one! on thy breast,
Pouring my heart forth ere I sink to rest!
But that were happiness, and unto me
Earth's gift is FAME. Yet I was form'd to be   110
So richly blest! With thee to watch the sky,
Speaking not, feeling but that thou wert nigh;
With thee to listen, while the tones of song
Swept ev'n as part of our sweet air along,
To listen silently;— with thee to gaze   115
On forms, the deified of olden days,
This had been joy enough;—and hour by hour,
From its glad well-springs drinking life and power,
How had my spirit soar'd, and made its fame
   A glory for thy brow! — Dreams, dreams! — the fire   120
Burns faint within me. Yet I leave my name —
   As a deep thrill may linger on the lyre
When its full chords are hush'd—awhile to live,
And one day haply in thy heart revive
Sad thoughts of me: — I leave it, with a sound,   125
A spell o'er memory, mournfully profound,
I leave it, on my country's air to dwell,—
Say proudly yet — "'Twas her's¹ who lov'd me well!"

PAULINE.[1]

To die for what we love!—Oh! there is power
In the true heart, and pride, and joy, for *this*;
It is to *live* without the vanish'd light
That strength is needed.[2]

Così trapassa al trapassar d'un Giorno
Della vita mortal il fiore e'l verde.

TASSO.[3]

ALONG the star-lit Seine[4] went music swelling,
    Till the air thrilled with its exulting mirth;
Proudly it floated, even as if no dwelling
    For cares or stricken hearts were found on earth;
5   And a glad sound the measure lightly beat,
    A happy chime of many dancing feet.

For in a palace of the land that night,
    Lamps, and fresh roses, and green leaves were hung,
And from the painted walls a stream of light,

---

1   a historical person; see Hemans's note to l. 12; first published in the *New Monthly Magazine* 19 (Feb. 1827): 155-57, with slight differences in spelling and punctuation (substantive variants are noted here), and an epigraph from Wordsworth.
2   lines probably by Hemans herself.
3   passage from Torquato Tasso's *Gerusalemme liberata* (canto 16, stanza 15), a widely read verse romance (1581) about Christian knights' expedition to take the Holy Land from its Muslim occupiers; translated: "Thus passes away in a day the flower and freshness of mortal life"; the epigraph in the *New Monthly Magazine* more directly addresses the theological problem of evil, seen in apparently meaningless death, in relation to a supposedly benevolent deity:

—One adequate support
For the calamities of mortal life
Exists, one only;—an assured belief
That the procession of our fate, howe'er
Sad or disturb'd, is order'd by a Being
Of infinite benevolence and power,
Whose everlasting purposes embrace
All accidents, converting them to good.
WORDSWORTH. [*The Excursion*, 4.11-18]
4   Seine] major river in France flowing through Paris.

On flying forms beneath soft splendour flung:
But loveliest far amidst the revel's pride
Was one, the lady from the Danube-side.[1]

Pauline, the meekly bright! — tho' now no more
　　Her clear eye flash'd with youth's all tameless glee,
Yet something holier than its dayspring wore,
　　There in soft rest lay beautiful to see;
A charm with graver, tenderer,[2] sweetness fraught—
The blending of deep love and matron thought.

Thro' the gay throng she moved, serenely fair,
　　And such calm joy as fills a moonlight sky,
Sate on her brow beneath its graceful hair,
　　As her young daughter in the dance went by,
With the fleet step of one that yet hath known
Smiles and kind voices in this world alone.

Lurk'd there no secret boding in her breast?
　　Did no faint whisper warn of evil nigh?
Such oft awake when most the heart seems blest
　　Midst the light laughter of festivity:
Whence come those tones! — Alas! enough we know,
To mingle fear with all triumphal show!

Who spoke of evil, when young feet were flying
　　In fairy rings around the echoing hall?
Soft airs thro' braided locks in perfume sighing,
　　Glad pulses beating unto music's call?

1　　　　　*But loveliest far amidst the revel's pride,*
　　　　　　Was she, the Lady from the Danube-side.
The Princess Pauline Schwartzenberg. The story of her fate is beautifully related in
L'Allemagne. Vol. iii. p. 336. [Hemans's endnote, referring to Germaine de Staël,
De l'Allemagne (1810, suppressed; republished at London, 1813), a major work of
Romantic cultural description, implicitly anti-Bonapartist and liberal; the account
of Pauline and the incident on which the poem is based is in ch. 6, "De la
douleur"; the Danube is the major river of central-southern Europe, flowing
through Vienna, Budapest, and other major cities.]
2　　the comma was removed in the 2nd edn to conform with normal usage.

35   Silence!—the minstrels pause—and hark! a sound,
      A strange quick rustling which their notes had drown'd!

      And lo! a light upon the dancers breaking—
          Not such their clear and silvery lamps had shed!
      From the gay dream of revelry awaking,
40   One moment holds them still in breathless dread;
      The wild fierce lustre grows—then bursts a cry—
      Fire! thro' the hall and round it gathering—fly!

      And forth they rush—as chased by sword and spear—
          To the green coverts of the garden-bowers;
45   A gorgeous masque of pageantry and fear,
          Startling the birds and trampling down the flowers:
      While from the dome behind, red sparkles driven
      Pierce the dark stillness of the midnight heaven.

      And where is she, Pauline?—the hurrying throng
50   Have swept her onward, as a stormy blast
      Might sweep some faint o'erwearied bird along—
          Till now the threshold of that death is past,
      And free she stands beneath the starry skies,
      Calling her child—but no sweet voice replies.

55   "Bertha! where art thou?—Speak, oh! speak, my own!"
          Alas! unconscious of her pangs the while,
      The gentle girl, in fear's cold grasp alone,
          Powerless hath sunk within[1] the blazing pile;
      A young bright form, deck'd gloriously for death,
60   With flowers all shrinking from[2] the flame's fierce breath!

      But oh! thy strength, deep love!—there is no power
          To stay the mother from that rolling grave,
      Tho' fast on high the fiery volumes tower,
          And forth, like banners, from each lattice wave.

---

1   within] *NMM*: amidst
2   from] *NMM*: at

Back, back she rushes thro' a host combined —   65
Mighty is anguish, with affection twined!

And what bold step may follow, midst the roar
   Of the red billows, o'er their prey that rise?
None! — Courage there stood still — and never more
   Did those fair forms emerge on human eyes!   70
Was one brief meeting theirs, one wild farewell?
And died they heart to heart? — Oh! who can tell?

Freshly and cloudlessly the morning broke
   On that sad palace, midst its pleasure-shades;
Its painted roofs had sunk — yet black with smoke   75
   And lonely stood its marble colonnades:
But yester-eve their shafts with wreaths were bound —
Now lay the scene one shrivell'd scroll around!

And bore the ruins no recording trace
   Of all that woman's heart had dared and done?   80
Yes! there were gems to mark its mortal place,
   That forth from dust and ashes dimly shone!
Those had the mother on her gentle breast,
Worn round her child's fair image, there at rest.[1]

And they were all! — the tender and the true   85
   Left this alone her sacrifice to prove,
Hallowing the spot where mirth once lightly flew,
   To deep, lone, chasten'd thoughts of grief and love.[2]
Oh! we have need of patient faith below,
To clear away the mysteries of such wo!   90

---

1   *NMM*: Hemans's footnote: "L'on n'a pu reconnoître ce qui restoit d'elle sur la terre, qu'au chiffre de ses enfans, qui marquoit encore la place où cet ange avoit péri." MADAME DE STAEL. ["Her earthly remains could not be recognized, except by the image of her children, which marked the spot where this angel perished."]
2   love.] *NMM*: love!

THE GRAVE OF A POETESS.[1]

"Ne me plaignez pas—si vous saviez
Combien de peines ce tombeau m'a epargnées!"[2]

I stood beside thy lowly grave;—
   Spring-odours breath'd around,
And music, in the river-wave,
   Pass'd with a lulling sound.

5   All happy things that love the sun
   In the bright air glanc'd by,
And a glad murmur seem'd to run
   Thro' the soft azure sky.

Fresh leaves were on the ivy-bough
10   That fring'd the ruins near;
Young voices were abroad—but thou
   Their sweetness couldst not hear.

And mournful grew my heart for thee,
   Thou in whose woman's mind
15   The ray that brightens earth and sea,
   The light of song was shrined.

---

1 Extrinsic interest has lately attached to the fine scenery of Woodstock, near Kilkenny, on account of its having been the last residence of the author of Psyche. Her grave is one of many in the church-yard of the village. The river runs smoothly by. The ruins of an ancient abbey that have been partially converted into a church, reverently throw their mantle of tender shadow over it. —*Tales by the O'Hara Family.* [Hemans's footnote; passage compressed and adapted from "The Fetches" in John and Michael Banim's *Tales by the O'Hara Family,* (1st series, 3 vols, 1825, 2.363-4), a collection of novellas depicting sympathetically the life of the Irish Catholic peasantry at a time when there were growing calls for granting them civil and religious rights and opportunities to improve their lot socially and economically; the "poetess" is Mary Tighe (1772-1810), author of *Psyche; or, The Legend of Love* (1805, republished 1811); Hemans's poem was originally published in the *New Monthly Magazine* 20 (July 1827): 69-70, with slight differences in punctuation and spelling, and with an additional sentence in the epigraph: "It is the very spot for the grave of a poetess." For context and commentary on this poem, see Introduction, p. 52.]

2 Germaine de Staël, *Corinne; ou, l'Italie* (3 vols, 1807, 3.283; book 18, ch. 3), where the phrase is on an epitaph in a church in Florence: "Don't feel sorry for me—if only you knew how much sorrow this tomb has saved me!"

Mournful, that thou wert slumbering low,
  With a dread curtain drawn
Between thee and the golden glow
  Of this world's vernal dawn.   20

Parted from all the song and bloom
  Thou wouldst have lov'd so well,
To thee the sunshine round thy tomb
  Was but a broken spell.

The bird, the insect on the wing,   25
  In their bright reckless play,
Might feel the flush and life of spring,—
  And thou wert pass'd away!

But then, ev'n then, a nobler thought
  O'er my vain sadness came;   30
Th' immortal spirit woke, and wrought
  Within my thrilling frame.

Surely on lovelier things, I said,
  Thou must have look'd ere now,
Than all that round our pathway shed   35
  Odours and hues below.[1]

The shadows of the tomb are here,
  Yet beautiful is earth!
What seest thou then where no dim fear,
  No haunting dream hath birth?   40

Here a vain love to passing flowers
  Thou gav'st—but where thou art,
The sway is not with changeful hours,
  There love and death must part.[2]

---

1 below.] in 2nd edn: below,
2 part.] *NMM*: part!

Thou hast left sorrow in thy song,
A voice not loud, but deep!
The glorious bowers of earth among,
How often didst thou weep!¹

Where couldst thou fix on mortal ground
Thy tender thoughts and high? —
Now peace the woman's heart hath found,
And joy the poet's eye.²

FROM "MISCELLANEOUS PIECES":

THE HOMES OF ENGLAND.³

Where's the coward that would not dare
To fight for such a land?

*Marmion.*⁴

THE stately Homes of England,
How beautiful they stand!

---

1   in July 1831 Hemans wrote to Clara Graves from the Hermitage, Kilkenny, revising her opinion of Tighe: "I was sorry to find that I must give up my beau idéal of Mrs. Tighe's Character; at least in a great measure; much of her domestic sorrow I learned, was caused by her excessive passion for shining in Society, which quite carried her away from all Home-enjoyments, until her Health gave way, and she was compelled to relinquish this career of dissipation. — How one is obliged to resign one's fair visions of excellence, my dear Clara, when the strong *daylight* of truth is thrown upon them; and how painful is the feeling with which we see them melt away! — I thought several times of Lord Byron's '*Implora pace*', whilst listening to these details, which were given me *at the tomb* itself ..." (Huntington Library MS HM 42533)

2   eye.] *NMM*: eye!

3   first published in *Blackwood's Magazine* 21 (April 1827): 392, with slight differences in spelling and punctuation and with a different epigraph, from Joanna Baillie's play *Ethwald* (1802), part 2, 1.2.76-82:

—————— A land of peace,
Where yellow fields unspoil'd, and pastures green,
Mottled with herds and flocks, who crop secure
Their native herbage, nor have ever known
A stranger's stall, smile gladly.
See through its tufted alleys to Heaven's roof
The curling smoke of quiet dwellings rise.

4   a popular poem (1808) by Walter Scott; passage from canto 4, stanza 30 (ll. 631-2), uttered by the noble Fitz-Eustace; the poem is set in the early 16th century and

Amidst their tall ancestral trees,
  O'er all the pleasant land.
The deer across their greensward bound   5
  Thro' shade and sunny gleam,
And the swan glides past them with the sound
  Of some rejoicing stream.

The merry Homes of England!
  Around their hearths by night,   10
What gladsome looks of household love
  Meet, in the ruddy light!
There woman's voice flows forth in song,
  Or childhood's tale is told,
Or lips move tunefully along   15
  Some glorious page of old.

The blessed Homes of England!
  How softly on their bowers
Is laid the holy quietness
  That breathes from Sabbath-hours!   20
Solemn, yet sweet, the church-bell's chime
  Floats thro' their woods at morn;
All other sounds, in that still time,
  Of breeze and leaf are born.

The Cottage Homes of England!   25
  By thousands on her plains,
They are smiling o'er the silvery brooks,
  And round the hamlet-fanes.
Thro' glowing orchards forth they peep,
  Each from its nook of leaves,   30
And fearless there the[1] lowly sleep,
  As the bird beneath their eaves.

---

deals with love and treachery at the time of the battle of Flodden Field (1513), dur-
ing the long struggle of Scotland to maintain its independence from England.
1 the] *BM*: they

The free, fair Homes of England!
  Long, long, in hut and hall,
35   May hearts of native proof be rear'd
  To guard each hallow'd wall!
And green for ever be the groves,
  And bright the flowery sod,
Where first the child's glad spirit loves
  Its country and its God![1]

TO WORDSWORTH.[2]

THINE is a strain to read among the hills,
  The old and full of voices;—by the source
Of some free stream, whose gladdening presence fills
  The solitude with sound; for in its course
5 Even such is thy deep song, that seems a part
Of those high scenes, a fountain from their heart.

Or its calm[3] spirit fitly may be taken
  To the still[4] breast, in sunny garden-bowers,[5]
Where vernal[6] winds each tree's low tones awaken,
10   And bud and bell with changes mark the hours.
There let thy thoughts be with me, while the day
Sinks with a golden and serene decay.

---

1   Originally published in Blackwood's Magazine. [Hemans's footnote]
2   first published as "To the Author of The Excursion and the Lyrical Ballads," in the
    Literary Magnet (new series, vol. 1, April 1826, pp. 169-70), with slight differences in
    punctuation, spelling, and wording, and numbered stanzas; substantive variants are
    recorded here; William Wordsworth (1770-1850) was receiving greater recognition
    in the 1820s, as shown by his being the first of the "The Living Poets of England"
    described in the *Literary Magnet* (n.s., 1, Jan. 1826, 17-22); Hemans was the first
    woman and second poet in the series (n.s., 1, March 1826, 113-21), and she sent her
    poem on Wordsworth to the *Literary Magnet* the following month; for context and
    commentary on this poem and Hemans's relationship to Wordsworth, see Intro-
    duction, p. 0.
3   calm] *LM*: pure
4   still] *LM*: calm
5   sunny garden-bowers] *LM*: some sweet Garden's bowers
6   vernal] *LM*: summer

Or by some hearth where happy faces meet,
   When night hath hush'd the woods, with all their birds,
There,[1] from some gentle voice, that lay were sweet   15
   As antique music, link'd with household words.
While, in pleased murmurs, woman's lip might move,
And the rais'd eye of childhood shine in[2] love.

Or where the shadows of dark solemn yews
   Brood silently o'er some lone burial-ground,   20
Thy verse hath power that brightly might diffuse
   A breath, a kindling, as of spring, around;
From its own glow of hope and courage high,
And steadfast faith's victorious constancy.

True bard, and holy! — thou art ev'n as one   25
   Who, by some secret gift of soul or eye,
In every spot beneath the smiling sun,
   Sees where the springs of living waters lie:[3]
Unseen awhile they sleep — till, touch'd by thee,[4]
Bright[5] healthful waves flow forth to each glad wanderer free.   30

KÖRNER AND HIS SISTER.[6]

Charles Theodore Körner, the celebrated young German poet
and soldier, was killed in a skirmish with a detachment of
French troops, on the 20th of August, 1813, a few hours after
the composition of his popular piece, "The Sword-song."[7] He
was buried at the village of Wöbbelin in Mecklenburg, under a
beautiful oak, in a recess of which he had frequently deposited

1   There] *LM*: *There*
2   in] *LM*: with
3   lie:] *LM*: lie!
4   line 29 in *LM*: Thou mov'st through nature's realm, and touched by thee,
5   Bright] *LM*: Clear
6   Karl Theodor Körner (1791-1813), German playwright, soldier, and poet, killed in
    the German Wars of Liberation against Napoleon; the refrain of the poem refers to
    one of his works, *Leyer und Schwerdt* (1814), a collection of his patriotic verse pub-
    lished after his death by his father and widely read through the nineteenth century.
7   a verse dialogue between a patriotic German soldier and his sword, figured as his
    bride-to-be, in which they enthusiastically anticipate their marriage on the field of

verses composed by him while campaigning in its vicinity. The monument erected to his memory is of cast iron, and the upper part is wrought into a lyre and sword, a favourite emblem of Körner's, from which one of his works had been entitled. Near the grave of the poet is that of his only sister, who died of grief for his loss, having only survived him long enough to complete his portrait, and a drawing of his burial-place. Over the gate of the cemetery is engraved one of his own lines:

"Vergiss die treuen Tödten nicht."
Forget not the faithful dead.

—*See Richardson's Translation of Körner's Life and Works, and Downes's Letters from Mecklenburg.*[1]

GREEN wave the oak for ever o'er thy rest,
    Thou that beneath its crowning foliage sleepest,
And, in the stillness of thy country's breast,
    Thy place of memory, as an altar keepest;
5   Brightly thy spirit o'er her hills was pour'd,
    Thou of the Lyre and Sword!

Rest, bard! rest, soldier!—by the father's hand
    Here shall the child of after-years be led,
With his wreath-offering silently to stand,
10   In the hush'd presence of the glorious dead.
Soldier and bard! for thou thy path hath trod
    With freedom and with God.

The oak wav'd proudly o'er thy burial-rite,
    On thy crown'd bier to slumber warriors bore thee,
15   And with true hearts thy brethren of the fight

---

battle; an English translation was published in *Blackwood's Magazine* 12 (Nov. 1822), 585-6.
1   Hemans's preface, referring to George Richardson, trans., *The Life of Carl Theodor Körner* (2 vols, London, 1827), and George Downes, *Letters from Mecklenburg and Holstein* … (London, 1822).

Wept as they vail'd[1] their drooping banners o'er thee.
And the deep guns with rolling peal gave token,
 That Lyre and Sword were broken.

Thou hast a hero's tomb: — a lowlier bed
 Is hers, the gentle girl beside thee lying,   20
The gentle girl, that bow'd her fair young head
 When thou wert gone, in silent sorrow dying.
Brother, true friend! the tender and the brave—
 She pined to share thy grave.

Fame was thy gift from others;—but for *her*,   25
 To whom the wide world held that only spot,
She loved thee! —lovely in your lives ye were,
 And in your early deaths divided not.
Thou hast thine oak, thy trophy: — what hath she? —
 Her own blest place by thee!   30

It was thy spirit, brother! which had made
 The bright earth glorious to her thoughtful eye,
Since first in childhood midst the vines ye play'd,
 And sent glad singing through the free blue sky.
Ye were but two — and when that spirit pass'd,   35
 Woe to the one, the last!

Woe, yet not long! —She linger'd but to trace
 Thine image from the image in her breast,
Once, once again to see that buried face
 But smile upon her, ere she went to rest.   40
Too sad a smile! its living light was o'er,
 It answer'd hers no more.

The earth grew silent when thy voice departed,
 The home too lonely whence thy step had fled;
What then was left for her, the faithful-hearted?   45
 Death, death, to still the yearning for the dead!

---

1 vail'd] lowered, as in salute, a 16th- and 17th-century usage that was revived in liter-
ature of the 1820s by Mary Shelley, Walter Scott, and others.

Softly she perish'd: —be the Flower deplor'd
Here with the Lyre and Sword!

Have ye not met ere now? —so let those trust
That meet for moments but to part for years,
That weep, watch, pray, to hold back dust from dust,
That love, where love is but a fount of tears.
Brother, sweet sister! peace around ye dwell—
Lyre, Sword, and Flower, farewell![1]

THE LANDING OF THE PILGRIM FATHERS IN NEW ENGLAND.[2]

Look now abroad—another race has fill'd
Those populous borders —wide the wood recedes,
And towns shoot up, and fertile realms are till'd;
The land is full of harvests and green meads.

BRYANT.[3]

---

1   [Hemans's footnote:] The following lines recently addressed to the author of the
    above, by the venerable father of Körner, who, with the mother, still survives the
    "Lyre, Sword, and Flower" here commemorated, may not be uninteresting to the
    German reader.
        Wohllaut tönt aus der Ferne von freundlichen Lüften getragen,
        Schmeichelt mit lindernder Kraft sich in der Trauernden Ohr,
        Stärkt den erhebenden Glauben an solcher seelen Verwandschaft,
        Die zum Tempel die brust nur für das Würdige weihn.
        Aus dem Lande zu dem sich stets der gefeyerte Jungling
        Hingezogen gefühlt, wird ihm ein gläzender Lohn.
        Heil dem Brittischen Volke, wenn ihm das Deutsche nicht fremd ist!
        Uber Länder und Meer reichen sich beyde die Hand.
                                                        Theodor Korner's Vater.
    [for English translation, see Henry Chorley, *The Lyre and the Sword* (1834), reprinted
    in Hughes, 57-8, and Hemans website]
2   first published in the *New Monthly Magazine* 14 (1825): 402, with slight differences
    in punctuation; the event to which the poem refers occurred in Dec. 1620 near
    what is now Plymouth, Massachusetts; the Pilgrims were a group of English Puri-
    tans who sought refuge from religious persecution first in Holland and then by
    founding a colony in the New World; the event was later mythologized as a found-
    ing moment in the development of the United States of America, and the original
    group came to be designated the Pilgrim Fathers; Hemans's poem was especially
    popular in the United States, where it was often used for public ceremonial occa-
    sions.
3   from *The Ages* (Cambridge, Mass., 1821, ll. 280-83; stanza 32), by the popular

THE breaking waves dash'd high
    On a stern and rock-bound coast,
And the woods against a stormy sky
    Their giant branches toss'd;

And the heavy night hung dark,   5
    The hills and waters o'er,
When a band of exiles moor'd their bark
    On the wild New-England shore.

Not as the conqueror comes,
    They, the true-hearted came;   10
Not with the roll of the stirring drums,
    And the trumpet that sings of fame:

Not as the flying come,
    In silence and in fear;—
They shook the depths of the desert[1] gloom   15
    With their hymns of lofty cheer.

Amidst the storm they sang,
    And the stars heard and the sea![2]
And the sounding[3] aisles of the dim woods rang
    To the anthem of the free.   20

The ocean-eagle soar'd
    From his nest by the white wave's foam,

American poet William Cullen Bryant (1794-1878), presenting history as a record
of despotism, superstition, and destruction until the emergence of liberty and toler-
ation in the New World; *NMM*: different epigraph:
> "Their dauntless hearts no meteor led
> In terror o'er the ocean;
> From fortune and from fame they fled
> To Heaven and its devotion."

An American Poet.
(ll. 11-14 from "Ode" by Robert Treat Paine, 1773-1811)

1 desert] *NMM*: desert's
2 sea!] *NMM*: sea;
3 sounding] *NMM*: surrounding

And the rocking pines of the forest roar'd—
 This was their welcome home!

25 There were men with hoary hair,
  Amidst that pilgrim band;—
Why had *they* come to wither there,[1]
 Away from their childhood's land?

There was woman's fearless eye,
30 Lit by her deep love's truth;
There was manhood's brow serenely high,
 And the fiery heart of youth.

What sought they thus afar?
  Bright jewels of the mine?
35 The wealth of seas, the spoils of war?—
 They sought a faith's pure shrine!

Ay, call it holy ground,
  The soil where first they trod!
They have left unstain'd[2] what there they found—
40 Freedom to worship God.

THE PALM-TREE.[3]

It wav'd not thro' an Eastern sky,
 Beside a fount of Araby;
It was not fann'd by southern breeze
 In some green isle of Indian seas,
5 Nor did its graceful shadow sleep

O'er stream of Afric, lone and deep.
 But fair the exil'd Palm-tree grew
 Midst foliage of no kindred hue;

---

1 there,] *NMM: there,*
2 unstain'd] *NMM:* undimm'd
3 This incident is, I think, recorded by De Lille, in his poem of "Les Jardins."
 [Hemans's footnote, referring to J. Delille, *Les Jardins,* 1782.]

Thro' the laburnum's dropping gold
Rose the light shaft of orient mould,   10
And Europe's violets, faintly sweet,
Purpled the moss-beds at its feet.

Strange look'd it there! — the willow stream'd
Where silvery waters near it gleam'd;
The lime-bough lured the honey-bee   15
To murmur by the Desert's Tree,
And showers of snowy roses made
A lustre in its fan-like shade.

There came an eve of festal hours —
Rich music fill'd that garden's bowers: 20
Lamps, that from flowering branches hung,
On sparks of dew soft colours flung,
And bright forms glanc'd — a fairy show —
Under the blossoms to and fro.

But one, a lone one, midst the throng,   20
Seem'd reckless all of dance or song:
He was a youth of dusky mien,
Whereon the Indian sun had been,
Of crested brow, and long black hair —
A stranger, like the Palm-tree there.   30

And slowly, sadly, mov'd his plumes,
Glittering athwart the leafy glooms:
He pass'd the pale green olives by,
Nor won the chestnut-flowers his eye;
But when to that sole Palm he came,   35
Then shot a rapture through his frame!

To him, to him, its rustling spoke,
The silence of his soul it broke!
It whisper'd of his own bright isle,
That lit the ocean with a smile;   40
Aye, to his ear that native tone
Had something of the sea-wave's moan!

His mother's cabin home, that lay
Where feathery cocoas fring'd the bay;
The dashing of his brethren's oar,
The conch-note heard along the shore;—
All thro' his wakening bosom swept:
He clasp'd his country's Tree and wept!

Oh! scorn him not!—the strength, whereby
The patriot girds himself to die,
Th' unconquerable power, which fills
The freeman battling on his hills,
These have one fountain deep and clear—
The same whence gush'd that child-like tear!

THE CHILD'S LAST SLEEP.[1]

SUGGESTED BY A MONUMENT OF CHANTREY'S.[2]

THOU sleepest—but when wilt thou wake, fair child?—
When the fawn awakes in the forest wild?
When the lark's wing mounts with the breeze of morn?
When the first rich breath of the rose is born?—
Lovely thou sleepest, yet something lies
Too deep and still on thy soft-seal'd eyes,

---

1 first published in the literary annual, *Friendship's Offering* (1826) with an epigraph from John Wilson:
> The lovely child is dead!
> All, all his innocent thoughts, like rose-leaves, scattered,
> And his glad childhood nothing but a dream.

Hemans probably wrote the poem to accompany an illustration of a sleeping child—usual practice in the literary annuals (see Paula Feldman, ed. Felicia Hemans, *Records of Woman*, pp. 206-7.)

2 Sir Francis Leggatt Chantrey (1781-1841), the most eminent English sculptor of his day, who executed many busts and statues of public figures, including George IV, George Washington, the Duke of Wellington, Wordsworth, and Walter Scott; Hemans is probably referring to what was, however, his best known monument, the "Sleeping Children" (1812) in the Cathedral Church of St Chad, Lichfield, the subject of her poem "The Sculptured Children: On Chantrey's Monument at Lichfield," first published in *The Forget-Me-Not* (1829); the monument was executed early in his career and depicts the two young Robinson girls as if asleep—a design influenced by information he gathered while visiting the children's grieving mother.

Mournful, tho' sweet, is thy rest to see —
When will the hour of thy rising be?

Not when the fawn wakes, not when the lark
On the crimson cloud of the morn floats dark —   10
Grief with vain passionate tears hath wet
The hair, shedding gleams from[1] thy pale brow yet;
Love with sad kisses, unfelt, hath press'd
Thy meek-dropt eyelids and quiet breast;
And the glad spring, calling out bird and bee,   15
Shall colour all blossoms, fair child! but thee.

Thou'rt gone from us, bright one! — that *thou* shouldst die,
And life be left to the butterfly![2]
Thou'rt gone as a dew-drop is swept from the bough —
Oh! for the world where thy home is now!   20
How may we love but in doubt and fear,
How may we anchor our fond hearts here,
How should e'en joy but a trembler be,
Beautiful dust! when we look on thee?

THE ILLUMINATED CITY.[3]

THE hills all glow'd with a festive light,
For the royal city rejoic'd by night:
There were lamps hung forth upon tower and tree,
Banners were lifted and streaming free;
Every tall pillar was wreath'd with fire,   5
Like a shooting meteor was every spire;

---

1   from] *Friendship's Offering*: o'er
2   A butterfly, as if resting on a flower, is sculptured on the monument. [Hemans's footnote]
3   first published in the *Monthly Magazine*, new series 2 (Nov. 1826): 515, with slight differences in spelling and punctuation; "illuminated" here refers to the practice of placing candles in windows of houses to mark a public celebration, such as a victory, coronation, or political event; partisan mobs would, however, force homeowners to illuminate their windows for various causes, to indicate support, and those who did not comply would have their windows broken.

And the outline of many a dome on high
Was traced, as in stars, on the clear dark sky.

I pass'd thro' the streets; there were throngs on throngs—
10   Like sounds of the deep were their mingled songs;
There was music forth from each palace borne—
A peal of the cymbal, the harp, and horn;
The forests heard it, the mountains rang,
The hamlets woke to its haughty clang;
15   Rich and victorious was every tone,
Telling the land of her foes o'erthrown.

Didst thou meet not a mourner for all the slain?
Thousands lie dead on their battle-plain!
Gallant and true were the hearts that fell—
20   Grief in the homes they have left must dwell;
Grief o'er the aspect of childhood spread,
And bowing the beauty of woman's head:
Didst thou hear, midst the songs, not one tender moan,
For the many brave to their slumbers gone?

25   I saw not the face of a weeper there—
Too strong, perchance, was the bright lamp's glare!—
I heard not a wail midst the joyous crowd—
The music of victory was all too loud!
Mighty it roll'd on the winds afar,
30   Shaking the streets like a conqueror's car;
Thro' torches and streamers[1] its floods swept by—
How could I listen for moan or sigh?

Turn then away from life's pageants,[2] turn,
If its deep story thy heart would learn![3]
35   Ever too bright is that outward show,
Dazzling the eyes till they see not wo.[4]

---

1   streamers] *MM*: streams
2   pageants,] *MM*: pageants!
3   learn!] *MM*: learn:
4   wo.] *MM*: woe!

But lift the proud mantle which hides from thy view
The things thou shouldst gaze on, the sad and true;
Nor fear to survey what its folds conceal,—
So must thy spirit be taught to feel!

THE GRAVES OF A HOUSEHOLD.[1]

THEY grew in beauty, side by side,
　　They fill'd one home[2] with glee;—
Their graves are sever'd, far and wide,
　　By mount, and stream, and sea.[3]

The same fond mother bent at night   5
　　O'er each fair sleeping brow;
She had each folded flower in sight,—
　　Where are those dreamers now?

One, midst the forests of the west,
　　By a dark stream is laid—   10
The Indian knows his place of rest,
　　Far in the cedar shade.

The sea, the blue lone sea, hath one,
　　He lies where pearls lie deep;
He[4] was the lov'd of all, yet none   15
　　O'er his low bed may weep.

One sleeps where southern vines are drest
　　Above the noble slain:
He wrapt his colours round his breast,
　　On a blood-red field of Spain.   20

And one—o'er *her* the myrtle showers
　　Its leaves, by soft winds fann'd;

1　first published in the *New Monthly Magazine* 14 (Dec. 1825): 534, with slight differences in punctuation and spelling; substantive differences are noted.
2　home] *NMM*: house
3　sea.] *NMM*: sea!
4　*He*] *NMM*: He

She faded midst Italian flowers,—
　　The last of that bright band.

25　And parted thus they[1] rest, who play'd
　　Beneath the same green tree;
　Whose voices mingled as they pray'd
　　Around one parent knee!

　They that with smiles lit up the hall,
30　　And cheer'd with song the hearth,—
　Alas![2] for love, if *thou* wert all,
　　And nought beyond, oh,[3] earth!

THE IMAGE IN LAVA.[4]

THOU thing of years departed!
　　What ages have gone by,
Since here the mournful seal was set
　　By love and agony!

5　Temple and tower have moulder'd,
　　Empires from earth have pass'd,—
　And woman's heart hath left a trace
　　Those glories to outlast!

　And childhood's fragile image
10　　Thus fearfully enshrin'd,
　Survives the proud memorials rear'd
　　By conquerors of mankind.

1　thus they] *NMM*: thus, *they*
2　Alas!] *NMM*: Alas
3　oh,] *NMM*: on
4　The impression of a woman's form, with an infant clasped to the bosom, found at
　the uncovering of Herculaneum. [Hemans's footnote; Herculaneum was one of the
　towns destroyed in the eruption of mount Vesuvius in AD 79; as the poem makes
　clear, the human victims were buried in volcanic ash rather than lava; see also
　Hemans's "The Festal Hour," l. 51 and note, from *The Siege of Valencia … with Other
　Poems* (1823); first published in the *New Monthly Magazine* 20 (Sept. 1827): 255-56,
　with slight differences in punctuation and spelling; substantive variants are noted.]

Babe! wert thou brightly[1] slumbering
   Upon thy mother's breast,
When suddenly the fiery tomb   15
   Shut round each gentle guest?

A strange dark fate o'ertook you,
   Fair babe and loving heart!
One moment of a thousand pangs —
   Yet better than to part!   20

Haply of that fond bosom,
   On ashes here impress'd,
Thou wert the only treasure, child!
   Whereon a hope might rest.

Perchance all vainly lavish'd,   25
   Its other love had been,
And where it trusted, nought remain'd
   But thorns on which[2] to lean.

Far better then to perish,
   Thy form within its clasp,
Than live and lose thee, precious one!   30
   From that impassion'd grasp.

Oh! I could pass all relics
   Left by the pomps of old,
To gaze on this rude monument,   35
   Cast in affection's mould.

Love, human love! what art thou?
   Thy print upon the dust
Outlives the cities of renown
   Wherein the mighty trust!   40

---

1 brightly] *NMM*: calmly
2 on which] *NMM*: whereon

Immortal, oh! immortal
    Thou art, whose earthly glow
Hath given these ashes holiness —
    It must, it *must* be so!

FROM
THE AMULET; OR, CHRISTIAN AND LITERARY REMEMBRANCER (1829):

WOMAN AND FAME.[1]

Happy — happier far than thou,
With the laurel on thy brow;
She that makes the humblest hearth,
Lovely but to one on earth.[2]

THOU hast a charmed cup, O Fame!
   A draught that mantles high,
And seems to lift this earthly frame
   Above mortality.
Away! to me — a woman — bring   5
Sweet waters from affection's spring.

Thou hast green laurel leaves, that twine
   Into so proud a wreath;
For that resplendent gift of thine,
   Heroes have smiled in death: 10
Give *me* from some kind hand a flower,
The record of one happy hour!

Thou hast a voice, whose thrilling tone
   Can bid each life-pulse beat
As when a trumpet's note hath blown,   15
   Calling the brave to meet:
But mine, let mine — a woman's breast,
By words of home-born love be bless'd.

---

1 *The Amulet* was a literary annual edited by S. C. Hall.
2 a slightly altered quotation from Hemans's own "Corinne at the Capitol" (ll. 45-8), published in *The Literary Souvenir* (1827) and in *Songs of the Affections* (1830); for context and commentary, see Introduction, pp. 53-4.

A hollow sound is in thy song,
20   A mockery in thine eye,
To the sick heart that doth but long
    For aid, for sympathy —
For kindly looks to cheer it on,
For tender accents that are gone.

25   Fame, Fame! thou canst not be the stay
    Unto the drooping reed,
The cool fresh fountain in the day
    Of the soul's feverish need:
Where must the lone one turn or flee? —
30   Not unto thee — oh! not to thee!

FROM *SONGS OF THE AFFECTIONS, WITH OTHER POEMS* (1830)[1]

FROM "SONGS OF THE AFFECTIONS"

WOMAN ON THE FIELD OF BATTLE.[2]

> Where hath not woman stood,
> Strong in affection's might? a reed, upborne
> By an o'ermastering current![3]

GENTLE and lovely form,
    What didst thou here,
When the fierce battle-storm
    Bore down the spear?

Banner and shiver'd crest,   5
    Beside thee strown,
Tell, that amidst the best,
    Thy work was done!

Yet strangely, sadly fair,
    O'er the wild scene,   10
Gleams, through its golden hair,
    That brow serene.

Low lies the stately head,—
    Earth-bound the free;
How gave those haughty dead   15
    A place to thee?

Slumberer! *thine*[4] early bier
    Friends should have crown'd,

---

1   texts from the 1st edition; for context and commentary, see Introduction, pp. 58–61.

2   first published in *Blackwood's Magazine* 22 (Nov. 1827): 585-6, with slight differences in spelling and punctuation.

3   the lines are probably by FH herself, a not uncommon practice at the time.

4   *thine*] BM: thine

Many a flower and tear
    Shedding around.

Soft voices, clear and young,
    Mingling their swell,
Should o'er thy dust have sung
    Earth's last farewell.

Sisters, above[1] the grave
    Of thy repose,
Should have bid violets wave
    With the white rose.

Now must the trumpet's note,
    Savage and shrill,
For requiem o'er thee float,
    Thou fair and still!

And the swift charger sweep,
    In full career,
Trampling thy place of sleep,—
    Why camest thou here?

Why?—ask the true heart why
    Woman hath been
Ever, where brave men die,
    Unshrinking seen?

Unto this harvest ground
    Proud reapers came,—
Some, for that stirring sound,
    A warrior's name;

Some, for the stormy play
    And joy of strife;
And some, to fling away
    A weary life;—

---

1   above] *BM*: about

But thou, pale sleeper, thou,
    With the slight frame,
And the rich locks, whose glow   50
    Death cannot tame;

Only one thought, one power,
    Thee could have led,
So, through the tempest's hour,   55
    To lift thy head!

Only the true, the strong,
    The love, whose trust
Woman's deep soul too long
    Pours on the dust!   60

FROM "MISCELLANEOUS POEMS":

CORINNE AT THE CAPITOL.[1]

Les femmes doivent penser qu'il est dans cette carrière bien peu
de sorte qui puissent valoir la plus obscure vie d'une femme
aimée et d'une mère heureuse.

MADAME DE STAEL.

DAUGHTER of th' Italian heaven!
Thou, to whom its fires are given,
Joyously thy car hath roll'd
Where the conqueror's pass'd of old;
And the festal sun that shone,   5

---

1 first published as "Corinna at the Capitol" in *The Literary Souvenir* (1827, pp. 189–
91), an annual, with minor variations in spelling and punctuation and numbered
stanzas; the poem refers to a scene in Germaine de Staël's novel *Corinne; ou, l'Italie*
(1807), one of FH's favourite works and with whose heroine she strongly identified
(see letters 1 and 28 here); the poem's epigraph is somewhat misquoted from Ger-
maine de Staël, *De l'Influence des passions sur le bonheur des individus et des nations*
(1796; *Œuvres complètes*, Paris, 1820, 3.107–8); translated: "Women ought to realize
that in this career [female authorship] there is very little that can equal in value the
most obscure life of a beloved wife and a happy mother."

O'er three[1] hundred triumphs gone,
Makes thy day of glory bright,

With a shower of golden light.
Now thou tread'st th' ascending road,
Freedom's foot so proudly trode;
While, from tombs of heroes borne,
From the dust of empire shorn,
Flowers upon thy graceful head,
Chaplets of all hues, are shed,
In a soft and rosy rain,

Touch'd with many a gemlike stain.
Thou hast gain'd the summit now!
Music hails thee from below;—
Music, whose rich notes might stir
Ashes of the sepulchre;
Shaking with victorious notes
All the bright air as it floats.
Well may woman's heart beat high

Unto that proud harmony!
Now afar it rolls — it dies —
And thy voice is heard to rise
With a low and lovely tone
In its thrilling power alone;
And thy lyre's deep silvery string,
Touch'd as by a breeze's wing,
Murmurs tremblingly at first,

Ere the tide of rapture burst.
All the spirit of thy sky
Now hath lit thy large dark eye,
And thy cheek a flush hath caught
From the joy of kindled thought;
And the burning words of song

---

1 The trebly hundred triumphs. — BYRON. [Hemans's footnote; quotation from *Childe Harold's Pilgrimage*, 4.731.]

From thy lip flow fast and strong,
With a rushing stream's delight

In the freedom of its might. 40
Radiant daughter of the sun!
Now thy living wreath is won.
Crown'd of Rome! — Oh! art thou not
Happy in that glorious lot? —
Happier, happier far than thou, 45
With the laurel on thy brow,
She that makes the humblest hearth
Lovely but to one on earth!

THE RUIN.

Oh! 'tis the *heart* that magnifies this life,
Making a truth and beauty of its own.
WORDSWORTH.[1]

Birth has gladden'd it: Death has sanctified it.
Guesses at Truth.[2]

No dower of storied song is thine,
    O desolate abode!
Forth from thy gates no glittering line
    Of lance and spear hath flow'd.
Banners of knighthood have not flung 5
    Proud drapery o'er thy walls,
Nor bugle notes to battle rung
    Through thy resounding halls.

Nor have rich bowers of *pleasaunce*[3] here
    By courtly hands been dress'd, 10

---

1 "Ode to Lycoris: To the Same," ll. 12-13.
2 a miscellany of aphorisms, reflections, and verses (2 vols, 1827; expanded in succes-
   sive editions) by Julius Charles Hare (1795-1855), dedicated to Wordsworth and
   dealing with issues of the day from an Anglican, progressive-conservative point of
   view.
3 pleasaunce] enjoyment, an archaism from medieval romance.

For Princes, from the chase of deer,
     Under green leaves to rest:
Only some rose, yet lingering bright
     Beside thy casements lone,
Tells where the spirit of delight
     Hath dwelt, and now is gone.

Yet minstrel tale of harp and sword,
     And sovereign beauty's lot,
House of quench'd light and silent board!
     For me thou needest not.
It is enough to know that *here*,
     Where thoughtfully I stand,
Sorrow and love, and hope and fear,
     Have link'd one kindred band.

Thou bindest me with mighty spells!
     —A solemnizing breath,
A presence all around thee dwells,
     Of human life and death.
I need but pluck yon garden flower
     From where the wild reeds rise,
To wake, with strange and sudden power,
     A thousand sympathies.

Thou hast heard many sounds, thou hearth!
     Deserted now by all!
Voices at eve here met in mirth
     Which eve may ne'er recall.
Youth's buoyant step, and woman's tone,
     And childhood's laughing glee,
And song and prayer, have all been known,
     Hearth of the dead! to thee.

Thou hast heard blessings fondly pour'd
     Upon the infant head,
As if in every fervent word
     The living soul were shed;
Thou hast seen partings, such as bear

The bloom from life away —
Alas! for love in changeful air,
   Where nought beloved can stay!

Here, by the restless bed of pain,
   The vigil hath been kept,   50
Till sunrise, bright with hope in vain,
   Burst forth on eyes that wept:
Here hath been felt the hush, the gloom,
   The breathless influence, shed
Through the dim dwelling, from the room   55
   Wherein reposed the dead.

The seat left void, the missing face,
   Have here been mark'd and mourn'd,
And time hath fill'd the vacant place,
   And gladness hath return'd;   60
Till from the narrowing household chain
   The links dropp'd one by one!
And homewards hither, o'er the main,
   Came the spring-birds alone.

Is there not cause, then — cause for thought,   65
   Fix'd eye and lingering tread,
Where, with their thousand mysteries fraught,
   Ev'n lowliest hearts have bled?
Where, in its ever-haunting thirst
   For draughts of purer day,   70
Man's soul, with fitful strength, hath burst
   The clouds that wrapt its way?

Holy to human nature seems
   The long-forsaken spot;
To deep affections, tender dreams,   75
   Hopes of a brighter lot!
Therefore in silent reverence here,
   Hearth of the dead! I stand,
Where joy and sorrow, smile and tear,
   Have link'd one household band.   80

THE SONG OF NIGHT.[1]

O night,
And storm, and darkness! ye are wondrous strong,
Yet lovely in your strength!

BYRON.[2]

I COME to thee, O Earth!
With all my gifts! —for every flower sweet dew,
In bell, and urn, and chalice, to renew
The glory of its birth.

5   Not one which glimmering lies
Far amidst folding hills, or forest leaves,
But, through its veins of beauty, so receives
A spirit of fresh dyes.

I come with every star;
10   Making thy streams, that on their noon-day track,
Give[3] but the moss, the reed, the lily back,
Mirrors of worlds afar.

I come with peace;—I shed
Sleep through thy wood-walks, o'er the honey-bee,
15   The lark's triumphant voice, the fawn's young glee,
The hyacinth's meek head.

---

1   Originally published in the Winter's Wreath for 1830. [Hemans's footnote at the
    end of the poem; The Winter's Wreath was a literary annual; minor differences in
    punctuation and spelling, with substantive differences noted here.]

2   Childe Harold's Pilgrimage, 3.859-61, where the quotation continues, "as is the light /
    Of a dark eye in Woman"; in The Winter's Wreath the poem had a different epi-
    graph, from Novalis (Friedrich von Hardenberg, (1772-1801): "Abwarts wend'ich
    mich zu der heiligen, unaussprechlichen, geheimnissvollen Nacht. Fernab liegt die
    Welt, in eine tiefe Gruft versenkt; in den Salten der Brust weht tiefe Wehmuth.
    Fernen der Erinnerung, der Kindheit Traume, der ganzen Lebens Freuden und
    Hoffnungen kommen in grauen Kleidern, wie Abendnebel nach der Sonne Unter-
    gang." Translation: "I turn toward the holy, ineffable, mysterious night. The world
    lies far off, sunk in a deep grave; through the folds [Falten for Salten] of my bosom
    wafts a deep melancholy. From afar come memory, childhood dreams, all of life's
    joys and hopes in grey attire, like evening mist at sunset."

3   Give] WW: Gave

On my own heart I lay
The weary babe; and sealing with a breath
Its eyes of love, send fairy dreams, beneath
    The shadowing lids to play.   20

    I come with mightier things!
Who calls me silent? I have many tones —
The dark skies thrill with low, mysterious moans,
    Borne on my sweeping wings.

    I waft them not alone   25
From the deep organ of the forest shades,
Or buried streams, unheard amidst their glades,
    Till the bright day is done;

    But in the human breast
A thousand still small voices[1] I awake,   30
Strong, in their sweetness, from the soul to shake
    The mantle of its rest.

    I bring them from the past:
From true hearts broken, gentle spirits torn,
From crush'd affections, which, though long o'erborne,   35
    Make their tones heard at last.

    I bring them from the tomb:
O'er the sad couch of late repentant love
They pass — though low as murmurs of a dove —
    Like trumpets through the gloom.   40

    I come with all my train:
Who calls me lonely? — Hosts around me tread,
The intensely bright, the beautiful, — the dead,[2] —
    Phantoms of heart and brain!

    Looks from departed eyes —   45
These are my lightnings! — fill'd with anguish vain,

---

1   still small voice] the Bible, 1 Kings 19.12
2   – the dead,] *WW*: the Dread

Or tenderness too piercing to sustain,
    They smite with agonies.

    I, that with soft control,
50 Shut the dim violet, hush the woodland song,
I am the avenging one! the arm'd—the strong,
    The searcher of the soul!

    I, that shower dewy light
Through slumbering leaves, bring storms!—the tempest-birth
55 Of memory, thought, remorse:—Be holy, earth!
    I am the solemn night!

THE DIVER.[1]

They learn in suffering what they teach in song.
                                SHELLEY.[2]

Thou hast been where the rocks of coral grow,
    Thou hast fought with the eddying waves;—
Thy cheek is pale, and thy heart beats low,
    Thou searcher of ocean's caves!

5   Thou hast look'd on the gleaming wealth of old,
    And wrecks where the brave have striven;
The deep is a strong and a fearful hold,[3]
    But thou its bar hast riven!

A wild and weary life is thine;
10   A wasting task and lone,
Though treasure-grots for thee may shine,
    To all besides unknown!

A weary life! but a swift decay

---

1   the poem is based on the belief that divers for pearls die an early death as the cost of
    their trade.
2   "Julian and Maddalo: A Dialogue," l. 546; said by Maddalo (who represents Byron)
    to Julian (Shelley).
3   hold] here, a fortified place, and particularly a prison there.

Soon, soon shall set thee free;
  Thou'rt passing fast from thy toils away,   15
Thou wrestler with the sea!

In thy dim eye, on thy hollow cheek,
  Well are the death-signs read—
Go! for the pearl in its cavern seek,
  Ere hope and power be fled!   20

And bright in beauty's coronal
  That glistening gem shall be;
A star to all in the festive hall—
  But who will think on *thee?*

None!—as it gleams from the queen-like head,   25
  Not one 'midst throngs will say,
"A life hath been like a rain-drop shed,
  For that pale quivering ray."

Woe for the wealth thus dearly bought!
  —And are not those like thee,   30
Who win for earth the gems of thought?
  O wrestler with the sea!

Down to the gulfs of the soul they go,
  Where the passion-fountains burn,
Gathering the jewels far below   35
  From many a buried urn:

Wringing from lava-veins the fire,
  That o'er bright words is pour'd;
Learning deep sounds, to make the lyre
  A spirit in each chord.   40

But, oh! the price of bitter tears,
  Paid for the lonely power
That throws at last, o'er desert years,
  A darkly-glorious dower!

Like flower-seeds, by the wild wind spread,
      So radiant thoughts are strew'd;
— The soul whence those high gifts are shed,
      May faint in solitude!

And who will think, when the strain is sung,
      Till a thousand hearts are stirr'd,
What life-drops, from the minstrel wrung,
      Have gush'd with every word?

None, none! —his treasures live like thine,
      He strives and dies like thee;
— Thou, that hast been to the pearl's dark shrine,
      O wrestler with the sea!

THE REQUIEM OF GENIUS.[1]

Les poètes dont l'imagination tient à la puissance d'aimer et de
souffrir, ne sont ils pas les bannis d'une autre region?
                    MADAME DE STAEL. *De L'Allemagne.*[2]

No tears for thee! —though light be from us gone
With thy soul's radiance, bright, yet restless one!
      No tears for thee!

---

1   first published in *Blackwood's Magazine* 27 (March 1830), with slight differences in
     punctuation and spelling and with a different epigraph, unattributed (see letter to
     Blackwood, 1 March 1828, National Library of Scotland), but a version of P. B.
     Shelley's "Alastor; or, The Spirit of Solitude" (ll. 686-95):
                         Thou art fled
               Like some frail exhalation, which the dawn
               Robes in its golden beams — ah! thou hast fled!
               The brave, the gentle, and the beautiful;
               The child of grace and genius. Heartless things
               Are done and said i' the world, and mighty earth,
               In vesper low or joyous orison,
               Lifts still her solemn voice — but thou art fled!
     Hemans omits half of Shelley's ll. 691-2 and l. 693, which read "Are done and said
     i' the world, and many worms / And beasts and men live on, and mighty Earth /
     From sea and mountain, city and wilderness."
2   in fact the passage is found in de Staël's *Corinne* (1807 edn), 2.338, where Corinne
     asks, "la fatalité ne poursuit-elle pas les ames exaltées, les poëtes dont l'imagination

They that have loved an exile, must not mourn
To see him parting for his native bourne   5
    O'er the dark sea.

All the high music of thy spirit here,
Breathed but the language of another sphere,
    Unechoed round;
And strange, though sweet, as 'midst our weeping skies   10
Some half-remember'd strain[1] of paradise
    Might sadly sound.

Hast thou been answer'd? thou, that from the night
And from the voices of the tempest's might,
    And from the past,   15
Wert seeking still some oracle's reply,
To pour the secrets of man's destiny
    Forth on the blast!

Hast thou been answer'd? — thou, that through the gloom,
And shadow, and stern silence of the tomb,   20
    A cry didst send,
So passionate and deep? to pierce, to move,
To win back token of unburied love
    From buried friend!

And hast thou found where living waters burst?   25
Thou, that didst pine amidst us, in the thirst
    Of fever-dreams!
Are the true fountains thine for evermore?
Oh! lured so long by shining mists, that wore
    The light of streams!   30

Speak! is it well with thee? — We call, as *thou*,
With thy lit eye, deep voice, and kindled brow,
    Wert wont to call

---

tient à la puissance d'aimer et de souffrir? Ils sont les bannis d'une autre région ..." ;
translation of FH's version: "Poets for whom imagination holds the power to love
and to suffer, are they not exiles from another world?"
1   strain] *BM*: song

On the departed! Art thou blest and free?
35   —Alas! the lips earth covers, even to *thee*,
              Were silent all!

Yet shall our hope rise fann'd by quenchless faith,
As a flame, foster'd by some warm wind's breath,
              In light upsprings:
40   Freed soul of song! yes,[1] thou hast found[2] the sought;
Borne to thy home of beauty and of thought,
              On morning's wings.

And we will dream[3] it is *thy* joy[4] we hear,
When life's young music, ringing far and clear,
45   O'erflows the sky:
—No tears for *thee!*[5] the lingering gloom is ours—
Thou art for converse with all glorious powers,
              Never to die!

SECOND SIGHT.[6]

Ne'er err'd the prophet heart that grief inspired,
Though joy's illusions mock their votarist.
                                        MATURIN.[7]

A MOURNFUL gift is mine, O friends!
      A mournful gift is mine!
A murmur of the soul which blends
      With the flow of song and wine.

5   An eye that through the triumph's hour,
              Beholds the coming woe,

---

1   yes,] *BM*: Yes!
2   found] *BM*: *found*
3   dream] *BM*: deem
4   joy] *BM*: voice
5   *thee!*] *BM*: thee!
6   first published in *The Literary Souvenir; or, Cabinet of Poetry and Romance* (1829), a lit-
      erary annual edited by Alaric Watts, with slight differences in punctuation and with
      numbered stanzas; second sight is the ability to see into the future.
7   from Charles Robert Maturin's play *Bertram; or, The Castle of St Aldobrand* (1816),
      4.2.144-5.

And dwells upon the faded flower
    'Midst the rich summer's glow.

Ye smile to view fair faces bloom
    Where the father's board is spread;   10
I see the stillness and the gloom
    Of a home whence all are fled.

I see the wither'd garlands lie
    Forsaken on the earth,
While the lamps yet burn, and the dancers fly   15
    Through the ringing hall of mirth.

I see the blood-red future stain
    On the warrior's gorgeous crest;
And the bier amidst the bridal train
    When they come with roses drest.   20

I hear the still small moan of Time,
    Through the ivy branches made,
Where the palace, in its glory's prime,
    With the sunshine stands array'd.

The thunder of the seas I hear,   25
    The shriek along the wave,
When the bark sweeps forth, and song and cheer
    Salute the parting brave.

With every breeze a spirit sends
    To me some warning sign: —   30
A mournful gift is mine, O friends!
    A mournful gift is mine!

Oh! prophet heart! thy grief, thy power,
    To all deep souls belong;
The shadow in the sunny hour,   35
    The wail in the mirthful song.

Their sight is all too sadly clear—
　　For them a veil is riven:
Their piercing thoughts repose not here,
　　Their home is but in Heaven.

40

FROM
HYMNS ON THE WORKS OF NATURE, FOR THE USE OF CHILDREN, BY MRS. FELICIA HEMANS. REPRINTED FROM THE AMERICAN EDITION (LONDON: JOHN MARDON, 1833)

TO A YOUNGER CHILD,
ON [HIS BIRTHDAY] 17 SEPTEMBER, 1825.[1]

WHERE sucks the bee now? — Summer is flying;
Leaves on the grass-plot faded are lying;
Violets are gone from the grassy dell,
With the cowslip-cups, where the fairies dwell;
The rose from the garden hath pass'd away —   5
Yet this,[2] happy, fair boy! is thy natal day.

For love bids it welcome, the love which hath smiled
Ever around thee, my gentle child!
Watching thy footsteps, and guarding thy bed,
And pouring out joy on thy sunny head.   10
Roses may vanish, but this will stay —
Happy and bright is thy natal day.

---

1 first published as "To a Child, on His Birthday," in *The New Year's Gift; and Juvenile Souvenir* (1829), a literary annual for young readers, edited by Mrs Alaric Watts; the text differs slightly in punctuation.

2 Yet this,] in *New Year's Gift*; in *Hymns on the Works of Nature*: Yet,

FROM THE *NEW MONTHLY MAGAZINE*, 40 (JAN. 1834): 1-8

GERMAN STUDIES.

BY MRS. HEMANS.

No. I. —Scenes and Passages from the "Tasso" of Goethe.[1]

THE dramatic poem of "Tasso," though presenting no changeful pageants of many-coloured life,—no combination of stirring incidents, nor conflict of tempestuous passions,—is yet rich in interest for those who find

> "The still small music of humanity
> ———————————of ample power
> To chasten and subdue."[2]

It is a picture of the struggle between elements which never can assimilate—powers whose dominion is over spheres essentially adverse; between the spirit of poetry and the spirit of the world. Why is it that this collision is almost invariably fatal to the gentler and the holier nature? Some master-minds have, indeed, winged their way through the tumults of crowded life,

---

1   the only one published; *Tasso* (1790), by Johann Wolfgang von Goethe (1749-1832), the leading German writer of the late 18th and early 19th century, dramatizes the conflict between creative genius and courtly society. It is based on the experiences of the young Torquato Tasso (1544-95) at the court of Ferrara in Italy, where he was a favourite but suffered episodes of mental illness and was confined; he escaped and wandered through Italy, seeking refuge with his sister; his major work, the chivalric romance *Gerusalemme liberata*, was published without his permission(1580-81). Romantic writers made him, with such other renaissance writers as Dante and Petrarch, a figure for the poet as exile from an inimical society; for context and commentary, see Introduction, pp. 73-5.

2   Wordsworth, "Tintern Abbey" (1798), ll. 92-4, where the poet lists compensations for the loss of the immediacy of youthful responsiveness to nature, including "The still, sad music of humanity, / Not harsh nor grating, though of ample power / To chasten and subdue."

like the sea-bird cleaving the storm from which its pinions come forth unstained; but there needs a celestial panoply, with which few indeed are gifted, to bear the heirs of genius not only unwounded, but unsoiled, through the battle; and too frequently the result of the poet's lingering afar from his better home has been mental degradation and untimely death. Let us not be understood as requiring for his well-being an absolute seclusion from the world and its interests. *His* nature, if the abiding place of the true light be indeed within him, is endowed above all others with the tenderest and most widely-embracing sympathies. Not alone from "the things of the everlasting hills," from the storms or the silence of midnight skies, will he seek the grandeur and the beauty which have their central residence in a far more majestic temple. Mountains, and rivers, and mighty woods, the cathedrals of nature—these will have their part in his picture; but their colouring and shadows will not be wholly the gift of rising or departing suns, nor of the night with all her stars; it will be a varying suffusion from the life within, from the glowing clouds of thought and feeling, which mantle with their changeful drapery all external creation,

> ———— "We receive but what we give,
> And in *our* life alone does nature live."[1]

Let the poet bear into the recesses of woods and shadowy hills a heart full-fraught with the sympathies which will have been fostered by intercourse with his kind, a memory covered with the secret inscriptions which joy and sorrow fail not indelibly to write,—then will the voice of every stream respond to him in tones of gladness or melancholy, accordant with those of his own soul; and he himself, by the might of feelings intensely human, may breathe the living spirit of the oracle into the resounding cavern or the whispering oak. We thus admit it essential to his high office, that the chambers of imagery in the heart of the poet must be filled with materials

---

1 Coleridge, "Dejection: An Ode," ll. 47-8, where the poet describes the creative interchange between perceiving mind and external world.

moulded from the sorrows, the affections, the fiery trials, and immortal longings of the human soul. Where love, and faith, and anguish, meet and contend; where the tones of prayer are wrung from the suffering spirit,—*there* lie his veins of treasure; there are the sweet waters ready to flow from the stricken rock. But he will not seek them through the gaudy and hurrying masque of artificial life; he will not be the fettered Sampson[1] to make sport for the sons and daughters of fashion. Whilst he shuns no brotherly communion with his kind, he will ever reserve to his nature the power of *self*-communion, silent hours for

> "The harvest of the quiet eye
> That broods and sleeps on his own heart;"[2]

and inviolate retreats in the depths of his being—fountains lone and still, upon which only the eye of Heaven shines down in its hallowed serenity. So have those who make us "heirs of truth and freedom by immortal lays," ever preserved the calm intellectual ether in which they live and move, from the taint of worldly infection; and it appears the object of Goethe, in the work before us, to make the gifted spirit sadder and wiser by the contemplation of one, which, having sold its birthright, and stooped from its "privacy of glorious light,"[3] is forced into perpetual contact with things essentially of the earth earthy. Dante[4] has spoken of what the Italian poets must have learned but too feelingly under their protecting princes—the bitter taste of another's bread, the weary steps by which the stairs of another's house are ascended; but it is suffering of a more spiri-

---

1 in the Bible, book of Judges, Samson the Israelite hero loses his strength when seduced by Delilah and is captured and publicly humiliated by his enemies the Philistines.

2 Wordsworth, "A Poet's Epitaph," ll. 51-2, where the poet celebrates the wisdom of a humble man after satirizing the intellectual pretensions of a series of professional men.

3 Wordsworth, "To a Sky-Lark," l. 8, where the poet addresses the bird, "Leave to the nightingale her shady wood; / A privacy of glorious light is thine ..."

4 Dante Alighieri (1265-1321), author of the major allegorical poem the *Divina Commedia*, was banished from his native Florence during factional political conflicts.

tual nature which is here pourtrayed. Would that the courtly patronage, at the shrine of which the Italian muse has so often waved her censer, had exposed no severer tasks upon its votaries than the fashioning of the snow-statue which it required from the genius of Michael Angelo! The story of Tasso is fraught with yet deeper meaning [....]

[criticizes Goethe for representing the earlier trials of Tasso at the court of Ferrara, before he went insane, and focuses on the sympathetic female characters, with translated excerpts from the dialogues; the essay concludes:]

The majestic lines in which Byron has embodied the thoughts of the captive Tasso will form a fine contrast and relief to the music of despair with which Goethe's work is closed: —

> "All this hath somewhat worn me, and may wear,
>   But must be borne. I stoop not to despair,
>   For I have battled with mine agony,
>   And made me wings wherewith to overfly
>   The narrow circus of my dungeon wall;
>   And freed the holy sepulchre from thrall;
>   And revell'd among men and things divine,
>   And pour'd my spirit over Palestine,
>   In honour of the sacred war for Him,
>   The God who was on earth and is in heaven;
>   For He hath strengthen'd me in heart and limb.
>   That through this sufferance I might be forgiven,
>   I have employ'd my penance to record
>   How Salem's shrine was won, and how adored."[1]

---

1   Byron, "The Lament of Tasso," ll. 19-32.

FROM
SCENES AND HYMNS OF LIFE, WITH OTHER RELIGIOUS POEMS (1834)[1]

PREFACE.

I TRUST I shall not be accused of presumption for the endeavour which I have here made to enlarge, in some degree, the sphere of Religious Poetry, by associating with its themes more of the emotions, the affections, and even the purer imaginative enjoyments of daily life, than may have been hitherto admitted within the hallowed circle.

It has been my wish to portray the religious spirit, not alone in its meditative joys and solitary aspirations, (the poetic embodying of which seems to require from the reader a state of mind already separated and exalted), but likewise in those active influences upon human life, so often called into victorious energy by trial and conflict, though too often also, like the upward-striving flame of a mountain watch-fire, borne down by tempest showers, or swayed by the current of opposing winds.

I have sought to represent that spirit as penetrating the gloom of the prison and the death-bed, bearing "healing on its wings"[2] to the agony of parting love — strengthening the heart

---

1 all texts from this edition; for context and commentary, see Introduction, pp. 71-3; on 5 November [1833] FH wrote to William Blackwood: "I now write chiefly to say, that my Volume of Sacred Poetry being nearly ready, it would perhaps be advisable that you should begin to advertise it – I wish to know which of these titles you would think best – "*Poetry of Religion*, or *Scenes and Hymns of Life, by Felicia Hemans*" – or this, "*Scenes and Hymns of Life, a volume of sacred Poetry, by F.H.*" (National Library of Scotland, MS 4036 fol. 80); the epigraph on the title-page is:
    "How beautiful this dome of sky,
    And the vast hills, in fluctuation fix'd
    At thy command, how awful! Shall the soul,
    Human and rational, report of Thee
    Even less than these?"
(spoken by the Wanderer in Wordsworth's *The Excursion*, 1814, 4.34-38).

2 from the Bible, Malachi, 4.2: "But unto you that fear my name shall the Sun of Righteousness arise with healing in his wings ..."; the phrase was used by several English poets, most relevantly Bernard Barton (1784-1849), whose work FH

of the wayfarer for "perils in the wilderness"[1]—gladdening the domestic walk through field and woodland—and springing to life in the soul of childhood, along with its earliest rejoicing perceptions of natural beauty.

Circumstances not altogether under my own control have, for the present, interfered to prevent the fuller developement of a plan which I yet hope more worthily to mature, and I lay this little volume before the public with that deep sense of deficiency which cannot be more impressively taught to human powers, than by their reverential application to things divine.

F. H.

FROM "SCENES AND HYMNS OF LIFE":

PRISONERS' EVENING SERVICE.[2]

A SCENE OF THE FRENCH REVOLUTION.[3]

From their spheres
The stars of human glory are cast down;
Perish the roses and the flowers of kings,
Princes and emperors, and the crown and palms

---

admired; e.g., "Jacob's Dream" from *Devotional Verses; Founded on and Illustrative of Select Texts of Scripture* (London, 1826), a project similar to FH's here.

1   the Bible, 2 Corinthians 11.26, where Paul is describing his sufferings during his travels.

2   first published in *Blackwood's Magazine* 35 (Feb. 1834): 269-72, with slight differences in punctuation and less capitalization of nouns; substantive differences are noted; *BM* title has PRISONER'S for PRISONERS'.

3   The last days of two prisoners in the Luxembourg, Sillery and La Source, so affectingly described by Helen Maria Williams, in her Letters from France, gave rise to this little scene. These two victims had composed a simple [*BM*: little] hymn, which they every night sung together in a low and restrained voice. [Hemans's footnote; in the 1790s Helen Maria Williams (1762-1827) published a series of *Letters* from France describing the events of the French Revolution and Napoleonic era; the story of Sillery and La Source, with their song of even, is recounted in Williams's *Letters Containing a Sketch of the Politics of France from the Thirty-first of May 1793, till the Twenty-eighth of July 1794, and of the Scenes which Have Passed in the Prisons of Paris* (2 vols, 1795, 1. 40-54) and occurred during the Jacobin "Reign of Terror" (1793-4), when Williams herself was imprisoned; she portrays the Jacobin regime as hostile to both the domestic affections and religion, here linked by FH.

Of all the mighty, withered and consumed!
Nor is power given to lowliest innocence
Long to protect her own.

WORDSWORTH.[1]

SCENE—*Prison of the Luxembourg, in Paris,*
during the Reign of Terror.
D'AUBIGNÉ, *an aged Royalist—*
BLANCHE, *his Daughter, a young girl.*

Blanche. What was our doom, my father?—In thine arms
I lay unconsciously through that dread hour.
Tell me the sentence!—Could our judges look,
Without relenting, on thy silvery hair?
5 Was there not mercy, father?—Will they not
Restore us to our home?
    D'Aubigné.   Yes, my poor child!
They send us home.
    Blanche.   Oh! shall we gaze again
On the bright Loire?—Will the old hamlet spire,
And the grey turret of our own château,
10 Look forth to greet us through the dusky elms?
Will the kind voices of our villagers,
The loving laughter in their children's eyes,
Welcome us back at last?—But how is this?—
Father! thy glance is clouded—on thy brow
There sits no joy!
15   *D'Aubigné.*   Upon my brow, dear girl,
There sits, I trust, such deep and solemn peace
As may befit the Christian, who receives
And recognizes, in submissive awe,
The summons of his God.
    Blanche.   Thou dost not mean—
20 No, no! it cannot be!—Didst thou not say
They sent us *home?*
    D'Aubigné.   Where is the spirit's home?—
Oh! most of all, in these dark evil days,

---

1 *The Excursion*, 7.978-84.

Where should it be—but in that world serene,
Beyond the sword's reach, and the tempest's power—
Where, but in Heaven?
    Blanche.   My father!
    D'Aubigné.   *We must die.*   25
We must look up to God, and calmly die. —
Come to my heart, and weep there!—for awhile
Give Nature's passion way, then brightly rise
In the still courage of a woman's heart!
Do I not know thee?—Do I ask too much   30
From mine own noble Blanche?
    Blanche, (*falling on his bosom.*) Oh! clasp me fast!
Thy trembling child!—Hide, hide me in thine arms—
Father!
    D'Aubigné. Alas! my flower, thou'rt young to go—
Young, and so fair!—Yet were it worse, methinks,
To leave thee where the gentle and the brave,   35
The loyal hearted and the chivalrous,
And they that lov'd their God, have all been swept,
Like the sere leaves, away.—For them no hearth
Through the wide land was left inviolate,
No altar holy;[1] therefore did they fall,   40
Rejoicing to depart.—The soil is steep'd
In noble blood; the temples are gone down;
The voice of prayer is hush'd, or fearfully
Mutter'd, like sounds of guilt.—Why, who would live?
Who hath not panted, as a dove, to flee,   45
To quit for ever the dishonour'd soil,
The burden'd air?—Our God upon the cross—
Our king upon the scaffold[2]—let us think

---

1   the Revolutionary governments confiscated property of aristocrats, the church, and
those deemed disloyal, and disestablished the church; in 1793-4 Catholicism was
banned in France, churches were closed, and politicians proposed state worship of
Reason

2   A French royalist officer, dying upon a field of battle, and hearing some one near
him uttering the most plaintive lamentations, turned towards the sufferer, and thus
addressed him: "My friend, whoever you may be, remember that your God expired
upon the cross – your king upon the scaffold – and he who now speaks to you has
had his limbs shot from under him. Meet your fate as becomes a man." [Hemans's

Of *these*—and fold endurance to our hearts,
And bravely die!

50   *Blanche.*   A dark and fearful way!
An evil doom for thy dear honour'd head!
Oh! thou, the kind, the gracious!—whom all eyes
Bless'd as they look'd upon !—Speak yet again—
Say, will they part us?

        D'Aubigné.   No, my Blanche; in death
We shall not be divided.

55   *Blanche.*   Thanks to God!
He, by thy glance, will aid me—I shall see
His light before me to the last. —And when—
Oh! pardon these weak shrinkings of thy child!—
When shall the hour befall?

        D'Aubigné.   Oh! swiftly now,

60 And suddenly, with brief dread interval,
Comes down the mortal stroke. —But of that hour
As yet I know not. —Each low throbbing pulse
Of the quick pendulum may usher in
Eternity!

        Blanche, (kneeling before him.) My father! lay thy hand

65 On thy poor Blanche's head, and once again
Bless her with thy deep voice of tenderness,
Thus breathing saintly courage through her soul,
Ere we are call'd.

        D'Aubigné.   If I may speak through tears!—
Well may I bless thee, fondly, fervently,

70 Child of my heart!—thou who dost[1] look on me
With thy lost mother's angel eyes of love!
Thou that hast been a brightness in my path,
A guest of Heaven unto my lonely soul,
A stainless lily in my widow'd house,

75 There springing up—with soft light round thee shed—
For immortality!—Meek child of God!
I bless thee—He will bless thee!—In his love
He calls thee now from this rude stormy world

---

note; Louis XVI was executed 21 Jan. 1793 and was later sentimentalized, like the
English king Charles II, as a royal martyr.]
1   dost] *BM*: didst

To thy Redeemer's breast. — And thou wilt die,
As thou hast lived — my duteous, holy Blanche!   80
In trusting and serene submissiveness,
Humble, yet full of Heaven.
   Blanche, (*rising.*)   Now is there strength
Infused through all my spirit. — I can rise
And say, "Thy will be done!"[1]
   D'Aubigné, (*pointing upwards.*) Seest thou, my child,
Yon faint light in the west? The signal star   85
Of our due vesper service, gleaming in
Through the close dungeon grating! — Mournfully[2]
It seems to quiver; yet shall this night pass,
This night alone, without the lifted voice
Of adoration in our narrow cell,   90
As if unworthy Fear or wavering Faith
Silenced the strain? — No! let it waft to Heaven
The prayer, the hope, of poor mortality,
In its dark hour once more! — And we will sleep —
Yes — calmly sleep, when our last rite is closed.   95
                          [*They sing together.*

PRISONERS EVENING HYMN.

We see no more, in thy pure skies,
How soft, O God! the sunset dies;
How every colour'd hill and wood
Seems melting in the golden flood:
Yet, by the precious memories won   100
From bright hours now for ever gone,
Father! o'er all thy works, we know,
Thou still art shedding beauty's glow;
Still touching every cloud and tree
With glory, eloquent of Thee;   105
Still feeding all thy flowers with light,
Though man hath barr'd it from our sight.
We know Thou reign'st, the Unchanging One, th' All Just,

---

1   the Bible, Matthew 6.10, Luke 11.2, from the Lord's prayer, part of Christ's sermon
     on the mount, just before his death by crucifixion.
2   Mournfully] *BM*: Fearfully

And bless thee still with free and boundless trust!

110   We read no more, O God! thy ways
On earth, in these wild evil days.
The red sword[1] in th' oppressor's hand
Is ruler of the weeping land;
Fallen are the faithful and the pure,
115   No shrine is spared, no hearth secure.
Yet, by the deep voice from the past,
Which tells us these things cannot last —
And by the hope which finds no ark,
Save in thy breast, when storms grow dark —
120   We trust thee! — As the sailor knows
That in its place of bright repose
His pole-star burns, though mist and cloud
May veil it with a midnight shroud.
We know thou reign'st! — All Holy One, All Just!
125   And bless thee still with love's own boundless trust.

We feel no more that aid is nigh,
When our faint hearts within us die.
We suffer — and we know our doom
Must be one suffering till the tomb.
130   Yet, by the anguish of thy Son
When his last hour came darkly on —
By his dread cry, the air which rent
In terror of abandonment —
And by his parting word, which rose
135   Through faith victorious o'er all woes[2] —
We know that Thou mayst wound, mayst break
The spirit, but wilt ne'er forsake!
Sad suppliants whom our brethren spurn,
In our deep need to Thee we turn!
140   To whom but Thee? — All Merciful, All Just!
In life, in death, we yield thee boundless trust!

---

1   red sword] *BM*: rod severe
2   when Christ was crucified he called out just before he died, "My God, my God,
why hast thou forsaken me?" (Matthew 27.46; cp. L. 133); after his resurrection he

FROM "MISCELLANEOUS POEMS":

FROM "FEMALE CHARACTERS OF SCRIPTURE":

FEMALE CHARACTERS OF SCRIPTURE.[1]

A SERIES OF SONNETS

Your tents are desolate; your stately steps,
Of all their choral dances, have not left
One trace beside the fountains: your full cup
Of gladness and of trembling, each alike
Is broken: yet, amidst undying things,
The mind still keeps your loveliness, and still
All the fresh glories of the early world
Hang round you in the spirit's pictured halls,
Never to change!²

I.

INVOCATION.

As the tired voyager on stormy seas
  Invokes the coming of bright birds from shore,
To waft him tidings, with the gentler breeze,
  Of dim sweet woods that hear no billows roar;
  So from the depth of days, when earth yet wore   5
Her solemn beauty and primeval dew,
  I call you, gracious Forms! Oh! come, restore
Awhile that holy freshness, and renew
Life's morning dreams. Come with the voice, the lyre,
  Daughters of Judah!³ with the timbrel rise!   10

---

   visited his disciples, to whom his last words were, "lo, I am with you alway, even
   unto the end of the world" (Matthew 28.20).
1 first published in *Blackwood's magazine* 33 (Apr. 1833): 593-95, and (May, 1833): 804-
   06, with slight differences in punctuation and spelling.
2 the passage seems to be by FH herself.
3 Judah] southern part of ancient Palestine, south of the kingdom of Israel.

Ye of the dark prophetic eastern eyes,
Imperial in their visionary fire;
Oh! steep my soul in that old glorious time,
When God's own whisper shook the cedars of your clime!

II.

INVOCATION CONTINUED.

And come, ye faithful! round Messiah[1] seen,
   With a soft harmony of tears and light
Streaming through all your spiritual mien,
   As in calm clouds of pearly stillness bright,
5   Showers weave with sunshine, and transpierce their slight
Ethereal cradle. — From *your* heart subdued
   All haughty dreams of power had wing'd their flight,
And left high place for martyr fortitude,
True faith, long suffering love. — Come to me, come!
10   And, as the seas beneath your master's tread
   Fell into crystal smoothness, round him spread
Like the clear pavement of his heavenly home;
   So in your presence, let the soul's great deep
   Sink to the gentleness of infant sleep.

IV.

RUTH.[2]

The plume-like swaying of the auburn corn,
   By soft winds to a dreamy motion fann'd,
Still brings me back thine image — Oh! forlorn,
   Yet not forsaken, Ruth! — I see thee stand

---

1 in the Bible, Jesus Christ; the poem addresses his disciples, and, taking up the
"daughters of Judah" of the first part of the Invocation, perhaps especially his
female followers, including his mother Mary and his follower Mary Magdalene.

2 in the book of the Bible named after her, Ruth is a widow who loyally follows her
widowed mother-in-law, Naomi, back to the latter's home and supports her by
gleaning in the fields; her loyalty attracts the landowner Boaz, who eventually mar-
ries her.

Lone, midst the gladness of the harvest band— 5
Lone as a wood-bird on the ocean's foam,
    Fall'n in its weariness. Thy father land[1]
Smiles far away! yet to the sense of home,
    That finest, purest, which can recognize
    Home in affection's glance, for ever true 10
Beats thy calm heart; and if thy gentle eyes
    Gleam tremulous through tears, 'tis not to rue
Those words, immortal in their deep Love's tone,
"*Thy people and thy God shall be mine own!*"[2]

VII.

THE ANUNCIATION.[3]

Lowliest of women, and most glorified!
    In thy still beauty sitting calm and lone,
A brightness round thee grew—and by thy side
    Kindling the air, a form ethereal shone,
    Solemn, yet breathing gladness. —From her throne 5
A queen had risen with more imperial eye,
A stately prophetess of victory
    From her proud lyre had struck a tempest's tone,
For such high tidings as to *thee* were brought,
    Chosen of Heaven! that hour: —but thou, O thou! 10
E'en as a flower with gracious rains o'erfraught,
    Thy virgin head beneath its crown didst bow,
And take to thy meek breast th' all holy word,
And own thyself *the handmaid of the Lord*.[4]

---

1 father land] *BM*: fatherland
2 slightly altered from the Bible (Ruth, 1.16), where Ruth says to her mother-in-law, who has bid her return to her own parents, "wither thou goest, I will go; ... thy people shall be my people, and thy God my God."
3 in the Bible, an angel ("form ethereal," l. 4) announces to the virgin Mary that she has been chosen from among all women to bear Jesus Christ, or god incarnate, referred to as the Saviour, Redeemer, or Lord (l. 14).
4 the Bible, Luke 1.38.

IX.

THE PENITENT ANOINTING CHRIST'S FEET.[1]

There was a mournfulness in angel eyes,
    That saw thee, woman! bright in this world's train,
Moving to pleasure's airy melodies,
    Thyself the idol of the enchanted strain.
5   But from thy beauty's garland, brief and vain,
When one by one the rose-leaves had been torn,
    When thy heart's core had quivered to the pain
Through every life-nerve sent by arrowy scorn;
When thou didst kneel to pour sweet odours forth
10   On the Redeemer's feet, with many a sigh,
And showering tear-drop, of yet richer worth
    Than all those costly balms of Araby;
    Then was there joy, a song of joy in Heaven,
For thee, the child won back, the penitent forgiven!

XV.

MARY MAGDALENE BEARING TIDINGS OF THE
RESURRECTION.

Then was a task of glory all thine own,
    Nobler than e'er the still small voice[2] assigned
To lips, in awful music making known
    The stormy splendours of some prophet's mind.
    "Christ is arisen!" —by thee, to wake mankind,
First from the sepulchre those words were brought!
    Thou wert to send the mighty rushing wind
First on its way, with those high tidings fraught—

---

1   the penitent is Mary Magdalene, who is supposed to have been a courtesan or pros-
titute but became Christ's follower; the poem refers to an incident recounted in the
Bible when an unnamed woman who was a sinner, mistakenly identified with
Mary Magdalene, bathed Christ's feet in tears, dried them with her hair, and
annointed them with costly oils; when Christ was criticized for permitting this
from such a woman, he defended her and forgave her her sins (Luke 7.37-49).
2   still small voice] the Bible, 1 Kings 19.12.

"*Christ is arisen!*" — Thou, *thou*, the sin enthralled,
Earth's outcast, Heaven's own ransomed one, wert called
    In human hearts to give that rapture birth:
Oh! raised from shame to brightness! —*there* doth lie
    The tenderest meaning of *His* ministry,
Whose undespairing love still owned the spirit's worth.

FROM "MISCELLANEOUS POEMS":

COMMUNINGS WITH THOUGHT.[1]

Could we but keep our spirits to that height,
We might be happy; but this clay will sink
Its spark immortal.

BYRON.[2]

RETURN my thoughts, come home!
Ye wild and wing'd! what do ye o'er the deep?
And wherefore thus th' abyss of time o'ersweep,
    As birds[3] the ocean foam?

Swifter than shooting star,   5
Swifter than lances of the northern light,
Upspringing through the purple heaven of night,
    Hath been your course afar!

Through the bright battle-clime,
Where laurel boughs make dim the Grecian streams,   10
And reeds are whispering of heroic themes,
    By temples of old time:[4]

---

1 first published in *Blackwood's Magazine* 29 (Feb. 1831): 260-61, with slight differ-
   ences in spelling and punctuation; substantive variants are noted.
2 *Childe Harold's Pilgrimage* 3.121-3: "He had been happy; but this clay will sink / Its
   spark immortal ..."
3 birds] *BM*: bird
4 *BM* has an additional stanza here:
            Through southern garden-bowers,
            Such as young Juliet look'd from, when her eye,
            Fill'd with the fervid soul of Italy,
                Watch'd for the starry hours:

Through the north's ancient halls,
Where banners thrill'd of yore, where harp strings rung,
15 But grass waves now o'er those that fought and sung—
      Hearth-light hath left their walls!

      Through forests old and dim,
Where o'er the leaves dread magic seems to brood,
And sometimes on the haunted solitude
20   Rises the pilgrim's hymn:

      Or where some fountain lies,
With lotus-cups through orient spice-woods gleaming!
There have ye been, ye wanderers! idly dreaming
      Of man's lost paradise!

25   Return, my thoughts, return!
Cares wait your presence in life's daily track,
And voices, not of music, call you back—
      Harsh voices, cold and stern!

      Oh! no, return ye not!
30 Still farther, loftier, let your soarings be!
Go, bring me strength from journeyings bright and free,
      O'er many a haunted spot.

      Go, seek the martyr's grave,
Midst the old mountains, and the deserts vast;
35 Or, through the ruin'd cities of the past,
      Follow the wise and brave!

      Go, visit cell and shrine!
Where woman hath endured!—through wrong, through
            scorn,
Uncheer'd by fame, yet silently upborne
40   By promptings more divine!

      Go, shoot the gulf of death!
Track the pure spirit where no chain can bind,

Where the heart's boundless love its rest may find,
  Where the storm sends no breath!

Higher, and yet more high!
Shake off the cumbering chain which earth would lay
On your victorious wings — mount, mount! — Your way
  Is through eternity!

FROM "SONNETS, DEVOTIONAL AND MEMORIAL":

I.

THE SACRED HARP

How shall the Harp of poesy regain
  That old victorious tone of prophet-years,[1]
  A spell divine o'er guilt's perturbing fears,
And all the hovering shadows of the brain?
Dark evil wings took flight before the strain,
  And showers of holy quiet, with its fall,
  Sank on the soul: — Oh! who may now recall
The mighty music's consecrated reign? —
Spirit of God! whose glory once o'erhung
  A throne, the Ark's dread cherubim[2] between,
  So let thy presence brood, though now unseen,
O'er those two powers by whom the harp is strung —
Feeling and Thought! — till the rekindled chords
Give the long buried tone back to immortal words!

---

1   prophet-years] in the Old Testament of the Bible, the era before Christ when
    prophets brought God's counsel and warnings to the Jews.
2   the Ark was a chest in which the Covenant or Decalogue (Ten Commandments)
    was carried by the Israelites into Palestine and kept in the temple at Jerusalem, and
    was supposed to be a dwelling-place of the divine spirit, guarded by cherubim, or
    angels.

FROM "MISCELLANEOUS POEMS":

ELYSIUM.[1]

"In the Elysium of the ancients, we find none but heroes and persons who had either been fortunate or distinguished on earth; the children, and apparently the slaves and lower classes, that is to say, Poverty, Misfortune, and Innocence, were banished to the infernal regions."

CHATEAUBRIAND, *Génie du Christianisme*.[2]

FAIR wert thou in the dreams
Of elder time, thou land of glorious flowers,
And summer winds, and low-toned silvery streams
Dim with the shadows of thy laurel-bowers!
5   Where as they passed, bright hours
Left no faint sense of parting, such as clings
To earthly love, and joy in loveliest things!

Fair wert thou, with the light
On thy blue hills and sleepy waters cast,
10   From purple skies ne'er deepening into night,
Yet soft, as if each moment were their last
     Of glory, fading fast
Along the mountains! — but *thy* golden day
Was not as those that warn us of decay.

---

1 placed as the last poem in the volume; in ancient mythology, Elysium was a paradis-al afterworld; the poem was first published, in somewhat different form, in *The Siege of Valencia … with other Poems* (1823); here FH added the following postscript: "This poem, written some years ago, is re-published from a volume now out of print; the train of thought it suggests appearing not unsuitable to the spirit of the present work."

2 from *Le Génie du christianisme; ou, les beautés poétiques et morales de la religion chrétienne* (1802; 1803 edn, ch. 6; p. 263) by François-René de Chateaubriand (1768-1848); the work contained the widely popular stories "Atala" and "René," and argues for the superiority of Christianity based on its theology (part 1), its poetic force (part 2), and its art (parts 3 and 4); its publication coincided with Napoleon's reinstituting Roman Catholicism as the French state religion, but it became more influential after the restoration of the monarchy and conservative state institutions in 1815.

And ever, through thy shades,   15
A swell of deep Æolian[1] sound went by,
From fountain-voices in their secret glades,
And low reed-whispers, making sweet reply
    To summer's breezy sigh!
And young leaves trembling to the wind's light breath   20
Which ne'er had touched them with a hue of death!

    And the transparent sky
Rang as a dome, all thrilling to the strain
Of harps that, midst the woods, made harmony
Solemn and sweet; yet troubling not the brain   25
    With dreams and yearnings vain,
And dim remembrances, that still draw birth
From the bewildering music of the earth.

    And who, with silent tread,
Moved o'er the plains of waving Asphodel?[2]   30
Called from the dim procession of the Dead,
Who, midst the shadowy amaranth-bowers might dwell,
    And listen to the swell
Of those majestic hymn-notes, and inhale
The spirit wandering in the immortal gale?   35

    They of the sword, whose praise,
With the bright wine at nations' feasts, went round!
They of the lyre, whose unforgotten lays
Forth on the winds had sent their mighty sound,
    And in all regions found   40
Their echoes midst the mountains!—and become
In man's deep heart as voices of his home!

    They of the daring thought!
Daring and powerful, yet to dust[3] allied—

---

1   Æolian] of the wind, from Eolus, Greek god of winds.
2   Asphodel] a kind of lily, but also, like amaranth (l. 32), a mythical never-fading
    flower of Elysium.
3   dust] common term in the Bible and literature for the mortal body.

45   Whose flight through stars, and seas, and depths had sought
     The soul's far birthplace—but without a guide!
         Sages and seers, who died,
     And left the world their high mysterious dreams,
     Born midst the olive-woods, by Grecian streams.

50   But the most *lov'd* are they
     Of whom Fame speaks not with her clarion voice
     In regal halls! the shades o'erhang their way,
     The vale, with its deep fountains, is their choice,
         And gentle hearts rejoice
55   Around their steps; till, silently, they die,
     As a stream shrinks from summer's burning eye.

         And these—of whose abode,
     Midst her green vallies, earth retained no trace,
     Save a flower springing from their burial-sod,
60   A shade of sadness on some kindred face,
         A dim and vacant place
     In some sweet home;—thou hadst no wreaths for *these*,
     Thou sunny land! with all thy deathless trees!

         The peasant at his door
65   Might sink to die when vintage feasts were spread,
     And songs on every wind! From *thy* bright shore
     No lovelier vision floated round his head—
         Thou wert for nobler dead!
     He heard the bounding steps which round him fell,
70   And sighed to bid the festal Sun farewell!

         The slave, whose very tears
     Were a forbidden luxury, and whose breast
     Kept the mute woes and burning thoughts of years,
     As embers in a burial urn compress'd;
75   *He* might not be thy guest!
     No gentle breathings from thy distant sky
     Came o'er *his* path, and whispered "Liberty!"

Calm, on its leaf-strewn bier,
Unlike a gift of nature to decay,
Too rose-like still, too beautiful, too dear,   80
The child at rest before the mother lay,
    E'en so to pass away,
With its bright smile!—Elysium ! what wert *thou*
To her, who wept o'er that young slumberer's brow?

    Thou hadst no home, green land!   85
For the fair creature from her bosom gone,
With life's fresh flowers just opening in its hand,
And all the lovely thoughts and dreams unknown,
    Which, in its clear eye, shone
Like spring's first wakening! but that light was past—   90
Where went the dew-drop swept before the blast?

    Not where *thy* soft winds play'd,
Not where thy waters lay in glassy sleep!
Fade with thy bowers, thou land of visions, fade!
From thee no voice came o'er the gloomy deep,   95
    And bade man cease to weep!
Fade, with the amaranth-plain, the myrtle-grove,
Which could not yield one hope to sorrowing love![1]

---

1   in the 1823 version, this stanza is followed by the present lines 50-6, in slightly diff-
    erent form, and by an additional stanza:
            And the world knows not then,
        Not then, nor ever, what pure thoughts are fled!
        Yet these are they, that on the souls of men
        Come back, when night her folding veil hath spread,
            The long-remember'd dead!
        But not with *thee* might aught save Glory dwell —
        — Fade, fade away, thou shore of Asphodel!

FROM *NATIONAL LYRICS, AND SONGS FOR MUSIC* (1834):

FROM "NATIONAL LYRICS":

INTRODUCTORY STANZAS

THE THEMES OF SONG.[1]

> Of truth, of grandeur, beauty, love, and hope,
> And melancholy fear subdued by faith.
> > WORDSWORTH.[2]

WHERE shall the minstrel find a theme?
— Where'er, for freedom shed,
Brave blood hath dyed some ancient stream,
Amidst the mountains, red.

5   Where'er a rock, a fount, a grove,
Bears record to the faith
Of love, deep, holy, fervent love,
Victor o'er fear and death.

Where'er a chieftain's crested brow
10   Too soon hath been struck down,
Or a bright virgin head laid low,
Wearing its youth's first crown.

Where'er a spire points up to heaven,
Through storm and summer air,
15   Telling, that all around have striven
Man's heart, and hope, and prayer.

---

1   first published, with slight differences in punctuation and spelling, and with stanzas 3 and 4 in reverse order, in *The Amulet* (1829), a literary annual edited by S.C. Hall.
2   from the opening of *The Excursion* (1814), in which the character of the Bard declares his subject matter.

Where'er a blessed Home[1] hath been,
    That now is Home[2] no more:
A place of ivy, darkly[3] green,
    Where laughter's light is o'er.   20

Where'er, by some forsaken grave,
    Some nameless greensward heap,
A bird may sing, a wild flower wave,
    A star its vigil keep.

Or where a yearning heart of old,   25
    A[4] dream of shepherd men,
With forms of more than earthly mould
    Hath peopled grot or glen.

There[5] may the bard's high themes be found —
    — We die, we pass away: 30
But faith, love, pity — these are bound
    To earth without decay.

The heart that burns, the cheek that glows,
    The tear from hidden springs,
The thorn and glory of the rose —   35
    These are undying things.

Wave after wave of mighty stream
    To the deep sea hath gone:
Yet not the less, like youth's bright dream,
    The exhaustless[6] flood rolls on.   40

---

1   blessed Home hath] *The Amulet*: home and hearth have
2   is Home] *The Amulet*: are man's
3   darkly] *The Amulet*: freshly
4   A] *The Amulet*: Or a
5   *There*] *The Amulet*: There
6   The exhaustless] *The Amulet*: Th' exhaustless

RHINE SONG

OF THE GERMAN SOLDIERS AFTER VICTORY.[1]

"I wish you could have heard Sir Walter Scott describe a glorious sight, which had been witnessed by a friend of his!—the crossing of the Rhine, at Ehrenbreitstein, by the German army of Liberators on their victorious return from France. 'At the first gleam of the river,' he said, 'they all burst forth into the national chaunt, "Am Rhein! Am Rhein!"' They were two days passing over; and the rocks and the castle were ringing to the song the whole time;—for each band renewed it while crossing; and the Cossacks, with the clash and the clang, and the roll of their stormy war-music, catching the enthusiasm of the scene, swelled forth the chorus, '*Am Rhein! Am Rhein!*'"

—MANUSCRIPT LETTER.[2]

TO THE AIR OF "AM RHEIN, AM RHEIN."

SINGLE VOICE

IT is the Rhine! our mountain vineyards laving,
   I see the bright flood shine, I see the bright flood shine!
Sing on the march, with every banner waving—
   Sing, brothers, 'tis the Rhine! Sing, brothers, 'tis the Rhine!

CHORUS

5 The Rhine! The Rhine! our own imperial River!
   Be glory on thy track, be glory on thy track!
We left thy shores, to die or to deliver;—
   We bear thee Freedom back, we bear thee Freedom back!

SINGLE VOICE

Hail! Hail! my childhood knew thy rush of water,

---

1   first published in *The Winter's Wreath* (1831), with structural differences, mainly in not repeating the refrain of the second and fourth lines of each stanza.

2   passage, with slight variations, from a letter by Hemans dated Chiefswood (Scotland), 13 July 1829, published in Chorley, *Memorials of Mrs. Hemans ...*, 2.31.

Ev'n as my mother's song; ev'n as my mother's song;
That sound went past me on the field of slaughter,
  And heart and arm grew strong! And heart and arm grew
    strong!

CHORUS

Roll proudly on!—brave blood is with thee sweeping,
  Poured out by sons of thine, poured out by sons of thine,
Where sword and spirit forth in joy were leaping,
  Like thee, victorious Rhine! Like thee, victorious Rhine!

SINGLE VOICE

Home!—Home!—thy glad wave hath a tone of greeting,
  Thy path is by my home, thy path is by my home:
Even now my children count the hours 'till meeting,
  O ransom'd ones, I come! O ransom'd ones, I come!

CHORUS

Go, tell the seas, that chain shall bind thee never,
  Sound on by hearth and shrine, sound on by hearth and
    shrine!
Sing through the hills, that thou art free for ever—
  Lift up thy voice, O Rhine! Lift up thy voice, O Rhine!

FROM "MISCELLANEOUS POEMS":

BOOKS AND FLOWERS.[1]

La vue d'une fleur caresse mon imagination, et flatte mes sens
à un point inexprimable. Sous le tranquille abri du toit paternel
j'etais nourrie des l'enfance avec des fleurs et des livres;—dans
l'etroite enceinte d'une prison, au mileiu des fers imposies par la
tyrannie, j'oublie l'injustice des hommes, leurs sottises et mes
maux avec des livres et des fleurs.

MADAME ROLAND.[2]

COME, let me make a sunny realm around thee,
  Of thought and beauty! Here are books and flowers,
With spells to loose the fetter which hath bound thee,
  The ravelled coil of this world's feverish hours.

5 The soul of song is in these deathless pages,
  Even as the odour in the flower enshrined;

---

1 first published in *The Winter's Wreath* (1832), a literary annual, with slight differ-
   ences in punctuation and spelling (more personifying capitalization of nouns such
   as Faith, Mind, and Nature) in the text, and some errors in the French epigraph
   ("un fleur" for "une fleur," "toil" for "toit," but the more correct "imposes" (proper-
   ly "imposés") for "imposies" in *National Lyrics*).

2 Marie-Jeanne Phlipon Roland (1754-93), wife of Jean-Marie Roland de la Platière
   (1734-93), French minister of the interior in the early French Revolutionary gov-
   ernment; they were leaders of the Girondins, or moderate revolutionary grouping,
   and she advised him behind the scenes; her role was attacked by the more radical
   Jacobin faction and she was executed after they seized government in spring 1793,
   whereupon he committed suicide. Her *Appel a l'impartiale postérité* (4 parts, 1795)
   was an autobiographical self-vindication, written while in prison and published
   after her death and the overthrow of the Jacobins. The passage comes from early in
   the first section of "Mémoires particulières," which comprise the third part of the
   Appel, retitled "Vie privée" in *Œuvres* (1800), and is somewhat censored by
   Hemans: after "inexprimable" Roland continues, "elle réveille avec volupté le
   sentiment de mon existence" ("it awakens voluptuously the sensation of my
   existence"); translation of Hemans's epigraph: "The sight of a flower pleases
   my imagination, and flatters my senses to an inexpressible degree. Under the tran-
   quil shelter of my paternal roof, I was happy from my infancy with flowers
   and books: in the narrow confines of a prison, amidst the chains imposed by tyran-
   ny, I forget the injustice of men, their follies, and my calamities with books and
   flowers."

Here the crown'd spirits of departed ages
   Have left the silent melodies of mind.

Their thoughts, that strove with time, and change, and anguish,
   For some high place where faith her wing might rest,   10
Are burning here; a flame that may not languish,
   Still pointing upward to that bright hill's crest!

Their grief, the veiled infinity exploring
   For treasures lost, is here;—their boundless love
Its mighty streams of gentleness outpouring   15
   On all things round, and clasping all above.

And the bright beings, their own heart's creations,
   Bright, yet all human, here are breathing still;
Conflicts, and agonies, and exultations
   Are here, and victories of prevailing will!   20

Listen, oh! listen, let their high words cheer thee!
   Their swan-like music ringing through all woes,
Let my voice bring their holy influence near thee,
   The Elysian air of their divine repose!

Or wouldst thou turn to earth? *Not* earth all furrowed   25
   By the old traces of man's toil and care,
But the green peaceful[1] world that never sorrowed,
   The world of leaves, and dews, and summer air!

Look on these flowers! As o'er an altar shedding,
   O'er Milton's page, soft light from coloured urns!   30
They are the links, man's heart to nature wedding,
   When to her breast the prodigal returns.

They are from lone wild places, forest dingles,
   Fresh banks of many a low voiced hidden stream,
Where the sweet star of eve looks down and mingles   35
   Faint lustre with the water-lily's gleam.

---

1   peaceful] *WW*: youthful.

They are from where the soft winds play in gladness,
  Covering the turf with flowery blossom-showers;
—Too richly dowered, O friend! are *we* for sadness—
  Look on an empire—mind and nature—ours!   40

SCENE IN A DALECARLIAN MINE.[1]

"Oh! fondly, fervently, those two had loved,
Had mingled minds in Love's own perfect trust:
Had watch'd bright sunsets, dreamt of blissful years:
—And thus they met.["]²

"HASTE, with your torches, haste! make firelight round!"
—They speed, they press—what hath the miner found?
Relic or treasure, giant sword of old?
Gems bedded deep, rich veins of burning gold?
5   —Not so—the dead, the dead! An awe-struck band,
In silence gathering round the silent stand,
Chained by one feeling, hushing e'en their breath,
Before the thing that, in the might of death,
Fearful, yet beautiful, amidst them lay—
10 A sleeper, dreaming not!—a youth with hair
Making a sunny gleam (how sadly fair!)
O'er his cold brow: no shadow of decay
Had touched those pale bright features—yet he wore
A mien of other days, a garb of yore.
15 Who could unfold that mystery? From the throng
A woman wildly broke; her eye was dim,
As if through many tears, through vigils long,
Through weary strainings:—all had been for him!
Those two had loved! And there he lay, the dead,
20 In his youth's flower—and she, the living, stood
With her grey hair, whence hue and gloss had fled—
And wasted form, and cheek, whose flushing blood

---

1   Dalecarlia (Dalarne) is a region in mid-west Sweden with iron and copper mines;
    the poem is based on the supposition that the coldness of a mine would perfectly
    preserve human remains.
2   lines probably by FH herself.

Had long since ebb'd — a meeting sad and strange!
— Oh! are not meetings in this world of change
Sadder than partings oft! She stood there, still, 25
And mute, and gazing, all her soul to fill
With the loved face once more — the young, fair face,
'Midst that rude cavern, touched with sculpture's grace,
By torchlight and by death: — until at last
From her deep heart the spirit of the past 30
Gushed in low broken tones: — "And there thou art!
And thus we meet, that loved, and did but part
As for a few brief hours! — My friend, my friend!
First-love, and only one! Is this the end
Of hope deferred, youth blighted? Yet thy brow 35
Still wears its own proud beauty, and thy cheek
Smiles — how unchanged! — while I, the worn, and weak,
And faded — oh! thou wouldst but scorn me now,
If thou couldst look on me! — a withered leaf,
Seared — though for thy sake — by the blast of grief! 40
Better to see thee thus! For thou didst go,
Bearing my image on thy heart, I know,
Unto the dead. My Ulric! through the night
How have I called thee! With the morning light
How have I watched for thee! — wept, wandered, prayed, 45
Met the fierce mountain tempest, undismayed,
In search of thee! Bound my worn life to one,
One torturing hope! Now let me die! 'Tis gone.
Take thy betrothed!" — And on his breast she fell —
— Oh! since their youth's last passionate farewell, 50
How changed in all but love! — the true, the strong,
Joining in death whom life had parted long!
— They had one grave — one lonely bridal bed —
No friend, no kinsman, there a tear to shed!
His name had ceased — *her* heart outlived each tie, 55
Once more to look on that dead face, and die.

FROM
THE *NEW MONTHLY MAGAZINE* (1835)

THOUGHTS DURING SICKNESS.

BY MRS. HEMEANS.[1]

I.

INTELLECTUAL POWERS.

O THOUGHT! O Memory! gems for ever heaping
High in the illumined chambers of the mind;
And thou, divine Imagination! keeping
Thy lamp's lone star mid shadowy hosts enshrined;
5   How, in one moment, rent and disentwined
At fever's fiery touch apart they fall,
Your glorious combinations! — broken all.
As the sand-pillars by the desert's wind
Scattered to whirling dust! — O soon uncrown'd!
10   Well may your parting swift, your strange return,
Subdue the soul to lowliness profound,
Guiding its chastened vision to discern
How by meek faith heaven's portals must be past
Ere it can hold your gifts inalienably fast.

II.

SICKNESS LIKE NIGHT

Thou art like night, O sickness! deeply stilling
Within my heart the world's disturbing sound,
And the dim quiet of my chamber filling
With low, sweet voices, by life's tumult drown'd.
5   Thou art like awful night! — thou gatherest round

---

1   first published in the *New Monthly Magazine* 43 (March 1835): 328-30.

The things that are unseen,—though close they lie,—
And with a truth, clear, startling, and profound,
Giv'st their dread presence to our mortal eye.
Thou art like starry, spiritual night!
High and immortal thoughts attend thy way,   10
And revelations, which the common light
Brings not, though wakening with its rosy ray
All outward life: —be welcome, then, thy rod,
Before whose touch my soul unfolds itself to God!

VII.

THE RECOVERY.

Back then, once more, to breast the waves of life,
To battle on against th' unceasing spray,
To sink o'erwearied in the stormy strife
And rise to strive again: yet on my way
Oh linger still, thou light of better day,   5
Born in the hours of loneliness; and you,
Ye childlike thoughts, the holy and the true,
Ye that came bearing, while subdued I lay,
The faith, the insight of life's vernal morn
Back on my soul, a clear, bright sense, new-born,   10
Now leave me not; but as profoundly pure
A blue stream rushes thro' a darker lake
Unchanged, e'en thus with me your journey take,
Wafting sweet airs of heaven thro' this low world obscure.

FROM
POETICAL REMAINS OF THE LATE
MRS HEMANS (1836)[1]

FROM
"RECORDS OF THE SPRING OF 1834":[2]

V.

A THOUGHT OF THE SEA.[3]

My earliest memories to thy shores are bound,
Thy solemn shores, thou ever-chaunting main!
The first rich sunsets, kindling thought profound
In my lone being, made thy restless plain
5 As the vast shining floor of some dread fane,
All paved with glass and fire.[4] Yet, O blue deep!
Thou that no trace of human hearts dost keep,
Never to thee did love with silvery chain
Draw my soul's dream, which thro' all nature sought
10 What waves deny;—some bower of[5] *stedfast* bliss,[6]

---

1 the volume was published after FH's death, but these texts were published in maga-
zines before that; it was her practice to collect her magazine poems into a volume,
and changes in wording seem to be hers; accordingly, the texts have been taken
from *Poetical Remains*, with substantive differences from the magazine versions
noted.

2 with prefatory note: "These sonnets, written in the months of April, May, and June,
were intended, together with the Records of the autumn of 1834, to form a contin-
uation of the series, entitled 'Sonnets Devotional and Memorial,' which appeared in
the Author's last published volume, 'Scenes and Hymns of Life.'" [First published
with slight differences in spelling, punctuation, and line indentation, in *New Month-
ly Magazine*, as "Records of Passing Thought."]

3 first published in the *New Monthly Magazine* 41 (Aug. 1834): 429, with slight differ-
ences in punctuation and spelling and different line indentation, as one in a series
of sonnets entitled "Records of Passing Thought."

4 fire.] *NMM*: fire!

5 of] *NMM*: for

6 in Spenser's *Fairie Queen* (1590-96, 2.12) the Bower of Bliss (i.e., pleasure) is the
home of Acrasia, figure for intemperance; it is destroyed by the knight Sir Guyon,
figure for temperance; but the phrase became proverbial and lost its negative
significance.

A *home* to twine with fancy, feeling, thought,
As with sweet flowers: — But chastened hope for this
Now turns from earth's green valleys, as from thee,
To that sole changeless world, where "there is no more sea."[1]

XII.

A REMEMBRANCE OF GRASMERE.[2]

O vale and lake, within your mountain-urn
Smiling so tranquilly, and set so deep!
Oft doth your dreamy loveliness return,
Colouring the tender shadows of my sleep
With light Elysian:[3]—for the hues that steep   5
Your shores in melting lustre, seem to float
On golden clouds from Spirit-lands remote,
Isles of the blest;—and in our memory keep
Their place with holiest harmonies: — Fair scene,
Most lov'd by evening and her dewy star![4]   10
Oh! ne'er may man, with touch unhallow'd, jar
The perfect music of the[5] charm serene!
Still, still unchanged, may *one* sweet region wear
Smiles that subdue the soul to love, and tears, and prayer!

---

1   from the Bible, Revelations of St John, 21.1-2: "And I saw a new heaven and a new
    earth: for the first heaven and the first earth were passed away; and there was no
    more sea. And I John saw the holy city, a new Jerusalem, coming down from God
    out of heaven, prepared as a bride for her husband."
2   early home of Wordsworth; poem first published in the *New Monthly Magazine* 42
    (Sept. 1834): 16, with slight differences in punctuation and spelling and different
    line indentation, in "Records of Passing Thought."
3   in classical mythology, Elysium is a paradisal world for the blessed after death, sup-
    posedly on islands to the west, and so associated with evening.
4   her dewy star!] *NMM*: the dewy star,
5   the] *NMM*: thy

XIII.

ON READING PAUL AND VIRGINIA IN CHILDHOOD.[1]

O gentle story of the Indian Isle!
I loved thee in my lonely childhood well
On the sea-shore, when day's last purple smile
Slept on the waters, and their hollow swell
5   And dying cadence lent a deeper spell
Unto thine ocean-pictures. 'Midst thy palms
And strange bright birds, my fancy joyed to dwell,
And watch the southern cross[2] thro' midnight calms,
And track the spicy woods. — Yet more I blessed
10 Thy vision of sweet love; kind, trustful, true,
Lighting the citron groves — a heavenly guest,
With such pure smiles as Paradise once knew.
Even then my young heart wept o'er the[3] world's power,
To reach and blight that holiest Eden-flower.[4]

---

1   first published in the *New Monthly Magazine* 42 (Sept. 1834): 17, in "Records of
Passing Thought," with slight differences in punctuation and spelling and different
line indentation; the title refers to *Paul et Virginie*, a highly descriptive Sentimental
novel by Bernardin de St Pierre, first published in his *Études de la nature* (1787) and
frequently on its own thereafter. There were English translations, including one by
Helen Maria Williams, which she claimed was done while she was imprisoned by
the Jacobins. The two title characters grow up together in nature on the French
colony of Ile de France (Mauritius), in the Indian ocean, and fall in love; when Vir-
ginie is called to France by her socially ambitious aunt, to make a figure in high
society, she is unhappy and returns, only to be lost in a shipwreck off the island;
Paul dies broken-hearted soon after; Mauritius was captured by Britain in 1810.
2   a constellation of stars visible from the southern hemisphere.
3   the] *NMM*: this
4   Eden is the paradise of the Bible, before humanity sinned and were expelled to a
fallen world of time, mortality, toil, and (for women) the pains of childbearing.

FROM
"RECORDS OF THE AUTUMN OF 1834":[1]

I.

THE RETURN TO POETRY.[2]

ONCE more the eternal melodies from far,
Woo me like songs of home: once more discerning
Through fitful clouds the pure majestic star,
Above the poet's world serenely burning,
Thither my soul, fresh-winged by love, is turning,   5
As o'er the waves the wood-bird seeks her nest,
For those green heights of dewy stillness yearning,
Whence glorious minds o'erlook the earth's unrest.
—Now be the spirit of Heaven's truth my guide
Through the bright land!—that no brief gladness, found   10
In passing bloom, rich odour, or sweet sound,
May lure my footsteps from their aim aside:
Their true, high quest—to seek, if ne'er to gain,
The inmost, purest shrine of that august domain.

II.

ON READING COLERIDGE'S EPITAPH
WRITTEN BY HIMSELF.[3]

Spirit! so oft in radiant freedom soaring,
High through seraphic mysteries unconfined,

---

1 first published in *Blackwood's Magazine* as "Sonnets, Devotional and Memorial."
2 first published in *Blackwood's Magazine* 36 (Dec. 1834): 800, with minor changes in use of dashes.
3 first published in *Blackwood's Magazine* 36 (Dec. 1834): 801, with slight differences in punctuation; substantive differences are noted; Coleridge's "Epitaph" was first published in his *Poetical Works* (1834):
      Stop, Christian passer-by! — Stop, child of God,
      And read with gentle breast. Beneath this sod
      A poet lies, or that which once seem'd he.
      O, lift one thought in prayer for S. T. C.;
      That he who many a year with toil of breath

And oft, a diver through the deep[1] of mind,
Its caverns, far below its waves, exploring;
5 And oft such strains of breezy music pouring,
As, with the floating sweetness of their sighs,
Could still all fevers of the heart, restoring
Awhile that freshness left in Paradise;
Say, of those[2] glorious wanderings what the goal?
10 What the rich fruitage to man's kindred soul
From wealth[3] of thine bequeathed? O strong, and high,
And sceptred intellect! thy goal confest
Was the Redeemer's Cross — thy last bequest
One lesson breathing thence profound humility!

VII.

DESIGN AND PERFORMANCE.[4]

They float before my soul, the fair designs
Which I would body forth to Life and Power,
Like clouds, that with their wavering hues and lines
Pourtray majestic buildings: — Dome and tower,
5 Bright spire, that through the rainbow and the shower
Points to th' unchanging stars; and high arcade
Far-sweeping to some glorious altar, made
For holiest rites: — meanwhile the waning hour
Melts from me, and by fervent dreams o'erwrought,
10 I sink: — O friend! O link'd with each high thought!

Found death in life, may here find life in death!
Mercy for praise — to be forgiven for fame
He ask'd, and hoped, through Christ. Do thou the same!
E. H. Coleridge states that "for" in the second last line means "instead of" (*The Complete Poetical Works of Samuel Taylor Coleridge*, 2 vols, 1912, 1.492n.1), though other senses of "for" (e.g., "in requital of"; "as a reward for"; "because of") could also apply here, and for FH.

1   deep] *BM*: deeps
2   those] *BM*: these
3   wealth] *BM*: toil
4   FH's use of an ecclesiastical architectural metaphor for her program as a poet resembles that used by Wordsworth in the Preface to *The Excursion* (1814); see also letter 34 in this edition (to Rose Lawrence).

Aid me, of those rich visions to detain
All I may grasp; until thou seest fulfill'd,
While time and strength allow, my hope to build,
For lowly hearts devout, but *one* enduring fane!

IX.

TO SILVIO PELLICO
ON READING HIS "PRIGIONE"[1]

There are who climb the mountain's heathery side,
Or, in life's vernal strength triumphant, urge
The bark's fleet rushing through the crested surge,
Or spur[2] the courser's fiery race of pride
Over the green savannas, gleaming wide   5
By some vast lake; yet thus, on foaming sea,
Or chainless wild, reign far less nobly free,
Than *thou*, in that lone dungeon, glorified
By thy brave suffering. — Thou from its dark cell
Fierce thought and baleful passion didst exclude,   10
Filling the dedicated solitude
With God; and where *His* spirit deigns to dwell,
Though the worn frame in fetters withering lie,
There — throned in *peace* divine is liberty!

---

1   first published, with the following poem, in *Blackwood's Magazine* 36 (Dec. 1834):
    800-01, with slight differences in punctuation; substantive differences are noted. Sil-
    vio Pellico (1789-1845) wrote neo-classical plays in the tradition of Alfieri and Fos-
    colo, writers admired by FH, and joined the Italian Romantic movement, which was
    closely associated with patriotic and nationalist movements and groups such as the
    Carbonari plotting for Italian independence from foreign rulers such as Austria; for
    these activities he was arrested in 1820 and condemned to death, but the sentence
    was commuted and he was imprisoned in Austria until 1830; there he underwent a
    religious crisis and on his release published an account, *Le mie prigioni* (1832).
    Though the book was more pious than protesting, as FH here indicates, it became
    widely read, especially by liberals, as a powerful representation of the sovereign sub-
    ject and as an assertion of the rights of the individual against despotism and state
    persecution; for context and commentary, see Introduction, p. 72.
2   spur] *BM*: spare

X.

How flows thy being now? — like some glad hymn,
One strain of solemn rapture? — doth thine eye
Wander through tears of voiceless feeling dim,
O'er the crowned Alps, that, 'midst the upper sky,
5 Steep[1] in the sunlight of thine Italy?
Or is thy gaze of reverent[2] love profound,
Unto those dear parental faces bound,
Which, with their silvery hair, so oft glanced by,
Haunting thy prison-dreams? — Where'er thou art,
10 Blessing be shed upon thine inmost heart,
Joy, from kind looks, blue skies, and flowery sod,
For that pure voice of thoughtful wisdom sent
Forth from thy cell, in sweetness eloquent,
Of love to man, and quenchless trust in God!

TO THE MOUNTAIN WINDS.[3]

——— How divine
The liberty, for frail, for mortal man,
To roam at large among unpeopled glens,
And mountainous retirements, only trod
By devious footsteps! — Regions consecrate
To oldest time! — And, reckless of the storm
That keeps the raven quiet in his nest,
Be as a presence or a motion — One
Among the many there.

WORDSWORTH.[4]

MOUNTAIN winds! oh! whither do ye call me?
Vainly, vainly would my steps pursue!

---

1 steep] *BM*: sleep
2 reverent] *BM*: innocent
3 first published in *Blackwood's Magazine* 28 (Nov. 1830): 750.
4 *The Excursion*, 4.513-21.

Chains of care to lower earth enthral me,
    Wherefore thus my weary spirit woo?

Oh! the strife of this divided being!   5
    Is there peace where ye are borne on high?
Could we soar to your proud eyeries[1] fleeing,
    In our hearts would haunting memories die?

Those wild places are not as a dwelling
    Whence the footsteps of the loved are gone!   10
Never from those rocky halls came swelling
    Voice of kindness in familiar tone!

Surely music of oblivion sweepeth
    In the pathways[2] of your wanderings free;
And the torrent, wildly as it leapeth,   15
    Sings of no lost home amidst its glee.

There the rushing of the falcon's pinion,
    Is not from some hidden pangs[3] to fly;
All things breathe of power and stern dominion—
    Not of hearts that in vain yearnings die.   20

Mountain winds! oh! is it, is it only
    Where man's trace hath been that we so pine?
Bear me up, to grow in thought less lonely,
    Even at nature's deepest, loneliest shrine!

Wild, and mighty, and mysterious singers!   25
    At whose tone my heart within me burns;
Bear me where the last red sunbeam lingers,
    Where the waters have their secret urns!

There to commune with a loftier spirit
    Than the troubling shadows of regret;   30

---

1 eyeries] *BM*: eyries
2 pathways] *BM*: pathway
3 pangs] *BM*: pang

There the wings of freedom to inherit,
　　Where the enduring and the wing'd are met.

Hush, proud voices! gentle be your falling!
　　Woman's lot thus chainless may not be;
35　　Hush! the heart your trumpet sounds are calling,
　　Darkly still may grow —but never free!

SABBATH SONNET.

Composed by Mrs HEMANS a few days before her death, and
dictated to her Brother.[1]

How many blessed groups this hour are bending
Through England's primrose meadow paths their way
Towards[2] spire and tower, 'midst shadowy elms ascending,
Whence the sweet chimes proclaim the hallowed day.
5　The Halls from old heroic ages grey
Pour their fair children forth; and hamlets low,
With whose thick orchard-blooms the soft winds play,
Send out their inmates in a happy flow,
Like a freed vernal stream. I may not tread
10　With them those pathways,—to the feverish bed
Of sickness bound;—yet, oh my God! I bless
Thy mercy, that with Sabbath peace hath filled
My chastened heart, and all its throbbings stilled
To one deep calm of lowliest thankfulness.

1　first published in *Blackwood's Magazine* 38 (July 1835): 96, with a memoir by Δ
　　(Delta, i.e., David Moir).
2　Towards] *BM*: Toward

Appendix A: Selected letters to, from, and about Felicia Hemans[1]

1. Felicia Browne to her aunt; 19 Dec. 1808

[illness; enthusiasm for Spanish cause in Peninsular War; anxiety over brother there; reading and writing]

The severe indisposition from which I have just recovered, has prevented me, my dear aunt, from fulfilling, so early as I could have wished, my promise of writing to you: I have suffered much pain, and should have continued an invalid much longer, but for the unremitting care and attention of my dear mother; my illness was a fever, entirely occasioned by cold. I can now appreciate the full value of health, and feel my heart glow with gratitude to the good Supreme, who bestows upon me so inestimable a blessing; so true it is, in the words of Shakspeare, "that what we have we prize not to the worth, *while we possess it*."[2] I am now quite restored, and my mind has recovered its usual energies. I never felt a more ardent emulation in the pursuit of excellence than at present. Knowledge, virtue, religion, are the exalted objects of my enthusiastic wishes and fervent prayers, in which I know you will unite with me....

You have, I know, perused the papers (as I have done,) with *anxiety*, though, perhaps, without the *tremors* which I continually experience. The noble Spaniards! surely, surely, they will be crowned with success: I have never given up the cause, notwithstanding the late disastrous intelligence; but I think their prospects begin to wear a brighter appearance, and we may hope that the star of freedom, though long obscured by clouds, will again shine with transcendent radiance. You will smile, my dear aunt, but you know not what an *enthusiast* I am in the cause of Castile and liberty: my whole heart and

---

1   editorial conventions used here: points of ellipsis in square brackets indicate omissions from source text; points of ellipsis not in square brackets indicate omissions made by source text; asterisks indicate omissions made by source text; words, letters, or punctuation in square brackets indicate material supplied by the present editor.

2   *Much Ado About Nothing*, 4.1.215-17; Friar: "... for it so falls out / That what we have we prize not to the worth / Whiles we enjoy it ..."

soul are interested for the gallant patriots, and though females are forbidden to interfere in politics, yet as I have a dear, dear brother, at present on the scene of action,[1] I may be allowed to feel some ardour on the occasion.

….You see I am writing on the anniversary of George's birthday; and I know you will pray that every year may see his progress in virtue and true heroism. I am proud that he is at present on the theatre of glory; and I hope he will have an opportunity of signalizing his courage, and of proving an honour to his family and an ornament to his profession. I am this very moment wishing that I possessed a small portion of that patience with which my mother is so eminently gifted, for the paper is not yet arrived, and you may imagine the petulance of your "*little obstreperous niece.*" I have been reading a most delightful French romance, by Madame de Genlis, "Le Siege de la Rochelle;"[2] you would be in raptures with it…. I think it excels "Corinne,"[3] which is certainly bestowing a very high eulogium upon any work. Lady Kirkwall paid us a long and highly agreeable visit a few days ago, and brought me these volumes, which I have perused with such enthusiasm: she bestowed great commendation upon

---

1   her two elder brothers were in the 23rd Royal Welsh Fusiliers; George, referred to here, was with the army of Sir John Moore, then being pursued by much superior French forces in north-west Spain, after a series of Spanish defeats by the French, culminating in the French capture of Madrid on 4 December, referred to in this letter; early in 1809 the British forces were withdrawn through the port of Corunna; George returned to Spain with Wellington's army and on 6 April 1812 was wounded in the leg during his regiment's successful but costly night assault on the bastion of La Trinidad, part of the walls of Badajoz; his brother seems to have been part of Wellington's headquarters staff (letter from Felicity Browne to Matthew Nicholson; Bronwhilfa, 26 May 1812; Liverpool, MS 920 NIC 29/112). After Badajoz fell, the British troops were allowed to rampage through the town for 29 hours, raping, killing, and looting, in one of the worst atrocities of the war.

2   Stéphanie Félicité, comtesse de Genlis (1746-1830), *Le Siège de La Rochelle, ou le malheur et la conscience* (1807); Genlis was a moralistic educational novelist, widely read in Britain.

3   Germaine de Staël (1766-1817), *Corinne, ou l'Italie* (1807), a novel about a woman who is half-English and half-Italian and whose ability to improvise lyrical public orations makes her the popular voice for the Italian people's spirit of and aspiration for independence; she finds love incompatible with her patriotic calling and eventually dies of unrequited passion for the melancholy Scottish nobleman, Lord Oswald Nelvil. The novel was very influential, and Staël was the most famous woman writer and political exile in Europe, a prominent liberal and opponent of Napoleon.

"Valour and Patriotism,"[1] and I hope it will justify her encomiums. I had a letter from Major Cox, dated 16th of November, and from Madrid: he wrote in good spirits, and looked forward to the ultimate success of the Spanish cause. Glorious, glorious Castilians! may victory crown your noble efforts. Excuse me for dwelling so much on this subject; for Spain is the subject of my thoughts and words — "my dream by night, my vision of the day."[2] Can you be surprised at my enthusiasm? My head is half turned, but still steady enough to assure you that I remain ever, my dearest aunt,

Your attached and affectionate

FELICIA.

[Chorley 1.29-31]

2. Felicia Browne to Matthew Nicholson, at Mrs. Parry's, Abergele;[3] Bronwhilfa, 11 Aug. 1810

[praise for a woman poet who upholds the cause of women]
[... expresses thanks for gift of poems by an unnamed woman:[4]]

I will defer, until I have the pleasure of seeing you, mentioning those beauties in the epistles with which I have been particularly struck; but I must say in general terms, that I have been extremely delighted with their perusal, and that I think the dignity & spirit of the sentiments, are equalled by the splendor of the imagery, and polish

---

1 her poem *England and Spain; or Valour and Patriotism* (1808).

2 Thomas Campbell, *The Pleasures of Hope* (1799), part 2, ll. 189-92:

> Above, below, in Ocean, Earth, and Sky,
> Thy fairy worlds, Imagination, lie,
> And Hope attends, companion of the way,
> Thy dream by night, thy visions of the day!

3 Nicholson was a family friend, who assisted in the publication of Felicia Browne's poems; Mrs Parry was possibly the wife or mother of John Parry, later the composer of music to accompany Hemans's *A Selection of Welsh Melodies* ... (1822).

4 probably Lucy Aikin (1781-1864), historian and poet, niece of the leading woman writer Anna Laetitia Barbauld, and author of *Epistles on Women, Exemplifying Their Character and Condition in Various Ages and Nations; with Miscellaneous Poems*, published in 1810 by the London firm of Joseph Johnson, who had strong Liverpool connections, who had published the leading feminist Mary Wollstonecraft in the 1780s and '90s, and whom Hemans later considered as possible publisher of her work (see letter 6 here). The subject matter and historical span of Aikin's book would be emulated by Hemans in *Tales, and Historic Scenes* (1819) and *Records of Woman* (1828), and in numerous shorter poems written throughout her career.

of the versification. Many of the apostrophes are remarkably striking, and the one beginning "Prophetic Spirits! that with ken sublime" &c is written with all that high enthusiasm which characterises the true poet. The claims of the Authoress in behalf of her sex are so tempered by sense & reason, that I think the *Lords of Creation* can hardly refuse *attending* to the grievances she states, however little they may be inclined to *redress* them.—Of this I am convinced, that few men of candour and liberality could read her work without feeling their esteem for the female character exalted into respect and tenderness.[1]
[...]
[McGill University Rare Books Library, Felicia Hemans Papers MS 458]

3. Felicia Browne to Matthew Nicholson; Bronwhilfa, 17 July 1811

[reading historical fiction; learning Spanish]

[...] Will you assume a very grave, *mentorial* face, & give me a long lecture, when I tell you I have also *been guilty* of reading a *Romance*? It is "The Scottish Chiefs," by Miss Porter,[2] & though I am by no means an Advocate for *Historical* Novels as they bewilder our ideas, by confounding truth with fiction, yet this animated Authoress has painted her Hero, the Patriot William Wallace, in such glowing colours, that you cannot avoid catching a spark of her own enthusiasm, as you follow him through the incidents of the Narrative—I am teaching myself Spanish, and find it much easier than I expected, but I envy all latin Scholars, for the great facility with which *they* must acquire every new language, in consequence of an advantage from which so many are debarred. [...]
[Liverpool, MS 920 NIC 29/96]

---

1   the terms of praise used here anticipate those later applied repeatedly to Hemans's poems by reviewers and critics; see selection of "Views and Reviews" in this edition.

2   Jane Porter (1776-1850), one of several women who pioneered the historical novel; her earlier novel, *Thaddeus of Warsaw* (1803) went through many editions and inspired the leaders of the Polish independence movement; *The Scottish Chiefs* (1810) fictionalised the career of the historical Scottish leader of resistance to English invasion, Sir William Wallace (?1272-1305), and anticipated the even more influential historical Waverley Novels of Walter Scott.

4. Felicity [Wagner] Browne[1] to Matthew Nicholson; Bronwhilfa, 7 Feb. 1812

[publication of her daughter's works; problems with publishers and marketing; Felicia's impending marriage; looking for works for Felicia to translate; concern for sons in military action in Spain]

[...] with regard to the offer of Messrs. Cadell & Davies,[2] I am such a novice on the subject, as to be quite incompetent to judge of its liberality; but I would much rather depend upon your judgment, & that of Mr. Roscoe,[3] than upon my own; & whatever you think most advisable, will certainly appear to me the most so — if you act as you would for yourself, you will most oblige Felicia & me, & you have unlimited discretionary powers on the occasion — I will, however, remark, that as Messrs. C. D have had the publication of the two first works,[4] it appears to me most *respectable* that *any* future productions should come out through the same channel; even though more liberal terms might be obtained from others & I am sure C. & D. have it fully as much in their power to promote the sale of a work & thereby make it popular, as any Book-sellers in London, if they would think it worth their while to exert themselves a little in the cause; but they have certainly been hitherto very supine, & I have no reason to speak of their liberality, *excepting* that they have not called upon me for the expences of printing "England & Spain" — What a number of copies of that work they must have on hand, which a very little exertion might have enabled them to dispose of — If it is thought advisable that Mr. Millar[5] should be spoken to, my friend & relation Mrs. Hurt, would write any letter for me to him, I am sure — she has a library worth some thousands of pounds, & he is her bookseller in London, so that it could not go through a more respectable channel; but I am

---

1 FH's mother.

2 Thomas Cadell the younger (1773-1836) took over his father's publishing business, with William Davies as his principal partner until the latter's death; the letter refers to Felicia Browne's *The Domestic Affections, and Other Poems*, published by Cadell and Davies in 1812.

3 William Stanley Roscoe (1782-1843), son of William Roscoe, leading citizen of Liverpool, was a partner in his father's bank and managed the publication by subscription of Hemans's first book.

4 *Poems* and *England and Spain* (1808).

5 William Miller (1769-1844), a leading publisher of the period; on his retirement in 1812 he was succeeded by John Murray, publisher of most of Hemans's works from *Modern Greece* (1817) to *The Forest Sanctuary* (1825).

decidedly of opinion that it would be better *eventually*, to remain with Messrs. C. D. & perhaps to accept the present offer—though again I repeat, that I would rather rely on your judgment than decide myself—

I must now, my dear Sir, expatiate with you upon a subject very near my heart, & which all your words & actions prove you to have a most sincere interest in—I need not say that this relates to the future hopes & fears for my beloved Felicia, whose youth & peculiar frame of mind, make her naturally an object of my most anxious maternal solicitations, on the present momentous occasion of her life—You will perhaps be surprised to hear that, young as she is, her present attachment has been the cause of much anxiety to herself & the object of it, for four years past; & perhaps I may say it has, in a great degree, alienated her mind from all delight in what the *world* generally calls *pleasure* & from every wish but that of domestic happiness—though she is a child in years, yet her mind is so mature, that I think her quite competent to decide for herself, on a subject wherein she alone, is most deeply concerned; & as splendor & riches were never objects of any consideration with her (nor with me for her) I trust she has as much prospect of happiness with the man of her choice, & I hope, a competence, as can reasonably be expected in this state of probation—

He is a man whose morals & manners are unexceptionable & in whom I feel an affectionate interest, very little, (if at all,) less, than in my own sons—this will, I know, have great weight with you in the judgment you will form on this occasion—& I trust the progress of Felicia's Genius towards perfection will not be impeded by the additional motive she will have to cultivate it & that the "Domestic Affections," beautiful as some of its ideas are, is but a humble pledge of what we are to receive from her future pen—She has been wishing to write to you herself, for some time past, but thought she could not do it without mentioning this subject & it was too delicate for her to touch upon—now that you have spoken upon it, you will hear from her soon—I saw in the paper some time ago, that two thousand pounds would be given for the best translation of Lucian Bonaparte's poem of Charlemagne[1]—Could you enquire where information

---

1 Lucien Bonaparte (1775-1841), younger brother of Napoleon, differed politically with him and embarked for the United States, but was interned by the British gov-

respecting this could be had?—it is a work for which Felicia's perfect knowledge of the French tongue & poetical genius would make her quite competent[1]—I read in the paper, of the fall of Ciudad Rodrigo & see four men of the 23d. wounded at the siege, but thank GOD the names of my sons are not in the fatal list & I hope soon to have George's account of the operations of the army—my last news from his brother & him were as favorable as I could possibly wish—Accept, my dear Sir, the best wishes & grateful expressions of the girls & myself, for all your goodness, & present our compliments & thanks to Mr. Roscoe[2]—

believe me your obliged friend F. D. Browne

[Liverpool, MS NIC 920, 29/104]

5. Felicia Browne to Matthew Nicholson, Richmond Row, Liverpool; Bronwhilfa, 12 March 1812

[impending marriage won't interfere with her writing; looking for works to translate]

[…] be assured no change of prospect or situation will ever lessen the pleasure and improvement I shall always derive from your letters—You seem to think, my dear Sir, in your last letter, that my having "concentrated my affections" will interfere with the pursuit of my favorite studies; on the contrary, as the object of those affections, (to whom they have been long devoted, with all the enthusiasm of a first attachment & an ardent mind;) will have delight in encouraging my progress, & will know how to appreciate excellence—if I should ever attain it, I shall have in his approbation, an additional stimulus to exert[ion.] Were you fully acquainted with him, (which I w[ish] you were,) you would feel satisfied, that the happiness of your young friend could not rest on a more secure basis than his worth & attachment; on which I rely with the most deserved confidence, for all that is to cheer & illumine my future life.

---

ernment at Ludlow, Shropshire, where he wrote a poem in 24 cantos dedicated to Pope Pius VIII, *Charlemagne; ou, l'église délivrée* (London, 1814; Paris, 1815).

1 a note in the Nicholson MSS (Liverpool, NIC 19/103) records a notice in the *Examiner* (number 196, 29 Sept. 1811, p. 626) that Lucien Bonaparte was anxious to have his poem translated into English and was said to have offered £2000 through a publisher to the poet Thomas Campbell to carry out the work.

2 William Stanley Roscoe.

———I have a particular desire to attempt a new style of writing, & think I should succeed in translation—could you, or would Mr. Roscoe, recommend any poem in French, Italian, or Spanish, which you think would be desirable?[1] I have so few books in any of those languages, that though I have acquired the two latter without any assistance, I am not sufficiently acquainted with their literature to know if they possess any work of merit which has not yet had an English dress—[...]

[Liverpool, MS 920 NIC 29/105]

6. FH to William Stanley Roscoe; Daventry, 22 Oct. 1813

[his help needed in publishing her works; her translations from Camoens and others]

Dear Sir,

I avail myself of your kind offer to undertake the disposal of my manuscripts for me, persuaded as I am that they cannot be in the hands of one who will make more disinterested exertions for a perfect stranger—I leave it entirely to you to offer them either to Messrs. Longman &c, or to Mr. Johnstone,[2] but I do not wish my name to appear on the occasion—if they should be inclined to purchase the copy-right, you will perhaps have the goodness to fix what you would consider as an adequate compensation—I know not what apology to make for thus troubling you, but that I am so little conversant with subjects of this nature, & that I have no literary friends to interest themselves in bringing me forward—I shall be extremely happy if this little work should obtain your approbation, in translating the *sonnets* of Camoens, &c which compose the greater part of the

---

1   in 1812 an English translation of Ugo Foscolo's *Ultime lettere di Jacopo Ortis* was published at London, signed "F.B." (Douglas Radcliffe-Umstead, *Ugo Foscolo's Ultime lettere di Jacopo Ortis, A Translation*, Chapel Hill: University of North Carolina Press, 1970, p. 14); possibly this was Felicia Browne; Foscolo's work expresses liberal yet anti-Napoleonic sentiments which would have corresponded with FH's own views at this time.

2   "Johnstone" is the firm established by Joseph Johnson (1738-1809), originally from Liverpool, and foremost publisher of the English provincial and Dissenting Enlightenments and of sympathisers with the French Revolution, including Mary Wollstonecraft. Thomas Norton Longman (1771-1842) was head of the long-established firm, with various partners, and published a number of leading Romantic writers.

volume,[1] I have not attempted any adherence to the rules of that species of composition, the difficulties of which determined me from endeavouring to overcome them in any continued series of translations—I should not have attempted to translate any of Camoens's sonnets, as Lord Strangford[2] had published so numerous a collection, if I had not compared his works with the originals without being able to discover any pretensions to fidelity. I shall be much indebted if you will inform me that you have received the manuscript safely, & remain,

Dear Sir

your obliged &c

Felicia Hemans

[Liverpool, Roscoe MSS 1991]

7. Felicia Hemans to B. P. Wagner; Bronwhilfa [Nov. 1819]

[good reception of her *Tales, and Historic Scenes*; planning a narrative poem different from those of Byron, Scott, and Moore; brother George's wife]

My dear Uncle,

Encouraged by your very gratifying encomiums on my former publication, I venture to offer you a copy of the last,[3] and need not say how highly I shall value your approbation, if you think the performance worthy of it—I have had the satisfaction of seeing it reviewed most favourably, in more than one popular work, and it has been honoured with the commendations of many who rank high in the literary World, but my pecuniary gains from it are all yet to come, and I fear I must not expect much from a production the style of which is little suited to the present fashionable taste—Our first poets, such as

---

1 *Translations from Camoens, and other Poets, with Original Poetry* was eventually offered to John Murray in November 1817 and published by him in 1818 (Paula Feldman, "The Poet and the Profits: Felicia Hemans and the Literary Marketplace," *Keats-Shelley Journal* 46 (1997): 148-76; p. 154).

2 Percy Clinton Sydney Smythe, 6th Viscount Strangford (1780-1855) was a diplomat, posted to Lisbon in 1802; in 1803 he published *Poems from the Portuguese of Camoens,* and went on to have a distinguished diplomatic career and a wide circle of literary friends; his version of Camoens was ridiculed by Byron in "English Bards and Scotch Reviewers."

3 *Tales, and Historic Scenes* (1819).

Lord Byron, Walter Scott, and Moore[1] have all set the example of writting [sic] what I call Novels in Verse, and those who hope for popularity and profit, must follow in the path these Leaders of the public taste, have marked out for them—I shall certainly ere long, make an attempt to write something in this popular style, though I must own it will be much against my inclination—Before you receive this you will I hope, have seen George and his Wife, & we shall be anxious to know your opinion of the latter—Though she possesses none of those brilliant qualities calculated to strike a superficial Observer she is amply endowed with all the less dazzling, but far more valuable ones of temper and heart which win and secure the affections, and her amiable disposition has endeared her to us all— [...]

[Huntington Library MS HM 2137]

8. FH to Miss [H.] Park [1820?]

[planning a long poem contrasting paganism with christianity]

I have been thinking a good deal of the plan we discussed together, of a poem on national superstitions. "Our thoughts are linked by many a hidden chain,"[2] and in the course of my lucubrations on this subject, an idea occurred to me, which I hope you will not think me too presumptuous in wishing to realize. Might not a poem of some extent and importance, if the execution were at all equal to the design, be produced, from contrasting the spirit and tenets of Paganism with those of Christianity? It would contain, of course, much classical allusion; and all the graceful and sportive fictions of ancient Greece and Italy, as well as the superstitions of more barbarous climes, might be introduced to prove how little consolation they could convey in the hour of affliction, or hope, in that of death. Many scenes from history might be portrayed in illustration of this idea; and the certainty of a future state, and of the immortality of the soul, which we derive from revelation, are surely subjects for poetry of the highest class. Descrip-

---

1   FH is referring to best-selling narrative poems such as Byron's *Childe Harold's Pilgrimage* (1812-18), *The Bride of Abydos* and *The Giaour* (1813), and *The Corsair* (1814); Sir Walter Scott's *Lay of the Last Minstrel* (1805), *Marmion* (1808), *Lady of the Lake* (1810), and *Rokeby* (1813); and Thomas Moore's *Lalla Rookh* (1817).

2   Samuel Rogers, *The Pleasures of Memory* (1792), Part 1, l. 172.

tions of those regions which are still strangers to the blessings of our region, such as the greatest part of Africa, India, &c., might contain much that is poetical; but the subject is almost boundless, and I think of it till I am startled by its magnitude.
[Hughes 40]

9. FH to Miss——; Bronwhilfa, 15 May 1823
[Joanna Baillie's female protagonists contrasted to those of other modern writers]

[...] I never, until very lately, met with a tragedy of Miss Baillie's, which is, I believe, less generally known than her other works; "The Family Legend."[1] I was much pleased with it, particularly her delineation of the heroine. Indeed, nothing in all her writings delights me so much as her general idea of what is beautiful in the female character. There is so much gentle fortitude, and deep self-devoting affection in the women whom she portrays, and they are so perfectly different from the pretty *"un-idea'd* girls," who seem to form the *beau ideal* of our whole sex in the works of some modern poets. The latter remind me of a foolish saying, I think of Diderot's,[2] that in order to describe a woman, you should write with a pen made of a peacock's feather, and dry the writing with the dust from butterflies' wings. [...]
[Chorley 1.99]

10. FH to Miss——; Bronwhilfa, 2 July 1823
[apolitical and pacifist character of ancient Welsh bards]

[...] I have not forgotten my promise of making you acquainted, at least as far as may be in my power, with the principles and system of the ancient British bards. The idea entertained of the bardic character appears to me particularly elevated and beautiful.[3] The bard was not

1   Joanna Baillie (1762-1851), poet and dramatist, caused a sensation with the anonymously published first series of her *Plays on the Passions* (1798; further series 1802, 1812), which aimed to reconstruct dramatic literature; *The Family Legend* (1810) was not part of the series; Baillie became a correspondent of FH, who dedicated *Records of Woman* (1828) to her.
2   Denis Diderot (1713-84), witty and libertine writer of the French Enlightenment.
3   by FH's day there was a considerable poetic literature on the ancient British bards, glamorising them as (doomed) cultural voices and patriotic leaders of their people,

allowed, in any way, to become a party in political or religious dispute; he was recognised so completely as the herald of peace, under the title of "Bard of the Isle of Britain," that a naked weapon was not allowed to be displayed in his presence. He passed unmolested from one hostile country to another, and if he appeared in his uni-coloured robe, (which was azure, being the emblem of peace and truth,) between two contending armies, the battle was immediately suspended. One of the general titles of the order was, "Those who are free throughout the world," and their motto, "The Truth against the World."

[Chorley 1.101; cf Hughes 65-6]

11. FH to Henry Hart Milman[1]; Bronwylfa, 16 Dec. 1823

[reaction to the failure of Charles Kemble's production of her *The Vespers of Palermo*[2]]

[...] As a female, I cannot help feeling rather depressed by the extreme severity with which I have been treated in the morning papers; I know not why this should be, for I am sure I should not have attached the slightest value to their praise, but I suppose it is only a proper chastisement for my temerity; for a female who shrinks from such things, has certainly no business to write tragedies. [...]

[Chorley 1.72-3; Hughes 72-3]

---

in implied analogy with the modern poet as (neglected) social critic; such poems include Thomas Gray's "The Bard" (1757), James Beattie's *The Minstrel* (1771-4), and James Macpherson's "Ossian" poems (1760; 1762; 1763). Romantic poets adapted the figure in such works as Walter Scott's *Lay of the Last Minstrel* (1805), Byron's *Childe Harold's Pilgrimage* (1812-18), and Wordsworth's *The Excursion* (1814); women writers represented female (and feminist) versions of the figure in such works as Germaine de Staël's novel *Corinne* (1807) and Laetitia Landon's poem *The Improvisatrice* (1824). These various versions of the "national" bard, ancient and modern, were theorised in such liberal Romantic treatises as Vittorio Alfieri's *Del Principe e delle lettere* (1785-6) and Staël's *De la Littérature considérée dans ses rapports avec les institutions sociales* (1800); FH had published bardic subjects and imitations in verse in *A Selection of Welsh Melodies ...* (1822).

1   (1791-1868), clergyman, poet, and historian, at the time of this letter author of Romantic orientalist poems such as *Samor* (1818), and *The Martyr of Antioch* and *Belshazzar* (1822), and a drama, *The Fall of Jerusalem* (1820); he later published a *History of the Jews* (1829).

2   at Covent Garden Theatre, London, 12 December 1823; apparently the audience was hostile to the poor performance of the actress who played the heroine, Constance.

12. FH to ?; 20 Nov. 1824

[interest in leader of Mexican independence; descriptions of South America; writing *The Forest Sanctuary*]

After the interest you had taught me to feel in the fortunes of poor Iturbide,[1] I really was shocked, as *you* must have been, in no ordinary degree, by the sudden intelligence of his violent death. It was impossible not to feel that his proposed attempt must be fraught with danger, yet there was something absolutely startling in so swift a transition from the pride of hope and enterprise to the end of all. Of the immediate circumstances which led to his death, I could obtain no clear idea from the newspapers in which I saw it mentioned, nor whether the act itself was sanctioned by the Mexican government. Perhaps you can tell me something of the fate of his widow and children. We are just reading Hall's work on South America,[2] which you mention in your last letter, and are exceedingly interested in it. How truly may that be called a *new* world to which he introduces us! I was particularly struck with his visit to the Araucanian territory, which the Spanish poet, Ercilla, has made a sort of classic ground.[3] The noble character of General San Martin,[4] which Captain Hall's temperate style of writing prevents our considering as the least exaggerated, is really, in our times and circumstances, not less surprising than interesting, and engages every feeling on his side. I am at present engaged on a poem of some length,[5] the idea of which was suggested to me by some passages in your friend Mr. Blanco White's delightful

---

1 Augustín de Iturbide (1783-1824); in 1810 he joined the royalist side during the Mexican war for independence from Spain and helped defeat the revolutionaries; in 1820 he joined the conservative side of the independence movement and secured the independence of his country, being declared emperor of Mexico; but his government was unpopular and he was forced to abdicate in 1823, moving to London; he returned to Mexico in 1824 but was captured and executed in July.

2 probably *Letters Written from Colombia During a Journey from Caracas to Bogotá and Thence to Santa Martha, in 1823* (London: G. Cowie and Co., 1824), by Col. Francis Hall.

3 *La Araucana* (1569), a poem by Alonso de Ercilla y Zúñiga (1533-94); there were editions in the early nineteenth century, and an English translation of extracts was published at New York in 1808.

4 José de San Martín (1778-1850), military leader who, with Simón Bolívar, helped achieve independence of much of South America from Spain in the 1810s and 1820s.

5 *The Forest Sanctuary* (1825).

writings.[1] It relates to the sufferings of a Spanish protestant in the time of Philip the Second; and is supposed to be narrated by the sufferer himself, who escapes to America. I am very much interested in my subject, and hope to complete the poem in the course of the winter. [...]

[Chorley 1.106-7; part in Hughes 81]

13. FH to Miss——; Rhyllon, 24 Nov. 1825

[first-hand information from Poland; interest in Polish independence]

[...] I owe you many thanks for your most interesting letter from Poland, which, besides the gratification such a proof of a friend's remembrance must always afford, gave me much information with regard to scenes and people hardly better known to us than those of another hemisphere. How much and how delightfully must your store of ideas and recollections have been enlarged by this interesting tour! I believe it was the perusal of Campbell's "Pleasures of Hope,"[2] in early childhood, which first excited my feelings of sympathy for the Poles.[3] My sister[4] became acquainted with some of that nation during her residence on the Continent, and the deep and indignant sense they entertained of their country's degradation made much the same impression on her mind as it appears to have done on yours. Such a feeling, if general, is surely the best pledge of eventual deliverance. [...]

[Chorley 1.109-10]

---

1 probably *Letters from Spain by Don Leucadio Doblado* (1822), by Joseph Blanco White (nom de plume of J.M. Blanco y Crespo, 1775-1841); he was born into a Spanish mercantile family but became a liberal and anti-Catholic and moved to England, where he supported the Spanish patriotic war against Napoleon, editing a Spanish-language periodical. He also published *A Letter upon the Mischievous Influence of the Spanish Inquisition* (1811), *Practical and Internal Evidence against Catholicism* (1825), *The Poor Man's Preservative against Popery: Addressed to the Lower Classes of Great Britain and Ireland* (1825), and probably a novel, *Vargas: A Tale of Spain* (1822).

2 a widely read survey of human history, on the theme of freedom, in heroic couplets, published in 1799 by Thomas Campbell (1777-1844); he was a Scottish poet and editor with liberal views, who published FH's poems in the *New Monthly Magazine*.

3 Poland ceased to be an independent state in 1795 when it was partitioned among Russia, Prussia, and Austria; during spring and summer 1825 there had been Polish attempts at protest against foreign rule; Poland did not regain independence until 1918.

4 Harriet Mary Browne Hughes, later Owen.

14. FH to Mary Mitford;[1] Rhyllon, 6 June 1827

[interest in Mitford's *Our Village*]

Madam,

   I can hardly feel that I am addressing an entire stranger in the author of *Our Village*,[2] and yet I know it is right and proper that I should apologize for the liberty I am taking. But really, after having accompanied you again and again, as I have done, in "violetting" and seeking for wood-sorrel; after having been with you to call upon Mrs Allen in "the dell," and becoming thoroughly acquainted with May and Lizzy, I cannot but hope that you will kindly pardon my intrusion, and that my name may be sufficiently known to you to plead my cause. There are some writers whose works we cannot read without feeling as if we really had looked with them upon the scenes they bring before us, and as if such communion had almost given us a claim to something more than the mere intercourse between author and "gentle reader." Will you allow me to say that your writings have this effect upon me, and that you have taught me, in making me know and love your *Village* so well, to wish for further knowledge, also of her who has so vividly impressed its dingles and coppices upon my imagination, and peopled them so cheerily with healthful and happy beings? I believe, if I could be personally introduced to you, that I should, in less than five minutes, begin to enquire about Lucy and the lilies of the valley, and whether you had succeeded in peopling that shady border in your own territories "with those shy flowers." My boys, the constant companions of my walks about *our* village, and along our two pretty rivers, the Elwy and the Clwyd, are not less interested in your gipsies young and old, your heroes of the cricket-ground, and, above all—Jack Hatch!—woeful and amazed did they look, when it was found that Jack Hatch could die! […]

[Hughes 122-3; cf. Chorley 1.150-2]

---

1   1787-1855, poet, dramatist, and novelist.
2   highly popular, semi-fictitious prose sketches first published in magazine form, then in book form from 1824 to 1832; the work has been reprinted down to the present and was very influential in creating an image of rural England as the "real" England and as essentially middle-class and almost free from social and economic conflict.

15. Felicia Hemans to William Blackwood, Edinburgh; St Asaph, 13 June [1827]

[agrees to contribute to *Blackwood's Magazine*; announces expected rate of payment]

[...] With regard to the subject of your letter, I really shall have pleasure in becoming an occasional contributor to a work possessing so many writers of talent, provided you should not object to the mode of remuneration to which I am accustomed, and which, in order to prevent any future mistake, it would perhaps be better that I should mention at once——I receive from the Publishers for whom I write, 24 guineas a sheet for poetry, with the liberty of drawing upon them for the value of the contributions, at my own convenience—The remote situation in which I live, renders this latter arrangement a particular convenience to me, and if it be not otherwise to you, I shall be happy sometimes to join the band of your writers. [...]
[National Library of Scotland MS 4019 fol. 183]

16. FH to Mr Owen [July 1827]

[Canning and clouds]

[...] You have heard I suppose to-day, of Mr. Canning's dangerous illness;[1] the next accounts are expected to bring tidings of his death; what a comment upon "all is Vanity!"[2]—Do you remember some time since, our watching some clouds that seemed to be battling in the air, and that melted away whilst we looked? I could not help thinking of them and their mimic conflict, when I heard the news.
[National Library of Scotland MS 581 no. 541]

---

1   George Canning (1770-1827) was from a politically liberal family but during the 1790s vigorously opposed Britons sympathetic to the French Revolution; after the fall of Napoleon he was a controversial government minister for foreign relations, keeping Britain from intervening in the suppression by France and Austria of liberal revolts in Spain and Italy; in 1827 he was manoeuvring to become head of government but died in August on the threshold of power; he was a liberal on trade, but opposed political reform.
2   the Bible, Ecclesiastes 1.2 and 12.8.

17. FH to Maria Jane Jewsbury[1] [1827 or 1828]

[enthusiasm for Wordsworth's poetry; recommends reading Sismondi]

The inclosed lines,[2] an effusion of deep and sincere admiration, will give you some idea of the enjoyment, and, I hope I may say, advantage, which you have been the means of imparting, by so kindly entrusting me with your precious copy of Wordsworth's Miscellaneous Poems.[3] It has opened to me such a treasure of thought and feeling, that I shall always associate your name with some of my pleasantest recollections, as having introduced me to the knowledge of what I can only regret should have been so long a "Yarrow unvisited."[4] I would not write to you sooner, because I wished to tell you that I had really *studied* these poems, and they have been the daily food of my mind ever since I borrowed them. There is hardly any scene of a happy, though serious, domestic life, or any mood of a reflective mind, with the spirit of which some one or other of them does not beautifully harmonize. This author is the *True Poet of Home*, and of all the lofty feelings which have their root in the soil of home affections. His fine sonnets to Liberty, and indeed, all his pieces which have any reference to political interest, remind me of the spirit in which Schiller has conceived the character of William Tell,[5] a calm, single-hearted herdsman of the hills, breaking forth into fiery and indignant eloquence, when the sanctity of his hearth is invaded. Then, what power Wordsworth condenses into single lines, like Lord Byron's "curdling a long life into one hour."[6]

---

1 (1800-33), writer of poetry, fiction, and essays and close friend of FH; she helped raise her sisters after her mother's death in 1819, and published in newspapers and magazines, including the *Athenaeum*; a volume of prose and verse, *Phantasmagoria* (1825), was dedicated to Wordsworth, and she dedicated *Lays of Leisure Hours* (1829) to FH; her prose character of "Egeria" in *The Three Histories* (1830) is supposed to be a portrait of FH. In 1832 she married the Rev. William Fletcher and they went to India as missionaries, where she died of cholera.

2 Those addressed "To the Poet Wordsworth." [Hughes's note]

3 published in 1820; in July or August 1826 Wordsworth wrote to Jewsbury asking her to pass on to Hemans his regret at being prevented from visiting the latter in north Wales (*The Letters of William and Dorothy Wordsworth: The Later Years*, ed. E. de Selincourt, 3 vols, Oxford: Clarendon Press, 1939, 1.252).

4 reference to a poem by Wordsworth.

5 *Wilhelm Tell* (1804), a play by Friedrich Schiller (1759-1805), one of FH's favourite German writers; see her "The Switzer's Wife" from *Records of Woman* (1828).

6 Byron, "The Dream," l. 26.

"The still sad music of humanity." —
"The river glideth at his own sweet will" —
"Over his own sweet voice the stock-dove broods." —[1]

And a thousand others, which we must some time, (and I hope not a very distant one,) talk over together. Many of these lines quite haunt me, and I have a strange feeling, as if I must have known them in my childhood, they come over me so like old melodies. I can hardly speak of *favourites* among so many things that delight me, but I think "The Narrow Glen," the Lines on "Corra Linn," the "Song for the Feast of Brougham Castle," "Yarrow visited," and "The Cuckoo," are among those which take hold of imagination the soonest, and recur most frequently to memory. ★ ★ I know not how I can have so long omitted to mention the "Ecclesiastical Sketches," [1822] which I have read, and do constantly read with deep interest. Their beauty grows upon you and develops as you study it, like that of the old pictures by the Italian masters. [...] I must, in a future letter, name to you, according to your wish, a few books, the perusal of which may be advantageous to you, though I can sincerely say that I should be far from discovering the deficiencies which you imagine in yourself, from any thing I have seen in your writings. I cannot help, however, mentioning, as works from which I have derived much clear and general information, those of Sismondi; in particular his "Littérature du Midi," and "Républiques Italiennes," but you are probably acquainted with both.[2] [...]
[Chorley 1.171-5; cf. Hughes 145-7]

---

1   the Wordsworth quotations come, respectively, from "Tintern Abbey," l. 92; "Composed upon Westminster Bridge, Sept. 3, 1802," l. 12; and "Resolution and Independence," l. 5.
2   Jean Charles Simonde de Sismondi, *De la Littérature du midi de l'Europe* (1813) and *Histoire des républiques italiennes du moyen age* (1807). Sismondi was a member of Germaine de Staël's circle and both works mentioned were influential with European liberals.

18. FH to Rev. S. Butler[1]; 19 Feb. 1828

[FH wishes Butler and his wife joy over the marriage of their daughter; FH's ill health and failure at the therapeutic horticulture advised by her doctor as a way of avoiding dangerous excitement]

[...] Still I can but too well imagine the mingled feelings with which you and Mrs Butler must look forward to the event, for I am about to lose in a similar manner, my only sister, and I may almost say, my only *Companion*; since we have for years been linked together in a community of thoughts and pursuits, which I must never hope to have renewed. Unfortunately for me, interchange of thought is an habitual *want* of my mind, and I pine without it, as the Swiss Exile does for his native Air, so that I look with a feeling almost of alarm, to the loneliness (not literal, but *mental* loneliness,) which seems awaiting me. —
[...] I *did* take to rearing Gera[niums] some time since, by way of a less exciting amusement than my usual ones; but I am almost ashamed to tell the result; in Summer I forgot to water them, and in Winter I forgot to shelter them, so the last frost, these my ill-used adopted Children all withered away. It would be too cruel to try similar experiments upon *live things* (though my conscience was sorely smitten upon reading the other day a gravely maintained opinion that plants can *feel*). So I fear I must not think of the Bees and Chickens. —[...]

[British Library Additional MSS 34587 g. 8]

19. FH to [member of the Chorley family?]; Rhyllon, 18 Sept. [1828]

[after a visit from James Montgomery[2]]

[...] He complained much in the course of conversation, and I heartily joined with him, of the fancy which wise people have in the

---

1 the Rev. Samuel Butler (1774-1839) was appointed headmaster of Shrewsbury school in 1798 and during the next 38 years made it one of the leading boys' schools in England; FH's sons attended the school; Butler left the school in 1836 on being made bishop of St Asaph and Coventry.

2 journalist and poet (1771-1854); in the 1790s he was a sympathiser with the French Revolution and later promoted parliamentary reform; he edited the *Sheffield Iris* newspaper and published well received poems such as *The Wanderer of Switzerland* (1806), critical of Napoleon's invasion of that country, and *Pelican Island* (1827).

present times, *for setting one right;* cheating one, that is, out of all the pretty old legends and stories, in the place of which they want to establish dull facts. We mutually grumbled about Fair Rosamond,[1] Queen Eleanor and the poisoned wound, Richard the Third and his hump-back; but agreed most resolutely that nothing *should* ever induce us to give up William Tell.[2] ...

[Chorley 1.202; Hughes 147]

20. To Mary Russell Mitford; St Asaph, 10 Nov. 1828

[Mitford's *Rienzi*; unwished-for independence; Mitford's *Our Village*]

My dear Miss Mitford,

Accept my late, though sincere and cordial congratulations on the brilliant success of Rienzi,[3] of which I have read with unfeigned gratification. I thought of your Father and Mother, and could not help imagining that your feelings must be like those of the Greek General who declared that his greatest delight in Victory arose from the thought of his Parents—I have no doubt that *your* enjoyment of your triumph has been of a similar Nature—I ought to have acknowledged long, long since, your kind present of the little Volume of plays[4] valued both for your sake and *theirs,* for they are indeed full of Beauty, but I have been a drooping creature for months, ill and suffering much from the dispersion of a little Band of Brothers and Sisters, amongst whom I had lived, and who are now all scattered— and strange as it may seem to say, I am now for the first time in my life holding *the reins of government*—independent—managing a House-

---

1   title of a long-popular chapbook, supposedly based on the misfortunes of a 12th-century historical figure, Rosamond de Clifford, mistress of king Henry 11.

2   Wilhelm Tell, a fifteenth-century figure about whom little is known, was made into a heroic leader of Swiss independence by late eighteenth-century historians, and dramatised by Schiller in his play of that name (1804).

3   *Rienzi* (1828), one of Mitford's most successful dramas, about the career of Cola di Rienzi (*c.* 1313-54), Roman politician who aimed to restore Rome to its former greatness; he seized control of the city in 1347 but, forced out by the nobles and the pope, he became an exile and turned to the German emperor for support; in 1354, with the support of a new pope, he retook the city from its aristocratic rulers, but he was murdered during a riot. In the nineteenth century various writers, including Mitford, glamorised him as a heroic precursor of liberal patriotism.

4   *Dramatic Scenes, Sonnets, and Other Poems* (1827), or a bound volume of Mitford's plays *Julian* (1823), *The Foscari* (1826), and *Rienzi.*

hold myself—and I never liked any thing *less* than "ce triste empire de Soi-même".[1] It really suits me as ill as the *Southron* climate did your wild Orkney School-girls whom perhaps, *you*, the creator of so many fine forms and images, may have forgotten but I have not. — I have changed my residence since I last wrote to you, and my address is now at Wavertree, near Liverpool, where I shall, as the Welsh country-people say, "Take it very kind" if you write to me; and I really cannot help venturing to hope that you *will*. — I have yet only read of Rienzi a few noble passages, given by the Newspapers and Magazines, but in a few days I hope to be acquainted with the whole—every Woman ought to be proud of your triumph—in this Age too, when dramatic triumph seems of all others the most difficult. — How are May and Mossy, and Lucy and Jack Hatch[2]—no—Jack Hatch actually *died*, to the astonishment of myself and my Boys, who thought I believe he had been "painted for Eternity"[3]—and Mrs. Allen, and all the rest of the dear Villagers?—And your Parents? I trust they are well—your Mother, I believe, is always an Invalid, but I hope she is able fully to enjoy the success of her Daughter as only a Mother *can* enjoy it. How hollow sounds the Voice of fame to an Orphan!—Farewell, my dear Miss Mitford, long may you have the delight of gladdening a Father and Mother!—Believe me, ever faithfully yours Felicia Hemans

[Liverpool, MS 920 HEM 10/1; published with slight alterations in Chorley 1.226-30 and Hughes 155-7]

21. FH to ? [1828?]

[Sismondi; identification with Staël's Corinne]

I send the first volume of the "Républiques Italiennes,"[4] for you and my cousin ———, and also the book with the "dernier chant de Corinne," that you may compare it with the poem in the "New Monthly;"[5] you will see that all the beauty and loftiness of the

---

1   this sad empire of oneself.
2   characters in Mitford's *Our Village*; see letter 14.
3   "As he that painted for eternity," in John Norris, "To the Memory of My Dear Neece, M.C.", l. 54; *A Collection of Miscellanies* ..., 2nd edn (1692).
4   by Sismondi; see letter 17.
5   FH's poem "Corinne at the Capitol" is inspired by the "last song of Corinne" in Staël's *Corinne*; see notes to Letter 1.

thoughts belong to Madame de Staël. That book, in particular towards its close, has a power over me which is quite indescribable; some passages seem to give me back my own thoughts and feelings, my whole inner being, with a mirror, more true than ever friend could hold up.[1]

I think I must have been *fey*, as the Scotch call it, last night at your house. I was in such strange wild spirits, I felt as if I could have taken wings to the stars. I believe it is an evil omen, for I have little cause to be light of heart. [...]

[Chorley 1. 295-6; cf Hughes 160, who does not give the first sentence or the second paragraph]

22. FH to [Maria Jane Jewsbury? Wavertree? 1828?]

[woman's mission; her intellectual aspirations and her private suffering]

You speak "high words" to me, dear friend! I gratefully feel them, and own their power. They remind me of Wordsworth's beautiful expression—

> "To teach us how divine a thing
> A woman may be made."[2]

And I, too, have high views, doubt it not. My very suffering proves it—for how much of this is occasioned by quenchless aspirations after intellectual and moral beauty, never to be found on earth! they

---

1 In Mrs Hemans' own copy of "Corinne," the following passage was marked with particular emphasis, and the words "*C'est moi.*"
"De toutes mes facultés la plus puissante est la faculté de souffrir. Je suis née pour le bonheur, mon caractère est co[n]fiant, mon imagination est animée; mais la peine excite en moi je ne sais quelle impétuosité qui peut troubler ma raison, ou me donner de la mort. Je vous le répète encore, ménagez-moi; la gaieté, la mobilité ne me servent qu'en apparence: mais il y a dans mon âme des abîmes de tristesse dont je ne pouvais me défendre qu'en me préservant de l'amour." Corinne, vol. 1. [Chorley's note; the passage is from *Corinne*, 1807 edn, 1.217-18; book 4, ch. 3; translation: "The strongest of my faculties is the capacity for suffering. I was born for happiness, I have a confident nature and a lively imagination; but suffering arouses in me some kind of impulse that disturbs my reason, or is killing to me. Again I repeat, be careful with me; gaiety and changeability are only an appearance with me: for I have in my soul depths of sadness that I can only protect myself against by avoiding love."]
2 slightly misquoted from "To a Young Lady, Who Had Been Reproached for Taking Long Walks in the Country," ll. 11-12.

seem to sever me from others, and make my lot more lonely than life has made it. Can you think that any fervent and aspiring mind ever passed through this world without suffering from that void which has been the complaint of all? "Les âmes dont l'imagination tient à la puissance d'aimer et de souffrir, ne sont-ils pas les bannis d'une autre region?"[1] I know that it must be so; that nothing earthly can fill it, and that it cannot be filled with the infinite, until infinity shall have opened upon it: — for these intense affections are human: they were given us to meet and answer human love; and though they may be "raised and solemnized"[2] even here, yet I do believe that it is only in the "Better Land"[3] they ever did, or will approximate to what is divine. Fear not any danger for me in the adulation which surrounds me. A moment's transient entertainment — scarcely even that at times, is the utmost effect of things that "come like shadows, so depart."[4] Of all things, never may I become that despicable thing, a woman living upon admiration! The village matron, *tidying up* for her husband and children at evening, is far, far more enviable and respectable.

[Hughes 174-5]

23. FH to ?; Chiefswood,[5] Roxburghshire, 13 July 1829
[outdoor adventures with Sir Walter Scott]

[…] At present I *can* only talk of Sir Walter Scott,[6] with whom I have been just taking a long, delightful walk through the "Rhymour's

---

1   Staël, *Corinne* (London, 1807 edn, 2.338, book 13, ch. 4), spoken by Corinne: "La fatalité … ne poursuit-elle pas les ames exaltées, les poëtes dont l'imagination tient à la puissance d'aimer et de souffrir? Ils sont les bannis d'une autre région …"; translation of Hemans's version: "Souls to whom imagination gives the power to love and to suffer — are they not exiles from another world?"

2   "Be thy affections raised and solemnised," Wordsworth, "Laodamia," 1. 144.

3   title of a poem published in FH's *Songs of the Affections* (1830).

4   Shakespeare, *Macbeth*, 4.1.111.

5   home of Thomas Hamilton (1789-1842), author of the novel *The Youth and Manhood of Cyril Thornton* (3 vols, 1827).

6   (1771-1832), one of the leading international literary figures of the period; he was a pioneering collector and imitator of folksongs and best-selling narrative poet and historical novelist; his fiction had an enormous influence on Romantic nationalism throughout Europe and beyond, throughout the nineteenth century and into the twentieth.

Glen." I came home, to be sure, in a rather disastrous state after my adventure, and was greeted by my maid, with that most disconsolate visage of hers, which invariably moves my hard heart to laughter; for I had got wet above my ancles in the haunted bourn, torn my gown in making my way through thickets of wild roses, stained my gloves with wood-strawberries, and even—direst misfortune of all! scratched my face with a *rowan* branch. But what of all this? Had I not been walking with Sir Walter Scott, and listening to tales of elves and bogles and brownies, and hearing him recite some of the Spanish ballads till they "stirred the heart like the sound of a trumpet["]? I must reserve many of these things to tell you when we meet, but one very *important* trait (since it proves a sympathy between the Great Unknown[1] and myself,) I cannot possibly defer to that period, but must record it now. You will expect something peculiarly impressive, I have no doubt. Well—we had reached a rustic seat in the wood, and were to rest there, but I, out of pure perverseness, chose to establish myself comfortably on a grass bank. "Would it not be more prudent for you, Mrs. Hemans," said Sir Walter, "to take the seat?" "I have no doubt that it would, Sir Walter, but, somehow or other, I always prefer the grass." "And so do I," replied the dear old gentleman, coming to sit there beside me, "and I really believe that I do it chiefly out of wicked wilfulness, because all my *good advisers* say that it will give me the rheumatism." Now was it not delightful? I mean for the future to take exactly my own way in all matters of this kind, and to say that Sir Walter Scott particularly recommended me to do so. I was rather agreeably surprised by his appearance, after all I had heard of its homeliness; the predominant expression of countenance, is, I think, a sort of arch good-nature, conveying a mingled impression of penetration and benevolence. [...][2]

[Chorley 2.27-9]

---

1   Scott was long called the Great Unknown because he published his enormously popular Waverley Novels (from 1814 on) anonymously and did not publicly admit authorship until 1827.

2   on 18 July 1823 Scott wrote to Joanna Baillie, "Miss Heman[s's poetry] is somewhat too poetical for my taste—too many flowers [i.e., figures such as metaphors and similes] I mean and too little fruit but that may be the cynical criticism of an elderly gentleman ..." (*The Letters of Sir Walter Scott*, ed. H.J.C. Grierson, vol. 8, 1835, 53). At the request of Baillie, Scott helped get Hemans's *Vespers of Palermo* staged in Edinburgh in 1824 (*Letters*, 8.174, 176, 179); during Hemans's visit, Scott wrote to

24. FH to ?; Rydal Mount, 22 June 1830

[Wordsworth at home]

[…] my nervous fear at the idea of presenting myself alone to Mr. Wordsworth, grew upon me so rapidly, that it was more than seven before I took courage to leave the inn.[1] I had indeed little cause for such trepidation. I was driven to a lovely cottage-like building, almost hidden by a profusion of roses and ivy; and a most benignant-looking old man greeted me in the porch: this was Mr. Wordsworth himself; and when I tell you that, having rather a large party of visitors in the house, he led me to a room apart from them, and brought in his family by degrees, I am sure that little trait will give you an idea of considerate kindness which you will both like and appreciate. In half an hour I felt myself as much at ease with him as I had been with Sir Walter in half a day. I laughed to find myself saying, on the occasion of some little domestic occurrence, "Mr. Wordsworth, how *could* you

---

his son-in-law J.G. Lockhart, "Mrs Hemans is here Sophia & [Anne, his daughters] are critical & do not like her. I am less fastidious and think her frank & pleasant in conversation & if Blue [i.e., a "Bluestocking," or intellectual woman, in a pejorative sense] not nineteen times dyed" (*Letters*, 11.218). To his journal Scott reported on 14 July, "… went to Chiefswood and had the pleasure of a long walk with a lady well known in the world of poetry, Mrs. Hemans. She is young and pretty though the mother of five children as she tells me. There is taste and spirit in her conversation. My daughters are critical and call her *blue* but I think they are hypercritical. I will know better when we meet again." Scott's daughter Sophia thought Hemans a "vulgar looking woman with a veil pinned in the mantilla fashion on her head" who was a burden to her hosts at Chiefswood, the Hamiltons (*The Journal of Sir Walter Scott*, ed. W.E.K. Anderson, Oxford: Clarendon Press, 1972, 586 and note).

1 Wordsworth was also apprehensive, though for a different reason: he wrote to the poet Samuel Rogers on 16 June 1830, just before Hemans was due to arrive, wishing Rogers were there to help entertain her, partly because "literary Ladies are apt to require a good deal of attention" (*Letters: Later Years*, ed. de Selincourt, 1.490). On 20 July he wrote to Sir Walter Scott reporting, "Mrs Hemans lately stayed a fortnight with us and is now lodged upon the banks of Windermere [at Dove Nest] along with 3 of her sons — all fine Boys" (1.501-2), and on 30 July he told Rogers, "We like Mrs Hemans much — her conversation is what might be expected from her Poetry, full of sensibility — and she enjoys the Country greatly" (1.503). Wordsworth and Hemans did correspond, but the connection seems to have lapsed, partly through Wordsworth's tardiness or neglect in replying (2. 588, 654), to be resumed in 1831 when Hemans sought Wordsworth's help in obtaining a church appointment in the Lake District for Robert Perceval Graves, son of her physician in Dublin (2.662, 669-70, 682; I.A. Williams, "Wordsworth, Mrs. Hemans, and Robert Perceval Graves," *London Mercury*, 6, Aug. 1922, 395-401).

be so giddy?" He has, undeniably, a lurking love of mischief, and would not, I think, be half so safely intrusted with the tied up bag of winds[1] as Mr. ——insisted that Dr. Channing[2] might be. There is an almost patriarchal simplicity, an absence of all pretension, about him, which I know you would like; all is free, unstudied—"the river winding at its own sweet will"[3]—in his manner and conversation there is more of impulse about them than I had expected, but in other respects I see much that I should have looked for in the poet of meditative life: frequently his head droops, his eyes half close, and he seems buried in quiet depths of thought. I have passed a delightful morning to-day in walking with him about his own richly-shaded grounds, and hearing him speak of the old English writers, particularly Spenser,[4] whom he loves, as he himself expresses it, for his "earnestness and devotedness." [...]

[Chorley 2.97-9; Hughes 206-7]

25. FH to [Mr L——?]; Rydal Mount, 25 June 1830
[Wordsworth on domesticity and genius]

[...] You will be pleased to hear that the more I see of Mr. Wordsworth, the more I admire, and I may almost say, love him. It is delightful to see a life in such perfect harmony with all that his writings express, "true to the kindred points of heaven and home!"[5] You may remember how much I disliked, and I think you agreed with me in reprobating that shallow theory of Mr. Moore's with regard to the unfitness of genius for domestic happiness.[6] I was speaking of it yes-

---

1 perhaps a reference to the classical legend of Pandora, who was entrusted with a jar or box containing numerous evils, which were released upon humanity when she ignored a warning not to open it; in another version the jar contains benefits for humanity which are lost when a curious person opens it.

2 William Ellery Channing (1780-1842), American liberal religious writer and leading promoter of Unitarianism, pacifism, abolition of slavery, and prohibition of alcohol; he corresponded with Hemans and helped promote her work in the United States; she stated that she valued his "counsel" highly (Chorley 1.132).

3 see p. 428 n1.

4 Edmund Spenser (1522-99), Elizabethan court poet and author of several important poems, including a religious and patriotic romance, *The Faerie Queen* (1590-96), which was widely read by Romantic poets, who adapted its stanza form, as FH did in *Modern Greece* and *The Forest Sanctuary*.

5 Wordsworth, "To a Sky-Lark," l. 12.

6 a view offered by Thomas Moore in his biography of Byron (1830).

terday to Mr. Wordsworth, and was pleased by his remark, "It is not because they *possess* genius that they make unhappy homes, but because they do not possess genius *enough;* a higher order of mind would enable them to see and feel all the beauty of domestic ties." He has himself been singularly fortunate in long years of almost untroubled domestic peace and union. [...]
[Chorley 2.105-6; cf Hughes 209-10]

26. FH to ?; Dove Nest[1] [July 1830]
[FH pursued by admirers, in person and by correspondence]

I have too long left unacknowledged your welcome letter, but the wicked world does so continue to persecute me with notes, and parcels and dispatches, that, even *here*, I cannot find half the leisure you would imagine. Yesterday I had three visiting cards — upon which I look with a fearful and boding eye — left at the house, whilst I was sitting, in the innocency of my heart, thinking no harm, by the side of the lake. Imagine visiting cards at Dove's Nest! Robinson Crusoe's dismay at seeing the print of the man's foot in the sand[2] could have been nothing, absolutely nothing, to mine, when these evil tokens of "young ladies with pink parasols"[3] met my distracted sight, on my return from the shore. *En revanche,*[4] however, I have just received the most exquisite letter ever indicted by the pen of man, from a young American, who being an inhabitant of No. ——,——, is certainly not likely to trouble me with anything more than his "spiritual attachment," as Mr. —— of —— is pleased to call it. He, that is, my American, must certainly not be the "walking-stick," but the very *leaping pole* of friendship. Pray read, mark, learn, and promul-

---

1   a small villa rented by Hemans and situated above and overlooking Lake Windermere, not far from Wordsworth's Grasmere; the building still exists; for a description of the place in the 1840s, including an illuminating conversation with the woman who kept the house and knew Hemans there, see William Howitt, *Homes and Haunts of the Most Eminent British Poets,* 2 vols (London, 1847), 2.116-22.
2   in Daniel Defoe's popular novel *Robinson Crusoe* (1719), Crusoe is shipwrecked on a desert island where he lives for years, and is panic-stricken one day to discover another man's footprint on the shore.
3   Thomas Moore, *Rhymes on the Road* (1819), a satire on English tourists abroad, Extract IX, l. 32-4: "Nor fear of Mamelukes forbids / Young ladies, with pink parasols, / To glide among the Pyramids …"
4   to compensate.

gate for the benefit of the family, the following delectable passage. "How often have I sung some touching stanza of your own, as I rode on horseback of a Saturday evening, from the village academy to my house a little distance out of town: and saw through the waving cedars and pines, the bark roof and the open door of some pleasant wigwam, where the young comely maidens were making their curious baskets, or mocasins, or wampum-belts, and singing their 'To-gas-a-wana, or evening song!' How often have I murmured 'Bring flowers' or the 'Voice of Spring,'[1] as thus I pondered along! How often have I stood on the shore of the Cayuga, the Seneca, the Oneida, and the Skaneateles,[2] and called to mind the sweetness of your strains!" I see you are enchanted, my dear——, but this is not all: "the lowliest of my admirers," as the amiable youth entitles himself, begs permission to be for once my "*cordonnier*,"[3] and is about to send me a pair of Indian *mocasins*, with my "illustrious name interwoved in the buckskin of which they are composed with wampum beads." If I receive this precious gift before I return to Liverpool, I shall positively make my appearance, *en squaw*, the very first evening I come to——street; and pray tell Dr.——that with these mocasins, and *a blanket to correspond*, I shall certainly be able to defy all the rigours of the ensuing winter. [...]
[Chorley 2.116-18]

27. FH to ?; Dove Nest [July 1830?]
[outdoor adventures; need for chocolate; domestic shame]

My dear——,

I must frankly own that it is my necessities which impel me so soon to address you again. From the various dilapidations which my wardrobe has endured since I came into this country, I am daily assuming more and more the appearance of "a decayed gentlewoman;" and if you could only behold me in a certain black gown, which came with me here in all the freshness of youth, your tender heart would be melted into tearful compassion. The ebony bloom of the said dress is departed for ever: the waters of Winandermere,

---

1 poems by Hemans published in *The Siege of Valencia ... with Other Poems* (1823).
2 lakes in north-west New York state.
3 shoemaker.

(thrown up by oars in unskilful hands,) have splashed and dashed over it, the rains of Rydal have soaked it, the winds from Helm-crag have wrinkled it, and it is altogether somewhat in the state of

> "Violets plucked, which sweetest showers,
> May ne'er make grow again."[1]

Three yards of black silk, however, will, I believe, restore me to respectability of appearance,..... if——will add a supply of chocolate, without which there is no getting through the fatigue of existence for me—and if——or your brother——will also send me a volume or two of Schiller—not the plays, but the poems—to read with Mr. Wordsworth, I shall then have a complete brown-paper-full of happiness. Imagine, my dear,——, a bridal present made by Mr. Wordsworth, to a young lady in whom he is much interested—a poet's daughter, too! You will be thinking of a broach in the shape of a lyre, or a butterfly-shaped aigrette, or a forget-me not ring, or some such "small gear;" —nothing of the sort, but a good, handsome, substantial, useful-looking pair of scales, to hang up in her store-room! "For you must be aware, my dear Mrs. Hemans," said he to me very gravely, "how necessary it is occasionally for every lady to see things weighed herself." "*Poveretta me!*"[2] I looked as *good as I could*, and, happily for me, the poetic eyes are not very clear-sighted, so that I believe no suspicion derogatory to my notability[3] of character, has yet flashed upon the mighty master's mind: indeed I told him that I looked upon scales as particularly graceful things, and had great thoughts of having my picture taken with a pair in my hand.[4] ...
[Chorley 2.124-6]

---

1 slightly misquoted from Thomas Percy's "The Friar of Orders Gray" (ll. 47-8), an imitation of a popular ballad, published in his influential collection of folksongs and street ballads, *Reliques of Ancient English Poetry* (1765, enlarged in successive editions to 1794).

2 Poor little me!

3 from the common phrase "notable woman," meaning a comprehensively skilled housekeeper.

4 in about 1830 FH wrote to Wordsworth's wife, Mary, but urged her not to bother replying since FH was sure that her correspondent had, "at this very moment, more affairs of domestic state upon your hands, than mortal human, except yourself,

28. FH [to member of Graves family; autumn 1830?]

[illness; sculpture of Sappho; female fame]

Since I wrote last, I have been quite confined to the house; but before I caught my last very judicious cold, I went to see an exquisite piece of sculpture, which has been lately sent to this neighbourhood from Rome by Gibson,[1] with whose name as an artist you are most likely familiar. It is a statue of Sappho, representing her at the moment she receives the tidings of Phaon's desertion.[2] I think I prefer it to almost any thing I ever saw of Canova's,[3] as it possesses all his delicacy and beauty of form, but is imbued with a far deeper sentiment. There is a sort of willowy drooping in the figure, which seems to express a weight of unutterable sadness, and one sinking arm holds the lyre so carelessly, that you almost fancy it will drop while you gaze. Altogether, it seems to speak piercingly and sorrowfully of the nothingness of Fame, at least to a woman. [...]

[Hughes 226; Chorley 2.156-7]

29. FH [to member of family of J.C. Graves?; the Hermitage, near Kilkenny, April 1831]

[illness; pestered by admirers in Dublin; dangerous and unsettled state of the country]

This is a very pretty little spot, and I should be really sorry that my brother is to leave it in two or three months, were it not that the

could ever get through. — I assure you I think with much admiration, and some little lurking envy, of the doing so much '*to warn, to comfort, to command*,' in the course of every day's work ..." (Huntington Library MS HM 11419). The quotation is from Wordsworth's "She was a Phantom of delight ..." (1807), l. 28.

1   John Gibson (1790-1866), neoclassical sculptor who lived in Liverpool until 1817, encouraged in his career by William Roscoe; he then went to Rome where he was influenced by Canova and Thorwaldsen, and where he executed a number of important commissions for patrons in England; later in his career he aroused controversy by reviving the ancient Greek practice of colouring sculptured human figures.

2   Sappho was a Greek poet (7th century BC) about whom little is known besides various legends, including her fatal passion for Phaon, which made her a figure for the woman artist disabled by feminine "weakness."

3   Antonio Canova (1757-1822), Italian sculptor and leading exponent of the neoclassical style, with an international reputation and clientele; his works were known for their smooth finish.

change will be one of great advantage to himself, as he is appointed to a trust of high responsibility. I have a blue mountain chain in sight of my window, and the voice of the river comes in to me delightfully. My health has been very unsettled, yet my friends are surprised to see me *looking* so well. I think that, on the whole, the soft climate agrees with me; my greatest foe is "the over-beating of the heart." My life in Dublin was what might have been expected—one of constant excitement, and more "broken into fragments"[1] than ever. I very nearly gave up letter-writing in despair. I must, however, gratefully acknowledge, that I met there much true kindness. The state of the country here, though Kilkenny is considered at present tranquil, is certainly, to say the least of it, very ominous. We paid a visit yesterday evening at a clergyman's house about five miles hence, and found a guard of eight armed policemen stationed at the gate: the window-ledges were all provided with great stones for the convenience of hurling down upon assailants; and the master of the house had not, for a fortnight, taken a walk without loaded pistols. You may imagine how the boys, who are all here for the holidays, were enchanted with this agreeable state of things; indeed, I believe, they were not a little disappointed that we reached home without having sustained an attack from the Whitefeet.[2] Do not, however, suppose that we are in the least danger, though there seems just possibility of danger enough all around us, to keep up a little pleasant excitement—(the tabooed word again!) There is this peculiarity in Irish disturbances, that those who are not obnoxious, from party or political motives, to the people, have really nothing to fear; and my brother is extremely popular. My sister-in-law and myself are often amused with the idea of what our English friends would think, did they know of our sitting, in this troubled land, with our doors and windows all open, till eleven o'clock at night.

[Hughes 235-7]

---

1   John Wilson (1785-1854), "Unimore: A Dream of the Highlands," Vision 1, l. 57: "Through the mist broken into fragments ..."

2   Whitefeet: members of an Irish Catholic secret society that carried out political murders and acts of violence around 1832-33.

30. FH [to a member of the Graves family? The Hermitage, Kilkenny; April 1831?]

[love in the pagan and Christian worlds]

It was with some difficulty that I refrained from making Alcestis[1] express the hope of an immortal reunion; I know this would be out of character, and yet could scarcely imagine how love, so infinite in its nature, could ever have existed without the hope (even if undefined and unacknowledged) of a heavenly country, an unchangeable rest-ing-place. This awoke in me many other thoughts with regard to the state of human affections, their hopes and their conflicts in the days of "the gay religions, full of pomp and gold,"[2] which, offering, as they did, so much of grace and beauty to the imagination, yet held out so little comfort to the heart. Then I thought how much these affections owed to a deeper and more spiritual faith, to the idea of a God who knows all our inward struggles, and pities our sufferings. I think I shall weave all these ideas into another little poem, which I will call *Love in the Ancient World*.[3]

[Hughes 240]

31. FH to ?; 4 May 1834

[increasingly religious and spiritual interest of her poetry]

[...] I have been busily employed in the completion of what I do hope you will think my best volume—the "Scenes and Hymns of Life;" though Blackwood's impatience to bring it out speedily has rather prevented my developing the plan as completely as I have wished. I regard it, however, as an undertaking to be carried on and thoroughly wrought out during several years; as the more I look for

---

1   in her poem "The Death Song of Alcestis"; Alcestis is the heroine of a Greek play of that title by Euripides (5th century BC); in it, Admetus is allowed a second life if he can find someone to die in his place, and his wife Alcestis makes the sacrifice, but Heracles brings her back to life.

2   Milton, *Paradise Lost*, 1.372.

3   This design was afterwards partly, and *but* partly, fulfilled, in the *Antique Greek Lament*, which was intended as one of a series of poems, illustrating the insufficien-cy of aught but Christianity to heal and comfort the broken in heart; and its all-sus-taining aid to those, "who, going through this vale of misery, use it for a well," and apply to its living waters for "the strengthening and refreshing of their souls." [Hughes's footnote]

indications of the connexion between the human spirit and its eternal Source, the more extensively I see those traces open before me, and the more indelibly they appear stamped upon our mysterious nature. I cannot but think that my mind has both expanded and strengthened during the contemplation of such things, and that it will thus by degrees arise to a higher and purer sphere of action than it has yet known. If any years of peace and affection be granted to my future life, I think I may prove that the *discipline of storms* has, at least, not been without purifying and ennobling influence. I shall not have wearied you, my dear friend, by what would have seemed mere egotism to most others, but I always feel, with reference to *you*, that your regard is really best repaid by a true unfolding of my mind, with its changeful inner life…. .
[Chorley 2.285-7]

32. FH to the Rev. S. Butler; 20 Dawson St., Dublin, 26 July 1834
[ambition for her religious poetry]

[…] I am anxious that my friends should see in it[1] some traces of that which I am ever earnestly and fervently seeking—*improvement.*—I look upon it also as but the opening of a plan which I hope to mature, if God grants me amended health. I would fain achieve some thing of *permanent* usefulness; of true, however lowly worth; but I have too much cause to feel in my troubled life what some old sacred Poet has affectingly said—

> "Our peaceful flame that *would point up to Heaven,*
> Is still disturb'd, and turn'd aside;
> And every blast of air
> Commits such waste in Man, as Man cannot repair."

[…]
[British Library Additional MSS 34589 ff. 95-6]

---

1 *Scenes and Hymns of Life, with Other Religious Poems* (1834).

33. Robert Peel to FH, Dublin; Whitehall Gardens [London], 7 Feb. 1835

[offers money and government post for her son Henry]

Madam

I have this moment heard from an authority which I fear I cannot question, that you are suffering from sickness, and from embar[r]assed pecuniary circumstances.

The position in which I am placed as Minister of the Crown, and the claims upon me in that capacity which high literary distinction establishes, will I trust entitle me to make a Communication which might otherwise from a stranger to you, appear somewhat abrupt, if not indelicate.

I hear that you have a son of about the age of 17, for whom you are anxious to provide, and I beg to assure you that if a Clerkship in a respectable public Department would be acceptable to you, I will place him with the greatest satisfaction in one of the first which becomes vacant.

For the relief of your own immediate wants, I beg your acceptance of the inclosed sum of £100. You need have no difficulty in accepting it. It imposes no personal obligation; it is only the fulfilment of a public duty, which I feel incumbent on me as the King's Minister, to prevent the reproach which would justly attach to me, if I could permit a Lady so distinguished for literary exertions, which have aided the cause of virtue, and have conferred honour on her Country and her sex, to suffer from privations, which official station gives me the opportunity of relieving.

I have the Honour &c

Robert Peel[1]

[British Library Additional MSS 40413 f. 291]

---

1 Hemans replied on 10 Feb., accepting Peel's offers (British Library Add. MSS 40414 f. 14). Peel was a reform-oriented Tory prime minister then struggling to maintain his minority government in power; according to Rose Lawrence, newspapers had carried accounts of FH's illness and poor financial straits, whereupon Dudley Ryder, Lord Sandon (1798-1882), M.P. for Liverpool and advocate of reform, arranged for Peel to make the offer, procuring an appointment for FH's son Henry in the Navy Office; her son Charles was appointed to a clerkship in H.M. Customs; in 1842 her son Claude wrote to Peel, calling him "the constant and powerful friend of Literature," and asking for a similar appointment, "for the sake of the name I bear" (British Library Additional MSS 40500 f. 15).

34. FH to Rose Lawrence; [Dublin] 10 Feb. 1835
[now free to pursue a higher poetic calling, after Peel's offer]

I hope my life, if it be spared, may now flow back into its native course of quiet thoughtfulness. You know in how rugged a channel the poor little stream has been forced, and through what rocks it has wrought its way; and it is now longing for repose in some still valley. It has ever been one of my regrets that the constant necessity of providing sums of money to meet the exigencies of the boys' education, has obliged me to waste my mind in what I consider mere desultory effusions:

> "Pouring myself away,
>   As a wild bird, amid'st the foliage, turns
>   That which within him thrills, and beats, and burns,
>   Into a fleeting lay."[1]

My wish ever was to concentrate all my mental energy in the production of some more noble and complete work; something of pure and holy excellence, (if there be not too much presumption in the thought,) which might permanently take its place as the work of a British poetess. I have always, hitherto, written as if in the breathing times of storms and billows. Perhaps it may not even yet be too late to accomplish what I wish, though I sometimes feel my health so deeply prostrated, that I cannot imagine how I am ever to be raised up again: but a greater freedom from those cares of which I have been obliged to bear up under the whole responsibility, may do much to restore me; and though my spirits are greatly subdued by long sickness, I feel the powers of my mind in full maturity.
[Lawrence, 387-8; 386n. and 407n.]

---

1   paradoxically, the passage is from one of FH's own "desultory effusions" — "The Dying Improvisatrice," ll. 31-3.

Appendix B: Views and Reviews of Hemans[1]

1. 1816: from review of *The Restoration of the Works of Art to Italy*, 2nd edn

This is a poem of no ordinary merit. The authoress is possessed of a powerful imagination and of a commanding mind. Her taste appears to have been cast in the mould of ancient days. Her periods are long, and generally well sustained; occasionally however they taper off towards the conclusion, which considerably diminishes the effect of the preceding beauties. [...]

[...] We were much pleased with the strain of piety in which the poem is concluded. This is the first time that we have met with any composition of our authoress. She has certainly great power and a mind truly classical. Her fault is that which a correct taste will remedy. She rises too often into the turgid, which is the more dangerous, as if the bubble bursts, the *bathos* most assuredly yawns below to receive the unfortunate victim.

[*British Critic*, new series, 7 (Sept. 1816): 311-13]

2. 1819: from review of *Tales, and Historic Scenes*

[Hemans in relation to her contemporaries and immediate predecessors, and to the recent "rage for poetry"]

The more we become acquainted with Mrs. Hemans as a poet, the more we are delighted with her productions, and astonished by her powers. She will, she must take her place among eminent poets. If she has a rival of her own sex, it is Johanna Baillie;[2] but even compared with the living *masters* of song—some of whom, be it remarked, were publishing poems when she was dressing dolls—she is entitled to a place of very high distinction. [...]

---

1 editor's additions and summaries enclosed in square brackets; editor's deletions indicated by ellipses enclosed in square brackets.

2 Joanna Baillie (1762-1851), poet and dramatist; her first *Series of Plays* on the passions (1798) created a sensation and shifted literary taste to drama for private reading rather than performance; Hemans greatly admired her work and corresponded with her.

Had Mrs. Hemans's birth and relative poetical maturity been ten or fifteen years earlier; had she appeared, in all her present strength and pride, when the late tide of poetical enthusiasm was at its flood; her name would now have been classical with all the readers of poetry. [...] Every one knows the recent remarkable history of poetry, and its present actual predicament. Eighty years of the last century had no doubt produced about as many bards, of worth enough to fill up the catalogue of what are called the British poets. Yet a very few names meet the eye in that roll, prominent like the greater beads in the rosary. When we have named Young, Gray, Chatterton, Akenside, Collins, Goldsmith, Beattie, Burns, and Cowper, we have named, if we mistake not, the whole poetical peerage of the 18th century, from Thomson to Campbell.[1] With Cowper commenced a decided change in the direction of the current of public taste. Had Mrs. Hemans started when "The Pleasures of Hope" were newly sung; when Scott appeared to the critics of the South a compiler of trash, and Byron was affectionately admonished by those of the North to forswear poetry like "thin potations;" when Moore was yet grovelling, and Southey was raving, and Wordsworth was puling;[2] had she

---

1   Edward Young (1683-1765), author of the widely read religious-didactic poem *Night Thoughts* (1742-45); Thomas Gray (1716-71), author of one of the best known 18th-century reflective poems, "Elegy in a Country Churchyard" (1751); Thomas Chatterton (1752-70) wrote several spuriously medieval poems and after his early death came to symbolize the disappointed and neglected author; Mark Akenside (1721-70) wrote the widely admired reflective poem, *Pleasures of the Imagination* (1744); William Collins (1721-59) helped revive interest in earlier poetic forms and was known especially for his *Odes* (1746); Oliver Goldsmith (1730-74), historian, essayist, dramatist, novelist, and poet, was known especially for his reflective Georgic poem *The Deserted Village* (1770); James Beattie (1735-1803), Scottish critic and poet, was known for his reflective poem *The Minstrel* (1771-74); Robert Burns (1759-96) helped revive interest in popular verse and balladry and was especially known for his poems in Scots dialect; William Cowper (1731-1800) wrote hymns and reflective-didactic poems, especially *The Task* (1785), an epic of everyday life; James Thomson (1700-48) wrote widely read descriptive and reflective poems in the tradition of classical republicanism, including *The Seasons* (1726-30) and *Liberty* (1735-36); Thomas Campbell (1777-1844) wrote the widely read *Pleasures of Hope* (1799) and *Gertrude of Wyoming* (1809), as well as numerous liberal and patriotic poems; he edited the *New Monthly Magazine* when Hemans published many poems there.

2   the reviewer refers to leading Romantic poets, including the best-selling historical novelist and narrative poet, Walter Scott (1771-1832); George Gordon, Lord Byron (1788-1824), who had a Europe-wide reputation and following, especially among liberals, for his narrative poems *Childe Harold's Pilgrimage* (1812-18) and *Don Juan*

launched at once such a fabric as her "Modern Greece," or "Abencer-rage," we should now have had cause to envy a tythe of her fame. We trust we are safe from the imputation of meaning that Mrs. Hemans would have been great, only had these poets never been great at all. She shines in the midst of them—uneclipsed by a constellated splendour in which no lesser star could live—steadily and beautifully visible in the very galaxy of their glory. But alas for poets in these surfeited, languid days! Never was more poetry written, and less poetry read. The multitude have had enough. The enthusiasm which has now cooled was founded on exhaustible feelings. Walter Scott at once awoke it and wore it out. Never was poet's career like his. He was a comet, and all eyes went heavenward. Yet many who came to gaze remained to feel; and, while his fable feasted their more vulgar appetite, the finer and the nobler essence of his song gave them a new delight equally unexpected and unaccountable. Tales were now too much in demand to give hopes to a poet who offered any thing else. All the poets of the age, accordingly, great and small, wrote tales, and the readers of poetry, as they were termed, multiplied beyond all former precedent.

It was nevertheless a grievous error to speculate upon the soundness and permanence of the foundation of this mere fashion, and to scare the lovers of mere tales, by a fearful array of new editions of the old poets, in all the impartiality of a general resurrection.[1] The high temperature of Lord Byron's poetry, for a time, kept from cooling the mass of public feeling. Mental is like bodily excitement; whatever produces it will, by repetition, lose its power of even causing sensation. It is a drunkard's history, but it is the recent history of the rage for poetry. Lord Byron supplied the strongest stimulus. By an exhibition of passions far beyond what we ought at least to sympathise with, he at once gloried in the field of his proper strength, and wooed and

---

(1819-24); his friend Thomas Moore (1779-1852), the Irish patriot poet; his opponent, the poet laureate and friend of Coleridge and Wordsworth, Robert Southey (1774-1843); and the leader of the early Romantic poets, William Wordsworth (1770-1850), who, like Southey and Coleridge, had been a reformist in the 1790s but later became more socially and politically conservative. The other main male writers of the Romantic movement, Keats and Percy Shelley, did not have established reputations at this time.

1 the early nineteenth century saw many reprint editions of the "British poets" for a newly book-conscious middle-class reading public.

won that darling popularity, which he has since scorned and loathed, till he has put his love of it, his dependence upon it, past a doubt. But even this concentrated poetry has lost its pungency[... .] Such is the unpropitious time of Mrs. Hemans' appearance as a poet. Her popularity and her merit are altogether distinct—we wish we could say that they are not *separate* considerations. If the multitude neglect her, they are alike neglecting the first poets of the age. They are off to novels of singularly powerful fascination, and to the poet they will not listen, however sweet his song. After all, there is a large class of readers of taste and feeling, to whom genuine poetry will ever afford the most exquisite delight. We invite *them* to do justice to Mrs. Hemans; and we promise them a more choice regale than any to which they have lately been called.

[turns to *Tales, and Historic Scenes* and quotes from several poems, with very brief commentary, except on "The Abencerrage," which is criticized for having an unclear narrative line: "It is an effort to the reader to have to gather a plot from interrogations, allusions, ellipses, apostrophes, inversions, and transitions."]

It appears to us that Mrs. Hemans has yielded her own to the public taste in conveying her poetry in the vehicle of tales. Her shorter pieces, which are scenes rather than plots, could not even in her hands take a better shape. We have already said, that in the narrative of her longer compositions she is not so happy. But truly, narrative is, in her style of poetry, a subordinate consideration. It is not her practice to exhaust our interest at first reading. She is aware that motion and action, shew and pageantry, surprizes and prodigies, will not bear a second perusal. She gains a much more permanent hold of our sympathies. She excites emotion which endures, and which gives fresh delight on repetition, by expressing natural feeling, in a sweet flow of tenderness, or a sustained and deep tone of pathos. And when she strikes her boldest chord, it is the true sublime of thrilling sentiment, in all the witchery of eloquence. [declares it is difficult to find technical faults in her work, approves of her name appearing on her title pages, deplores the prosaic character of her titles, and recommends putting "The Abencerrage" first in *Tales*]

We cannot help thinking that Mrs. Hemans fritters away her great powers, by bestowing them upon a number of small poems, instead of concentrating them in one great effort. [...] We hope to hail Mrs.

Hemans' muse in still a higher and more extended flight than any which she has hitherto achieved. Poetical nobility she has already attained; nevertheless her honours may yet be far more distinguished and illustrious. But we do most cordially wish, for her sake, that her destined title of one of the first poets of the age, were something more than rank without fortune.

[*Edinburgh Monthly Review*,[1] 2 (Aug. 1819): 194-209]

3. 1819: from review of *Tales, and Historic Scenes*

When we consider the cultivation of the female mind in the present day, and the great taste and relish which exist among the ladies of our country for the finest and highest department of literature, it is certainly strange that we find so few poetesses of celebrity. The beautiful story of Psyche, indeed, raised the name of Tighe[2] to an enviable and well-merited height in the public estimation: but, although since the publication of that poem we have had several fair candidates for public favour whose merits have been very considerable, we think that none can offer such strong claims to it as the writer of these "Tales and Historic Scenes." —Mrs. Hemans is in fact no stranger in the literary world, but has long wandered in the Olympian bowers; and her previous offerings at the shrine of feeling and taste have met with well deserved encouragement. [...]

Mrs. Hemans's talents, however, are not of the highest order. Her poetry is graceful, and in many parts rises into the finer and more impassioned soundings of the lyre: but her verses do not possess that uniform deep colour of poetic feeling, by which the touch of a master-poet is so easily distinguished: they contain little of the "breathing and burning," or of that powerful strength of expression which stamps itself on our imagination, and makes our memory faithful even though we do not strive to remember. We should be unjust, indeed, if we required from Mrs. Hemans that which has at all times been possessed by so very few, and of which perhaps one only of the many living poets of our country can now be called the possessor; and, with the exception of this great qualification, we think that Mrs. Hemans

---

1 a short-lived periodical.
2 on Tighe see "The Grave of a Poetess" from *Records of Woman*.

has all the requisites which make a poet. She displays a strain of high and pure feeling, a great power of poetical expression, a correct taste, and a fund of good sense: which last is perhaps as essential to the poet as any of the former qualities, in order to prevent him from running into that affectation and mannerism which so many writers of the present day conceive to be the distinguishing mark of true genius. To these excellences may also be added a flowing and correct versification, and a careful propriety of style and arrangement.

[...] The Abencerrage is the longest, and in our opinion the best: — the others being rather poetical pictures than tales, and presenting to the reader a single scene of action rather than a chain of continued events. [...]

In the design and execution of this tale, as well as in some of the sentiments, we perceive a resemblance to the Fire-Worshippers of Moore.[1] Of the other tales, "The Widow of Crescentius" is perhaps the best [...] .

Mrs. Hemans is rather too fond of description: but her delineation of the scenes which are enriched by classical association is masterly[2] and touching. Of this power, the commencement of "Alaric in Italy" may be mentioned as an example. When Liberty strings her lyre, she frequently rises into a more elevated and impressive strain of poetry, of which we could give many proofs from the present volume.

We shall always greet with gladness the appearance of this lady before the public; feeling assured that we shall never receive any production from her pen which is not consonant to pure feelings and correct taste.

[*Monthly Review*, 2nd series, 90 (Dec. 1819): 408-12]

4. 1817-20: Byron on Hemans

a. dislikes Modern Greece:
Modern Greece Good for nothing—written by some one who has never been there—and not being able to manage the Spenser Stanza has invented a thing of it's own—consisting of two elegiac stanzas a

---

1 "The Fire-Worshippers" is one of the inset verse tales in Thomas Moore's very popular Orientalist prose-verse novel, *Lalla Rookh* (1817).

2 May we use this word with application to a female? [reviewer's footnote]

heroic line and an Alexandrine twisted on a string—besides why "*modern*"?—you may say *modern Greeks* but surely *Greece* itself is rather more ancient than ever it was.
[Byron to John Murray, 4 Sept. 1817; in *Byron's Letters and Journals*, ed. Leslie A. Marchand, vol. 5, London: John Murray, 1976, 262-3]

b. response to The Sceptic:[1]

Mrs. Hemans is a poet also—but too stiltified, & apostrophic[2]—& quite wrong—men died calmly before the Christian æra—& since without Christianity—witness the Romans[3]—& lately Thistle-wood—Sandt—& Louvel[4]—*men who ought to have* been weighed down with their crimes—even had they believed.—A deathbed is a matter of nerves & constitution—& not of religion;—Voltaire was frightened[5]—Frederick of Prussia not.[6]—Christians the same according to their strength rather than their creed.
[Byron to John Murray; Ravenna, 7 June 1820; in Marchand, 7.113-14]

---

1 a poem by Hemans (1820) published by John Murray.
2 that is, too elevated ("on stilts") in language and style, and with too many instances of direct second-person address (apostrophe), a rhetorical device often used by poets to achieve intensity.
3 standard histories had long represented the ancient Romans, especially of the pre-Christian republican era, facing death calmly because of their stoical philosophy, which some theologians saw as anticipating central elements of Christianity.
4 Arthur Thistlewood (1774-1820), supposed leader of an attempted violent revolution in 1816 and, in 1820, of the so-called Cato Street Conspiracy, a plot to assassinate the government ministers, but in fact engineered by government agents to catch leading radicals; he was hung with four others on 1 May 1820; in 1819 Karl Sandt, or Sand, a liberal theology student, assassinated the German diplomat and dramatist August Kotzebue, who had become a spokesman for opponents of reform; Louis Pierre Louvel, a saddle-maker, assassinated the Duke of Berry, a member of the French royal family, at Paris on 13 February 1820.
5 Voltaire, or François Marie Arouet (1694-1778), was a leading figure of the French Enlightenment, social critic, and religious freethinker; when he thought he was near death in February 1778 he called for a priest, but upon recovering he ridiculed his own action; when about to die a few months later he first called for a priest and then refused his ministrations.
6 Frederick II (1712-86), king of Prussia, was a major administrative modernizer and military leader, guided by Enlightenment ideas, and he invited Voltaire to his court; he ridiculed Christianity and the church, and died as a result of stoically reviewing his troops throughout a rainstorm.

c. sees Hemans as a follower of "Turdsworth":

—but no *more modern* poesy—I pray—neither Mrs. Hewoman's—
nor any female or male Tadpole of Poet Turdsworth's[1]—nor any of
his ragamuffins.

[Byron to John Murray; Ravenna, 12 Aug. 1820; in Marchand, 7.158]

d. Hemans a Bluestocking:

—I do not despise Mrs. Heman [sic]—but if [she] knit blue stock-
ings[2] instead of wearing them it would be better. —

[Byron to John Murray; Ravenna, 28 Sept. 1820; in Marchand, 7.182]

5. 1820: from review of *The Restoration of the Works of Art to Italy* and *The Sceptic*

We know not whether the Authoress of these Poems will consider it
a compliment, or otherwise, when we state that in examining her
"Modern Greece" [...] we conceived it to be the work of an academ-
ical,[3] and certainly not a female, pen. It is not to disparage either sex
to say that as they usually live in different worlds, so they must natu-
rally write in different styles. Mrs. Hemans's productions, however,
possess much of that chaste correctness and classical spirit which
characterize Pope's Messiah, or Heber's Palestine,[4] poems which have
furnished a sort of accredited model for our university prize compo-
sitions. From being early and deeply imbued with the elegant litera-
ture of Greece and Rome, the poetry of men of education, even
when it does not rise much above mediocrity in other respects, often
evinces an elaborate finish which does not usually fall to the lot of

---

1   the first two letters replace crossed out "Wo."

2   "bluestocking" was a term adopted by the intellectual circle of men and women led
    by Elizabeth Montagu (1718-1800), referring to the informal blue worsted stock-
    ings worn by men of the circle as a sign of their egalitarian sociability; the term
    came to be used by others, usually disparagingly, to describe an intellectual woman.

3   of members of a college or university, all of whom at that time would have been
    male.

4   Reginald Heber (1783-1826) won an Oxford University student poetry competi-
    tion in 1803 with *Palestine* (published 1807); he became cathedral prebendary at St
    Asaph, where Hemans lived, and later bishop of Calcutta; he corresponded with
    Hemans; Alexander Pope (1688-1744), leading early 18th-century poet, published
    his *Messiah* in 1712.

female writers. Perhaps we may be thought incorrect both in the fact and its solution; but we have been surprised to observe how little really first rate versification has come from a quarter so fertile in other fruits of elegant literature, especially fictitious narrative.[1] We are not willing to refer the deficiency, for certainly we think there is a deficiency, to any disparaging cause. We would rather impute it to their mode of education, their reading, and their habits of life. While our sons are drinking deep in their very childhood at the fountains of classical literature, and forming their taste on the purest models of poesy, our daughters are spending their best hours in very different occupations. [...]

In most respects the education of women is unfavourable to the cultivation of the higher branches of poetry. The standards with which they are most conversant are usually defective; and they do not learn early in life that mental discipline which true poetry requires even when it seems most unconstrained. We might perhaps add to this that the mind of women is not usually favourable to that deep-toned emotion which constitutes the very essence of the higher kinds of poetry. Tenderness, which is a very necessary quality of poetry, will not of course be denied to that sex, one of whose characteristic epithets, in common parlance, is that of "tender;"[2] but poetry is in truth a thing of study; strong feeling is indeed necessary to its perfection; but it is the feeling of a *spectator* rather than of a *sufferer*. Those who feel most acutely, are at least able to analyse their sensations; nor are the ladies usually in the habit of examining so closely into the springs of human emotion as to touch them at their pleasure. [...]

[...] Perhaps in all instances of this kind we might make a useful distinction between what might be called *sentimental* emotion and *passionate* emotion.[3] [...]

---

1 fictitious narrative] the novel, which was at that time often represented (and often negatively) as a feminine genre, though women writers also pioneered the late 18th- and early 19th-century narrative poem.

2 in fact the word "tender" and its variants are used over 80 times in Hemans's works.

3 by the early 19th century, Sentimentalism, or Sensibility, which was a culturally avant garde movement of the later 18th century, came to be disparaged as emotionally excessive and validating other forms of excess, including even revolutionary violence. Sensibility was also associated with feminized culture and literature, at first positively but then negatively, so that by the early 19th century a positively

Mrs. Hemans's productions certainly betray no want of labour or finish; but are truly classical in their model, and evince a highly respectable share both of poetical and moral feeling. [...]

A striking transition occurs towards the close of the poem [*The Restoration of the Works of Art to Italy*] from the "gods of illusion, fancies of a dream," the "powerful idols of departed time," to the subjects from *sacred writ* which in after ages employed the chisel and pencil of the sons of Italy. Contrary to the example of most poets, Mrs. Hemans never treads so nobly as on sacred ground. [...]

[*British Review and London Critical Journal*, 15 (June 1820): 299-310]

6. 1823: from review of *The Siege of Valencia*

[...] By the selection of subjects for her muse, Mrs. Hemans has in this volume displayed considerable tact and knowledge of her own powers of verse. A chivalrous and even a martial strain flows freely from her lyre, which never sends forth nobler sounds than when it celebrates the battles of freedom or the achievements of romance. With such dispositions, the fame of the Cid[1] naturally attracted her regards. Indeed, the history of that hero possesses a singular charm, celebrated as he has been in the rude but fascinating ballads of his country; and we know not any writer by whom the high romantic character of that old poetry has been more successfully caught than by Mrs. Hemans, who has transferred it into her elegant and polished verse with great fidelity and happiness. We would instance the lyrical songs with which the "Siege of Valencia" is interspersed, as specimens of this kind of composition in which she has been most successful; and which have an air of romantic magnificence and grandeur thrown around them, that is admirably suited to the subject.

When we contemplate the achievements of this illustrious hero, whether it be in the rude but splendid ballads of his native land or in the fine imitations of them which Mrs. Hemans has produced,[2] we cannot refrain from expressing a sentiment of degradation and shame

---

valued and implicitly masculinized "passion" came to displace a disparaged (and still disparaged) and implicitly feminized "sentimentality" in critical criteria.

1 on El Cid, see notes to "Songs of the Cid."
2 "Songs of the Cid."

at the fate with which Spain is at this moment visited.[1] Is there not, among her nobility or her captains, one unyielding arm or one faithful heart to emulate the heroic virtues of "the Campeador?"[2] Apathy seems to have unnerved the hands of her soldiers, and treason to have corrupted the hearts of her commanders. [...]

In conclusion, we can only exhort this fair votary of the muses to persevere in the course which she has hitherto pursued with so much success. When we review the progress which she has made, and more especially when we turn to this last production of her pen, we feel assured that she cannot be under better guidance than that of her own taste and judgment. Let her continue to study, with the same devotion and fervour as heretofore, the works of our great poets: — let her cherish that high moral sense which pervades all her writings;—and we do not doubt that we shall see her assume her merited station among the leading poets of her age.

[*Monthly Review*, 2nd series, 102 (Oct. 1823) 177-81]

7. 1820s: Anne MacVicar Grant[3] to and on FH:

a. Anne Macvicar Grant to FH [*mid or late 1820s?*]
Shenstone complains of his hard fate, in wasting a lonely existence, "not loved, not praised, not known."[4] How very different is your case! Praised by all that read you,—loved by all that praise you,—and known, in some degree, wherever our language is spoken.
[Hughes 120]

b. Anne MacVicar Grant to ? [*c. 30 July 1829?*]
Mrs Hemans is here just now at Lady Wedderburn's, and is in person, mind, & manners the most charming person I ever met with, & that

---

1 despite British protests, a French army invaded Spain in April 1823 at the request of the reactionary Spanish king, Ferdinand VII, to suppress the insurrection led by "liberales" demanding a constitutional monarchy.
2 Campeador] a nickname of El Cid.
3 (1755-1838), early writer on folklore and folk culture, in *Letters from the Mountains: Being the Real Correspondence of a Lady, between the Years 1773 and 1803* (1806) and *Essays on the Superstitions of the Highlanders of Scotland ...* (1811); she celebrated what she saw as the purity and nobility of Scottish Highland culture but also called for social, cultural, and economic modernization of the Highlands.
4 slightly misquoted from William Shenstone (1714-63), "A Pastoral Ode, to the Honourable Richard Lyttelton," l. 12.

inclusive of her talents. She is feminine & natural, & very pretty. But she sings like a nightingale with a thorn at her breast[1]——Anne Grant
[Huntington Library MS HM 42515]

8. 1829: from Francis Jeffrey,[2] review of 2nd editions of *Records of Woman* and *The Forest Sanctuary*

Women, we fear, cannot do every thing; nor even every thing they attempt. But what they can do, they do, for the most part, excellently—and much more frequently with an absolute and perfect success, than the aspirants of our rougher and more ambitious sex. They cannot, we think, represent naturally the fierce and sullen passions of men—nor their coarser vices—nor even scenes of actual business or contention—and the mixed motives, and strong and faulty characters, by which affairs of moment are usually conducted on the great theatre of the world. For much of this they are disqualified by the delicacy of their training and habits, and the still more disabling delicacy which pervaded their conceptions and feelings; and from much they are excluded by their actual inexperience of the realities they might wish to describe—by their substantial and incurable ignorance of business—of the way in which serious affairs are actually managed—and the true nature of the agents and impulses that give movement and direction to the stronger currents of ordinary life. Perhaps they are also incapable of long moral or political investigations, where many complex and indeterminate elements are to be taken into account, and a variety of opposite probabilities to be weighed before coming to a conclusion. They are generally too impatient to get at the ultimate results, to go well through with such discussions;

---

1 in classical mythology, as retold in book 6 of Ovid's *Metamorphoses*, Philomel was raped by her sister's husband, Tereus, who cut out her tongue to prevent her telling of the crime; but she wove the story in cloth and with her sister obtained revenge by killing his son and serving him to Tereus in a meal; Philomel was transformed into a nightingale and, according to various literary versions (e.g., Byron, *Don Juan*, canto 6, stanza 87), kept herself awake at night by leaning against a thorn, so that she could continue to sing her plaintive song.

2 Jeffrey (1773-1850) was a judge, editor of the Whig-oriented *Edinburgh Review*, and leading literary critic, sympathetic to reform and liberalism, but known for trenchant attacks on what he saw as the excesses in such Romantic poets as Keats and Shelley.

and either stop short at some imperfect view of the truth, or turn aside to repose in the shadow of some plausible error. This, however, we are persuaded, arises entirely from their being seldom set on such tedious tasks. Their proper and natural business is the practical regulation of private life, in all its bearings, affections, and concerns; and the questions with which they have to deal in that most important department, though often of the utmost difficulty and nicety, involve, for the most part, but few elements; and may generally be better described as delicate than intricate;—requiring for their solution rather a quick tact and fine perception than a patient or laborious examination. For the same reason, they rarely succeed in long works, even on subjects the best suited to their genius; their natural training rendering them equally averse to long doubt and long labour.

For all other intellectual efforts, however, either of the understanding or the fancy, and requiring a thorough knowledge either of man's strength or his weakness, we apprehend them to be, in all respects, as well qualified as their brethren of the stronger sex; while, in their perceptions of grace, propriety, ridicule—their power of detecting artifice, hypocrisy, and affectation—the force and promptitude of their sympathy, and their capacity of noble and devoted attachment, and of the efforts and sacrifices it may require, they are, beyond all doubt, our superiors.

Their business being, as we have said, with actual or social life, and the colours it receives from the conduct and dispositions of individuals, they unconsciously acquire, at a very early age, the finest perception of character and manners, and are almost as soon instinctively schooled in the deep and dangerous learning of feeling and emotion; while the very minuteness with which they make and meditate on these interesting observations, and the finer shades and variations of sentiment which are thus treasured and recorded, trains their whole faculties to a nicety and precision of operation, which often discloses itself to advantage in their application to studies of a very different character. When women, accordingly, have turned their minds—as they have done but too seldom—to the exposition or arrangement of any branch of knowledge, they have commonly exhibited, we think, a more beautiful accuracy, and a more uniform and complete justness of thinking, than their less discriminating brethren. There is a finish and completeness about every thing they put out of their hands, which indicates not only an inherent taste for elegance and neatness, but a habit of nice observation, and singular exactness of judgment.

It has been so little the fashion, at any time, to encourage women to write for publication, that it is more difficult than it should be, to prove these truths by examples. Yet there are enough, within the reach of a very careless and superficial glance over the open field of literature, to enable us to explain, at least, and illustrate, if not entirely to verify, our assertions. No *man*, we will venture to say, could have written the Letters of Madame de Sevigné, or the Novels of Miss Austin, or the Hymns and Early Lessons of Mrs. Barbauld, or the Conversations of Mrs Marcet.[1] These performances, too, are not only essentially and intensely feminine, but they are, in our judgment, decidedly more perfect than any masculine productions with which they can be brought into comparison. They accomplish more completely all the ends at which they aim, and are worked out with a gracefulness and felicity of execution which excludes all idea of failure, and entirely satisfies the expectations they may have raised. We might easily have added to these instances. There are many parts of Miss Edgeworth's earlier stories, and of Miss Mitford's sketches and descriptions, and not a little of Mrs Opie's,[2] that exhibit the same fine and penetrating spirit of observation, the same softness and delicacy of hand, and unerring truth of delineation, to which we have alluded as characterising the purer specimens of female art. The same distin-

1   Marie de Rabutin-Chantal, Marquise de Sévigné (1626-1696), whose letters were considered a source for examples of both fashionable conduct and epistolary style; the novels of Jane Austen (1775-1817) were only just being accorded "classic" literary status at the time of Jeffrey's review; Anna Laetitia Barbauld (1743-1825) was a widely read writer of books for children and a leading literary and political voice of reform-oriented English religious Dissent; Jane Marcet (1769-1858) was known for a series of science texts, in the form of conversations, directed mainly to young female readers, and including *Conversations on Political Economy* (1816).

2   Maria Edgeworth (1767-1849), published moralistic stories for children from the late 1790s, and widely read tales and novellas for adults; Mary Mitford (1787-1859) published poems and plays but was known for a series of country anecdotes, published in a magazine and collected as *Our Village* (1824-32); much admired by Hemans, it depicted rural life as predominantly middle-class and had a powerful influence in representing such a countryside as the essential England; Amelia Opie (1769-1853), writer of poetry and prose fiction, came from reform-oriented English religious Dissent and, with Edgeworth, was the most respected English woman novelist of the 1800s and 1810s.

guishing traits of a woman's spirit are visible through the grief and the piety of Lady Russel, and the gaiety, the spite, and the venturesomeness of Lady Mary Wortley.[1] We have not as yet much female poetry; but there is a truly feminine tenderness, purity, and elegance, in the Psyche of Mrs Tighe, and in some of the smaller pieces of Lady Craven.[2] On some of the works of Madame de Staël[3]—her Corinne especially—there is a still deeper stamp of the genius of her sex. Her pictures of its boundless devotedness—its depth and capacity of suffering—its high aspirations—its painful irritability, and inextinguishable thirst for emotion, are powerful specimens of that morbid anatomy of the heart, which no hand but that of a woman's was fine enough to have laid open, or skilful enough to have recommended to our sympathy and love. There is the same exquisite and inimitable delicacy, if not the same power, in many of the happier passages of Madame de Souza and Madame Cottin—to say nothing of the more lively and yet melancholy records of Madame de Staal, during her long penance in the court of the Duchesse de Maine.[4]

[...] We think the poetry of Mrs Hemans a fine exemplification of Female Poetry—and we think it has much of the perfection which we have ventured to ascribe to the happier productions of female genius.

It may not be the best imaginable poetry, and may not indicate the very highest or most commanding genius; but it embraces a great deal of that which gives the very best poetry its chief power of pleasing; and would strike us, perhaps, as more impassioned and exalted, if it

---

1 the letters of Lady Rachel Russell (1636-1723) to her husband, who was executed for treason by Charles 11, were published in 1817; Lady Mary Wortley Montagu (1689-1762) wrote essays, poetry, and letters.

2 for Tighe, see Hemans's "Grave of a Poetess," from *Records of Woman*; Lady Elizabeth Craven (1750-1828) published travels and plays.

3 Germaine de Staël (1766-1817) was the most famous woman writer in Europe at this time; her novel *Corinne; ou, l'Italie* (1807) depicts its eponymous poet-heroine as the embodiment of Italy and was widely read and highly influential, especially among patriotic liberals and other women writers, including Hemans.

4 Marie Risteau, known as "Sophie" Cottin (1770-1807), published numerous widely read and translated French sentimental novels; Adélaïde Filleul, marquise de Sousa-Botelho (1761-1836) wrote partly autobiographical sentimental novels depicting upper-class French society; Marguerite Cordier de Launay, Mme de Staal (1684-1750), published memoirs (1755), translated and frequently reprinted, of her unfortunate experiences as attendant to the duchesse du Maine.

were not regulated and harmonized by the most beautiful taste. It is infinitely sweet, elegant, and tender—touching, perhaps, and contemplative, rather than vehement and overpowering; and not only finished throughout with an exquisite delicacy, and even serenity of execution, but informed with a purity and loftiness of feeling, and a certain sober and humble tone of indulgence and piety, which must satisfy all judgments, and allay the apprehensions of those who are most afraid of the passionate exaggerations of poetry. The diction is always beautiful, harmonious, and free—and the themes, though of infinite variety, uniformly treated with a grace, originality and judgment, which mark the same master hand. These themes she has borrowed, with the peculiar interest and imagery that belong to them, from the legends of different nations, and the most opposite states of society; and has contrived to retain much of what is interesting and peculiar in each of them, without adopting, along with it, any of the revolting or extravagant excesses which may characterise the taste or manners of the people or the age from which it has been derived. […] Though occasionally expatiating, somewhat fondly and at large, amongst the sweets of her own planting, there is, on the whole, a great condensation and brevity in most of her pieces, and, almost without exception, a most judicious and vigorous conclusion. The great merit, however, of her poetry, is undoubtedly in its tenderness and its beautiful imagery. The first requires no explanation; but we must be allowed to add a word as to the peculiar charm and character of the latter.

It has always been our opinion, that the very essence of poetry, apart from the pathos, the wit, or the brilliant description which may be embodied in it, but may exist equally in prose, consists in the fine perception and vivid expression of that subtle and mysterious analogy which exists between the physical and the moral world—which makes outward things and qualities the natural types and emblems of inward gifts and emotions, and leads us to ascribe life and sentiment to every thing that interests us in the aspects of external nature. The feeling of this analogy, obscure and inexplicable as the theory of it may be, is so deep and universal in our nature, that it has stamped itself on the ordinary language of men of every kindred and speech: and that to such an extent, that one half of the epithets by which we familiarly designate moral and physical qualities, are in reality so many metaphors, borrowed reciprocally, upon this analogy, from those opposite forms of existence. [...]

[Metaphor] has substantially two functions, and operates in two directions. In the *first* place, it strikes vividly out, and flashes at once on our minds, the conception of an inward feeling or emotion, which it might otherwise have been difficult to convey, by the presentment of some bodily form or quality, which is instantly felt to be its true representative, and enables us to fix and comprehend it with a force and clearness not otherwise attainable; and, in the *second* place, it vivifies dead and inanimate matter with the attributes of living and sentient mind, and fills the whole visible universe around us with objects of interest and sympathy, by tinging them with the hues of life, and associating them with our own passions and affections. This magical operation the poet too performs, for the most part, in one of two ways—either by the direct agency of similes and metaphors, more or less condensed or developed, or by the mere graceful presentment of such visible objects on the scene of his passionate dialogues or adventures, as partake of the character of the emotion he wishes to excite, and thus form an appropriate accompaniment or preparation for its direct indulgence or display. The former of those methods has perhaps been most frequently employed, and certainly has most attracted attention. But the latter, though less obtrusive, and perhaps less frequently resorted to of set purpose, is, we are inclined to think, the most natural and efficacious of the two; and is often adopted, we believe, unconsciously by poets of the highest order [... .]

[...] we think the fair writer before us is eminently a mistress of this poetical secret [... .] Almost all her poems are rich with fine descriptions, and studded over with images of visible beauty. But these are never idle ornaments: All her pomps have a meaning; and her flowers and her gems are arranged, as they are said to be among Eastern lovers, so as to speak the language of truth and of passion. This is peculiarly remarkable in some little pieces, which seem at first sight to be purely descriptive—but are soon found to tell upon the heart, with a deep moral and pathetic impression. But it is a truth nearly as conspicuous in the greater part of her productions; where we scarcely meet with any striking sentiment that is not ushered in by some such symphony of external nature—and scarcely a lovely picture that does not serve as a foreground to some deep or lofty emotion. [quotes "The Palm-Tree" and "Graves of a Household" from *Records of Woman*, commenting on the "exquisite lines" of the former and on "how well the graphic and the pathetic may be made to set off each other," as seen in the latter; then discusses her longer poems, quoting from several poems to illustrate Hemans's "graceful narrative along with her pathetic descriptions"; he comments on the "great force and sweetness" of "The Lady of the Castle" and on how "Joan of Arc, in Rheims" is "in a loftier and more ambitious vein; but sustained with equal grace, and as touching in its solemn tenderness"; he points to the "more passionate character" of "Arabella Stuart" and "Properzia Rossi" and then considers some of the shorter poems in the volume; he comments on how "The Hour of Romance" "breathes the very spirit of poetry, in its bright and vague picturings," "though it has no very distinct object or moral"; and he remarks on the "great sweetness" seen in lines from "Evening Prayer at a Girls' School," the "fine and stately solemnity" of a passage from "The Lost Pleiad," and the "rich lyrical cadence, and glow of deep feeling" of a passage from "The Dying Improvisatore"]

[…] there are few to whom our pages are likely to come, who are not already familiar with their beauties; and, in fact, we have made these extracts, less with the presumptuous belief that we are introducing Mrs Hemans for the first time to the knowledge or admiration of our readers, than from a desire of illustrating, by means of them, the singular felicity in the choice and employment of her imagery, of which we have already spoken so much at large;—that fine accord she has established between the world of sense and of soul—that delicate blending of our deep inward emotions with their splendid symbols and emblems without.

We have seen too much of the perishable nature of modern literary fame, to venture to predict to Mrs Hemans that hers will be immortal, or even of very long duration. Since the beginning of our critical career, we have seen a vast deal of beautiful poetry pass into oblivion, in spite of our feeble efforts to recall or retain it in remembrance.[1] The tuneful quartos of Southey are already little better than

---

1   Jeffrey now refers to male poets prominent from the 1790s to the early 1820s, including Robert Southey (1774-1843), John Keats (1795-1821), Percy Bysshe Shelley (1792-1822), William Wordsworth (1770-1850), George Crabbe (1754-

lumber: —and the rich melodies of Keats and Shelley,—and the fantastical emphasis of Wordsworth,—and the plebeian pathos of Crabbe, are melting fast from the fields of our vision. The novels of Scott have put out his poetry. Even the splendid strains of Moore are fading into distance and dimness, except where they have been married to immortal music; and the blazing star of Byron himself is receding from its place of pride. We need say nothing of Milman, and Croly, and Atherstone, and Hood, and a legion of others, who, with no ordinary gifts of taste and fancy, have not so properly survived their fame, as been excluded by some hard fatality from what seemed their just inheritance. The two who have the longest withstood this rapid withering of the laurel, and with the least marks of decay on their branches, are Rogers and Campbell; neither of them, it may be remarked, voluminous writers, and both distinguished rather for the fine taste and consummate elegance of their writings, than for that fiery passion, and disdainful vehemence, which seemed for a time to be so much more in favour with the public.

If taste and elegance, however, be titles to enduring fame, we might venture securely to promise that rich boon to the author before us; who adds to those great merits a tenderness and loftiness of feeling, and an ethereal purity of sentiment, which could only emanate from the soul of a woman. She must beware of becoming too voluminous; and must not venture again on anything so long as the "Forest Sanctuary." But, if the next generation inherits our taste for short poems, we are persuaded it will not readily allow her to be forgotten. For we do not hesitate to say, that she is, beyond all comparison, the most touching and accomplished writer of occasional verses that our literature has yet to boast of.

[*Edinburgh Review*, 50 (Oct. 1829): 32-47]

9. 1831: from Maria Jane Jewsbury, "Literary Sketches No. 1: Felicia Hemans"

[feminine and English character of Hemans and her poetry]

1832), Walter Scott (1771-1832), Thomas Moore (1779-1853), Byron (1788-1824), Henry Hart Milman (1791-1868), George Croly (1780-1860), Edwin Atherstone (1788-1872), Thomas Hood (1799-1845), Samuel Rogers (1763-1855), and Thomas Campbell (1777-1844).

Were there to be a feminine literary house of commons, Felicia Hemans might very worthily be called to fill the chair as the speaker—a representative of the whole body, as distinguished from the other estates of the intellectual realm. […]

[divides her work into two kinds—"the classic and the romantic":] Up to the publication of the "Siege of Valencia," her poetry was correct, classical, and highly polished—but it wanted warmth; it partook more of the nature of statuary than of painting. She fettered her mind with facts and authorities, and drew upon her memory when she should have relied upon her imagination:—she did not possess too much knowledge, but she made too much use of it. She was diffident of herself, and, to quote her own admission, "loved to repose under the shadow of mighty names":—Since then she has acquired the courage which leads to simplicity. Those were the days when she translated, and when her own poetry had somewhat the air of translation:—see the "Restoration of the Works of Art to Italy"—the "Tales and Historic Scenes"—"Modern Greece"—"The Greek Songs"—"The Last Constantine"—and "Dartmoor." But now this is no longer the case. The sun of feeling has risen upon her song—noon has followed morning [… .] She writes from and to the heart, putting her memory to its fitting use—that of supplying materials for imagination to fashion and build with. It is ridiculous to compare poets who have no points in common—equally vain to settle their priority of rank: each has his own character and his own station without reference to others. There will always be a difference between the poetry of men and women—so let it be; we have two kinds of excellence instead of one; we have also the pleasure of contrast: we discover that power is the element of man's genius—beauty that of woman's:—and occasionally we reciprocate their respective influence, by discerning the beauty of power, and feeling the power of beauty.

Mrs. Hemans has written pieces that combine power and beauty in an equal degree:—"Cœur de Lion at the Bier of his Father"—"England's Dead"—"The Pilgrim Fathers"—"The Lady of Provence"—"The Vaudois Wife"—and numbers of the same stamp, are "lumps of pure gold:" poems full of heroism, full of strength, and full of spirit; but the most distinctive feature in the mind and poetry of Mrs. Hemans, is their bias toward the supernatural of thought.

Most of her later poems breathe of midnight fancies and lone questionings—of a spirit that muses much and mournfully on the grave, not as for ever shrouding beloved objects from the living, but as a shrine whence high unearthly oracles may be won; and all the magnificence of this universal frame, the stars, the mountains, the deep forest, and the ever-sounding sea, are made ministrants to this form of imagination.

"The Address to a Departed Spirit"—"The Message to the Dead"—"The Spirit's Return," are express embodyings of this longing after visible signs of immortality—this turning inward and looking outward for proof that the dead dream in their long sleep, and dream of *us*; whilst incidental breathings of the same nature continually occur through her volumes.

As poetry, the productions thus characterized are exquisite; but we deeply regret the habit of thought they embody and display. With the dead we have nothing to do: we shall go to them, but they shall not return to us; and to invest anything like a wish for such return—anything like belief in its possibility—with the charms and subtleties of imagination, fancy, or feeling, is neither wise nor safe. [turns to the feelings Hemans "loves to pourtray":]—they are the purest, most profound, or, in other words, the most poetic of our nature: —look again at the characters she delights to honour—the wise, the virtuous, the heroic, the self-devoted, the single-hearted; those who have been faithful unto death in a noble cause; those who have triumphed over suffering and led on to holy deeds; those who have lived, and those who have died for others. PASSION is a poetical watchword of the day;—unfortunately, it is also something worse—a species of literary Goule[1] that preys upon good sense, good feeling, and good taste. Nothing now is considered to be said strongly that is said simply— every line must produce "effect"—every word must "tell" [... .]

[...] POWERFUL is another watchword, which palms off every delineation that is monstrous and absurd. Thus, language is powerful when epithets succeed each other as fast and heavily as the strokes of a blacksmith's hammer; ideas are powerful when, like Ossian's ghosts,[2] they reveal themselves in mists and shadow; and characters and

---

1   Goule] ghoul: in Eastern legend and literature a spirit that preys on corpses.
2   Ossian was the supposed author of Gaelic poems "translated" and published in the early 1760s by their actual author, James Macpherson.

incidents are powerful when they are worthy of the Newgate Calendar.[1] Those who catered for the nursery in olden times had very correct notions on these points: Jack the Giant-killer is truly "powerful"; Blue Beard is fraught with "passion."[2]

The admirable taste possessed by Mrs. Hemans has entirely preserved her from these, the besetting sins of our imaginative literature; she always writes like one who feels that the heart is a sacred thing, not rashly to be wounded, whilst she scorns to lower her own intellectual dignity by an ambitious straining after effect. Her matronly delicacy of thought, her chastened style of expression, her hallowed ideas of happiness as connected with home, and home-enjoyments;— to condense all in one emphatic word, her *womanliness* is to her intellectual qualities as the morning mist to the landscape, or the evening dew to the flower—that which enhances loveliness without diminishing lustre. To speak confidentially to our trusted friend the public, Mrs. Hemans throws herself into her poetry, and the said self is an English gentlewoman. Now this proves the exceeding good sense of Imagination, a faculty that Utilitarians are so apt to libel:[3] Imagination says, that a poetess ought to be ladylike, claiming acquaintance with the Graces no less than with the muses; and if it were not so, Imagination would conceive he had a right to be sulky. We appeal to any one who is imaginative. If, after sighing away your soul over some poetic effusion of female genius, a personal introduction took place, and you found the fair author a dashing dragoon-kind of woman— one who could with ease rid her house of a couple of robbers— would you not be startled? Or, if she called upon you to listen to a discussion on Petrarch's love in a voice that brayed upon your sense of hearing, would you not feel that nature had made a mistake? Without a doubt you would. Your understanding might in time be converted;

---

1 *The Newgate Calendar*, named after a London prison, was a popular 18th-century anthology of famous crimes.

2 Jack the Giant-killer is the hero of a long-popular chapbook and Blue Beard the villain of another popular chapbook who kills a succession of his wives; by the 1820s such forms of traditional working-class literature were widely dismissed by middle-class critics as sensational and childish, and in any case were being displaced by cheap Gothic thrillers, adventure stories, and so on.

3 Utilitarianism was a movement for wide-ranging reform, promulgated by such social critics as Jeremy Bentham and James Mill, and supposedly based on rational and scientific methods and criteria of utility, or providing the greatest benefit for the largest number of people.

you might bow at the very feet, and solicit the very hand, the proportions of which at first inspired terror, but your Imagination, a recreant to the last, would die maintaining that a poetess ought to be feminine. All that we know are so; and Mrs. Hemans especially. Her Italian extraction somewhat accounts for the passion which, even in childhood, she displayed for sculpture and melody; but her taste for the beautiful, so fastidious, so universal, so unsleeping—(we are not discussing how far such a taste contributes to happiness, but in what way it modifies genius,)—is that, to which may mainly be attributed Mrs. Hemans's separation from all other sisters of the lyre. [...]

[goes on to claim that poems such as "The Voice of Spring," "Bring Flowers," "The Death-song of the Nightingale," "Music of Yesterday," and "The Song of Night" "seem like some of Shelley's— less written than dreamed"]

[comments on "poetry as connected or unconnected with moral truth":] It is not necessary that every poem should be a homily in verse, or a sermon written for music; but it *is* necessary that the bias of a poet's own mind should be towards the beneficial. It has been finely said, that the intention of poetry, like that of christianity, is "to spiritualize our nature" [....] Great improvement has taken place in this respect; there is a holier spirit abroad in our poetry of an imaginative nature; and, in common with some other poets, Mrs. Hemans has given us many poems destined we trust, in better than a human sense, to "shine as the stars for ever"[1] [such as "The Hebrew Mother," "Cross in the Wilderness," "The Trumpet," "The Fountain of Marah," "The Penitent," "The Graves of the Martyrs."] To our minds Mrs. Hemans always succeeds best when her "strain is of a higher mood;"[2] when she sings to us of "melancholy fear subdued by faith";[3] and, when, through the tender gloom that habitually hangs over her poetry (twilight on a rose-bed) we have glimpses of that future which alone can "make us less forlorn."[4] For this reason the "Forest Sanctuary" is our first favourite [....]

---

1   from Edward Perronet, *The Mitre* (1757): the "reward ... reserved [in Heaven] for *all* such as turn many to righteousness, *viz.* to shine as the stars for ever and ever!" (2.1320n.)

2   Milton, "Lycidas," l. 87: "That strain I heard was of a higher mood."

3   Wordsworth, "Prospectus" to *The Excursion* (l. 15).

4   Wordsworth, "The World Is Too Much with Us; Late and Soon" (l. 12).

[comments on Hemans's song-writing and quotes "The Lyre and Flower"]

[...] Mrs. Hemans often partakes, it is true, of the modern faults of diffuseness, over-ornament, and want of force; but, taken for all in all, and judged by her best productions, she is a permanent accession to the literature of her country; she has strengthened intellectual refinement, and beautified the cause of virtue. The superb creeping-plants of America often fling themselves across the arms of mighty rivers, uniting the opposite banks by a blooming arch: so should every poet do to truth and goodness — so has Felicia Hemans often done, and been, poetically speaking, a Bridge of Flowers.

[*The Athenæum, Journal of English and Foreign Literature, Science, and the Fine Arts* (5 Feb. 1831): 104-5[1]]

10. 1833: a transatlantic, trans-hemispheric verse tribute

A fair correspondent has transmitted to us the following poem from the other side of the Atlantic. It is pleasant to see one lady-poet praising another; and on this account, as well as for its own merits, we give it insertion.[2]

TO MRS. HEMANS.

BY THE HON. MRS. ERSKINE NORTON.[3]

WHENCE dost thou fill thy golden urn?
What fountain is unseal'd for thee?
Thou mistress of the mighty thought!
Daughter of Poesy!

Tranquil and deep that fountain flows,   5
And flowers of rarest, richest dye
Droop o'er to view themselves as stars
Set in its pure blue sky.

---

1 The *Athenæum* (1828-1921) was one of the leading 19th-century literary and intellectual periodicals.

2 prefatory note by editor of *New Monthly Magazine*.

3 Eliza Bland, the Hon. Mrs Esme Steuart Erskine (born *c.* 1795), author of *Isabel: A Tale, in Two Cantos; and Other Poems* (London, 1814) and *Alcon Malanzore: A Moorish Tale* (Brussels, 1815); she also published political journalism from South America in the *New Monthly Magazine*.

Beneath the lofty shades around,
Forms of simple grandeur move;
Such forms as youthful Greece conceived
In her all-glorying love.

Such is thy spirit's dwelling-place;
With Beauty shrined — serene — alone:
Breathing forth tenderness and truth —
Thou highly-favoured one!

I ask not whether this world's pomp
Be thine or not: a perfect bliss
Springs with each life-gush of thy heart;—
Canst thou have more than this?

No gem that glows, no bird that sings,
No leaf that glitters in the dew;
No gift of love in air, earth, skies,
But hath a voice for you.

Poetess! we thank thee — in thy strains
Of melting melody *that voice*
To us thou dost pour forth; with thee
We worship and rejoice!
Rio de Janeiro, December, 1832.

[*New Monthly Magazine*, 39 (Sept. 1833): 93-4]

11. 1835: Letitia Elizabeth Landon,[1] "On the Character of Mrs. Hemans's Writings"

"OH! mes amis, rappellez-vous quelquefois mes vers; mon ame y est empreinte." "Mon ame y est empreinte."[2] Such is the secret of poetry. There cannot be a greater error than to suppose that the poet does not feel what he writes. What an extraordinary, I might say, impossible view, is this to take of an art more connected with emotion than any of its sister sciences. What—the depths of the heart are to be sounded, its mysteries unveiled, and its beatings numbered by those whose own heart is made by this strange doctrine—a mere machine wound up by the clock-work of rhythm! No; poetry is even more a passion than a power, and nothing is so strongly impressed on composition as the character of the writer. I should almost define poetry to be the necessity of feeling strongly in the first instance, and the as strong necessity of confiding in the second.

It is curious to observe the intimate relation that subsists between the poet and the public. "Distance lends enchantment to the view,"[3] and those who would shrink from avowing what and how much they feel to even the most trusted friend, yet rely upon and crave for the sympathy of the many. The belief that it exists in the far off and unknown is inherent as love or death. [...] Suffering discourses eloquent music, and it believes that such music will find an echo and reply where the music only is known, and the maker loved for its sake. [...]

I believe that no poet ever made his readers feel unless he had

---

1   Landon (1802-38), known by her literary signature "L. E. L.," rivalled Hemans as widely read female poet during the 1820s and '30s, developing the dramatic monologue and the set of poems framed within a larger narrative poem, with such works as *The Fate of Adelaide* (1821), *The Improvisatrice* (1824), *The Troubadour* (1825), and *The Golden Violet* (1826); like Hemans, she contributed many poems to the literary annuals, including an elegy to Hemans, included below.

2   Germaine de Staël, *Corinne; ou, l'Italie* (1807), from "Le Dernier Chant de Corinne," the heroine's last public improvisation: "Rappelez-vous quelquefois mes vers, mon ame y est empreinte; mais des muses fatales, l'amour et le malheur, ont inspiré mes derniers chants" (3.431 (book 20, ch. 5): "Remember my poems sometimes—my soul is imprinted there; but deadly muses, love and unhappiness, have inspired my last songs."

3   Thomas Campbell, "The Pleasures of Hope," 1.7.

himself felt. The many touching poems which most memories keep as favourites originated in some strong personal sensation. [...]

I have said that the writer's character is in his writings: Mrs. Hemans is strongly impressed upon hers. The sensitiveness of the poet is deepened by the tenderness of the woman. [...]

No emotion is more truly, or more often pictured in her song, than that craving for affection which answers not unto the call. The very power that she possesses, and which, in early youth, she perhaps deemed would both attract and keep, is, in reality, a drawback. Nothing can stand its test. The love which the spirit hath painted has too much of its native heaven for earth. In how many and exquisite shapes is this vain longing introduced on her page. Some slight incident gives the framework, but she casts her own colour upon the picture. In this consists the difference between painting and poetry: the painter reproduces others,—the poet reproduces himself. We would draw attention especially to one or two poems in which the sentiment is too true for Mrs. Hemans not to have been her own inspiration. [quotes from "Properzia Rossi," epigraph and ll. 1-25]

Did we not know this world to be but a place of trial—our bitter probation for another and for a better—how strange in its severity would seem the lot of genius in a woman. The keen feeling—the generous enthusiasm—the lofty aspiration—and the delicate perception—are given but to make the possessor unfitted for her actual position. It is well; such gifts, in their very contrast to the selfishness and the evil with which they are surrounded, inform us of another world—they breathe of their home, which is Heaven; the spiritual and the inspired in this life but fit us to believe in that which is to come. With what a sublime faith is this divine reliance expressed in all Mrs. Hemans's later writings. [...]

We have noticed this yearning for affection—unsatisfied, but still unsubdued—as one characteristic of Mrs. Hemans's poetry: the rich picturesque was another. Highly accomplished, the varied stores that she possessed were all subservient to one master science. Mistress both of German and Spanish, the latter country appears to have peculiarly captivated her imagination. At that period when the fancy is peculiarly alive to impression—when girlhood is so new, that the eagerness of childhood is still in its delights—Spain was, of all others, the country on which public attention was fixed: victory after victory carried the British flag from the ocean to the Pyrenees; but, with that craving for the ideal which is so great a feature in her writings, the present was insufficient, and she went back to the past; the romantic history of the Moors was like a storehouse, with treasures gorgeous like those of its own Alhambra.[1] [...]

Besides the ideal and the picturesque, Mrs. Hemans is distinguished by her harmony. I use the word harmony advisedly, in contradistinction to melody. Melody implies something more careless, more simple, than belongs to her style [... .] Now, Mrs. Hemans has the most perfect skill in her science; nothing can be more polished than her versification. Every poem is like a piece of music, with its eloquent pauses, its rich combinations, and its swelling chords. [...] It is like the finest order of Italian singing—pure, high, and scientific.

I can never sufficiently regret that it was not my good fortune to know Mrs. Hemans personally; it was an honour I should have estimated so highly—a happiness that I should have enjoyed so keenly. I never even met with an acquaintance of hers but once; that once, however, was much. I knew Miss Jewsbury, the late lamented Mrs. Fletcher.[2] She delighted in speaking of Mrs. Hemans: she spoke of her with the appreciation of one fine mind comprehending another, and with the earnest affection of a woman and a friend. She described her conversation as singularly fascinating—full of poetry, very felicitous in illustration by anecdote, happy, too, in quotation, and very rich in imagery; "in short, her own poem on 'The Treasures of the Deep' would best describe it." [...] I asked her if she thought Mrs. Hemans a happy person; and she said, "No; her enjoyment is feverish, and she desponds. She is like a lamp whose oil is consumed by the very light which it yields." [...]

To the three characteristics of Mrs. Hemans's poetry which have already been mentioned—viz., the ideal, the picturesque, and the harmonious—a fourth must be added,—the moral. Nothing can be more pure, more feminine and exalted, than the spirit which pervades the whole: it is the intuitive sense of right, elevated and strengthened into a principle. It is a glorious and beautiful memory to bequeath; but she who left it is little to be envied. Open the volumes which she

---

1 a fortified palace, famed for its beautiful architecture, gardens, and ornament, built by the Moors at Granada, in southern Spain, during the 13th and 14th centuries.
2 Maria Jane Jewsbury.

has left, legacies from many various hours, and what a record of wasted feelings and disappointed hopes may be traced in their sad and sweet complainings! Yet Mrs. Hemans was spared some of the keenest mortifications of a literary career. She knew nothing of it as a profession which has to make its way through poverty, neglect, and obstacles: she lived apart in a small, affectionate circle of friends. The high road of life, with its crowds and contention—its heat, its noise, and its dust that rests on all—was for her happily at a distance; yet even in such green nest, the bird could not fold its wings, and sleep to its own music. There came the aspiring, the unrest, the aching sense of being misunderstood, the consciousness that those a thousand times inferior were yet more beloved. Genius places a woman in an unnatural position; notoriety frightens away affection; and superiority has for its attendant fear, not love. Its pleasantest emotions are too vivid to be lasting: hope may sometimes,

> "Raising its bright face,
> With a free gush of sunny tears, erase
> The characters of anguish;"[1]

but, like the azure glimpses between thunder-showers, the clouds gather more darkly around for the passing sunshine. The heart sinks back on its solitary desolation. In every page of Mrs. Hemans's writings is this sentiment impressed; what is the conclusion of "Corinne crowned at the Capitol?" [quotes ll. 41-8]

What is poetry, and what is a poetical career? The first is to have an organization of extreme sensibility, which the second exposes bareheaded to the rudest weather. The original impulse is irresistible—all professions are engrossing when once began; and acting with perpetual stimulus, nothing takes more complete possession of its follower than literature. But never can success repay its cost. The work appears—it lives in the light of popular applause; but truly might the writer exclaim—

> "It is my youth—it is my bloom—it is my glad free heart
> I cast away for thee—for thee—ill fated as thou art."[2]

---

1 Hemans, "Arabella Stuart," 37-9.
2 Hemans, "The Chamois Hunter's Love," 17-18.

If this be true even of one sex, how much more true of the other. Ah! Fame to a woman is indeed but a royal mourning in purple for happiness. [...]

L. E. L.

[*New Monthly Magazine*, 44 (Aug. 1835): 425-33]

12. 1835: Letitia Elizabeth Landon: "Stanzas on the Death of Mrs. Hemans"[1]

"The rose—the glorious rose is gone." —*Lays of Many Lands.*[2]

BRING flowers to crown the cup and lute,—
    Bring flowers,—the bride is near;
Bring flowers to soothe the captive's cell,
    Bring flowers to strew the bier!
Bring flowers! thus said the lovely song;[3]   5
    And shall they not be brought
To her who linked the offering
    With feeling and with thought?

Bring flowers,—the perfumed and the pure,—
    Those with the morning dew,   10
A sigh in every fragrant leaf,
    A tear on every hue.
So pure, so sweet thy life has been,
    So filling earth and air
With odours and with loveliness,   15
    Till common scenes grew fair.

Thy song around our daily path
    Flung beauty born of dreams,
That shadows on the actual world
    The spirit's sunny gleams.   20

---

1 first published *New Monthly Magazine* 44 (May-Aug. 1835), 286-88.
2 Hemans, "The Nightingale's Death-Song," 3.
3 song] Hemans's poem "Bring Flowers," which is summarized in Landon's first 4 lines and which, like Landon's poem, also suggests the ultimate futility of the celebratory act of bringing flowers.

Mysterious influence, that to earth
    Brings down the heaven above,
And fills the universal heart
    With universal love.

25   Such gifts were thine,—as from the block,
    The unformed and the cold,
The sculptor calls to breathing life
    Some shape of perfect mould,
So thou from common thoughts and things
30   Didst call a charmed song,
Which on a sweet and swelling tide
    Bore the full soul along.

And thou from far and foreign lands
    Didst bring back many a tone,
35   And giving such new music still,
    A music of thine own.
A lofty strain of generous thoughts,
    And yet subdued and sweet,—
An angel's song, who sings of earth,
40   Whose cares are at his feet.

And yet thy song is sorrowful,
    Its beauty is not bloom;
The hopes of which it breathes, are hopes
    That look beyond the tomb.
45   Thy song is sorrowful as winds
    That wander o'er the plain,
And ask for summer's vanished flowers,
    And ask for them in vain.

Ah! dearly purchased is the gift,
50   The gift of song like thine;
A fated doom is hers who stands
    The priestess of the shrine.
The crowd—they only see the crown,
    They only hear the hymn;—

They mark not that the cheek is pale,   55
    And that the eye is dim.[1]

Wound to a pitch too exquisite,
    The soul's fine chords are wrung;
With misery and melody
    They are too tightly strung.   60
The heart is made too sensitive
    Life's daily pain to bear;
It beats in music, but it beats
    Beneath a deep despair.

It never meets the love it paints,   65
    The love for which it pines;
Too much of Heaven is in the faith
    That such a heart enshrines.
The meteor wreath[2] the poet wears
    Must make a lonely lot;   70
It dazzles, only to divide
    From those who wear it not.

Didst thou not tremble at thy fame,
    And loathe its bitter prize,
While what to others triumph seemed,   75
    To thee was sacrifice?
Oh, Flower brought from Paradise
    To this cold world of ours,
Shadows of beauty such as thine
    Recall thy native bowers.   80

Let others thank thee —'twas for them
    Thy soft leaves thou didst wreathe;
The red rose wastes itself in sighs

---

1   this stanza recalls the heroine in Germaine de Staël's novel *Corinne* (1807), which
    inspired both Hemans and Landon, as well as many other women writers.
2   meteor wreath] Landon seems to mean spectacular but transient fame, as the mete-
    or is a flashing but fleeting natural phenomenon, and the wreath is the convention-
    al crown of the public poet, as in de Staël's *Corinne*.

Whose sweetness others breathe!
85   And they have thanked thee — many a lip
            Has asked of thine for words,
        When thoughts, life's finer thoughts, have touched
            The spirit's inmost chords.

        How many loved and honoured thee
90   Who only knew thy name;
        Which o'er the weary working world
            Like starry music came!
        With what still hours of calm delight
            Thy songs and image blend;
95   I cannot chuse but think thou wert
            An old familiar friend.

        The charm that dwelt in songs of thine
            My inmost spirit moved;
        And yet I feel as thou hadst been
100   Not half enough beloved.
        They say that thou wert faint, and worn
            With suffering and with care;
        What music must have filled the soul
            That had so much to spare!

105   Oh, weary One! since thou art laid
            Within thy mother's breast —
        The green, the quiet mother-earth —
            Thrice blessed be thy rest!
        Thy heart is left within our hearts,
110   Although life's pang is o'er;
        But the quick tears are in my eyes,
            And I can write no more.

[*Letitia Elizabeth Landon: Selected Writings*, ed. Jerome McGann and Daniel Riess (Peterborough, Ont.: Broadview Press, 1997), pp. 169-72]

13. 1845: a tribute from a Chartist poet
[addresses Woman]

> That mind is of no sex,—when thou art freed,
> Thy thought-deeds shall proclaim: our Edgeworth's sense,
> Our Baillie's truthful skill, Felicia's meed
> Of grace with perfectest mellifluence
> Of music joined,—or thy magnificence
> Of heart and reason, Necker's glorious child![1]—
> Problems shall be no more: Woman's intense
> Inherent claim to mind-rank, when befoiled
> No more by Man, she will display with glow unsoiled.

[Thomas Cooper, *The Purgatory of Suicides: A Prison-Rhyme* (London),[2] book 9, stanza 17]

14. 1847: from George Gilfillan,[3] "Female Authors. No. I.— Mrs. Hemans"

[...] The works of British women have now taken up, not by courtesy but by right, a full and conspicuous place in our literature. They constitute an elegant library in themselves; and there is hardly a department in science, in philosophy, in morals, in politics, in the belles lettres, in fiction, or in the fine arts, but has been occupied, and ably occupied by a lady. This certainly proclaims a high state of cultivation on the part of the many which has thus flowered out into composition in the case of the few. It exhibits an extension and refinement of that element of female influence which, in the private intercourse of society, has been productive of such blessed effects—it

---

1 Maria Edgeworth (1768-1849) wrote numerous tales for children and tales for adults and was the most respected woman novelist in English during the first two decades of the 19th century; Joanna Baillie (1762-1851) published a widely-read *Series of Plays* on the passions from 1798 and corresponded with Hemans; "Necker's glorious child" is Germaine de Staël (1766-1817), one of Hemans's favourite authors.

2 Cooper (1805-92) was a working-class poet and Chartist campaigner who wrote the poem while jailed for political activities.

3 (1813-78) Scottish Dissenting minister and critic, best known for his *Gallery of Literary Portraits* (1845, 1850, 1854), originally published in *Tait's Edinburgh Magazine*, a Whig-leaning periodical.

mingles with the harsh tone of general literature, "as the lute pierceth through the cymbal's clash"[1]—it blends with it a vein of delicate discrimination, of mild charity, and of purity of morals—gives it a healthy and happy tone, the tone of the fireside; it is in the chamber of our literature, a quiet and lovely presence; by its very gentleness, overawing as well as refining and beautifying it all. One principal characteristic of female writing in our age is its sterling sense. [...] Indeed, on all questions affecting proprieties, decorums, what we may call the *ethics* of sentimentalism, minor as well as major morals, their verdict may be considered oracular, and without appeal. But we dare not say that we consider them entitled to speak with equal authority on those higher and deeper questions, where not instinct nor heart, but severe and tried intellect is qualified to return the responses. We remark, too, in the writings of females, a tone of greater generosity than in those of men. They are more candid and amiable in their judgments of authors and of books. [...] We have selected Mrs. Hemans as our first specimen of Female Authors, not because we consider her the best, but because we consider her by far the most feminine writer of the age. [...]

Sometimes, indeed, Mrs. Hemans herself seems reduced, through the warmth of her temperament, the facility and rapidity of her execution, and the intensely lyrical tone of her genius, to dream that the shadow of the Pythoness[2] is waving behind her, and controlling the motions of her song. To herself she appears to be uttering oracular deliverance. Alas! "oracles speak," and her poetry, as to all effective utterance of original truth, is silent. It is emotion only that is audible to the sharpest ear that listens to her song. [...] We are reluctantly compelled, therefore, to deny her, in its highest sense, the name of poet—a word often abused, often misapplied in mere compliment or courtesy, but which ought ever to retain its stern and original signification. [...]

[...] Mrs. Hemans had something more than the common belief of all poets in the existence of the beautiful. She was a genuine woman, and, therefore, the sequence (as we shall see speedily) is irresistible, a true Christian. Nor has she feared to set her creed to music in her poetry. But it was as a betrayal, rather than as a purpose, that she

---

1 Byron, *Sardanapalus: A Tragedy*, 3.1.393.
2 priestess and oracle of the Greek god Apollo.

so did. She was more the organ of sentiment and sensibility than of high and solemn truth [... .]

[...] In many poets we see the germ of greatness, which might in happier circumstances, or in a more genial season, have been developed. But no such germ can the most microscopic survey discover in her, and we feel that at her death her beautiful but tiny task was done. Indeed, with such delicate organization, and such intense susceptiveness as hers, the elaboration, the long reach of thought, the slow *cumulative* advance, the deep-curbed, yet cherished ambition which a great work requires and implies, are, we fear, incompatible.

It follows, naturally from this, that her largest are her worst productions. They labour under the fatal defect of tedium. They are a surfeit of sweets. [...] Hence few, comparatively, have taken refuge in her "forest sanctuary," reluctant and rare the ears which have listened to her "Vespers of Palermo," her "Siege of Valencia," has stormed no hearts, and her "Sceptic" made, we fear, few converts. But who has not wept over her "Graves of a Household," or hushed his heart to hear her "Treasures of the Deep," in which the old Sea himself seems to speak, or wished to take the left hand of the Hebrew child and lead him up, along with his mother, to the temple service; or thrilled and shouted in the gorge of "Morgarten," or trembled at the stroke of her "Hour of Death?" Such poems are of the kind which win their way into every house, and every collection, and every heart. [...]

Mrs. Hemans's poems are strictly effusions. And not a little of their charm springs from their unstudied and extempore character. This, too, is in fine keeping with the sex of the writer. You are saved the ludicrous image of a double-dyed Blue,[1] in papers and morning wrapper, sweating at some stupendous treatise or tragedy from morn to noon, and from noon to dewy eve[2]— you see a graceful and gifted woman, passing from the cares of her family, and the enjoyments of society, to inscribe on her tablets some fine thought or feeling, which had throughout the day existed as a still sunshine upon her countenance, or perhaps as a quiet unshed tear in her eye. In this case, the transition is so natural and graceful, from the duties or delights of the day to the employments of the desk, that there is as little pedantry in

---

1   Blue] bluestocking, see note to Byron's comment (item 4d) above.
2   Milton, *Paradise Lost* 1.742-43, describing the duration of the rebel angel Mulciber's fall from Heaven.

writing a poem as in writing a letter, and the authoress appears only the lady in *flower*. Indeed, to recur to a former remark, Mrs. Hemans is distinguished above all others by her intense womanliness. And as her own character is so true to her sex, so her sympathies with her sex are very peculiar and profound. Of the joys and the sorrows, the difficulties and the duties, the trials and the temptations, the hopes and the fears, the proper sphere and mission of woman, and of those peculiar consolations which the "world cannot give nor take away"[1] that sustain her even when baffled, she has a true and thorough appreciation; and her "Records of Woman," and her "Songs of the Affections," are just audible beatings of the deep female heart. In our judgment, Mrs. Ellis's idea of Woman[2] is trite, vulgar, and limited, compared with that of "Egeria," as Miss Jewsbury used fondly to denote her beloved friend.[3] [...]

Next to her pictures of the domestic affections stand Mrs. Hemans's pictures of nature. These are less minute than passionate, less sublime than beautiful, less studious than free, broad, and rapid sketches. [...]

In many points Mrs. Hemans reminds us of a poet just named, and whom she passionately admired, namely, Shelley. Like him, drooping, fragile, a reed shaken by the wind,[4] a mighty wind, in sooth, too powerful for the tremulous reed on which it discoursed its music; like him, the victim of exquisite nervous organization; like him, verse flowed for and from her, and the sweet sound often overpowered the meaning, kissing it, as it were, to death; like him, she was melancholy, but the sadness of both was musical, tearful, active, not stony, silent and motionless, still less misanthropical and disdainful; like him, she was gentle, playful, they could both run about their prison garden, and dally with the dark chains which, they knew, bound them till death. Mrs. Hemans, indeed, was not like Shelley, a vates[5]; she has never reached his heights, nor sounded his depths, yet they are, to our

1 in the Bible, Jesus promises that God will send a Comforter giving peace that the "world cannot give nor take away" (John 14.27).

2 Sarah Stickney Ellis (1799-1872), noted author of conduct books for women, including *The Women of England* (1838).

3 for Maria Jane Jewsbury's portrait of Hemans as "Egeria," see above, item 11.

4 phrase used in the Bible to describe John the Baptist, who prophesied the coming of Christ the saviour.

5 vates] poet-prophet.

thought, so strikingly alike, as to seem brother and sister, in one beautiful, but delicate and dying family. Their very appearance must have been similar. [...]

In Mrs. Hemans's melancholy, one "simple"[1] was wanting, which was largely mixed in Shelley's, that of faithless despondency. Her spirit was cheered by faith—by a soft and noble form—of the softest noblest faith [... .] Although, as we have said, her poetry is not, of prepense and purpose, the express image of her religious thought, yet it is a rich illustration of the religious tendency of the female mind. Indeed, females may be called the natural guardians of morality and faith. [...]

In Mrs. Hemans's writings you find this pious tendency of her sex unsoiled by an atom of cant, or bigotry, or exclusiveness; and shaded only by so much pensiveness as attests its divinity and its depth [....]

[...] If not, in a transcendent sense, a poet, her life was a poem. Poetry coloured all her existence with a golden light—poetry presided at her needlework—poetry mingled with her domestic and her maternal duties—poetry sat down with her to her piano—poetry fluttered her hair and flushed her cheek in her mountain rambles—poetry quivered in her voice, which was a "sweet sad melody"—poetry accompanied her to the orchard, as she read the "Talisman,"[2] in that long glorious summer day, which she has made immortal—and poetry attended her to the house of God, and listened with her to the proud pealing organ, as to an echo from within the veil. Poetry performed for her a still tenderer ministry; it soothed the deep sorrows, on which we dare not enter, which shaded the tissue of her history [....]

Thus lived, wrote, suffered, and died "Egeria." Without farther seeking to weigh the worth, or settle the future place of her works, let us be thankful to have had her among us, and that she did what she could, in her bright, sorely-tried, yet triumphant passage. She grew in beauty; was blasted where she grew; rained around her poetry, like bright tears from her eyes; learned in suffering what she taught in song;[3] died, and all hearts to which she ever ministered delight, have

---

1 simple] a medicinal herb.
2 a novel (1825) by Walter Scott.
3 Shelley, "Julian and Maddalo," "Most wretched men / Are cradled into poetry by wrong, / They learn in suffering what they teach in song" (544-46), lines used by Hemans as epigraph to "The Diver."

obeyed the call of Wordsworth, to

> "Mourn rather for that holy spirit,
> Mild as the spring, as ocean deep;—
> For her who, ere her summer faded,
> Has sunk into a dreamless sleep."[1]

[*Tait's Edinburgh Magazine*, new series, 14 (June, 1847): 359-63]

15. 1861: from Jane Williams, *The Literary Women of England*
[takes issue with Jewsbury's portrait of Hemans as "Egeria," and comments on her career and characteristic style]

[...] That there was no room in the mind of Mrs. Hemans for philosophy because it was filled with imagination is certainly a mistaken assertion; for her imagination, in the form of poetry, was itself intuitive philosophy. Truth could scarcely be announced before her mind had fully penetrated and seized upon it: though for discursive reasoning, the deduction of conclusions from the application of principles to facts, she had little ability. The general tenor of her writings was, in truth, philosophical, serving more or less to illustrate the adaptation of external nature to the intellectual and moral constitution of man. [...]

The poetical life of Mrs. Hemans divides itself into four periods.

First. The juvenile: including the earliest efforts of her childhood, with the imitative and prelusive strains in various styles, chiefly chivalrous, which she poured forth during the spring-time of her existence.

Second. The classic: when her taste being refined and set by the pure models of ancient Greece, her natural utterance was in some degree constrained and chilled.

Third. The romantic: when, retaining all the correctness of classic types, the exuberant richness of her imagination burst forth, like luxuriant vines overrunning trellis-work; and her sadness gave to every glowing object a tinge of its own hue.

Fourth. Her mature style: when the foliage, buds, and flowers of the preceding periods gave way to fruitage, golden fruitage, more beautiful, and far more precious. Her world-wide sympathies, mental

---

1 description of Hemans in Wordsworth, "Extempore Effusion upon the Death of James Hogg," ll. 37-40.

interests, home affections, and heart-wearing sorrows being all sup-
planted, absorbed, or etherialized by the increase of Divine knowl-
edge and love.

Even if Mrs. Hemans had not survived the second of these peri-
ods, she would have left an honoured name to posterity. The third
was that of her greatest popularity, and by the productions of that
period she still continues to be best known to the world at large. [...]

It cannot be denied that her style, in its most popular and florid
period, was in its general effect monotonous. The monotony, howev-
er, resembled woodland scenery, which tires the cursory beholder
with superficial sameness, while to the naturalist and the artist, its
recesses and interstices, its nooks and crevices, supply endless diversi-
ties of minutely delicate and beautiful objects. The more her poems
are studied the more various do they appear; shining out like a tuft of
moss to a beam of sunshine, words, which seemed casual adjuncts of
the cadence of verse, show meanings which attest the most exact and
thoughtful observation. [...]

Her descriptions of natural objects are not ornamental disserta-
tions, but inseparably belong to the human interest of her poems; and
her notice of those objects, exhibiting a ceaseless alacrity of observa-
tion, presupposes a certain degree of cheerfulness which tends to
abate the mournful effect of her poetry.

External nature is for her a standing simile; a background against
which the human figures appear in relief; or, perhaps, it may be
termed the symphony, the accompaniment, and the voluntary of
every subject, carrying it through with a flowing ease and apparent
artlessness, like the soft, free sweep of streams through a valley, or of
winds over flowers. The perfect accordance of the melody of the ver-
sification with the predominating idea of each poem captivates the
ear and wins the mind to unresisting sympathy. [...]

Wherever her poems may be localized, she peoples them with
heroic men, devoted women, and children such as to a poet-mother
her own appeared.

Any incident which impressed her, in the course of her reading,
incited her to give it a poetic paraphrase; and whenever the theme
admitted of expansion, illustration, and the infusion of pathetic inter-
est, she made it thoroughly her own.

She had no particular faculty for narration, and consequently told a short story much better than a long one. Her tales are languid streams, loitering in eddies, and soon merging in lakes; meditative retrospections rather than moving accidents. Nevertheless, they are in their kind unrivalled in beauty. Never, before or since, has so much deep and passionate feeling found utterance so fervid, so tender, and yet so chastened by sober judgment, in the language of poetry. [...]

In those peculiar qualities which distinguish the poetry of women from that of men, in the revelation of feminine modes of thought and tones of feeling, in fine and minutely delicate observation, tender pathos, deep affection, and sublimely blended purity and piety, she excelled all preceding authoresses. Of a mother's protecting and self-sacrificing fondness, of the endeared attachment of the sister, the grateful devotedness of the daughter, the loving faithfulness of the wife, of genial sympathy with human nature in all its forms of being and suffering, of subjection to every passing change in the sky, the air, the earth, and human aspect, blended with the conscious independence of a hidden life for immortality, never before had such an eloquent exponent arisen. [...]

Machiavelli, in his "Reflections on Livy," remarks: — "I have often thought that the cause of every man's success in life is due to the adaptation of his mind to the times in which he lives." This may with equal propriety be asserted of books; and the proposition in an enlarged form is likewise indisputable, — that the adaptation of books to those principles of human nature which continue unchanged throughout the fluctuations of ages will render them permanently acceptable. The writings of Mrs. Hemans met with immediate and extensive popularity, alike in the most distant and alienated colonial settlements and in the old home of the British race. Their suitability to more than one condition of social life has thus been manifested. Their writer died more than a quarter of a century ago, and many of them have now been more than forty years before the public in undiminished favour. These are good auguries. Perhaps when the century has run its course, and a critical reviewer, like a gardener at the breaking up of winter, examines the ground and sorts out surviving plants from those which have perished in the frost of time, two-thirds of those produced by Mrs. Hemans will be found to possess perennial vitality.

[*The Literary Women of England Including a Biographical Epitome of all the*

16. 1873: from William Michael Rossetti, "Prefatory Notice"

Sentiment without passion, and suffering without abjection—these, along with a deep religious sense, and with the gifts of a brilliant mind taking the poetical direction through eager sympathy and some genuine vocation, constitute the life of Mrs. Hemans. Whatever may be the deservings of the poems in other respects, they do not fail to convey to the reader a certain impression of beauty, felt to be inherent as much in the personality of the authoress as in her writings; they show as being the outcome of a beautiful life, and in fact they are so. [goes on to review the facts of her life, from Hughes and Chorley, and gives a summary of her character:]

[...] Her accomplishments were considerable, and not merely superficial. She knew French, Italian, Spanish, Portuguese, and in mature life German, and was not unacquainted with Latin. She had some taste and facility not only in music [...] but likewise in drawing [... .] Byron, Shelley, and Madame de Staël, were among the writers she was in the habit of quoting. Jealousy of contemporary female writers, prominent in the public eye, was unknown to her gentle and true-hearted nature [goes on to quote Maria Jane Jewsbury's portrait of "Egeria" as Hemans.]

In Mrs. Hemans's poetry there is [...] a large measure of beauty, and, along with this, very considerable skill. Aptitude and delicacy in versification, and a harmonious balance in the treatment of the sub-ject, are very generally apparent: if we accept the key-note as right, we may with little misgiving acquiesce in what follows on to the close. Her skill, however, hardly rises into the loftier region of art: there is a gift, and culture added to the gift, but not a great native fac-ulty working in splendid independence, or yet more splendid self-dis-cipline. Her sources of inspiration being genuine, and the tone of her mind feminine in an intense degree, the product has no lack of sin-cerity: and yet it leaves a certain artificial impression, rather perhaps through a cloying flow of "right-minded" perceptions of moral and material beauty than through any other defect. "Balmy" it may be: but the atmosphere of her verse is by no means bracing. One might sum up the weak points in Mrs. Hemans's poetry by saying that it is not only "feminine" poetry (which under the circumstances can be no imputation, rather an encomium) but also "female" poetry: besides exhibiting the fineness and charm of womanhood, it has the monotone of mere sex. [...] She is a leader in that very modern phalanx of poets who persistently coordinate the impulse of sentiment with the guiding power of morals or religion. Everything must convey its "lesson," and is indeed set forth for the sake of its lesson: but must at the same time have the emotional gush of spontaneous sentiment. The poet must not write because he has something of his own to say, but because he has something *right* to feel and say. Lamartine was a prophet in this line. After allowing all proper deductions, however, it may be gratefully acknowledged that Mrs. Hemans takes a very honourable rank among poetesses [....]

[*The Poetical Works of Mrs. Felicia Hemans*, ed. W. M. Rossetti (London: E. Moxon and Son, 1873)]

Select Bibliography

Hemans's Works—Lifetime and Posthumous Collected Editions

Poems. Liverpool and London: T. Cadell and W. Davies, 1808.

England and Spain; or Valour and Patriotism. Liverpool and London: T. Cadell and W. Davies, 1808.

The Domestic Affections, and Other Poems. London: T. Cadell and W. Davies, 1812.

The Restoration of the Works of Art to Italy: A Poem. Oxford: R. Pearson; J. Ebers, London, 1816; 2nd ed, rev. London: John Murray, 1816.

Modern Greece: A Poem. London: John Murray, 1817; 2nd ed, 1821.

Translations from Camoens, and Other Poets, with Original Poetry. Oxford: J. Parker; London: John Murray, 1818.

Tales, and Historic Scenes, in Verse. London: John Murray, 1819; 2nd ed, 1823.

The Sceptic; A Poem. London: John Murray, 1820; 2nd ed, 1821.

Stanzas to the Memory of the Late King. London: John Murray, 1820.

Wallace's Invocation to Bruce. Edinburgh: Blackwood; T. Cadell and W. Davies, London; 1820, dated 1819; 2nd ed, 1821.

Dartmoor; A Poem. London: The Royal Society of Literature, 1821.

A Selection of Welsh Melodies, with Symphonies and Accompaniments by John Parry, and Characteristic Words By Mrs. Hemans. London: J. Power, 1822.

The Siege of Valencia: A Dramatic Poem; The Last Constantine: with Other Poems. London: John Murray, 1823.

The Vespers of Palermo: A Tragedy, in Five Acts. London: John Murray, 1823.

The Forest Sanctuary: and Other Poems. London: John Murray, 1825; 2nd ed, 1829; 3rd ed, 1835.

Hymns for Childhood. Boston: Hilliard, Gray, Little, and Wilkins, 1827.

Records of Woman: with Other Poems. Edinburgh: William Blackwood; London: T. Cadell, 1828; 2nd ed, 1828; 3rd ed, 1830; 4th ed, 1834.

Songs of the Affections, with Other Poems. Edinburgh: William Black-
wood; London: T. Cadell, 1830; 2nd ed, 1835.

Hymns on the Works of Nature, for the Use of Children. London: John
Mardon, 1833.

Scenes and Hymns of Life, with Other Religious Poems. Edinburgh:
William Blackwood; London: T. Cadell, 1834.

National Lyrics, and Songs for Music. Dublin: William Curry Jr. and Co.;
London: Simpkin and Marshall, 1834.

Poetical Remains of the Late Mrs Hemans. Edinburgh: William Black-
wood and Sons; London: T. Cadell, 1836.

The Works of Mrs Hemans, 7 vols. Edinburgh and London: William
Blackwood and Sons, 1839.

Biographical

Chorley, Henry F. *Memorials of Mrs. Hemans with Illustrations of Her Lit-
erary Character from Her Private Correspondence*, 2nd ed, 2 vols.
London: Saunders and Otley, 1837.

[Hughes, Harriet Mary Browne, later Owen,] "Memoir of the Life
and Writings of Mrs Hemans: By Her Sister," in *The Works of
Mrs Hemans*, 7 vols (1839), vol. 1.

Lawrence, Rose. *The Last Autumn at a Favourite Residence, with Other
Poems; and Recollections of Mrs. Hemans*. Liverpool: G. and J.
Robinson, and Evans, Chegwin, and Hall; London: John Mur-
ray, 1836.

Critical (see also Views and Reviews in this edition)

Approaches to Teaching British Women Poets of the Romantic Period, ed.
Stephen C. Behrendt and Harriet Kramer Linkin. New York:
Modern Language Association of America, 1997.

Armstrong, Isobel. "The Gush of the Feminine: How Can We Read
Women's Poetry of the Romantic Period?", in *Romantic Women
Writers*, 13–32.

Blain, Virginia. "'Thou with Earth's Music Answerest to the Sky':
Felicia Hemans, Mary Ann Browne, and the Myth of Poetic
Sisterhood," *Women's Writing*, 2:3 (1995): 251–69.

Clarke, Norma. *Ambitious Heights: Writing, Friendship, Love—The Jews-
bury Sisters, Felicia Hemans, and Jane Welsh Carlyle*. London and
New York: Routledge, 1990.

Curran, Stuart. "The I Altered," in *Romanticism and Feminism*, ed. Anne K. Mellor. Bloomington and Indianapolis: Indiana UP, 1988. 185-207.

Eubanks, Kevin. "Minerva's Veil: Hemans, Critics, and the Construction of Gender," *European Romantic Review*, 8 (Fall 1997): 341-59

Feldman, Paula R. "The Poet and the Profits: Felicia Hemans and the Literary Marketplace," *Keats-Shelley Journal*, 46 (1997): 148-76.

———. Introduction, Felicia Hemans, *Records of Woman with Other Poems*, ed. Paula R. Feldman. Lexington: UP of Kentucky, 1999.

———. "Endurance and Forgetting: What the Evidence Suggests," in *Romanticism and Women Poets*, 15-21.

Harding, Anthony John. "Felicia Hemans and the Effacement of Woman," in *Romantic Women Writers*, 138-49.

Kelly, Gary. "Feminine Romanticism, Masculine History, and the Founding of the Modern Liberal State," in *Essays and Studies* (1998), "Romanticism and Gender," ed. Anne Janowitz, 1-18.

———. "Gender and Memory in Post-Revolutionary Women's Writing," in *Memory and Memorials, 1789-1914: Literary and Cultural Perspectives*, ed. Matthew Campbell, Jacqueline M. Labbe, and Sally Shuttleworth. London and New York: Routledge, 1998. 119-31, 220.

Kennedy, Deborah. "Hemans, Wordsworth, and the 'Literary Lady'," *Victorian Poetry*, 33 (Fall 1997): 267-86.

———. "Introducing Felicia Hemans in the First-Year Course," in *Approaches to Teaching British Women Poets of the Romantic Period*, 153-56.

Leighton, Angela. *Victorian Women Poets: Writing Against the Heart*. Charlottesville and London: UP of Virginia, 1992.

Linley, Margaret. "Sappho's Conversions in Felicia Hemans, Letitia Landon, and Christina Rossetti," *Prism(s): Essays in Romanticism*, 4 (1996): 15-42.

Lootens, Tricia. "Hemans and Home: Victorianism, Feminine 'Internal Enemies,' and the Domestication of National Identity," *PMLA*, 109 (March 1994): 238-53.

———. "Hemans and her American Heirs: Nineteenth-Century Women's Poetry and National Identity," in *Women's Poetry, Late Romantic to Late Victorian: Gender and Genre, 1830-1900*, ed. Isobel Armstrong and Virginia Blain. Basingstoke: Macmillan Press, 1999. 243-60.

McGann, Jerome. *The Poetics of Sensibility: A Revolution in Literary Style*. Oxford: Clarendon Press, 1996.

Mellor, Anne K. *Romanticism and Gender*. New York and London: Routledge, 1993.

Morlier, Margaret M. "Elizabeth Barrett Browning and Felicia Hemans: The 'Poetess' Problem," *Studies in Browning and His Circle*, 20 (1993): 70-79.

Reiman, Donald H. Introduction, Felicia Dorothea Hemans, *Tales and Historic Scenes*, etc. New York and London: Garland Publishing, 1978.

Romantic Women Writers: Voices and Countervoices, ed. Paula R. Feldman and Theresa M. Kelley. Hanover, NH, and London: UP of New England, 1995.

Romanticism and Women Poets: Opening the Doors of Reception, ed. Harriet Kramer Linkin and Stephen C. Behrendt. Lexington: UP of Kentucky, 1999.

Ross, Marlon. *The Contours of Masculine Desire: Romanticism and the Rise of Women's Poetry*. New York and Oxford: Oxford UP, 1989.

Ruwe, Donelle R. "The Canon-Maker: Felicia Hemans and Torquato Tasso's Sister," in *Comparative Romanticisms: Power, Gender, Subjectivity*, ed. Larry H. Peer and Diane Long Hoeveler. Columbia, SC: Camden House, 1998. 133-57.

Saglia, Diego. "Epic or Domestic?: Felicia Hemans's Heroic Poetry and the Myth of the Victorian Poetess," *Rivista di Studi Vittoriani*, 2 (July 1997): 125-47.

Sweet, Nanora. "History, Imperialism, and the Aesthetics of the Beautiful," in *At the Limits of Romanticism: Essays in Cultural, Feminist, and Materialist Criticism*, ed. Mary A. Favret and Nicola J. Watson. Bloomington and Indianapolis: Indiana UP, 1994. 170-84.

———. "'Hitherto closed to British enterprise': Trading and Writing the Hispanic World circa 1815," *European Romantic Review*, 8 (Spring 1997): 139-47.

———. "Hemans's 'The Widow of Crescentius': Beauty, Sublimity, and the Woman Hero," in *Approaches to Teaching British Women Poets of the Romantic Period*, 101-05.

———. "'Lorenzo's' Liverpool and 'Corinne's' Coppet: The Italianate Salon and Romantic Education," in *Lessons of Romanticism: A Critical Companion*, ed. Thomas Pfau and Robert F. Gleckner. Durham and London: Duke UP, 1998. 244-60.

Stephenson, Glennis. "Poet Construction: Mrs Hemans, L.E.L., and the Image of the Nineteenth-Century Woman Poet," in *ReImagining Women: Representations of Women in Culture*, ed. Shirley Neuman and Glennis Stephenson. Toronto: U of Toronto P, 1993. 61-73.

Trinder, Peter. *Mrs. Hemans*. Cardiff: U of Wales P, 1984.

Wolfson, Susan J. "'Domestic Affections' and 'the spear of Minerva': Felicia Hemans and the Dilemma of Gender," in *Re-Visioning Romanticism: British Women Writers, 1776-1837*, ed. Carol Shiner Wilson and Joel Hafner. Philadelphia: U of Pennsylvania P, 1994. 128-66.

———. "Gendering the Soul," in *Romantic Women Writers*, 33-68.

———. "Men, Women, and 'Fame': Teaching Felicia Hemans," in *Approaches to Teaching British Women Poets of the Romantic Period*, 110-20.

———. "Felicia Hemans and the Revolving Doors of Reception," in *Romanticism and Women Poets*, 214-41.